Working with Trauma-Exposed Children and Adolescents

Far too often, children and youth experience trauma, from rare events such as mass shootings, terrorism attacks, and school lockdowns, to very common occurrences such as bullying, exposure to drugs and alcohol, or various mental health issues. They can experience these events both directly and indirectly (from surfing the Internet, watching television, or through their friends). Our children spend a large portion of their day at school interacting with other students, teachers, and school personnel, where these topics are raised and discussed. This edited volume addresses how our teachers and school personnel can help students deal with these potentially traumatic events to reach the most positive possible outcomes.

This collection brings together leading experts, including academics and professionals working in the field, to provide the most current evidence-based practices on how to help students who may have experienced or witnessed trauma. It presents research and advice on how to respond to traumatic events regarding bullying; drugs and alcohol; sexual abuse; mental health; lesbian, gay, bisexual, transgender, and queer (LGBTQ) safety; stranger danger; childhood disruptive behaviors; school shootings and lockdowns; and terrorism. It also includes a chapter focused on how to implement a school safety program. Schools cannot deal with these issues alone; effective strategies must engage family members and the broader community. Hence, the collection includes a chapter on how schools can partner with families and the communities they reside in to bring about positive change. All this work pays close attention to cultural and religious sensitivity, socio-economic variabilities, diversity issues, and developmental stages.

Joanna Pozzulo is a Full Professor and the Chair of the Department of Psychology at Carleton University. Dr. Pozzulo's research and teaching broadly falls under the domain of Forensic Psychology (borrowing from developmental, social, and cognitive psychology). Dr. Pozzulo has published widely on the "young eyewitness".

Craig Bennell is a Full Professor in the Department of Psychology at Carleton University. Dr. Bennell teaches in the areas of Forensic Psychology and Police Psychology. His research focuses on police use of force, police training, police investigations, and evidence-based policing.

Working with Trauma-Exposed Children and Adolescents

Evidence-Based and Age-Appropriate Practices

EDITED BY JOANNA POZZULO AND CRAIG BENNELL

Routledge
Taylor & Francis Group

NEW YORK AND LONDON

First published 2019
by Routledge
52 Vanderbilt Avenue, New York, NY 10017

and by Routledge
2 Park Square, Milton Park, Abingdon, Oxon, OX14 4RN

Routledge is an imprint of the Taylor & Francis Group, an informa business

Library of Congress Cataloging-in-Publication Data
Names: Pozzulo, Joanna, editor. | Bennell, Craig, editor.
Title: Working with trauma-exposed children and adolescents : evidence-
    based and age-appropriate practices / edited by Joanna Pozzulo and
    Craig Bennell.
Description: New York, NY : Routledge, 2019. | Includes bibliographical
    references and index. |
Identifiers: LCCN 2018033733 (print) | LCCN 2018046871 (ebook) |
    ISBN 9780429423017 (master ebook) | ISBN 9780429750717 (pdf) |
    ISBN 9780429750700 (epub) | ISBN 9780429750694 (mobi) | ISBN
    9781138099180 (hbk : alk. paper) | ISBN 9781138099197
    (pbk : alk. paper) | ISBN 9780429423017 (ebk)
Subjects: LCSH: Psychic trauma in children—Treatment. | School
    children—Mental health. | Schools—Sociological aspects.
Classification: LCC RJ506.P66 (ebook) | LCC RJ506.P66 W66 2019 (print) |
    DDC 618.9285/21—dc23
LC record available at https://lccn.loc.gov/2018033733

ISBN: 978-1-138-09918-0 (hbk)
ISBN: 978-1-138-09919-7 (pbk)
ISBN: 978-0-429-42301-7 (ebk)

Typeset in Avenir and Dante
by Apex CoVantage, LLC

MIX
Paper from
responsible sources
FSC
www.fsc.org   FSC® C013056

Printed and bound in Great Britain by
TJ International Ltd, Padstow, Cornwall

Contents

Contributors

Brittany J. Allen University of Wisconsin School of Medicine and Public Health, USA

Leena Augimeri Child Development Institute, Canada

Andrea Blackman Child Development Institute, Canada

Jeffrey A. Daniels West Virginia University, USA

Tina Daniels Carleton University, Canada

Kristin Duval Royal Canadian Mounted Police, Canada

Diana E. Gal Arizona State University, USA

Julie A. Gocey University of Wisconsin, USA

Abby L. Goldstein Ontario Institute for Studies in Education, Canada

Sherie Hohs Madison Metropolitan School District, USA

Whitney Hyatt West Virginia University, USA

Maureen C. Kenny Florida International University, USA

Judith A. Myers-Walls Purdue University, USA

Jonathan Pettigrew Arizona State University, USA

Erin Rajca Child Development Institute, Canada

Philip J. Ritchie Children's Hospital of Eastern Ontario, Canada

Roberta Sinclair Royal Canadian Mounted Police, Canada

Mauranne Ste-Marie Royal Canadian Mounted Police, Canada

Nicole Summers Carleton University, Canada

Kara Thompson St. Francis Xavier University, Canada

Monique Verpoort Child Development Institute, Canada

Margaret Walsh Child Development Institute, Canada

Shanda R. Wells University of Wisconsin, USA

Sandy K. Wurtele University of Colorado, USA

Introduction

Joanna Pozzulo and Craig Bennell

Mass shootings, terrorism attacks, and cyberbullying are just a few examples of trauma that our children and youth may experience. Whether children or youth are surfing the Internet or watching television, it is all too common for them to be faced with tragedy. At a minimum, children and youth will have questions about these events; alternatively, these events may impact them on a deeper, more personal level. Our children/youth spend a large portion of their day at school interacting with other students, teachers, and school personnel, where these topics are raised and discussed. How are teachers and school personnel to help students deal with these events so the most positive outcomes are possible?

This edited book defines the "traumas" that children/youth are confronted with, both common and uncommon, with the goal of equipping school personnel (and parents) with the tools needed to address these issues with age-appropriate approaches and from a systemic, research-based perspective. Although children/youth may not directly experience some of the traumas discussed in this book (e.g., terrorism), exposure through the media to these types of traumas/events may have psychological consequences (and will certainly lead to many tough conversations at school and at home). Having to explain or deal with a child or youth who may be experiencing or even witnessing such events can be difficult to navigate. Often, teachers (and parents) are unsure how to talk to their students about a number of events that may be traumatic. Our goal was to bring together leading experts on the various types of dangers or traumas children and youth may experience to provide evidence-based best practices for school personnel (and parents) to deal with the issues that arise.

Who Should Read This Book?

Our main target audience for this book is school personnel (teachers, school staff, school psychologists, consultants to schools, school board members, and faculty members at universities and colleges who conduct research on related topics), so they can effectively deal with issues that arise at school around the traumas covered in this book. The chapters are mindful of the challenges school personnel may face when trying to help their students through the trauma. Such challenges consider that students come from different cultures, religious affiliations, and socio-economic groups. In addition, a particular student's social support system may vary from single-parent to extended family with few or many connections within the community. We think it is critical that those interacting with students who have either witnessed, experienced, or know about a particular trauma are engaged with sensitivity within the diversity present in the class, school, and community. We have provided some concrete examples on how to address the trauma being experienced and deal with some of the challenges that school personnel will encounter when having these conversations. Each chapter ends with a set of key messages that can be used as a quick guide for school personnel to ensure they are aware of essential points that should be considered when addressing the trauma. Each chapter also includes a list of resources for further reading and programming, should the reader wish to pursue more in-depth information.

How Is the Book Structured?

Each chapter is dedicated to a particular trauma for a total of nine topics. These topic chapters explain the trauma (e.g., school lockdowns) and discuss how to talk to children about the trauma, from the perspective of school personnel. Each chapter: (1) describes the particular trauma and its effects on children/youth, (2) describes practical methods for dealing with the particular trauma in the moment, and (3) describes practical methods for dealing with the trauma in the aftermath (i.e., over the long term). Each chapter informs the reader on the possible short and long-term consequences of the trauma, which may not necessarily be obvious if just looking at a child/youth. Chapters also highlight how the background of the child/youth (e.g., with respect to culture) may need to be considered when attempting to engage children/youth in conversations about traumatic experiences. When dealing with young people, we understand that what may be appropriate for an adolescent may not be appropriate for a first grader; as such, we have identified the age groups appropriate for each strategy. The traumas covered include: (1) bullying, (2) drugs and alcohol, (3) sexual abuse, (4) mental health, (5) lesbian, gay, bisexual, transgender, and queer (LGBTQ) safety, (6) stranger danger, (7) childhood disruptive behaviors, (8) school shootings and lockdowns, and (9) exposure to terrorism.

To increase the likelihood that school personnel will have the information they need to engage their students in conversations about these topics, and be able to do so in an effective manner, an Implementation chapter is included that describes how school boards, schools, and school professionals can implement the strategies discussed in the topic chapters. This chapter answers the question, "How do you accomplish what is described in this book without unduly harming children/youth?"

Traumas are multifaceted; as a consequence, we require a broad-based approach that includes not only the school but caregivers and the larger community. The penultimate chapter examines how schools can partner with and educate parents so they can effectively deal with issues arising at home (and school) around the sorts of trauma focused on throughout the book.

The Conclusion chapter highlights take-home messages, identifies remaining challenges, and provides closing remarks.

Why This Book?

To the best of our knowledge, there is no one book that deals with all these issues from the perspective of what school personnel need to know to help their students navigate the trauma. Although books are available on particular topics, these may not be "evidence-based". We sought to ensure that the suggestions provided in the chapters are based on the current research available and presented in a manner that can be implemented by school personnel. When possible, best practice guidelines are provided.

How Should You Use This Book?

This book provides teachers and school personnel with an understanding of various traumas, indicates the possible short- and long-term consequences that can be associated with these traumas, and offers concrete strategies that can be implemented by school professionals (and parents) for producing better outcomes for our children/youth. Each trauma is a stand-alone chapter and can therefore be read on its own; but, of course, the book can be read cover to cover. If you are interested in more information about a particular trauma, or want more specific details around particular programs that have been mentioned by the contributors, details about where to find that material is included in each appendix. As a quick "cheat sheet", each chapter ends with a set of key messages.

Conclusion

Although in an ideal world, this type of book would not be necessary, given that the traumas discussed in this book are very real and can be prevalent, we sought to equip school personnel with the latest, evidence-based recommendations on how to support their students. We hope this book will be used either on its own or as part of a larger school-based approach to helping our children and youth as they navigate life's challenges and come to understand the trauma they have encountered. We applaud all our school professionals for trying to ensure their students experience a healthy development.

Talking About Bullying in the Classroom and Beyond

1

Tina Daniels and Nicole Summers

Bullying has become an important topic of conversation with youth today. It is not a new phenomenon, but how we perceive and deal with it has changed extensively over the last 20 years. Today, bullying is understood as harmful behaviors and interactions that cannot be ignored.

A recent meta-analysis of 80 studies analyzing bullying involvement rates (for both bullying others and being bullied) for 12–18 year olds found on average 35% of peers were involved in traditional bullying and 15% were involved in cyberbullying (Modecki, Minchin, Harbaugh, Guerra, & Runions, 2014). Despite these high rates of bullying behavior, many who work with youth are not sure how or what they should do when bullying situations arise. Professionals are hesitant to talk with youth about bullying for fear of making things worse and because they lack confidence in their abilities to deal effectively with these behaviors. One research study asked 735 US teachers and school counselors "What do you think you might do?" in response to the following bullying scenario (Bauman, Rigby, & Hoppa, 2008):

> A 12-year-old student is being repeatedly teased and called unpleasant names by another, more "powerful" student [i.e., possessing greater or enhanced social or physical power such as greater physical strength, access to embarrassing information, higher peer status, or popularity], who has successfully persuaded other students to avoid the targeted

person as much as possible. As a result, the victim of this behavior is feeling angry, miserable, and often isolated.

(p. 839)

Before discussing what others thought they might do, take a minute to think about this situation:

- What would you do? Do you have a clear idea of how to handle this situation?
- Are you sure that this is what you should do?
- Do you have confidence in your abilities to address this issue in an effective way?

The teachers and counselors who completed this survey most often reported they would "discipline the bully". Although this strategy may be considered justifiable in some cases of severe bullying, it is not applicable in this situation, which is relatively low in severity. In fact, punitive approaches are currently not considered best for dealing with bullying behavior (APA's Zero Tolerance Task Force, 2008). Teachers had the least agreement about what should be done to help the victim. Many said they would "teach the victim to stand up to the bully", a strategy that places the targeted youth in danger, and others said they would "work to increase the self-esteem of the bully", a strategy that is not supported by research (Rigby, 1996; Seals & Young, 2003). Thus, it appears that, despite the best intentions, there is a lack of knowledge as to how best to address bullying behaviors.

A study by Fekkes, Pijpers, and Verloove-Vanhorick (2005) found that among the 58% of children who had been bullied several times a week and reported the incident to a teacher, only 28% reported that their teacher was successful in stopping the bullying; 20% said the teacher tried to stop it to no effect; 10% said the teacher tried to stop the bullying but it became worse; and 8% responded that the teacher did not try to stop the bullying. Findings from these types of studies provide grounds for concern regarding the ability of professionals who work with youth to effectively address bullying behaviors. Most adults have the same concerns that children express regarding dealing with bullying: they are not sure what to do, are fearful of making it worse, and hope that if they just ignore it, the bullying will stop. Unfortunately, the nature of bullying behavior is such that just ignoring it, or telling kids they should learn to solve their own problems, will not reduce bullying. By definition, bullying starts off as small insidious acts that over time escalate if nothing is done.

This chapter focuses on the nature and impact of bullying and cyberbullying on youth and how those who work with youth can help reduce these behaviors. To make changes in the rates of bullying behavior requires knowledge, motivation, self-efficacy, attitude change, school climate change, and cultural change. Bullying is a complex social phenomenon and because of these complexities, it is not easily eradicated, but that does not mean it is impossible to effectively intervene and even prevent such behaviors from occurring. In fact, the most important variable in producing change is buy-in from school staff and administration (Limber, 2004; Rigby, 2011). The more invested agencies are in addressing bullying, the more successful they will be. Because you are reading this chapter, you are already on your way to effectively addressing bullying for the youth you work with. At the end of this chapter, you will find that additional bullying prevention resources have been provided in Appendix 1. Where relevant, they have been noted in the text using an asterisk and the corresponding number from Appendix 1. Please refer to these for additional information regarding tools, resources, and support.

Establishing a Common Definition of Bullying

Youth have multiple ways in which they are able to hurtfully engage with their peers. They might say mean things in face-to-face interactions, use indirect actions such as exclusion and eye-rolling, or use the vastly expanding cyberworld to hurt each other by sharing private pictures or messages with unintended recipients, sending mean texts, or writing nasty tweets or other social media posts. The definition of bullying has changed over the years to account for the growing number of environments and mediums in which bullying may occur. Recently, in an effort to establish a uniform definition of bullying, the Centers for Disease Control and Prevention (Violence Prevention Division) and the United States Department of Education engaged in a consultative process with leading bullying experts and practitioners (Gladden, Vivolo-Kantor, Hamburger, & Lumpkin, 2014). These organizations have recommended that the following definition be used universally:

> [Bullying is] any unwanted aggressive behavior(s) by another youth or group of youths, who are not siblings or current dating partners, that involves an observed or perceived power imbalance (i.e. physical size, social status, high influence on the peer group) and is repeated multiple times or is highly likely to be repeated. Bullying may inflict harm or distress through many behaviors intended to cause physical, psychological, social, or educational harm.

(p. 7)

Bullying is a learned aggressive behavior and is not a reflection of the child's innate nature. It is important not to label children as "bullies" or "victims", as these labels are stigmatizing and can lead to children being perceived and perceiving themselves as nothing more than this label (Reiney & Limber, 2013; Swearer & Espelage, 2004). These labels also do not reflect the dynamic nature of bullying, which often involves a group of children who sometimes bully others and are sometimes victimized and often are witnesses to these acts. Regardless of the role played, addressing bullying must involve changing the way youth understand, perceive, and react to bullying behavior. Adults who work with youth must support and help them develop effective strategies for developing healthy relationships, interacting with peers, and dealing with conflict (1, 2, 6*).

The environment in which bullying behaviors may be used is not restricted to the school or school yard. Bullying is not only a school problem, but also a community and societal problem that requires community effort, including teachers, parents, and peers, for prevention and intervention to be effective. Moreover, bullying is not a normal part of development and is not a problem that children can solve on their own (Pepler & Craig, 2014). Youth spend a large amount of time in school, where adults can model positive behaviors and positive relationships; however, to effectively address bullying behavior, children need to receive a consistent message from all those they interact with that bullying is not ok and that adults will be able to effectively help them address these behaviors to develop positive relationship skills. This begins with understanding what bullying behavior is and looks like.

What IS and Is NOT Bullying?

It is important to distinguish bullying from other hurtful behaviors such as accidently hurting someone's feelings or saying or doing mean things. Bullying and violence are subcategories of aggressive behavior that overlap and there are situations in which violence is used in the context of bullying. Importantly, not all forms of bullying (e.g., rumor spreading, online bullying) involve violent behavior (Olweus, 1996). Understanding what bullying is and recognizing that not all hurtful behavior is bullying is an important step towards addressing this problem (Hinduja & Patchin, 2014).

What differentiates aggression from bullying? Sometimes, youth reactively aggress against another person because they are unable to control their anger (e.g., a child is accidently hit with a ball in the hall, they infer negative intent, and react in the situation by hitting the person who threw the ball). This type of situation is referred to as reactive aggression. It differs from bullying in several important ways: (1) it is not planned, (2) it is not directed towards a particular person, (3) it does not occur repeatedly over time, nor is there the perceived threat that it may, and (4) there is not an established power differential between those involved. These are hurtful acts of aggression and may be mean, but they are not considered bullying. Not all aggression is bullying.

Although relationships can involve a level of conflict and teasing, it is important to identify and intervene when teasing becomes bullying. Teasing can be a playful interaction used to evoke a response from a peer, provide feedback to a peer regarding their behaviors, or resolve a conflict in an indirect manner; however, teasing also can be used to cause harm by embarrassing, criticizing, or isolating a peer. The words "just teasing" also can be used to cover mean or hurtful intent from the adults who are present. Teasing becomes bullying when the teasing causes stress, hostility, and harm to the person being teased, when it occurs repeatedly, and when there is a power imbalance between the peers. Further information can be found in an informative article written by Dess, White, Jaffe, and Jaffe (2011).

The Nature of Bullying Behavior

There are many different forms or ways that children can be bullied. Bullying is often defined using four categories: physical, verbal, social, and cyber/online bullying. Physical bullying involves hitting, kicking, shoving, spitting, damaging someone's property, and/or stealing. Although certainly not limited to boys, boys are more likely than girls to partake in physical bullying and this form of bullying is most prevalent during preschool-early elementary school years and tends to decrease over time (Silva, Pereira, Mendonça, Nunes, & de Oliveira, 2013; Veenstra et al., 2013). Verbal bullying includes name-calling, mocking, hurtful teasing, humiliation, threatening someone, making racist comments, and sexual harassment. Boys and girls are equally likely to verbally bully and these behaviors can start as early as preschool, but also tend to gradually decline over time. A more indirect form of bullying is social or relational bullying, which is characterized by using the peer group to harm another individual's social status, relationships, or reputation. Examples of social/relational bullying include excluding others from the group, gossiping or spreading rumors about others, and damaging friendships (Coyne et al., 2006; Galen & Underwood, 1997). Girls tend to partake in social/

relational bullying more when they are younger, but by high school, boys and girls engage in social bullying at equal rates (Crick, 1996; Crick & Grotpeter, 1995; Li, 2006). By adolescence and into adulthood, social bullying becomes one of the most frequent forms of bullying, with a focus on manipulating social relationships.

A newer form of bullying, labeled "cyberbullying", has gained attention in both the media and research. Cyberbullying occurs through modern technological devices, specifically mobile phones or the Internet (Slonje & Smith, 2008). Cyberbullying may take the form of mean or nasty messages or comments, rumor spreading through posts or creation of groups, exclusion by groups of peers online, and the posting of embarrassing photographs. Cyberbullying has been found to be less prevalent than traditional bullying; however, Pornari and Wood (2010) have found that high levels of traditional bullying and victimization are related to high frequencies of cyberbullying and becoming a victim of cyberbullying (Merrill & Hanson, 2016). Cyberbullying has been argued to be similar to traditional bullying in intent to harm, and the behaviors used to cause harm (Dooley, Pyżalski, & Cross, 2009; Smith et al., 2008); however, it differs from traditional bullying in three important ways: (1) it can reach the victims without requiring face-to face interaction, (2) it has the potential to reach an infinite audience, and (3) because of the perceived anonymity, youth report that they would engage in more hurtful and harmful behaviors than they would face-to-face (Felix, Green, & Sharkey, 2014; Li, 2006). What is posted online is permanent, has the potential to reach a vast audience, and can victimize a peer across many different environments (e.g., school, home, the mall). The permanency of cyberbullying posts enables them to re-victimize a person over and over as each new person sees/reads it. One of the defining features of cyberbullying is the inability of victims to escape it (Slonje & Smith, 2008). Because it also does not include any face-to-face interaction, those who engage in harmful behavior do not receive any immediate feedback in regards to the target's emotional reaction to the hurtful behaviors. This lack of feedback may contribute to youth reports that bullying is more hurtful online than face-to-face. In addition, some researchers have found that cyberbullying may be less planned than traditional bullying and may be more fluid, shifting between engaging in bullying behavior, experiencing victimizing behaviors, and witnessing bullying online (Shapka & Amos, 2012) (3, 7, 22, 23, 24, 25*).

Despite these differences in bullying behavior, research to date suggests that it is the content of the bullying that causes the harm, not the delivery method that is most detrimental to youth (Bauman & Newman, 2013; Modecki et al., 2014; Vandebosch & van Cleemput, 2008). In addition, there is a strong relationship between involvement in traditional bullying behaviors and involvement in cyberbullying behaviors. Research has also shown that cyberbullying decreases after the implementation of anti-bullying programs that contain no cyber-specific content (Salmivalli, Karna, & Poskiparta, 2011). Thus, at this time, it appears that strategies to address traditional bullying behaviors also have a positive impact on reducing rates of cyberbullying (32*).

Who Is at Risk?

Often, when we think of those who are victimized, we think of stereotypes such as "the little red-haired boy with glasses"; however, there is not a clear profile of those who are the targets of bullying behavior (Card & Hodges, 2008). This is because there is no single reason why a child may be bullied. There are many different factors that could increase the likelihood of a child being victimized. For the most part, these risk factors represent individual qualities that make a child or youth different from their peers (e.g., LGBTQ youth, children with exceptionalities, and children with mental health challenges or behavioral problems) (Blake et al., 2012; Espelage et al., 2008; Kumpulainen, Rasanen, & Henttonen, 1999; Rivers, 2001).

These vulnerabilities create an opportunity for those using bullying behavior to gain power by deriding their target. Although research has indicated that youth who are different are more vulnerable to bullying, everyone has vulnerabilities and, thus, the possible pool of targets for bullying behavior is endless. Further, those who engage in bullying behavior are typically good at identifying and targeting these vulnerabilities. Any child may participate in bullying behavior or be the target of these behaviors. Often, children "try on" these behaviors to see if they are effective in gaining power. Thus, trying to identify the characteristics of those who will engage in bullying behavior or be targeted by their peers is not an effective strategy. Rather, strategies that attempt to change the attitudes and beliefs of the peer group to be more accepting of diversity and more supportive of minority youth hold more promise (Salmivalli, 2010).

Bullying: A Relationship Problem

Bullying was once considered to be a problem related to an individual's aggressive behavior. Now, bullying is understood as a relationship problem that requires relationship solutions (Craig & Pepler, 1998; O'Connell et al.,

1999; Trach, Hymel, Waterhouse, & Neale, 2010). Research has shown that bullying happens within the context of the peer group, as a group process, involving more than just the individual engaging in bullying behaviors and the peer being victimized (Gini, 2006; Gini et al., 2008; Obermann, 2011; Salmivalli, 1999). Rarely does bullying occur in isolation. Most often, other youth are present (85–88% of the time; Atlas & Pepler, 1998; Pepler & Craig, 1995; Hawkins, Pepler, & Craig, 2001). When other youth are present, they are often drawn into the situation and actively participate in the bullying behavior (22–30% of the time; Pepler & Craig, 1995). Most bystanders, those who witness a bullying episode, report that they find watching bullying disturbing, are against bullying, and admire those who intervene and defend others. Despite this, it is rare that youth step up to defend the peer being victimized (11–19%; Atlas & Pepler, 1998; Pepler & Craig, 1995; Hawkins, Pepler, & Craig, 2001). There is a disconnect between the intentions of bystanders and their actions (Salmivalli, 2010). It is in this way that peers play an active role in the problem of bullying.

How bystanders respond in bullying situations effects those who are victimized. Those who use bullying behaviors carefully select who to target, the time, and the place to maximize their chances of demonstrating their power to peers and gain social status (Juvonen Graham, & Schuster, 2003; Salmivalli, 2010). When bystanders reinforce these behaviors, either by supporting the person engaging in the bullying behavior or by doing nothing, the severity and length of the bullying episode increases (Pepler & Craig, 1999). The more classmates reinforce the person engaging in bullying behavior, the more bullying behavior takes place (Kärnä, Salmivalli, Poskiparta & Voeten, 2008, as cited in Salmivalli, 2010). In contrast, increased rates of defending behavior have been found to be related to lower frequencies of bullying in the classroom (Salmivalli, Voeten, & Poskiparta, 2011). When bystanders support the youth who is the target of bullying behavior, this buffers the negative impact of bullying, shortening the bullying episode and substantially reducing the impact. Those who are victimized and have classmates supporting and defending them are better off than those without defenders; they are less depressed and anxious, have higher self-esteem, and are less rejected by peers (Sainio, Veenstra, Huitsing, & Salmivalli, 2011; Salmivalli, 2014). Thus, it is not the victimization per se that leads to the negative consequences of bullying, but rather the message that the larger peer group believes that the individual is deserving of the bullying. In turn, those who are targeted by these hurtful behaviors may internalize these messages, which can lead to an erosion of self-esteem, feelings of helplessness and hopelessness, anxiety and depression, loneliness and isolation, and physical ill health (Hawker &

Boulton, 2000; McDougall & Vaillancourt, 2015; Ladd & Troop-Gordon, 2003; Rigby, 2001, 2003).

Having friends can protect against further harm as well as the negative effects of victimization (Boulton, Trueman, Chau, Whitehand, & Amatya, 1999; Hodges, Boivin, Vitaro, & Bukowski, 1999). Greater perceived caring by friends also has been demonstrated to be a protective factor (Kendrick, Jutengren, & Stattin, 2012). These findings suggest that prevention efforts should focus on increasing perceptions of support and caring within existing friendships and within the classroom (31*).

Finally, bystanders themselves can be negatively impacted by witnessing bullying behavior. Watching and participating in harmful behavior can lead to feeling scared, anxious, and helpless. Witnesses to bullying behavior may become highly aroused and excited, experience a breakdown in inner controls against antisocial behavior, and may not be aware of the potentially serious consequences of their behavior when they are drawn into participating (Dovidio, Pilavin, Gaertner, Schroeder, & Clark, 1991). Youth risk becoming desensitized to cruelty (Gini, 2006; Hymel, Rocke-Henderson, & Bonanno, 2005; Obermann, 2011). They may perceive the target as deserving of abuse and dislike for the target can increase over time (Hodges & Perry, 1999). Witnessing high levels of victimization can hinder the development of empathy and compassion. Thus, evidence suggests that those who witness acts of bullying are as harmed as those who are the targets (Kärnä, Voeten, Poskiparta, & Salmivalli, 2010; Rivers, Poteat, Noret, & Ashurst, 2009).

Short- and Long-Term Consequences of Bullying

Bullying is a major risk factor for poor physical and mental health, and reduced adaptation to adult roles, including forming lasting relationships, integrating into work, and being economically independent (for a comprehensive review, see Card & Hodges, 2008). Negative consequences have been clearly demonstrated for all roles of bullying (i.e., engaging in bullying behavior, experiencing victimization, and witnessing bullying). Children who are the targets of bullying have consistently been found to be at higher risk for internalizing problems, anxiety disorders, and depression (Wolke et al., 2014), as well as the physical expression of the stress experience such as colds and somatic complaints (e.g., headaches, stomach aches, body pain, tiredness, and sleeping problems), poorer academic performance, and more school absenteeism (Card, 2010; Faris & Felmlee, 2014; Hawker & Boulton, 2000; Rigby, 2001, 2003). Children who are involved in bullying behavior experience an erosion in their self-esteem, have poorer social relationships, and fewer friends both in the short and long term (Wolke & Lereya, 2015). Research also has shown that children who are bullied or engaged in bullying behavior are significantly more likely to contemplate or attempt suicide (Espelage & Goldblum, 2015). Suicide in youth arises from a complex interplay of various biological, psychological, and social factors of which bullying can be one contributing factor (Sinyor, Schaffer, & Cheung, 2014) (22, 23*).

Engaging in bullying behavior, witnessing these behaviors, or experiencing these behaviors can be very stressful. The human body is not designed to experience the prolonged levels of stress induced from chronic victimization. This chronic buildup of stress-response chemicals can have harmful effects on physical and mental health for all those involved in bullying (Vaillancourt et al., 2008). Bullying has serious deleterious effects on health both immediate and over the lifespan (Vaillancourt, Hymel, & McDougall, 2013). To prevent these effects, it is essential to understand the role that each member of a community must play in bullying prevention and intervention efforts.

Bullying Behavior Is Preventable

Bullying is a serious issue in schools and organizations today and when we consider strategies for reducing bullying, it is important to remember that these behaviors: (1) are learned, (2) are being "tried on" by children and youth to see how they work and how others react, and (3) can be changed. Bullying is about behaviors, not character traits. This is important to understand when attempting to reduce bullying behaviors among youth. There are two general approaches for addressing issues of bullying. One is to *intervene* by focusing on the perpetrator and the target of the behaviors when acts of bullying occur to prevent their reoccurrence (i.e., secondary prevention). The other is to focus on the *prevention* of these behaviors, so they do not occur to begin with, by teaching all youth skills incompatible with bullying behavior (i.e., primary prevention) (Srabstein et al., 2008).

Historical Intervention and Prevention Practices

Many of the early efforts to address bullying focused on intervention, targeting those who were the instigators and receivers of bullying behavior. Strategies focused on a feature or quality belonging to the individual and were designed to bolster self-esteem, assertiveness, and strength of character for those who were the targets of bullying behavior and counseling, social skills training, and behavioral approaches for those who perpetrated the bullying behaviors (Swearer & Hymel, 2015; Volk, Camilleri, Dane, & Marini, 2012). Although these strategies may be beneficial to some youth, they have not been found to be effective in addressing rates of bullying behavior. For example, Fox and Boulton (2003) found that social skills training for victimized youth improved global self-worth, but did not change victim status. This may be a result of bullying being more than just the attributes of the perpetrator or the target; it is also about those who witness and respond to these behaviors. Youth engaging in bullying behaviors who have successfully gained social status and popularity will continue to use these behaviors if the people whose opinion they value the most (i.e., their peers) support and encourage them by actively engaging in the bullying behavior, or by only standing and watching without trying to stop the bullying. Without changing the social climate in which bullying takes place, and the attitudes and beliefs of the peer group, the social dynamics that support bullying will not change. Only when interventions are directed towards the entire peer group can we be successful in reducing bullying rates (Salmivalli, 1999). O'Connell, Pepler, and Craig (1999) suggest that intervention is unlikely to be effective unless it is part of a wider, whole-school, anti-bullying program targeted at the individual, dyad, peer, classroom, school, family, and community level.

In addition, intervention strategies solely focused on changing attributes of the individual who has been targeted may be perceived as "victim blaming", as the onus is placed on the child who is victimized to change their behavior to be less impacted and less vulnerable as a target. Unfortunately, only training the target will not reduce the incidence of bullying behavior (Card & Hodges, 2008; Green, 2006). It is the environment that supports bullying behavior that needs to change as well.

Other previous efforts have included strict punishment strategies, such as "zero tolerance". This approach is based on the belief that a clear message must be given to youth that bullying behaviors will not be tolerated and there will be harsh consequences for those who perpetrate these behaviors. Zero-tolerance bullying policies became widespread in the 1990s and 2000s in both Canada and the United States as a way to use harsh punishment to deter bullying. By the late 1990s, 79% of American schools had some form of a zero-tolerance policy in effect to address school violence, drugs, and alcohol use (Boccanfuso & Kuhfeld, 2011). In Ontario, Canada, the adoption of a zero-tolerance policy by the Ministry of Education in 2000 led to a significant increase in suspensions (7.2% increase from 2001 to 2004), but no reduction in rates of bullying; furthermore, a significant proportion of youth that were suspended were students with exceptionalities (18% of suspended students represented 8.8% of all students with exceptionalities) (Brent, 2007). In 2005, the Ontario Human Rights Commission alleged that these school board policies discriminated against students with disabilities and those from racial minorities. The American Academy of Pediatrics issued a policy statement announcing they do not support the concept of zero tolerance for the developing child (Lamont, 2013). Today, zero-tolerance policies are considered a failed approach that has not been shown to improve school climate or school safety.

The message that bullying behavior will not be tolerated is critical to intervention and prevention; however, the consequences for engaging in such behavior must be clearly established, consistent, and fair (APA's Zero Tolerance Task Force, 2008). In 2006, the Ontario Safe Schools Action Team recommended that disciplinary measures shift from punitive to supportive and corrective in nature. Specifically, when inappropriate behavior occurs, schools employ a range of developmentally appropriate consequences, including opportunities to learn from mistakes, and focus on improving behavior. Additionally, it was recommended that the behavior be judged, not the student— we must be hard on the problem but soft on the person (Fisher, Ury, & Patton, 1991).

When discussing how to impact bullying behaviors, there are several terms that have been used in the field. The early years saw the use of *anti-bullying* strategies. More recently, there has been a move to focus on bullying *prevention* strategies (Quigley, 2017). It is a subtle language choice, but one that is meaningful, as it reflects a change in thinking about bullying as attributional to focusing on changing behavior. For many children, bullying reflects a "trying on" of some unkind or hurtful behaviors that they have seen used effectively by others. Whether they will continue to use these behaviors depends on the reaction and perceived support of those who witness the behavior.

There are some common misconceptions about children who use or "try on" bullying behaviors that are important to take into consideration when determining how to effectively prevent the use of these behaviors in the future. Those who use bullying behaviors are not maladjusted or marginalized by their peers (Vaillancourt, Hymel, & McDougall, 2003; Veenstra et al., 2005). They have a high degree of status and power within the group (Pellegrini, 2002; Salmivalli & Peet, 2008). Despite being disliked, they are perceived as cool and popular and have friends (Rodkin, Farmer, Pearl, & Van Acker, 2000; Salmivalli, 2010). They report higher social self-efficacy and social and physical self-concepts (Salmivalli, 1998) and are often perceived to be leaders (Peeters, Cillessen, & Scholte, 2010). Bullies report feeling good about themselves and their peer interactions. This can make it difficult to convince youth, who believe themselves to be popular and cool, to reduce their bullying behavior (Vaillancourt, Hymel, & McDougall, 2003). In fact, because of these talents and strengths, teachers often do not recognize those who are using bullying behaviors in their classroom. Research indicates that teachers identify fewer than half the bullies identified by youth (Vaillancourt et al., 2003; Leff, Kupersmidt, Patterson, & Power, 1999).

Bystanders Matter, a Lot!

Why do youth who we believe to be good and caring individuals behave in ways that condone or maintain bullying behaviors? When youth interact with peers that accept and condone bullying behaviors, this can lead to changes in the way they see and interact with others in their world. They begin by experimenting with harmful behavior and gradually move from small hurtful acts to more serious harm without experiencing negative emotions such as guilt and shame.

When thinking about how to prevent bullying behavior, it is important to consider what maintains or supports these behaviors. There are three things that drive the need to use aggressive behaviors to bully others: (1) desire for power and control, (2) the need for status within the peer group, and (3) the approval of these behaviors by peers and the community as an acceptable means to achieve these desires (Pellegrini, 2002; Salmivalli & Peets, 2008). Children who use bullying behaviors have learned to use their interpersonal power in an aggressive way. They may possess power as a function of their physical size and strength, but more often, the power they wield is social in nature, achieved because of their status within the group, their ability to know another person's vulnerability, and/or because they have the support of others. These youths have learned that power and aggression lead to dominance and status among those whose opinions they value the most—their peers. Those who use bullying behavior are dependent on the peer group to attain their desire for power, popularity, and status (Salmivalli, 2010). Over time, this power imbalance becomes larger, making it more difficult for the person who is being targeted to extricate themselves from the situation. Youth who watch this occurring learn to align themselves with their peers and engage in the aggressive behavior for protection and status.

In thinking about how to effectively intervene to disrupt this process, it becomes important to consider why youth currently do not act to defend or support others. There are several good reasons why youth may fail to support targets of bullying behavior. They might be fearful that if they attempt to intervene, they may be targeted next. They could be unsure of what they should do and afraid they might do the wrong thing (Thornberg et al., 2012). Others may feel powerless and unable to act, and feel they need help from adults to deal with these situations (36*).

Bystanders have been found to be the most successful and powerful focus for intervention but it is often difficult for youth to intervene effectively and engage as defenders when witnessing bullying. Attitudes and beliefs play a significant role in supporting bullying behavior. If we teach children only to be concerned for themselves, we will raise a generation of youth who are desensitized to others' pain, who fail to develop empathy and compassion. For example, in the words of one eighth-grade girl, "No offense to you, lady, but why should I care? It's not happening to me". Youth need to be taught to challenge these beliefs. This includes developing and enhancing empathy for those targeted by bullying and raising bystanders' sense of moral agency and their belief in their ability to make a difference. It may be helpful to think about building in youth a set of skills incompatible with bullying behavior. These include empathy, inclusivity, and acceptance of diversity (5, 37*). Youth who understand how others feel, are welcoming to others, and accept and value diversity are unlikely to engage in bullying behavior or support it when they see it (34*).

Prevention Efforts Should Focus on the Peer Group

High status and powerful individuals who have used bullying behaviors to achieve their status will be particularly resistant to change, especially if they perceive their interactions to be socially accepted by their peers. Peers are a critical and untapped resource in school-based bullying prevention efforts, but may be difficult to engage because of their concern that they may risk losing their popularity and status within the peer group (Vaillancourt et al., 2003). The peer group as a whole must be taught not to empower the peer who is using bullying behaviors by supporting him/her.

Thornberg and colleagues (2012), and Salmivalli (2010), have identified four important strategies for helping youth take an active role in preventing bullying behavior:

1. *Increase empathy.* Adults need to give a clear message that they expect bystanders to intervene when they see bullying. This means talking with youth about bullying and raising awareness of the role they play in the

bullying process. It means building empathy for those who are the target of bullying behaviors.

2. *Develop self-efficacy.* Youth must be taught how to effectively intervene without causing risk to themselves. Often, role-play exercises can be useful for preparing what to do or say when such situations arise. Without practice, in the highly emotionally laden situation of bullying, youth may freeze. High levels of emotion can also shut off the thinking side of the brain, making it difficult to access strategies and solutions. Unless they are well prepared, youth may not be able to respond effectively in the moment (Thornberg et al., 2012). When working with youth, adults can support the development of skills such as recognizing negative behaviors, and provide them with quick, acceptable solutions to increase their self-efficacy (2, 11, 30*).

3. *Change the reward structure of the classroom.* Children that belong to groups that endorse bullying model these behaviors because they see them rewarded and admired by their peers and wish to be accepted. In the same way, supporting and defending can become the norm, and even valued and rewarded in the peer group (Salmivalli, 2010). Youth must believe that they can make a difference and have the confidence to stand up to their peers. Conversations with youth can bring awareness to the power of social norms and aid them in developing skills to be assertive, model positive behaviors, and recognize and value positive relationships.

4. *Change the normative attitudes and beliefs.* It is important to encourage conversations with youth about bullying to establish a common belief that bullying is wrong, and for adults to model this belief. These conversations and effort should also encourage the targeted youth to use pro-social behaviors.

One example of a current evidence-based program founded on these premises is KiVa, which is being implemented in Finland schools (Salmivalli, 2010). A central goal of the KiVa program is for bystanders to show they are against bullying and support the victim. Having been extensively researched, KiVa has been found to successfully decrease bullying and victimizing behaviors (Kärnä et al., 2011). Over a 9-month period of implementation, reductions of 15% and 14% in the prevalence rates of victimization and bullying were found. The intervention effects increased from grade 1 until grade 4, where the effects were largest. After grade 4, the effects decreased into the secondary grades. This program has been found to influence multiple forms of victimizing behavior, including verbal, relational, physical, and cyberbullying, and improve favorable feelings towards school, academic motivation, and achievement, as well as reduce anxiety and depression.

Why does KiVa work? KiVa is designed to prevent bullying and relies on evidenced-based strategies, but it also provides strategies to address incidents of bullying behavior when they arise (see https://www.kivaprogram.net). KiVa provides extensive materials for teachers, students, and parents, including teachers' manuals, videos, online games, student and staff surveys, posters, vests, and parents' guides. KiVa is not a one-shot approach to bullying, but rather is intended to be a permanent part of a school's strategy for prevention. Currently, KiVa is being implemented predominately in European countries, but has recently started to be implemented and evaluated in the US (for additional evidence-informed prevention and intervention programs, see 10, 11, 12, 13, 16, 20*).

How Might You Establish This in Your School or Youth Setting?

Felix, Greif-Green, and Sharkey (2014) provide a review of best practices and a case study that provides practical direction for implementing bullying prevention strategies that can be used to help determine what this might look like in your setting (30, 33, 34, 35*). The most effective programs use a whole-school or community approach to prevention. They offer training for school staff, involvement of parents, and assistance to help the school improve its response to bullying concerns and reports. An important first step is to conduct a needs assessment to determine where your school or agency is in the process of moving towards a comprehensive approach to preventing bullying behavior. Next, identify a team of committed advocates who will take the lead in creating a shared vision and implementing a bullying prevention school policy and action plan. Research evidence indicates that administration and teacher commitment to any approach to bullying behavior is critical to program success. Be prepared to educate everyone (including the lunch room monitors, those who provide schoolyard supervision, the bus drivers, etc.) and teach new skills to both the adults and youth in your setting.

Empathy, acceptance of diversity, and inclusion are important aspects of social-emotional learning that can go a long way towards preventing bullying behavior. The bullying prevention program that you consider should include some combination of education, classroom discussion, and role-playing. Youth need an opportunity to talk about bullying and be heard. They also need to practice their new skills to be able to rely on them in the moment. Finally, any successful efforts to reduce bullying behavior require changing the school climate and the normative attitudes and values of youth towards these behaviors. To achieve this change, both adults and youth need to develop the knowledge and self-confidence that they can make a difference and must be equipped with the necessary skills and strategies. A positive school climate includes attitudes, norms, and values that support social, emotional, and physical safety. Creating a positive school climate is not easy but not impossible.

Bullying is a triadic relationship (Card, Rodkin, & Garandeau, 2010; Twemlow, Fonagy, & Sacco, 2004) that includes those who perpetrate bullying behavior, those who are the target of these behaviors, and those who witness these acts. Any effective intervention effort needs to focus on all these individuals. Those who perpetrate bullying behavior do not act as an individual—they become the agent of the bystanding audience, and the responses of each individual can affect the outcome (Salmivalli, 2010). If these rewards are removed by eliminating the attention and social regard awarded to bullies by peers, the payoff for the use of these behaviors is also significantly reduced. Without a payoff, there is little to sustain these behaviors. In talking to youth about the bullying dynamic, the key to a reduction in the incidence of bullying behavior is raising awareness of the contribution they make to the perpetration of the behaviors, even when they seemingly "only stand and watch". In Appendix 1, you will find an annotated list of resource materials (i.e., websites, books, and videos) for parents, teachers, school administrators, pediatricians, and others who work with youth that may be beneficial in your next steps towards bullying prevention.

The purpose of this chapter was to identify the prevention strategies that have been proven effective in decreasing bullying behavior. A strong argument has been made that interventions against bullying should be targeted at the peer-group level rather than at individual bullies and victims (Rigby & Slee, 2008; Salmivalli, 2010). Those strategies that include strong adult models, a focus on positive relationships, peer group engagement, and the endorsement of nonaggressive norms have been shown to have positive effects on problem behavior.

Conclusion

What does all this mean for those who work with children and youth? You must challenge every incidence of bullying that comes to your attention. Bullying is a learned behavior and can be prevented but children need to see that adults, teachers, and principals mean business, and that they are effective in their interventions.

Bullying is a relationship problem that requires relationship solutions. Informed parents, caregivers, teachers, and others who work with youth can build safe, supportive environments that do not endorse bullying behavior. This is accomplished when all members are on the same page and share a consistent message about what bullying is, when it is happening, how to act to stop it, and how to support those involved. It is critical for adults to manage incidents that have a serious impact on individuals and/or the school in effective ways, and build skills incompatible with bullying (i.e., empathy, inclusion, and acceptance of diversity). Bystanders are important to the social dynamic that is bullying. Our goal must be to influence group norms, build capacity in all youth, and effectively address bullying when it occurs (2*).

In conclusion, adults cannot mandate friendships, but can ensure that all youth feel included as members of their (school) community. When having conversations with youth around bullying behavior, it is essential to ensure the understanding that bullying is a learned behavior that is preventable when community members and youth come together. Bullying is a relationship problem that requires the engagement of all youth, including those who are not directly involved in the bullying behavior. Therefore, prevention and intervention efforts should focus on changing the climate and relationship dynamics of the peer group through mobilizing bystanders, modeling positive relationship skills, and endorsing powerful skills such as empathy and self-efficacy. In having conservations with youth, it is important to remember they do not have to be friends with everyone but it is NOT ok to be hurtful or harmful to anyone. Together, as a community, we should ensure that all youth develop the skills necessary for healthy social relationships—being respectful to others, regardless of differences.

Key Messages

What you need to know before you can talk to youth about bullying behavior:

1. Bullying is a learned behavior.
2. Bullying is a relationship problem requiring relationship solutions.
3. Bullying behavior is preventable.
4. Bystanders matter, a lot!
5. Prevention and intervention efforts should be focused on the peer group.

Appendix 1

Resource Materials for Parents, Teachers, School Administrators, Pediatricians, and Others Who Work with Youth

Tools to Educate

1. Authoritative information on bullying in Canada, including extensive downloadable resources for teachers and school administrators, and selective and comprehensive links to websites featuring Canadian school-based programs, can be found at: http://www.prevnet.ca

2. Pepler and Craig's (2014) Bully Prevention and Intervention in the School Environment: Factsheet and Tools is available at: http://www.prevnet.ca/sites/prevnet.ca/files/prevnet_facts_and_tools_for_schools.pdf

3. Detailed information about what to do if you are receiving hurtful messages via technology is given at: http://www.cyberbullying.ca

4. The Ontario Teacher's Federation (OTF) and the Centre Ontarien de Prévention des Agressions (COPA) are involved in putting together information for teachers on topics related to bullying and victim blaming at: https://www.safeatschool.ca/plm/bullying-prevention/understanding-bullying/victim-blaming

5. The University of British Columbia's Social & Emotional Learning (SEL) Resource Finder includes a collection of resources for educators on fostering social-emotional learning (SEL) and mental well-being in educational settings. These can be found at: http://www.selresources.com/

6. The American Academy of Pediatrics (AAP) provides information to parents on different topics of bullying, including how it differs from fighting and teasing, how to respond to bullying, and what to do if your child is the bully. This can be found at: https://www.healthychildren.org/English/safety-prevention/at-play/Pages/Bullying-Its-Not-Ok.aspx

7. Included within their website, the AAP relays important information to parents on cyberbullying, such as how to know if one's child is being cyberbullied, why it is on the rise, what to do, and when to call the police, as well as additional resources for parents to visit at: https://www.healthychildren.org/English/family-life/Media/Pages/Cyberbullying.aspx

8. The US Department of Health and Human Services manages a website dedicated to the topic of bullying and geared towards different audiences, such as parents, educators, the community, teens, and kids. State policies and laws are included as well as featured videos. These resources can be found at: https://www.stopbullying.gov/

9. The Ontario Human Rights Commission's website regarding the Ontario Safe Schools Act speaks about regulations on school safety and discriminatory and disproportionate disciplinary actions taken against minority students. This can be found at: http://www.ohrc.on.ca/en/ontario-safe-schools-act-school-discipline-and-discrimination/i-introduction

10. The Clemson University website for the Olweus Bullying Prevention Program (OBPP) focuses on bullying prevention from elementary school to grade 12, and includes research and training information. Included on their webpage is a link to their recently published "Bullying in US Schools: 2014 Status Report", which relates recent data on students' experiences and opinions on bullying during the 2013–2014 school year: http://olweus.sites.clemson.edu

11. The WITS program website includes relevant information and training guides for the prevention of peer victimization. The website includes user-friendly tools for students, families, community leaders, and kids, including books and lessons, online training, a resource guide, videos, songs, and much more: http://www.witsprogram.ca

12. The following link describes a technique for resolving bullying issues with students called the Method of Shared Concern, first suggested by Pikas (2002). It involves a series of meetings with an authority figure and the students suspected of bullying, and concludes with a statement on their behalf to resolve the issue or an apology to the target, and a promise to improve their behavior: http://www.kenrigby.net/11e-Shared-Concern-Method-How-it-Works

13. One of the main objectives of the Roots of Empathy program is to reduce levels of bullying, aggression, and violence, and promote children's pro-social behaviors. A significant reduction in levels of aggression and bullying among school children has been shown subsequent to this method. Further information on this can be found at: http://www.rootsofempathy.org

14. The Ontario Centre of Excellence for Child and Youth Mental Health works with different agencies in Ontario to strengthen services catering to youths with mental health concerns. Their website is designed

to shed light on evidence-informed practices geared towards practitioners and leaders in the field to improve the quality of care for youths at the community level: http://www.excellenceforchildandyouth.ca/resource-hub/evidence-based-strategies-mobilize-communities

15. The following web link touches on the different styles of teaching by educators, specifically on a democratic approach and its advantages to the management of student behavior. High school teacher Marcos Torres shares his personal experience on the effectiveness of changing from an authoritative teaching style to a democratic one: http://www.tolerance.org/supplement/democratic-classrooms

Websites

16. The Anti-Bullying Alliance's website describes a number of programs that focus on specific aspects of bullying behavior, and includes advice to parents and their children on taking action against bullying, as well as training for teachers on this topic: https://www.anti-bullyingalliance.org.uk

17. The Australian National Centre against Bullying website includes advice for parents, schools, and kids, the latest research on bullying, and online seminars and workshops: https://www.ncab.org.au

18. Kidscape includes online training for professionals on bullying and mentorship programs. The website includes advice for parents, young people, and professionals, as well as suggestions for protecting yourself online: https://www.kidscape.org.uk

19. The International Bullying Prevention Association website has links to published articles (outlining current research), books, websites, videos, bullying conferences, presentations and workshops: https://ibpaworld.org

20. Ken Rigby is a renowned international authority in bullying and victimization in schools with over 100 peer-refereed papers and publications. This link is useful in briefly describing Dr. Rigby's teachings for schools and parents on bullying and how to access further resources on the topic: http://www.kenrigby.net/Home

21. This link leads to an article titled "Role of the Pediatrician in Youth Violence Prevention", which urges pediatricians to take a direct role in youth violence prevention by familiarizing themselves with the American Academy of Pediatrics' primary care violence prevention protocol: http://pediatrics.aappublications.org/content/124/1/393

The Impact of Social Media on Children, Adolescents, and Families

Cyberbullying

22. *Together to Live* is a toolkit for addressing youth suicide, including prevention, postvention, risk management, and policies and protocols: http://www.togethertolive.ca/bullying-and-cyberbullying

23. Suzanne McLeod's factsheet provides a comprehensive definition of cyberbullying and relevant facts and statistics, suggestions for solutions, recommendations by professionals, and online resources: http://www.suicideinfo.ca/LinkClick.aspx?fileticket=U9Oo1Hz3LCs=&tabid=516

24. The Cyberbullying Research Centre Fact Sheet covers issues spanning the topic of cyberbullying, including the nature and extent, and solutions for preventative action: http://cyberbullying.org/cyberbullying_fact_sheet.pdf

25. This web page offers suggestions to parents on what to do if their child is a cyberbully: http://www.puresight.com/Cyberbullying/what-should-i-do-if-my-child-is-a-cyber-bully.html

Book Recommendations

For more recommendations, see PREVnet (https://www.prevnet.ca/node/1078).

Bullying in Preschool

26. Froschl, M. & Hinitz, B.S.F. (2005). *The anti-bullying and teasing book for preschool classrooms*. Lewisville, NC: Gryphon House, Inc.

    This book is comprised of 128 pages and is an easy and simple way for preschool children to understand that teasing and bullying is considered hurtful behavior. Quotes in the book give children clear messages about how to interact with other children; for example, "If you are alone, you are welcome to join a game".

27. Katch, J. (2004). *They don't like me: Lessons on bullying and teasing from a preschool classroom*. Boston, MA: Beacon Press.

    Katch offers her readers insight into the day-to-day interactions of her preschool classroom. Throughout her book, the author writes about instances that happen in her classroom and the methods she uses to resolve issues and empower her children.

28. Paley, V. (2009). *You can't say you can't play*. Cambridge, MA: Harvard University Press.

      "You can't say, you can't play"; this is the new rule that Paley enforced on her school children from kindergarten to grade 5. Through this social experiment, Paley discusses and listens to the opinions of her kids, which gives readers an insight into what kids believe constitutes as hurtful and ostracizing behavior.

29. Storey, K. & Slaby, R., G. (2013). *Eyes on bullying in early childhood*. Waltham, MA: Education Development Centre, Inc. Retrieved from http://www.eyesonbullying.org/pdfs/eob-early-childhood-508.pdf

      A 58-page pdf file on bullying in early childhood. The target audience is for early educators or any adult with children under their care. It is separated into five main sections: Understanding Bullying, What You Can Do, Activities for Building Children's Skills, Intervention Action Plan, and Resources.

30. Storey, K., Slaby, R. G., Adler, M., Minotti, J., Katz, R., Edd, K. S., & Pioneering, H. (2008, 2013). *Eyes on bullying toolkit*. Waltham, MA: Education Development Center, Inc. Retrieved from http://www.eyesonbullying.org/pdfs/toolkit.pdf

      A comprehensive 35-page toolkit complete with descriptions of terminology, quizzes, role-playing activities, and suggested approaches to prevent and stop bullying. Can be applied to youths and adults.

Bullying in Elementary School

31. Bean, A. (2005). *The bully free classroom: Over 100 tips and strategies for teachers K-8 (updated edition)*. Golden Valley, MN: Free Spirit Publishing Inc.

      An extensive resource for teachers and parents with tips and strategies to use to combat a bullying mentality. It poses thoughtful questions that are good discussion material for classrooms, such as "How would you feel if you were the new kid at school?"

32. Hinduja, S. & Patchin, J. W. (2014). *Bullying beyond the schoolyard: Preventing and responding to cyberbullying* (2nd edition). Thousand Oaks, CA: Crowin/A SAGE Company.

      This book addresses the serious issue of cyberbullying and offers suggestions for schools and policymakers to consider as they try to cope with rapidly changing social media interfaces. It provides best practices in strategy implementation, real-life examples, statistics, and effective ways of dealing with arising problems.

33. Patchin, J. W. & Hinduja, S. (2016). *Bullying today: Bullet points & best practices*. Thousand Oaks, CA: Corwin/A SAGE Company.

A small and concise book aimed at educators on creating a positive atmosphere in the school, delivered in 800-word chapters. The book includes ways to distinguish bullying from other hurtful behaviors, between cyberbullying and in-person bullying, and lists prevention strategies for teachers to incorporate.

34. Rigby, K. (2002). *Stop the bullying: A handbook for teachers.* London, England: Jessica Kingsley Publishers.

    Rigby's handbook for teachers is based on research that helps educators make the right decisions in supporting victims of bullying and dealing with children who bully. There are a number of activities that teachers can refer to and reproduce in their own classrooms.

35. Roberts, W. B. (2016). *Working with kids who bully: New perspectives on prevention and intervention.* Thousands Oaks, CA: Corwin / A SAGE Company.

    A book specific to ameliorating the behavior of children with problem behaviors and bullying tendencies. The author provides information on cyberbullying, relational aggression, and mediation. The aim of the book is to help educators and parents of bullies to understand how to better manage their children's behavior.

Bullying in Adolescence

36. Bazelon, E. (2013). *Sticks and stones: Defeating the culture of bullying and rediscovering the power of character and empathy.* New York, NY: Random House, Inc.

    The author takes us into a detailed account of the dynamics at play during bullying situations. Readers are given information on real-life stories from the perspectives of bullies and their victims.

37. Wiseman, R. (2016). *Owning up: Empowering adolescents to confront social cruelty, bullying and injustice.* Thousand Oaks, California: Corwin / A SAGE Company.

    This book imparts knowledge on several important themes that impact young people's lives and helps them better understand how to navigate through their issues. It includes material for group leaders to share with students, such as discussion topics, group activities, and games.

Videos

Glazier, L. (2004). *It's a girl's world.* Retrieved from https://www.nfb.ca/film/its_a_girls_world/

This documentary is about a "popular" clique formed from a handful of ten-year-old girls that shows us a vicious reality of the verbal abuse perpetrated towards their own friends in the hopes of gaining more social power. It is a stand-alone series of six modules, ranging from 5 to 10 minutes, about different aspects of social bullying. Intermissions between modules are intended to prompt classroom discussion to raise awareness on the serious consequences of bullying.

Hirsch, L. (2011). *Bully*. Retrieved from https://docur.co/documentary/the-bully-project
The filmmaker of this documentary executed a very realistic take on what bullying looks like in America every day for an average of 13 million kids in school. This 90-minute documentary includes personal accounts of students and their families on how bullying has affected their lives.

Ibrahim, F. (2012). *Web of hate*. Retrieved from http://documentarylovers.com/film/web-of-hate/
Australia is rated one of the top countries with issues in cyberbullying. This documentary takes a close look at what it is like for youths who are continuously victimized by this seemingly inescapable form of bullying.

Books for Youth

Preschoolers–Grade 2:

Bateman, T. (2004). *The bully blockers club. Park Ridge*, IL: Albert Whitman Prairie Books.
This 32-page illustrated storybook is about Lotty Raccoon and the different ways she tries to overcome her bully at school.

Button, L. (2013). *Willow finds a way*. Toronto, ON: Kids Can Press.
This picture book depicts the story of a shy and quiet student, Willow, and how she deals with her bossy classmate who has her classmates under her thumb by threat of uninviting guests to her awesome birthday party. This book offers great lessons to students on how to emulate the actions of Willow and stand up to manipulative bullies.

Henkes, K. (2008). *Chrysanthemum*. New York, NY: Greenwillow Books. (Discussion questions can be found at: http://www.witsprogram.ca/pdfs/schools/books/chrysanthemum/chrysanthemum.pdf)
Henkes's *Chrysanthemum* was named a Notable Book for Children by the American Library Association and depicts the story of a girl whose self-esteem was challenged when teased about her name on the first day of school. This story speaks to the negative effects of teasing, self-esteem issues, and the power of acceptance.

McCain, B. (2001). *Nobody knew what to do: A story about bullying*. Park Ridge, IL: Albert Whitman & Company.
A young boy, although fearful, steps up and tells his teacher about his friend being bullied and subsequently puts an immediate stop to it. McCain's book tackles the issue of the bystander effect and teaches young children to speak up when they witness bullying.

Moss, P. (2004). *Say something*. Thomaston, ME: Tilbury House Publishers.
Say Something is about a girl who witnesses multiple acts of bullying at her school but never does anything about it. One day, she becomes the target of a joke herself and feels frustrated by the silence of her schoolmates. Through this incident, the protagonist

realizes the power of speaking up when others are being bullied. The book includes topics for discussion at the back of the book, as well as advice for kids on bullying.

Munson, D. (2000). *Enemy pie*. San Francisco, CA: Chronicle Books. (Discussion questions can be found at: http://www.witsprogram.ca/pdfs/schools/books/enemy-pie/enemy-pie.pdf)
This story is about a boy whose father sneakily teaches him how to make a friend out of his enemy by having him spend the day with him. The boy quickly realizes that he and his "enemy" have much in common and subsequently learns the importance of giving people the "benefit of the doubt".

O'Neill, A. (2002). *The recess queen*. New York, NY: Scholastic Press. (Discussion questions can be found at: http://www.witsprogram.ca/pdfs/schools/books/recess-queen/the-recess-queen.pdf)
This short story is about Mean Jean, who lords over the playground and inspires fear from other students. A new student by the name of Katie Sue is not intimidated by Mean Jean but instead asks her to jump rope with her. This story teaches children that sometimes bullies are simply lonely and want to play, and that a bully's power is reinforced by others' fear of them.

Roberts, J. (2014). *The smallest girl in the smallest grade*. London, England: G.P. Putnam's Sons Books for Young Readers.
This story is about a small girl who goes mostly unnoticed by everyone and yet notices everything around her, including the bullying of her peer. In this story, readers will realize that a person's size has little to do with their courage and that everyone can make a difference.

Sornson, B., & Dismondy, M. (2010) *Juice box bully: Empowering kids to stand up for others*. Northville, MI: Ferne Press.
Pete decides to become the school bully at his new school. However, his classmates have made a "promise" at the beginning of the year to get involved if they witness bullying. Needless to say, Pete's bullying antics do not go as planned when his actions are met with kindness.

Woodson, J. (2012). *Each kindness*. New York, NY: Nancy Paulsen Books, Penguin Young Readers.
Woodson's book is written in a realistic tone about a young girl, Maya, who is shunned by her classmates because she is different. Chloe sees this happening but does not do anything about it until, eventually, Maya stops coming to school. When her teacher gives them a lesson on the power of small acts of kindness, Chloe is filled with regret due to her inaction. Woodson's ending leaves readers feeling powerless to rectify the situation and teaches people to always take action before it is too late.

Grades 3–6

Blume, J. (1980). *Blubber*. Basingstoke, Hampshire, UK: Macmillan Children's Books. (Discussion questions and activities can be found at: http://www.witsprogram.ca/pdfs/schools/books/blubber/blubber.pdf)
Blubber is a story about bullying from the perspective of one of the bullies. It is a realistic portrayal of the life of a fifth grader and the pressures they feel to act a certain way towards others simply to fit in.

Estes, E. (2004). *The hundred dresses*. San Diego, CA: Harcourt Brace & Company. (Discussion questions and activities can be found at: http://www.witsprogram.ca/pdfs/schools/books/the-hundred-dresses/the-hundred-dresses.pdf)

This book depicts the story of a girl who is ridiculed by her classmates for always wearing the same dress to school every day, despite adamantly telling everyone that she has a hundred different dresses in her closet. This story teaches an important lesson about never judging others based on their appearance.

Goldblatt, M. (2014) *Twerp*. New York, NY: Yearling Books, Random House Books for Young Readers.

Twerp is about a boy who makes a deal with his teacher to write a journal on him and his friends instead of an essay on Julius Caesar. Julian readily agrees and writes about the happenings of his schoolmates and the subtle and not-so-subtle manipulations and bullying that take place in a 1969 New York neighborhood.

Ludwig, T. (2005). *My secret bully*. Berkeley, CA: Tricycle Press.

Ludwig's *My Secret Bully* deals with relational aggression; a form of emotional bullying that often goes unnoticed by people except for the target of the bullying. This story delivers a clear message about bullying, that it is not always loud and physical, but can sometimes be verbal and quiet and can still cause significant damage.

Ludwig, T. (2006). *Just kidding*. Berkeley, CA: Tricycle Press. (Discussion questions and activities can be found at: http://www.witsprogram.ca/pdfs/schools/books/just-kidding/just-kidding.pdf)

Ludwig delivers another great read about relational aggression in her book *Just Kidding*, which is about a boy who is teased by his friend in a joking manner and is afraid to speak up about his frustration lest his friends think he cannot take a joke. This relatable story delivers a crucial message about the power of words to hurt others.

Ludwig, T. (2006). *Sorry*. Berkeley, CA: Tricycle Press.

Jack's friend Charlie overuses the word "sorry" to apologize for his wrongdoings, despite not meaning it. Jack decides to emulate his actions to remain his friend. However, Jack and Charlie both learn a lesson about the importance of a heartfelt apology.

Ludwig, T. (2012). *Confessions of a former bully*. Berkeley, CA: Tricycle Press.

This story is narrated from the point of view of the bully. Katie is called to the guidance counselor's office to rectify her behavior after she is caught teasing a classmate. This book gives kids practical ways to deal with bullying. Its pages are designed in a creative way to clarify important terms such as the distinction between "tattling" and "reporting".

Madonna (2003). *The English roses*, New York, NY: Callaway Editions. (Discussion questions and activities can be found at: http://www.witsprogram.ca/pdfs/schools/books/the-english-roses/the-english-roses.pdf).

The English Roses is about four best friends who do everything together. Binah, the new girl, is seemingly perfect and loved by everyone, which frustrates the four girls and makes her the target of all their envy. A fairy godmother appears and takes the four girls on a magical journey to teach them about the importance of compassion and friendship. This book highlights the use of social aggression as a way to exclude someone from the group.

Polacco, P. (2012). *Bully*. London, England: G.P. Putnam's Sons Books for Young Readers, Penguin Publishing Group.

Lyla is invited to join the popular clique at her new school. This new friendship soon loses its appeal when Lyla realizes they are bullying other students on Facebook. When she decides to leave them, they quickly turn their ire on her. The book ends with a question posed to the reader about how they would react in the same situation.

Romain, T. (1997). *Bullies are a pain in the brain*. Golden Valley, MN: Free Spirit Publishing.
Romain combines fun wit and practical advice for kids dealing with bullies in his book *Bullies are a Pain in the Brain*. He describes some ways to become "bully-proof" and get help in dangerous situations.

Adolescence

Anderson, L. (1999). *Speak*. New York, NY: Square Fish/Macmillan Publishing.
Melinda is an outcast at her school because she called the police to break up an end-of-summer party for the students. In reality, Melinda was raped by one of the students at her school that night and is afraid to say anything about it. When her attacker starts to harass her once more, Melinda finally embraces her ability to speak up.

Asher, J. (2011). *Thirteen reasons why*. New York, NY: Razorbill, Penguin Young Readers.
Prior to her suicide, Hannah Baker left recorded messages to Clay Jensen detailing the 13 reasons that pushed her to commit suicide. Her recordings help him uncover realities happening in Clay's town that will change his life forever.

Goldman Koss, A. (2000) *The girls*. London, UK: Puffin Books.
Maya's new clique decides to exclude her based on the whims of Candace, the head of the group. Although the other girls do not understand why they have to stop being friends with Maya, they blindly follow Candace's orders. This book takes on multiple character viewpoints and gives the reader better insight on each girl's emotions and thought processes.

Preller, J. (2011). *Bystander*. New York, NY: Square Fish/Macmillan Publishing.
Eric befriends Griffin, a charismatic and seemingly nice boy who is at the center of a wild group of boys. Unbeknownst to the adults, Griffin is in actuality a big bully who constantly picks on other students. Eric quickly finds himself in the position of a bystander and needs to come up with a solution to stop the bully.

Darer Littman, S. (2015). *Backlash*. New York, NY: Scholastic Press.
Backlash takes on the perspective of four emotionally vulnerable teenagers as they navigate through life with their insecurities. Some of the topics it discusses are cyberbullying, suicide/mental illness, sexuality, and sibling and parent relationships.

References

APA's Zero Tolerance Task Force. (2008). Are zero tolerance policies effective in the schools? An evidentiary review and recommendations. *American Psychologist*, *63*(9), 852–862. doi:10.1037/0003–066X.63.9.852

Atlas, R. S., & Pepler, D. J. (1998). Observations of bullying in the classroom. *The Journal of Educational Research*, *92*(2), 86–99.

Bauman, S., & Newman, M. L. (2013). Testing assumptions about cyberbullying: Perceived distress associated with acts of conventional and cyber bullying. *Psychology of Violence, 3*(1), 27–38. doi:10.1037/a0029867

Bauman, S., Rigby, K., & Hoppa, K. (2008). US teachers' and school counsellors' strategies for handling school bullying incidents. *Educational Psychology, 28*(7), 837–856. doi:10.1080/01443410802379085

Bazelon, E. (2013). *Sticks and stones: Defeating the culture of bullying and rediscovering the power of character and empathy.* New York, NY: Random House, Inc.

Blake, J. J., Lund, E. M., Zhou, Q., Kwok, O., & Benz, M. R. (2012). National prevalence rates of bully victimization among students with disabilities in the United States. *School Psychology Quarterly, 27*(4), 210–222. doi:10.1037/spq0000008

Boccanfuso, C., & Kuhfeld, M. (2011). Multiple responses, promising results: Evidence-based, nonpunitive alternatives to zero tolerance. *Child Trends, 9*, 1–12, Retrieved from www.childtrends.org/wp-content/uploads/2011/03/Child_Trends-2011_03_01_RB_Alt-ToZeroTolerance.pdf

Boulton, M. J., Trueman, M., Chau, C., Whitehand, C., & Amatya, K. (1999). Concurrent and longitudinal links between friendship and peer victimization: Implications for befriending interventions. *Journal of Adolescence, 22*(4), 461–466.

Brent, R. H. (2007). Safety and Security in Schools: Update on the Safe Schools Act—Beyond Zero Tolerance? Retrieved from http://litigationstudent.com/sites/default/files/Safety-and-Security-in-Schools-presentation.PDF

Card, N. (2010). Antipathetic relationships in child and adolescent development: A meta-analytic review and recommendations for an emerging area of study. *Developmental Psychology, 46*(2), 516–529. doi:10.1037/a0017199

Card, N. A., & Hodges, E. V. E. (2008). Peer victimization among schoolchildren: Correlations, causes, consequences, and considerations in assessment and intervention. *School Psychology Quarterly, 23*(4), 451–461. doi:10.1037/a0012769

Card, N., Rodkin, P., & Garandeau, C. (2010). A description and illustration of the triadic relations model: Who perceived whom as bullying whom? *International Journal of Behavioral Development, 34*(4), 374–383. doi:10.1177/0165025410371418

Coyne, S. M., Archer, J., & Eslea, M. (2006). "We're not friends anymore! Unless. . .": The frequency and harmfulness of indirect, relational, and social aggression. *Aggressive Behavior, 32*(4), 294–307. doi:10.1002/ab.20126

Craig, W. M., & Pepler, D. J. (1998). Observations of bullying and victimization in the school yard. *Canadian Journal of School Psychology, 13*, 41–59. doi:10.1177/082957359801300205

Crick, N. R. (1996). The role of overt aggression, relational aggression, and prosocial behavior in the prediction of children's future social adjustment. *Child Development, 67*(5), 2317–2327. doi:10.1111/j.1467–8624.1996.tb01859.x

Crick, N. R., & Grotpeter, J. K. (1995). Relational aggression, gender, and social-psychological adjustment. *Child Development, 66*(3), 710–722.

Dess, J., White, T., Jaffe, E. M., & Jaffe, S. L. (2011). *Understanding playful vs. hurtful teasing and bullying behavior.* Marietta, GA: The Prevention Intervention Center for Cobb Country School District.

Dooley, J. J., Pyżalski, J., & Cross, D. (2009). Cyberbullying versus face-to-face bullying: A theoretical and conceptual review. *Zeitschrift für Psychologie/Journal of Psychology, 217*(4), 182–188. doi:10.1080/00221325.2014.934653

Dovidio, J. F., Pilavin, J. A., Gaertner, S. L., Schroeder, D. A., & Clark, R. D. (1991). The arousal: cost-reward model and the process of intervention: A review of the evidence.

Review of Personality and Social Psychology, 12, 83–118. Retrieved from http://psr. sagepub.com/

Espelage, D. L., Aragon, S. R., Birkett, M., & Koenig, B. W. (2008). Homophobic teasing, psychological outcomes, and sexual orientation among high school students: What influence do parents and schools have? *School Psychology Review, 37*(2), 202.

Espelage, D. L., & Goldblum, P. (2015). *Youth suicide and bullying: Challenges and strategies for prevention and intervention.* New York, NY: Oxford University Press.

Faris, R., & Felmlee, D. (2014). Casualties of social combat: School networks of peer victimization and their consequences. *American Sociological Review, 79*(2), 228–257. doi:10.1177/0003122414524573

Fekkes, M., Pijpers, F. I. M., & Verloove-Vanhorick, S. P. (2005). Bullying: Who does what, when and where? Involvement of children, teachers and parents in bullying behavior. *Health Education Research, 20*(1), 81–91. doi:10.1093/her/cyg100

Felix, E. D., Greif-Green, J., & Sharkey, J. (2014). Best practices in bullying prevention. In *Best practices in school psychology* (pp. 245–258). Bethesda, MD: National Association of School Psychologists.

Fisher, R., Ury, W., & Patton, B. (1991). *Getting to yes: Negotiating agreement without giving in* (2nd ed.). Boston, MA: Houghton Mifflin.

Fox, C., & Boulton, M. (2003). Evaluating the effectiveness of a social skills training (SST) program for victims of bullying. *Educational Research, 45*(3), 231–247. doi. org/10.1080/0013188032000137238

Galen, B. R., & Underwood, M. K. (1997). A developmental investigation of social aggression among children. *Developmental Psychology, 33*(4), 589–600.

Gini, G. (2006). Social cognition and moral cognition in bullying: What's wrong? *Aggressive Behavior, 32,* 528–539. doi:10.1002/ab.20153

Gini, G., Albeiro, P., Benelli, B., & Altoe, G. (2008). Determinants of adolescents' active and passive bystanding behavior in bullying. *Journal of Adolescence, 31,* 93–105. doi:10.1002/ab.20204

Gladden, R. M., Vivolo-Kantor, A. M., Hamburger, M. E., & Lumpkin, C. D. (2014). *Bullying surveillance among youths: Uniform definitions for public health and recommended data elements* (version 1.0). Atlanta, GA: National Center for Injury Prevention and Control, Centers for Disease Control and Prevention and U.S. Department of Education.

Green, M. (2006). Bullying in schools: A plea for measure of rights. *Journal of Social Issues, 62*(1), 63–79.

Hawkins, D. L., Pepler, D. J., & Craig, W. M. (2001). Naturalistic observations of peer interventions in bullying. *Social Development, 10,* 512–527.

Hawker, D. S. J., & Boulton, M. J. (2000). Twenty years' research on peer victimization and psychosocial maladjustment: A meta-analytic review of cross-sectional studies. *The Journal of Child Psychology and Psychiatry and Allied Disciplines, 41*(4), 441–455. doi:10.1017/S0021963099005545

Hinduja, S., & Patchin, J. W. (2014). *Bullying beyond the schoolyard: Preventing and responding to cyberbullying.* Thousand Oaks, CA: Corwin Press.

Hodges, E., Boivin, M., Vitaro, F., & Bukowski, W. (1999). The power of friendship: Protection against an escalating cycle of peer victimization. *Developmental Psychology, 35,* 94–101.

Hodges, E. V. E., & Perry, D. G. (1999). Personal and interpersonal antecedents and consequences of victimization by peers. *Journal of Personality and Social Psychology, 76,* 677–685.

Hymel, S., Rocke-Henderson, N., & Bonanno, R. A. (2005). Moral disengagement: A framework for understanding bullying among adolescents. *Journal of Social Sciences*, *8*, 1–11.

Juvonen, J., Graham, S., & Schuster, M. A. (2003). Bullying among young adolescents: The strong, the weak, and the troubled. *Pediatrics*, *112*(6), 1231–1237. doi:10.1542/peds.112.6.1231

Kärnä, A., Voeten, M., Little, T., Poskiparta, E., Kaljonen, A., & Salmivalli, K. (2011). A large-scale evaluation of the KiVa antibullying program. *Child Development*, *82*, 311–330. doi:10.1111/j.1467-8624.2010.01557.x

Kärnä, A., Voeten, M., Poskiparta, E., & Salmivalli, K. (2010). Vulnerable children in varying classroom contexts bystanders' behaviors moderate the effects of risk factors on victimization. *Merrill-Palmer Quarterly*, *56*(3), 261–282. doi:10.1353/mpq.0.0052

Kendrick, K., Jutengren, G., & Stattin, H. (2012). The protective role of supportive friends against bullying perpetration and victimization. *Journal of Adolescence*, *35*, 1069–1080. doi:10.1016/j.adolescence.2012.02.014

Kumpulainen, K., Räsänen, E., & Henttonen, I. (1999). Children involved in bullying: Psychological disturbance and the persistence of the involvement. *Child Abuse & Neglect*, *23*(12), 1253–1262. doi:10.1016/S0145-2134(99)00098-8

Ladd, G. W., & Troop-Gordon, W. (2003). The role of chronic peer difficulties in the development of children's psychological adjustment problems. *Child Development*, *74*(5), 1344–1367. doi:10.1111/1467-8624.00611

Lamont, J. (2013). Policy statement, American Academy of pediatrics: Out-of-school suspension and expulsion. *Pediatrics*, *131*(3), 1001–1008. doi:10.1542/peds.2012-3932.

Li, Q. (2006). Cyberbullying in schools: A research of gender differences. *School Psychology International*, *27*(2), 157–170. doi:10.1177/0143034306064547

Limber, S. P. (2004). Implementation of the Olweus bullying prevention program in American schools: Lessons learned from the field. In D. L. Espelage & S. M. Swearer (Eds.), *Bullying in American schools* (pp. 351–364). Mahwah, NJ: Erlbaum.

Leff, S., Kupersmidt, J., Patterson, C., & Power, T. (1999). Factors influencing teacher identification of peer bullies and victims. *School Psychology Review*, *28*(3), 505–517.

McDougall, P., & Vaillancourt, T. (2015). Long-term adult outcomes of peer victimization in childhood and adolescence: Pathways to adjustment and maladjustment. *The American Psychologist*, *70*(4), 300. doi:10.1037/a0039174

Merrill, R., & Hanson, C. (2016). Risk and protective factors associated with being bullied on school property compared with cyberbullied. *BioMedCentral Public*, *16*(1), 145. doi:10.1186/s12889-016-2833-3

Modecki, K. L., Minchin, J., Harbaugh, A. G., Guerra, N. G., & Runions, K. C. (2014). Bullying prevalence across contexts: A meta-analysis measuring cyber and traditional bullying. *Journal of Adolescent Health*, *55*, 602–611. doi:http://dx.doi.org/10.1016/j.jadohealth.2014.06.007

Obermann, M. L. (2011). Moral disengagement among bystanders to school bullying. *Journal of School Violence*, *10*, 239–257. doi:10.1080/15388220.2011.578276

O'Connell, P., Pepler, D., & Craig, W. (1999). Peer involvement in bullying: Insights and challenges for intervention. *Journal of Adolescence*, *22*, 437–452.

Olweus, D. (1996). Bullying at school: Knowledge base and an effective intervention program. *Annals of the New York Academy of Sciences*, *794*, 265–276. doi:10.1111/j.1749-6632.1996.tb32527.x

Ontario Safe Schools Action Team. (2006). *Safe schools policy and practice: An agenda for action*. Toronto, ON: Queen's Printer for Ontario. Retrieved from www.edu.gov.on.ca/eng/ssareview/report0626.pdf

Patchin, J. W. (2016). Distinguishing bullying from other hurtful behaviors. In J. W. Patchin & S. Hinduja (Eds.), *Bullying today: Bullet points & best practices* (Ch.2). Thousand Oaks, CA: Corwin/A SAGE Company.

Peeters, M., Cillessen, A., & Scholte, R. (2010). Clueless, or powerful? Identifying subtypes of bullies in adolescence. *Journal of Youth and Adolescence, 39*(9), 1041–1052. doi:10.1007/s10964-009-9478-9

Pellegrini, A. D. (2002). Bullying, victimization, and sexual harassment during the transition to middle school. *Educational Psychologist, 37*, 151–163. doi:10.1207/S15326985EP3703_2

Pepler, D. J., & Craig, W. M. (1995). A peek behind the fence: Naturalistic observations of aggressive children with remote audiovisual recording. *Developmental Psychology, 31*(4), 548. doi:10.1037/0012–1649.31.4.548

Pepler, D. J., & Craig, W. M. (1999). Children who bully: Will they just grow out of it? *Orbit, 29*(4), 16.

Pepler, D., & Craig, W. (2014) *Bully prevention and intervention in the school environment: Factsheet and tools*. Retrieved from www.prevnet.ca/bullying/facts-and-solutions

Pikas, A. (2002). New developments of the shared concern method. *School Psychology International, 23*(3), 307–326. doi:10.1177/0143034302023003234

Pornari, C. D., & Wood, J. (2010). Peer and cyber aggression in secondary school students: The role of moral disengagement, hostile attribution bias, and outcome expectancies. *Aggressive Behavior, 36*(2), 81–94. doi:10.1002/ab.20336 PREVNet. (2017). Retrieved from www.prevnet.ca/

Quigley, D. (2017, May 17). Anti-bullying vs. bullying prevention: Do the terms we use make a difference? *Promoting Relationships and Eliminating Violence Network (PREVNet)*. Retrieved from https://www.prevnet.ca/blog/general/anti-bullying-vs-bullying-prevention-do-the-terms-we-use-make-a-difference.

Reiney, E., & Limber, S. (2013) *Why we don't use the word "bully" to label Kids*. Retrieved from www.stopbullying.gov/blog/2013/10/23/why-we-don%25E2%2580%2599t-use-word-%25E2%2580%259Cbully%25E2%2580%259D-label-kids

Rigby, K. (2001). Health consequences of bullying and its prevention in schools. In J. Juvonen & S. Graham (Eds.), *Peer harassment in school. The plight of the vulnerable and victimized* (pp. 310–331.). New York, NY: Guilford Press.

Rigby, K. (2003). Consequences of bullying in schools. *The Canadian Journal of Psychiatry, 48*(9), 583–590. doi:https://doi.org/10.1177/070674370304800904

Rigby, K. (2011). What can schools do about cases of bullying? *Pastoral Care in Education, 29*(4), 273–285. doi:10.1080/02643944.2011.626068

Rigby, K., & Cox, I. (1996). The contribution of bullying at school and low self-esteem to acts of delinquency among Australian teenagers. *Personality and Individual Differences, 21*(4), 609–612. doi:10.1016/0191–8869(96)00105–5

Rigby, K., & Slee, P. (2008). Interventions to reduce bullying. *International Journal of Adolescent Medicine and Health, 20*(2), 165–184. doi:10.1515/IJAMH.2008.20.2.165

Rivers, I. (2001). The bullying of sexual minorities at school: Its nature and long-term correlates. *Educational and Child Psychology, 18*(1), 32–46.

Rivers, I., Poteat, V. P., Noret, N., & Ashurst, N. (2009). Observing bullying at school: The mental health implications of witness status. *School Psychology Quarterly, 24*, 211–223. doi:10.1037/a0018164

Rodkin, P., Farmer, T., Pearl, R., & Van Acker, R. (2000). Heterogeneity of popular boys: Antisocial and prosocial configurations. *Developmental Psychology, 36,* 14–24. doi:i0.1037//OOI2–1649.36.1.14

Safe Schools Action Team. (2006). *Safe schools policy and practice: An agenda for action.* Retrieved from www.edu.gov.on.ca

Sainio, M., Veenstra, R., Huitsing, G., & Salmivalli, C. (2011). Victims and their defenders: A dyadic approach. *International Journal of Behavioral Development, 35,* 442–455. doi:10.1177/0165025410378068

Salmivalli, C. (1998). Intelligent, attractive, well behaving, unhappy: The structure of adolescents' self-concept and its relation to their social behavior. *Journal of Research on Adolescence, 8*(3), 333–354.

Salmivalli, C. (1999). Participant role approach to school bullying: Implications for intervention. *Journal of Adolescence, 22*(4), 453–459. doi:10.1006/jado.1999.0239

Salmivalli, C. (2010). Bullying and the peer group: A review. *Aggression and Violent Behavior, 15*(2), 112–120. doi:10.1016/j.avb.2009.08.007

Salmivalli, C., Kärnä, A., & Poskiparta, E. (2011). Counteracting bullying in Finland: The KiVa program and its effects on different forms of being bullied. *International Journal of Behavioral Development, 35*(5), 405–411. doi:10.1177/0165025411407457

Salmivalli, C., & Peets, K. (2008). Bullies, victims, and bully—Victim relationships. In K. Rubin, W. Bukowski, & B. Laursen (Eds.), *Handbook of peer interactions, relationships, and groups* (pp. 322–340). New York, NY: Guilford Press.

Salmivalli, C. C., Voeten, M., & Poskiparta, E. (2011). Bystanders matter: Associations between reinforcing, defending, and the frequency of bullying behavior in classrooms. *Journal of Clinical Child & Adolescent Psychology, 40*(5), 668–676. doi:10.1080/15374416.2011.597090

Salmivalli, C. (2014). Participant roles in bullying: How can peer bystanders be utilized in interventions? *Theory into Practice, 53*(4), 286–292. doi:10.1080/00405841.2014.947222

Schenk, A. M., & Fremouw, W. J. (2012). Prevalence, psychological impact, and coping of cyberbully victims among college students. *Journal of School Violence, 11*(1), 21–37. doi:10.1080/15388220.2011.630310

Seals, D., & Young, J. (2003). Bullying and victimization: Prevalence and relationship to gender, grade level, ethnicity, self-esteem, and depression. *Adolescence, 38*(152), 735.

Shapka, J., & Amos, H. (2012). Cyberbullying and bullying are not the same: UBC research. *NewsRx Health & Science.* Retrived from http://news.ubc.ca/2012/04/13/cyberbullying-and-bullying-are-not-the-same-ubc-research/

Silva, M. A. I., Pereira, B., Mendonça, D., Nunes, B., & de Oliveira, W. A. (2013). The involvement of girls and boys with bullying: An analysis of gender differences. *International Journal of Environmental Research and Public Health, 10*(12), 6820–6831. doi:10.3390/ijerph10126820

Sinyor, M., Schaffer, A., & Cheung, A. H. (2014). An observational study of bullying as a contributing factor in youth suicide in Toronto. *The Canadian Journal of Psychiatry, 59*(12), 632–638. doi:10.1177/070674371405901204

Slonje, R., & Smith, P. K. (2008). Cyberbullying: Another main type of bullying? *Scandinavian Journal of Psychology, 49*(2), 147–154. doi:10.1111/j.1467-9450.2007.00611.x

Smith, P. K., Mahdavi, J., Carvalho, M., Fisher, S., Russell, S., & Tippett, N. (2008). Cyberbullying: Its nature and impact in secondary school pupils. *Journal of Child Psychology and Psychiatry, 49*(4), 376–385. doi:10.1111/j.1469-7610.2007.01846.x

Srabstein, J., Joshi, P., Due, P., Wright, J., Leventhal, B., Merrick, J., . . . Riibner, K. (2008). Prevention of public health risks linked to bullying: A need for a whole community approach. *International Journal of Adolescence Medical Health, 20*(2), 185–199.

Swearer, S., & Espelage, D. (2004) Introduction: A social-ecological framework of bullying among youth. In D. Espelage & S. Swearer (Eds.), *Bullying in American schools: A social-ecological perspective on prevention and intervention* (pp. 1–12). Mahwah, NJ: Laurence Erlbaum Associates.

Swearer, S. M., & Hymel, S. (2015). Understanding the psychology of bullying: Moving toward a social-ecological diathesis-stress model. *The American Psychologist, 70*(4), 344–353. doi:10.1037/a0038929

Thornberg, R., Tenenbaum, L., Varjas, K., Meyers, J., Jungert, T., & Vanegas, G., . . . Filosofiska fakulteten. (2012). Bystander motivation in bullying incidents: To intervene or not to intervene?. *The Western Journal of Emergency Medicine, 13*(3), 247–252. doi:https://doi.org/10.5811/westjem.2012.3.11792

Trach, J., Hymel, S., Waterhouse, T., & Neale, K. (2010). Bystander responses to school bullying: A cross-sectional investigation of grade and sex differences. *Canadian Journal of School Psychology, 25*, 114–130. doi:10.1177/0829573509357553

Twemlow, S. W., Fonagy, P., & Sacco, F. C., (2004). The role of the bystander in the social architecture of bullying and violence in schools and communities. *Annals of the New York Academy of Sciences, 1036*, 215–232. doi:10.1196/annals.1330.014.

Vaillancourt, T., Duku, E., Decatanzaro, D., Macmillan, H., Muir, C., & Schmidt, L. A. (2008). Variation in hypothalamic—pituitary—adrenal axis activity among bullied and non-bullied children. *Aggressive Behavior, 34*(3), 294–305. doi:10.1002/ab.20240.

Vaillancourt, T., Hymel, S., & McDougall, P. (2003). Bullying is power: Implications for school-based intervention strategies. *Journal of Applied School Psychology, 19*(2), 157–176. doi:10.1300/J008v19n02_10.

Vaillancourt, T., Hymel, S., & McDougall, P. (2013). The biological underpinnings of peer victimization: Understanding why and how the effects of bullying can last a lifetime. *Theory into Practice, 52*(4), 241–248. doi:10.1080/00405841.2013.829726

Vandebosch, H., & Van Cleemput, K. (2008). Defining cyberbullying: A qualitative research into the perceptions of youngsters. *CyberPsychology & Behavior, 11*(4), 499–503. doi:10.1089/cpb.2007.0042

Veenstra, R., Lindenberg, S., Oldehinkel, A., De Winter, A., Verhulst, F., & Ormel, J. (2005). Bullying and victimization in elementary schools: A comparison of bullies, victims, bully/victims, and uninvolved preadolescents. *Developmental Psychology, 41*(4), 672–682.

Veenstra, R., Verlinden, M., Huitsing, G., Verhulst, F. C., & Tiemeier, H. (2013). Behind bullying and defending: Same-sex and other-sex relations and their associations with acceptance and rejection. *Aggressive Behavior, 39*, 462–471.

Volk, A. A., Camilleri, J. A., Dane, A. V., & Marini, Z. A. (2012). Is adolescent bullying an evolutionary adaptation? *Aggressive Behavior, 38*(3), 222–238. doi:10.1002/ab.21418

Wiseman, R. (2016). *Owning up: Empowering adolescents to confront social cruelty, bullying and injustice.* Thousand Oaks, CA: Corwin Press.

Wolke, D., & Lereya, S. T. (2015). Long-term effects of bullying. *Archives of Disease in Childhood, 100*(9), 879–885. doi:10.1136/archdischild-2014-306667

Wolke, D., Lereya, S. T., Fisher, H. L., Lewis, G., & Zammit, S. (2014). Bullying in elementary school and psychotic experiences at 18 years: A longitudinal, population-based cohort study. *Psychological Medicine, 44*(10), 2199–2211. doi:10.1017/S0033291713002912

Addressing Problematic Substance Use in Adolescence

2

What Works?

Kara Thompson and Abby L. Goldstein

Adolescence is a critical time for the establishment of healthy behaviors but it is also a key time for experimentation and self-discovery. The use of alcohol and drugs is often a part of this experimentation and is largely the norm by the end of high school. Alcohol is by far the most commonly used substance, with approximately 40% of Canadian and American youth in grades 7 through 12 reporting drinking in the last year[1] (Health Canada, 2016; Miech, Johnston, O'Malley, Bachman, & Schulenberg, 2016). Most adolescents initiate substance use between 13 and 14 years of age, and the proportion of youth who use substances increases dramatically across the high school years (Health Canada, 2016; Kann et al., 2016; Miech et al., 2016). For example, the proportion of students drinking alcohol increased from approximately 20% of junior high students (in grades 7 through 9) to nearly 60% of students in grade 12 in both Canadian and US samples (Health Canada, 2016; Miech et al., 2016). Marijuana is the second most commonly used substance among youth (Canadian youth = 17%; US youth = 23%) and the most commonly used illicit drug. However, few students use tobacco, with only 4% of Canadian youth and 3.5% of US youth reporting smoking regularly, and relatively few engage in other types of illicit drug use (5% of Canadian youth; 10.5% of

US youth) (Health Canada, 2016; Miech et al., 2016). The rates of substance use are similar for girls and boys in Canadian samples, but in US samples, boys tend to use at slightly higher rates than girls and these gender differences tend to grow over time (Health Canada, 2016; Miech et al., 2016).

The good news is that the prevalence of alcohol and drug use among Canadian and American teens has been on the decline over the past decade (Health Canada, 2016; Miech et al., 2016). Contrary to popular belief, the prevalence of marijuana use among Canadian youth is at its lowest in the last 20 years, dropping from 27% in 2008–2009 to 17% in 2014–2015 (Health Canada, 2016). Moreover, the vast majority of adolescents do not use alcohol and drugs (Health Canada, 2016; Miech et al., 2016). Of those who do, many use them only occasionally or experimentally and are at low risk for experiencing harmful consequences. However, others engage in more frequent heavy use and have pre-existing vulnerabilities (e.g., behavioral problems) that increase their risk of experiencing significant health and social harms (Committee on Substance Abuse, 2010). Youth are also more vulnerable to the negative consequences of substance use than adults because of the significant social, psychological, and physiological changes occurring during this developmental period (Brown et al., 2009). Addressing youth substance use in the context of these changes is important for helping young people successfully navigate the transition to adulthood.

Schools and teachers are uniquely situated to identify young people at risk for problematic substance use and implement interventions to minimize the likelihood of substance-related harm. Effectively reducing harm from adolescent alcohol and drug use requires an understanding of the developmental precursors of substance use and the multiple risk factors that contribute to problematic substance use patterns. This chapter focuses on increasing your knowledge of how and why youth use substances, and how to engage productively with youth about their substance use and implement evidence-based, developmentally appropriate strategies. We focus specifically on alcohol and marijuana, the two most commonly used substances. However, many of the risk factors, consequences, and prevention strategies discussed herein are equally applicable to other substances used by adolescents.

Distinguishing Between Problematic and Non-Problematic Use

How do you know if an adolescent's substance use is a problem or a normative part of adolescent development? Knowing that a young person has ever used a substance does not give any insight into *how* they are using (i.e., how much or how often) or whether there are any problems with their use. Use is not equivalent to misuse, and certain patterns of alcohol and drug use are riskier than others. In fact, patterns of use characterized by occasional use and low dosages are rarely associated with harmful outcomes (Stockwell et al., 2016). Canada's low-risk drinking guidelines for youth recommend consuming no more than one or two drinks per occasion, no more than once or twice a week, to minimize their likelihood of alcohol-related harm (Butt, Beirness, Gliksman, Paradis, & Stockwell, 2011). American drinking guidelines do not specify low-risk levels for youth, but suggest no more than one drink per occasion for adult women and two drinks for adult men over the age of 21 (US Department of Health & Human Services, 2018). However, youth often exceed these guidelines and the drinking patterns of young people differ significantly from that of adults in ways that increase their risk for harm (Health Canada, 2015; Miech et al., 2016).

Adult drinking tends to be characterized by frequent (e.g., 1–3 times a week), low levels of consumption (e.g., one or two drinks). In contrast, adolescents tend to drink relatively infrequently, often consuming alcohol only a few times a month (Freeman, King, & Pickett, 2016). However, when they drink, youth consume alcohol in much higher quantities. Approximately, 24% of Canadian youth report binge drinking in the last 12 months, defined as five or more drinks in one event for males and four or more for females (Health Canada, 2015). For US youth, 18% report binge drinking in the last 30 days (Kann et al., 2016). Heavy use of marijuana is typically considered daily or almost daily use (Hall & Pacula, 2010) and between 2% and 6% of Canadian and American teens use marijuana this frequently (George & Vaccarino, 2015; Miech et al., 2016). The recently developed *Lower Risk Cannabis Use Guidelines for Canada* publication recommends limiting use to once a week (Fischer et al., 2017). However, it is still unclear if there is a "safe" level of marijuana use for youth. Importantly, most substance-related harm experienced by adolescents result from these high-frequency, high-quantity use patterns.

Other concerning patterns of substance use among adolescents include an early age of onset (e.g., < 15) and polysubstance use. Research consistently shows that the earlier an adolescent uses alcohol or marijuana, and the more regular and higher levels they use, the more likely they are to develop a substance use disorder in adulthood, and experience other health and social harms, such as poor educational and occupational outcomes, injuries, and negative impacts on cognitive abilities, brain structure, and function (Griffin, Bang, & Botvin, 2010; Hingson & Zha, 2009; Kim et al., 2017; Lisdahl, Gilbart, Wright, & Shollenbarger, 2013; Moss, Chen, & Yi, 2014; Nelson, Van Ryzin, &

Dishion, 2015; Patte, Qian, & Leatherdale, 2017). There is no "normal" age to begin substance use, but delaying substance use is associated with better short- and long-term outcomes for young people, and public health recommendations encourage delaying use as long as possible.

Young people also rarely use substances in isolation. Most youth who engage in marijuana use are also using alcohol (Conway et al., 2013). For example, only 1% of Canadian youth who used marijuana in the last year reported that they did not use alcohol (Health Canada, 2016). Canadian (15%) and American adolescents (13%) also commonly report mixing alcohol with energy drinks (Health Canada, 2016; Miech et al., 2016). Combining alcohol with other substances can lead to greater impairment over using either substance alone because they can interact and cause dangerous and unpredictable effects in the body (Yurasek et al., 2017). Youth who use multiple substances have higher levels of substance use, engage in more risk-taking activities, and experience more consequences from their use compared to those using single substances (McKetin, Coen, & Kaye, 2015; Moss, Chen, & Yi, 2014; Patrick et al., 2017; Peacock, Pennay, Droste, Bruno, & Lubman, 2014; Subbaraman & Kerr, 2015; Terry-McElrath, O'Malley, & Johnston, 2013).

Thus, *problematic* (sometimes also referred to as hazardous, harmful, risky use, or misuse) substance use, which increases a youth's likelihood of experiencing negative consequences, tends to be characterized by an early age of use onset (particularly before age 13), high frequency, and/or high quantity use patterns (i.e., daily or almost daily marijuana use or binge drinking) and using more than one substance. Engaging in problematic alcohol and drug use patterns substantially increase youths' risk of developing a substance use disorder; however, problematic use does not necessarily imply that a student has or will develop a substance use disorder.

What differentiates *problematic use* from an *addiction*? Problematic use is a pattern of use that has a high likelihood of resulting in harm (World Health Organization, 1994). An addiction or substance use disorder is a clinically diagnosed condition characterized by harm from use and/or physical and psychological dependence on a drug (American Psychiatric Association, 2013). Those addicted to a substance tend to lack control over their use (i.e., they use more than intended and/or have trouble stopping or reducing their use), use in high-risk contexts (e.g., drinking and driving), continue to use the drug despite experiencing significant harmful consequences from their use, and show signs of physiological dependence, such as needing more of the drug to get the same effect (i.e., tolerance) or experiencing withdrawal symptoms when not using the drug (American Psychiatric Association, 2013). Data suggests that approximately 12% of Canadian youth and 5% of American youth have a substance use disorder, most commonly related to alcohol (Center for Behavioral Health Statistics and Quality, 2016; Pearson, Janz, & Ali, 2013). Marijuana is generally perceived to be less addictive then alcohol, but research evidence indicates that marijuana use *can* lead to addiction. In fact, approximately 5% of Canadian youth and 2.5% of American youth will develop an addiction to marijuana and the likelihood of developing a marijuana addiction triples for those who start using in adolescence (Center for Behavioral Health Statistics and Quality, 2016; George & Vaccarino, 2015). Both problematic use patterns and substance use disorders are *not* a normal part of development and place youth at considerable risk for short- and long-term health and social harm (Brown et al., 2008; Committee on Substance Abuse, 2010). Understanding the distinction between experimental or non-problematic use, problematic use, and addiction are key to identifying *which* youth are most in need of intervention.

Risks Versus Rewards: Why Do Adolescents Use Substances?

Understanding *why* youth use alcohol and other drugs is essential to developing more effective strategies for prevention and treatment. It is important to remember that all substance use is goal-directed, meaning that, just like adults, adolescents use substances to achieve specific benefits or meet certain needs. Most commonly, youth report using alcohol and marijuana for social reasons, to have fun and feel connected with peers (Kuntche et al., 2014; McKiernan & Fleming, 2017). Some youth also use alcohol and marijuana as a means of seeking peer acceptance and avoiding feeling left out. Peers play an important role in shaping adolescents' beliefs and behaviors. Across adolescence, youth increasingly spend more time with peers as they seek greater social and emotional autonomy from their parents (Christie & Viner, 2005). At the same time, adolescents' brains are still developing. During adolescence, activity in the reward-sensitive regions of the brain (limbic system) are well developed, but regions of the brain responsible for decision-making, judgment, planning, and impulse control (pre-frontal cortex) are still developing (Brown et al., 2008; Casey, Jones, & Hare, 2008). These developmental changes result in heightened sensitivity to the influence of peers and a biological propensity to perceive greater rewards from engaging in substance use relative to risks. Together, these changes make it more likely that adolescents will engage in substance use, particularly when with peers, despite knowledge of the potential risks (Sawyer et al., 2012).

Some youth also use alcohol and marijuana because they believe it will make them feel better by reducing stress, relieving pain, improving sleep, or reducing symptoms associated with mental health problems such as anxiety and depression (Roditis & Halpern-Felsher, 2015). Recent studies report that many youth mistakenly perceive marijuana use to be relatively harmless and a more "natural" remedy for relieving physical and mental health problems (McKiernan & Fleming, 2017; Miech et al., 2016). However, the research clearly shows that youth who use alcohol and/or marijuana to cope with negative emotional states are at the greatest risk of experiencing harmful consequences from their substance use, compared to those who use for other reasons (Kuntche et al., 2014; Patrick, Bray, & Berglund, 2016), although, in early adolescence, social reasons are also associated with heavier use of alcohol and drunkenness, which can also increase risk of harm (Kuntche et al., 2014). When engaging with youth about their substance use, it is important to consider what is motivating the young person to use alcohol or marijuana in the first place.

Who Is at Risk?

Substance use is a complex social phenomenon influenced by various dimensions of the environment (Ennett et al., 2008; Sitnick, Shaw & Hyde, 2014; Trucco, Colder, Wieczorek, Lengua, & Hawk, 2014). As a result, there is no single factor that predicts who will go on to develop problematic substance use. We know a great deal about what places youth at risk for problematic substance use. These include a multitude of biological, social, and psychological risk factors such as genetic vulnerability, pre-existing mental health and behavioral problems, relationships with peers and parents, and social determinants such as socio-economic status (Brown et al., 2008; Sitnick, Shaw, & Hyde, 2014). For example, we know that youth engaged in problematic substance use are more likely to have a family history of substance abuse, have pre-existing behavioral problems such as conduct disorder or ADHD, engage with deviant peers, have parents who fail to adequately monitor their whereabouts, and have high levels of sensation seeking and poor self-regulation. Importantly, many of these risk factors also interact and co-occur, creating profiles of risk for young people. Each of these factors are indications that young people may be at risk for problematic use of alcohol and other drugs, as well as other, often co-occurring, problems such as poor mental health, unsafe sex, and interpersonal violence (Boden & Fergusson, 2011; Elliott, Huizinga, & Menard, 2012). Of specific relevance to this chapter is the importance of how youth act, feel, and think about school—collectively termed *school engagement*.

During adolescence, attachment and engagement with school can wane. Youth often transition into larger schools with multiple classes and teachers, resulting in fewer personal interactions with teachers and lower academic motivation (Li & Learner, 2011). Research consistently shows that feeling emotionally connected to school and generally liking school is associated with lower levels of alcohol and drug use (Wang & Fredricks, 2014). Having good-quality relationships with teachers is particularly salient to school connectedness. When adolescents feel safe, supported, and respected by adults at school, they are much less likely to become associated with deviant peer groups or engage in alcohol and drug use. Peers also contribute to feelings of school connectedness (Zaharakis et al., 2017). Adolescents who feel socially isolated and rejected by peers and those who are bullied report lower school connectedness and are at increased risk for problematic substance use (O'Brennan & Furlong, 2010) (also see Chapter 1 on bullying).

Beyond feeling emotionally connected, being actively involved and engaged in school activities (e.g., participating in class, paying attention, doing homework) and higher academic achievement are also associated with lower levels of alcohol and drug use (Wang & Fredricks, 2014). Engagement in academic activities may limit the time and energy youth have available for engaging in alcohol and drug use and strengthen feelings of connection to the school. In sum, research supports that youth who believe they have adults and peers at school who care about them are more positively oriented to school, have good grades and future plans, are less likely to engage in alcohol or marijuana use, and are more likely to delay use onset. In contrast, youth who tend to display cynicism towards school, feel isolated and disconnected from teachers and peers, and present with school-related problems (e.g., lower grades, absenteeism, misconduct) are more likely to become engaged in alcohol and drug use. These should be regarded as warning signs for the development of problematic alcohol and drug use, as well as other negative outcomes, such as school dropout, delinquency, and depression (Li & Learner, 2011; Trenz, Dunne, Zur, & Latimer, 2015).

Short- and Long-Term Consequences of Substance Use

Decades of research have documented the many negative consequences associated with problematic adolescent substance use patterns (e.g., Boden & Fergusson, 2011; Committee on Substance Abuse, 2010; Hall, 2015). Typically, there is a dose-response relationship between alcohol and marijuana use and risk of negative outcomes, such that higher levels of use are associated with a greater likelihood of experiencing harm and a greater severity of harm (Boden & Fergusson, 2011; Hall, 2015). Some harmful outcomes result from acute intoxication; that is, they are a result of the immediate impairing effects of alcohol and marijuana and occur while youth are under the influence of the substances (Hall, 2015). Other harmful consequences result from chronic heavy use of alcohol and marijuana over time; that is, they result from cumulative, long-term, heavy exposure to the substance (Hall, 2015). We know more about the harmful consequences of alcohol use than marijuana. Alcohol is the main risk factor for injury and death among adolescents (World Health Organization, 2014), but marijuana is far from harmless. There are both similarities and differences in the risk of harm from alcohol and marijuana. Next, we outline some main acute and chronic risks associated with *problematic* alcohol and marijuana use patterns among young people.

Acute Risks

For both alcohol and marijuana, the most acute safety concern for youth is risk of injury, specifically, motor vehicle crashes. Road traffic accidents are the number one cause of death for young people (World Health Organization, 2014). Between 10% and 20% of youth report driving under the influence of alcohol and/or marijuana and many more (~35%) report riding in a vehicle with a driver who has been drinking or is high (George & Vaccarino, 2015; Minaker et al., 2017). Riding or driving while impaired more than doubles the risk of crashes and injury because of the acute cognitive impairments associated with alcohol and marijuana intoxication, particularly among youth who are still very early in their driving careers. Both alcohol and marijuana intoxication produce impairments in reaction time, attention, motor coordination, and information processing, which can lead to poor decision-making and increased risk-taking behavior, such as risky driving, risky sexual behavior (e.g., having unprotected sex and multiple partners), other drug use, physical and sexual assault, and suicide (Boden & Fergusson, 2011; Brown et al., 2009; Hall, 2015; Volkow et al., 2014). Using both alcohol and cannabis simultaneously heightens these acute risks (Yurasek, Aston, & Metrik, 2017).

Alcohol intoxication has additional acute effects beyond cognitive impairment. Intoxication can lead to blackouts, vomiting, slurred speech, reduced coordination, and overdose (Taylor, 2016). Alcohol poisoning occurs when there is so much alcohol in the bloodstream that areas of the brain controlling basic life-support functions, such as breathing, heart rate, and temperature control, begin to shut down (Taylor, 2016). Youth are particularly vulnerable to overdose risk because of their inexperience with alcohol and their tendency to engage in risky use patterns like binge drinking (Committee on Substance Abuse, 2010). Alcohol is the number one substance responsible for overdose and can lead to brain damage and death (White, Hingson, Pan, & Yi, 2011). In contrast, marijuana intoxication is not typically accompanied by many of the negative physical effects seen with alcohol, and risk of overdose for marijuana use is low, even at very high levels of use (George & Vaccarino, 2015). However, some studies suggest that marijuana intoxication may be associated with negative feelings of anxiety, panic, and paranoia for youth inexperienced with it, or those who have pre-existing vulnerability to mental health problems (Hall, 2015).

Chronic Risks

Persistent problematic alcohol and marijuana use in adolescence is also associated with various negative outcomes across the life-course (Hall, 2015; Taylor, 2016). Research suggests that the developing adolescent brain is particularly vulnerable to the neurotoxic effects of alcohol and marijuana, and that long-term heavy use of these substances is associated with damage to cognitive abilities, such as memory and attention, which may have implications for learning (Brown et al., 2009; Hall, 2015; Jacobus & Tapert, 2013). Heavy use of alcohol and marijuana have both been found to lower the chance of completing high school and pursuing post-secondary education (Boden & Fergusson, 2011; Homel, Thompson, & Leadbeater, 2014). These relationships may reflect cognitive impairment that interferes with a youth's ability to learn in school. Association with heavy-using peers may also reduce school engagement, leading to dropout or poor performance that creates barriers for pursuing post-secondary training. Regardless of the mechanism, poor educational attainment creates barriers for achieving occupational success. Adolescent substance use has been linked to lower income, unemployment, and problems paying for basic necessities (Fergusson & Boden, 2008; Thompson, Leadbeater, Ames, & Merrin, 2018).

Problematic use of alcohol and marijuana in adolescence is also one of the strongest predictors of substance use in adulthood, increasing youths' risk for developing substance use disorders, as well as creating further vulnerabilities for negative long-term health outcomes (Brown et al., 2008; Hall, 2015; Thompson, Merrin, Ames, & Leadbeater, 2018). Problematic alcohol use is associated with over 200 different chronic diseases and linked to eight different types of cancer (World Health Organization, 2014b). Regular marijuana use is associated with risks of developing chronic bronchitis and doubles the risk of being diagnosed with schizophrenia (Hall, 2015; Volkow, 2014). Moreover, both alcohol and marijuana have been associated with increased risk for depression and anxiety and studies report that heavy use exacerbates mental health symptoms for young people already coping with these disorders (George & Vaccarino, 2015; Thompson, Leadbeater, & Ames, 2015; Volkow, 2014). Overall, heavy adolescent substance use often sets young people on a path incompatible with long-term success in adulthood.

Prevention and Intervention Strategies

Schools are an ideal setting for the delivery of substance abuse prevention programming. No other institution offers access to such a large number of children and youth at an age at which alcohol and other drug use has yet to be initiated (Stigler, Neusel, & Perry, 2011). Schools may incorporate substance abuse prevention programming in several ways. Substance abuse prevention might be delivered within the current curriculum (e.g., as part of the health curriculum), as an add-on to the current curriculum, or even outside of school hours—in after-school programs delivered by external facilitators (e.g., D'Amico et al., 2012). There are also different levels of prevention programs that may be implemented for youth substance use behavior, which follow. First, *universal programs* are those that are applied to everyone—the same program is delivered to all students, regardless of their risk or involvement in substance use. Second, *selective programs* are those that target at-risk youth. Youth may be identified as at-risk based on a variety of factors (e.g., previous history of externalizing disorders, family history of substance abuse, academic underachievement, placement in an alternative school). Finally, *indicated programs* are analogous to treatment and target those who are already experiencing problems with alcohol or other drugs. Indicated programs are generally outside the scope of school prevention programming. The discussion that follows focuses on universal and selective prevention programs. A list of prevention resources and databases are provided in Appendix 2, along with a few examples of universal and selective prevention programs.

The majority of school-based prevention programs are universal, with the goal of delaying the initiation of substance use or reducing it to prevent problematic use or substance-related harm (Stigler et al., 2011). However, universal prevention programs are less effective for students who are most at-risk for developing problematic substance use, highlighting the need for selective programs to better target different groups within the broader population (Gottfredson & Wilson, 2003).

What Is the Teacher's Role?

Teachers may be involved in substance abuse prevention in several ways. They may be trained to deliver a particular prevention curriculum, which involves adhering to the content of lesson plans and activities outlined in the prevention guidelines. Teachers may also play a role in the identification and referral of students who are already experiencing substance-related problems. As noted previously, teachers are in a unique position to identify the effects of substance use on their students' behavior, appearance, relationships, and academic performance, and facilitate getting help when they see a student struggling. Table 2.1 lists some changes that might indicate a student is struggling with an alcohol or drug problem. It is important to note that this is not an exhaustive list of potential signs of a substance use problem and many of these signs are not specific to a substance use issue—they may be indications of other concerns, such as separation, divorce or loss of parents, anxiety or depression, bullying, or other interpersonal issues.

Table 2.1   Signs That a Student May Be Struggling With Problematic Substance Use

Behavior	Appearance	Relationships	Academics
Increasing aggression	Unkempt or poor hygiene	Avoiding peers	Decline in grades
Frequent tardiness	Frequent illness	Changes in peer group	Late assignments, missing tests
Frequent absences	Slurred or incoherent speech	Intense emotions (crying or yelling)	Short attention span
Fatigue or drowsiness	Bloodshot eyes	Affiliation with older crowd	Daydreaming or zoning out
Difficulty staying awake in class	Runny nose		Hyperactive
Excessive energy	Weight loss		No motivation
Withdrawn			
Erratic, mood swings			

Because these signs may reflect other areas of difficulty (besides substance use) or multiple difficulties (e.g., substance use and a mental health concern), when talking to a student about a potential substance use issue, it is important to express concern in broad or neutral terms ("I notice that you've been falling asleep in class lately and that you've been much quieter than usual. I wonder if it might be helpful to talk to someone?"). Teachers are in an excellent position to listen, affirm, and support the student's decision to discuss their concerns and seek further support, without taking on a counseling role. Teachers and school counselors (or social work staff) can work together to help the student access the support that he or she needs, including youth-focused treatment services. Before starting any prevention programming, teachers should be aware of substance abuse resources in their school and community because discussion of the topic might raise concerns for students who need a place to talk about these feelings.

Early Approaches to Substance Abuse Prevention: What Does Not Work

Although there is extensive literature on substance abuse prevention in schools, early attempts at delivering prevention programs were largely ineffective and based on intuitive notions about what *should* work rather than on research about what *does* work (Botvin, 2000; Midford, 2010). These early methods were often based on information dissemination approaches, in which the goal was to increase knowledge of drug use and consequences and promote anti-drug attitudes through instruction, school assemblies, discussions, and dissemination of videos and written materials on the harms of drug use (Shin, 2001). Teachers and allied professionals (e.g., public health nurses, police officers) often used scare tactics to inform students about the dangers of drug use. These approaches assumed that decisions not to use drugs are based on full knowledge of drug use consequences. Despite the popularity of information dissemination approaches, these approaches targeted knowledge and attitudes about substance use, but were ineffective for reducing tobacco, alcohol, or other drug use behavior (Botvin & Botvin, 1992). As a result, programs using information dissemination only are no longer delivered in schools. Instead, where substance abuse prevention programming includes information dissemination, this is usually part of a multi-component intervention and delivery is accomplished through interactive means (e.g., group discussion, presented as a trivia game).

Turning to Theory and Evidence for Prevention: What Does Work?

Given the lack of evidence that changing attitudes and knowledge about substance use has an impact on behavior, there has been a shift towards prevention programming that targets the social impacts or influences of substance use. These approaches are largely based on research highlighting the important influence of peers and other social forces (e.g., mass media) on adolescent substance use and are typically categorized as either social influence or social competence approaches, although many programs include a combination of these two frameworks as well as information regarding the harmful effects of substance use.

Social influence approaches address the social factors most likely to influence drug use among youth, including offers from their peers to engage in drug use, particularly in situations in which alcohol or drugs are highly accessible (e.g., at a party, at a friend's house when parents are away). Social influence approaches typically involve three components: psychological inoculation, social resistance training, and social norms education (Botvin, 2000). Psychological inoculation (McGuire, 1964) is based on the premise that exposing youth to increasingly stronger pro-drug influences will build resistance to these messages and prepare students to resist these influences once they reach adolescence. These approaches are often combined with social resistance, so when faced with pro-drug influences, students have the skills to deal with them. Social resistance training involves teaching students to first identify situations likely to be high-risk in terms of peer pressure to engage in substance use and then use social skills to either avoid these situations or effectively communicate their intention not to participate in substance use. Students are taught how to refuse offers to use alcohol or other drugs, and given opportunities to practice their refusal skills during role-play situations. Finally, students are provided with information regarding normative rates of substance use (smoking, alcohol use, marijuana use, and other drug use) among their peers. This is intended as corrective information, as most youth overestimate the prevalence of substance use among their peers and believe that the majority are using alcohol or other substances. For example, in one study, Perkins and Craig (2003) found that middle and high school students overestimated the prevalence of tobacco use in their school by 16% and 17%, respectively. For marijuana use, middle school and high school students overestimated the rate of ever using marijuana by 19% and 20%, respectively. These overestimates are predictive of higher levels of one's own substance use behavior

(Brooks-Russell, Simons-Morton, Haynie, Farhat, & Wang, 2014; Clapp & McDonnell, 2000). Correcting these misperceptions provides students with a more realistic appraisal of the social consequences of not engaging in alcohol or other drug use. Social influence approaches make use of a variety of strategies for prevention, including instruction and discussion, skills training and behavioral rehearsal of drug refusal skills, and involvement of same-age or older peer leaders.

Although social influence approaches are based on strong theoretical evidence and were initially deemed effective for reducing alcohol and marijuana use, there is limited evidence to support their effectiveness for reducing substance use behaviors when used on their own (i.e., not in combination with other approaches) (Faggiano, Minozzi, Versino, & Buscemi, 2014). This may be because these approaches assume that youth do not want to use alcohol or drugs and will be motivated to refuse offers to engage in substance use when faced with a high-risk situation (Botvin & Griffin, 2003). This largely ignores the function that alcohol or drugs serve for youth.

Beliefs about the functions that alcohol and drugs serve are formed well in advance of actual alcohol or drug use, although these beliefs may be reinforced once substance use is initiated. For example, holding positive beliefs about alcohol's effects on social functioning (e.g., alcohol will help me make new friends) and relaxation (e.g., alcohol will help me forget my problems) by middle childhood is associated with greater problematic alcohol use in adolescence (Jester et al., 2015). Thus, effective prevention programming needs to consider that some youth may already have positive perceptions about the effects of alcohol or drugs and may not be motivated to refuse them, even if they have the skills to do so.

Social competence approaches address this limitation by focusing on improving social and personal competence to reduce vulnerability to social and motivational forces that typically contribute to substance use (Botvin & Griffin, 2007). Social competence approaches are based on social learning (Bandura, 1977) and problem behavior theory (Jessor & Jessor, 1977), and consider drug use to reflect the interaction between exposure to others who model drug use and its associated rewards, and positive perceptions about the effects of drug use. Social competence approaches address a range of behaviors that contribute to healthy and positive decision-making, including: perceptions about drug use; problem solving, self-management, anxiety management and coping skills; and social and assertiveness skills. Social competence approaches utilize cognitive-behavioral skills training, which includes instruction, demonstrations, opportunities to practice new skills and receive feedback, and reinforcement of gains in the skill development areas. Research on the effectiveness of prevention programs has found that social competence or combined social competence + social influence programs are the most effective, at least for reducing alcohol and marijuana use (Faggiano et al., 2014; Lemstra et al., 2010; Porath-Waller, Beasley, & Beirness, 2010).

The Life Skills Training (LST) program developed by Gilbert Botvin (Botvin & Griffin, 2004) is largely based on the social competence model, but also includes elements of the social influence model (e.g., drug resistance skills). The LST uses different curricula for elementary, middle, and high school students, but the program has been used most widely with 11–14 year olds in middle schools. The program is delivered by a trained facilitator, usually a teacher or school counselor. The program extends over 3 years and consists of 30 classroom periods lasting 45 minutes each. The curriculum includes three components: (1) drug resistance skills; (2) personal self-management skills; and (3) general social skills. A typical session will start with the teacher introducing the topic and facilitating a discussion to help students link the topic with their own personal experiences. Students are then taught a relevant skill (e.g., effective decision-making) and are provided with examples and practice situations to apply this skill. Students work on the skill individually and together with the larger group. Students have opportunities to practice skills and receive feedback from the facilitator and their peers. At the end of every session, students are given homework to help prepare for the next session.

Is Abstinence the Only Option?

It is well established that the majority of youth have initiated alcohol or other drug use by the time they finish high school. As a result, teachers and other prevention program facilitators are faced with the challenge of addressing substance use in a way that resonates with youth, but also acknowledges its illegal status. Historically, the primary message for alcohol and drug use programming was to encourage abstinence only ("just say no"). In light of the changing landscape for legalization of cannabis and the reality of substance use experimentation among youth, a more comprehensive approach is required (Rosenbaum, 2016). Harm reduction approaches offer an alternative to abstinence-only approaches by attending to the negative impacts of alcohol and other drug use, rather than alcohol or drug use itself. From a harm reduction perspective, the difference between substance use and substance abuse or problematic use is an important one and should be included in discussions with youth to allow for a realistic and credible discussion. There are, naturally, some controversies associated with taking a harm reduction approach, primarily due to the illegal status of alcohol and cannabis for youth. In addition, many argue that youth are a particularly vulnerable group who need very clear messages around alcohol and drugs. In considering prevention approaches that take a harm reduction perspective, the message regarding abstinence is neutral—use is not condoned or condemned. It is generally agreed that there should be a balance between reducing harm from a hazardous behavior and continuing to present non-use as a health-promoting option.

Program Implementation

Although we have come a long way in understanding what works (and what does not work) for preventing substance abuse, there are several other factors besides the content of the prevention program that influence outcomes. These include the timing, structure, and methods for implementing the program. These factors are described in more detail next and should be considered in any discussion regarding the implementation of substance abuse prevention programming in schools. Of note, the best approaches are those that take a whole-school approach and engage parents and the wider school community (Cuijpers, 2002). The publication *Building on Our Strengths: Canadian Standards for School-Based Substance Abuse Prevention*, developed by the Canadian Centre for Substance Abuse and Addiction (CCSA, 2010; see Appendix 2 for web link), provides a good overview of the whole-school approach, which exists in the context of a comprehensive health-promotion framework supported at all levels of leadership (administration, teachers, staff, students, parents), fully integrated into the core mission of the school, and infused in all aspects of the school climate (e.g., through school safety policies and procedures, promoting positive relationships and inclusiveness, attending to social-emotional skills). Community involvement can vary considerably and may include media campaigns, in which prevention messages are distributed through the community (e.g., on community message boards), as well as outreach and collaboration with community-based services. Parents are also a critical resource for enhancing the effectiveness of prevention programming. For younger students, parents may be actively involved in prevention programming, in which parent training and positive parenting skills may be included to improve parent-child bonds (Flay, 2000). For older students (middle and high school), parent engagement may include seeking parent input on school policies and procedures and providing parents with guidance and information on how to address substance use in their families (CCSA, 2010).

Developmental Timing of the Intervention

The developmental progression of alcohol and other drug use from childhood to adolescence is important to consider when implementing substance
abuse prevention programming. As noted previously, the likelihood of initiating alcohol and marijuana use increases rapidly from grade 7 to grade 12. As a
result, prevention programming that aims to delay the initiation of substance
use is best delivered during middle school, when there is greater awareness
and curiosity regarding the effects of alcohol and other drugs, but limited substance use initiation (Newton, Conrod, Teesson, & Faggiano, 2012). Although
the majority of prevention programming is delivered in middle school (Stigler,
Neusel, & Perry, 2011), there is still value to delivering prevention programs in
elementary and high school, as long as the specific goals of the program are
aligned with the developmental timing of their delivery.

In elementary school, most effective programs are those that do not
address substance use per se, but focus instead on the development of basic
skills necessary for healthy functioning in childhood, including problem solving, social skills, and self-control (Botvin, 2000; Hopfer et al., 2010; Onrust,
Otten, Lammers, & Smit, 2016). One of the most profound changes in the
transition from elementary to middle school is the increasing amount of time
youth spend with peers. Social acceptance is critical, resulting in greater vulnerability to peer conformity. From a cognitive perspective, this is also the
"age of reason", when youth begin to think abstractly, make inferences, and
engage in moral reasoning that extends beyond "good vs. bad". They begin
to realize there must be some benefits to alcohol or drugs, otherwise people
would not choose to use them. Onrust et al. (2016) found that social influence
approaches alone were not effective for reducing alcohol or other drug use
in early and middle adolescents, likely due to their concerns regarding peer
conformity and acceptance. However, the addition of a social norms component enhanced the effectiveness of these programs, meaning that students
responded when they were told that most of their peers did not engage in
substance use.

In high school, peer relationships often guide morality and what is "right"
is what is approved by others. The primary task of middle to late adolescence
is separation and individuation. Older adolescents look to their peers for assistance regarding their identity formation, and social relationships play a central role in substance use, with peer alienation contributing to problematic
substance use in particular. At this age, social influence approaches have a
greater impact (Onrust et al., 2016). These are the students who likely have

the most opportunities to refuse substances (e.g., at parties or friends' homes) and may feel most comfortable with alcohol or drug refusal as part of asserting their independence.

Who Is Delivering the Intervention?

For the most part, interventions are delivered by teachers or school counselors who receive training in the substance abuse prevention curriculum. However, in one study examining the extent to which teachers consistently delivered the program materials, only 15% of teachers reported that they followed the curriculum *very closely*. Factors that impacted adherence included: the extent to which teachers believed they had discretion in what topics they could cover in the substance use lessons, their feeling that the curriculum was (in)effective, and feeling well prepared to deliver the curriculum. Lack of support from the school principal was also an important factor (Ringwalt et al., 2003). Thus, teachers need to feel that they have adequate preparation and support to effectively deliver prevention programming and the programming needs to be structured to ensure that all content and lessons can be feasibly delivered within the classroom.

There is also some support for having peers involved in delivering substance abuse prevention programming. Compared to teachers, peers often have greater credibility when it comes to discussions around substance use and pressures to use substances. There is evidence to support the effectiveness of peer leaders in substance use prevention programming, although some researchers believe that having a peer leader is only one element of effective prevention and must be combined with other elements (Cuijpers, 2002). There are several important factors to consider when using peer-led interventions, including the nomination and training of peer leaders, who must have the necessary skills to deliver the materials effectively and answer any sensitive questions that might arise during discussions. If peer leaders are involved, they should be trained and supported by experienced teachers to ensure they adhere to the prevention model and seek assistance regarding challenging issues (MacArthur, Harrison, Caldwell, Hickman, & Campbell, 2016).

How Is the Intervention Delivered?

The most effective prevention programs involve interactive delivery of program content. The delivery of the materials should foster interaction among peers and encourage active discussion. When the intervention involves learning new behaviors, students should have the opportunity to practice their skills and receive feedback to improve performance (Cuijpers, 2002). Small-group activities and class discussions are a good way to introduce program content and promote the acquisition of new skills. For example, students may be provided with a scenario that outlines a situation in which a teen is required to make a choice about using or not using alcohol at a party or other social event. In small groups, students discuss the scenario and review the options—exploring the possible benefits and consequences associated with choosing each option. Students then share their conclusions with the class and the facilitator, providing an opportunity for students to be exposed to various points of view, reflect on possible outcomes, and receive feedback from the facilitator. In all cases, information should be provided in a nonjudgmental and non-confrontational manner (Herman, Reinke, Frey, & Shepard, 2013).

Over the last few decades, there has been increasing interest in using computers to deliver substance abuse prevention programming. Computer-based programs have several advantages: they do not require professionals trained in intervention delivery, which reduces the burden on teachers to learn and deliver the materials; they are readily available and easily accessible to those with a computer and Internet connection and can therefore be delivered to a larger number of schools; they can be updated to reflect recent advances or knowledge; and there is a guarantee that the material will be delivered as intended, reducing any concerns around implementation fidelity (Wood et al., 2014). Recent reviews of computer-delivered prevention programs show promising results (Champion, Newton, Barrett, & Teesson, 2013), but there is a need for additional research on how these programs can be delivered to maximize efficacy. One example of an online substance abuse prevention program that has been shown to reduce alcohol use and binge drinking among youth (compared to a control condition) is the CLIMATE intervention (Newton, Teesson, Vogl, & Andrews, 2010). The CLIMATE intervention was developed in Australia and is based on the social influence model of prevention. The program can be delivered on its own or integrated within the health curriculum. Each online lesson depicts a 15-minute scenario in which a group of animated teens are involved with a challenging substance abuse situation (e.g., making a decision about whether to drink, responding to an alcohol-related emergency involving a friend). Through the scenarios, students learn about substance use norms, the consequences of alcohol and drug use, how to identify and respond to an emergency situation involving alcohol or drugs, and how to use drug refusal skills. After each online module, teachers have the option of delivering a 20-minute activity to reinforce the concepts and skills depicted in the online scenarios.

Cross-Cultural Perspectives

Effective prevention programming must be culturally sensitive and relevant to the target audience (Botvin & Griffin, 2007). Unfortunately, there is limited research on whether prevention programming has cross-cultural applicability. Although studies suggest there are similar risk factors for substance abuse across cultures, it is important to tailor interventions based on the composition of the community. In fact, enhancing the cultural relevance of prevention programming is one of the primary reasons for program adaptations (Colby et al., 2013) and previous research has found that prevention programs must consider the social context to maximize effectiveness (Midford, Munro, McBride, Snow, & Ladzinski, 2002).

Conclusion

Alcohol and marijuana use is common in adolescence. It is a goal-directed behavior for young people and its use is motivated by a variety of factors, such as a desire to fit in with peers, facilitate social engagement, or cope with the negative effects of other traumatic experiences (e.g., divorce, mental health problems, bullying). For many, this use will be experimental, occasional, and largely harmless, but for those who progress to problematic use patterns (high frequency/high quantity), or use to cope with negative affect, the potential short- and long-term costs are high.

Addressing adolescent substance use is complicated by the fact that the onset of alcohol and marijuana coincides with significant physical, neurological, and social changes in adolescence. Development itself works against us in the battle to prevent *any* substance use from occurring. Youth tend to have permissive attitudes about the potential harms from alcohol and marijuana use and, on average, take more risks than adults (Brown et al., 2008). Studies have shown that just telling youth about the potential harms associated with using alcohol and marijuana is unlikely to change behavior—education will *not* be enough.

Teachers play an important role in helping create supportive school environments incompatible with problematic substance use behavior and identifying youth in need of additional support to address their use. Teachers do not need to be experts on substance use to deliver effective prevention programming. As discussed, the most effective substance use prevention programs focus on building skills in social and personal competence—such as problem solving, coping skills, and social skills—that mitigate some of the motivational forces driving these behaviors. But we must be mindful that how these programs are delivered is also important. Implementation must take into consideration development stage and the role of parents, peers, and community members in shaping and preventing substance use behaviors. The best approaches are those that take a whole-school approach and allow youth to engage and interact with each other and the content. When having conversations with youth, it is important to remember that they have reasons for engaging in substance use and we should neither condone nor condemn use. The goal is to support youth in making healthier decisions and the cumulative evidence suggests that our efforts may be better spent focusing on reducing harm from use, rather than attempting to prevent use altogether.

Key Messages

1. Substance use is a goal-directed behavior.
2. Not ALL substance use is problematic.
3. Teachers play a role in identification of "at-risk" youth.
4. Social competence programs are the most effective.
5. The timing, structure, and methods for implementation matter.

Appendix 2

Resource Materials for Teachers, Parents, and School Administrators

1. National Crime Prevention Centre. (2009). *School-based drug abuse prevention: Promising and successful programs.* Ottawa, ON: National Crime Prevention Centre. Overview of risk and protective factors for drug abuse and listing of school-based prevention programs. https://www.publicsafety. gc.ca/cnt/rsrcs/pblctns/sclbsd-drgbs/sclbsd-drgbs-eng.pdf

2. National Institute on Drug Abuse. (2003). *Preventing drug use among children and adolescents: A research-based guide for parents, educators, and community leaders.* https://www.drugabuse.gov/sites/default/files/redbook_0.pdf

3. Canadian Centre on Substance Abuse and Addiction (CCSA). (2010). *Building on our strengths: Canadian standards for school-based youth substance abuse prevention* (version 2.0). Ottawa, ON: Canadian Centre on Substance Abuse and Addiction. http://www.ccsa.ca/Resource%20Library/ ccsa-011815-2010.pdf#search=all%28Canadian%20Standards%20for%20 School-Based%20Substance%20Abuse%20Prevention%29

4. Substance Abuse and Mental Health Services Administration National Registry of Evidence-based Programs and Practices. A searchable database listing evidence-based substance abuse programs, including school-based prevention. https://www.samhsa.gov/ebp-resource-center

5. United Nations Office for Drug Control and Crime Prevention. (2002). *A participatory handbook for youth drug abuse preventin programmes: A guide for development and improvement.* New York, NY: United Nations. https:// www.unodc.org/documents/drug-prevention-and-treatment/E_hand book.pdf

6. Blueprints for Healthy Youth Development is an online registry of evidence-based programs that promote the health and well-being of youth, including youth substance abuse prevention programming. https://www.blue printsprograms.org/

7. Centre for Addiction and Mental Health Educating Students About Drug Use and Mental Health—Building Teacher Confidence and Comfort about Substance Use and Abuse: Grades 1–10. Components of the Ontario Curriculum focusing on substance use and abuse. http://2017.camh.ca/en/ education/teachers_school_programs/resources_for_teachers_and_ schools/Pages/curriculum_buildingconfidence.aspx

8. National Institute on Drug Abuse resources for parents and educators. https://www.drugabuse.gov/parents-educators

Sample Evidence-Based Programs

Primary Prevention Programs

1. Life Skills Training: lifeskillstraining.com

    Life Skills Training (LST) is an evidence-based program that combines social influence and social competence approaches. With programs for elementary, middle, and high school students, LST addresses substance use issues across stages of development.

2. Project Alert: https://www.projectalert.com/

    Project ALERT is a classroom-based substance abuse prevention program for middle school students based on the social influence model. The program is delivered by trained facilitators (teachers, counselors, nurses, school resource officers) across 11 sessions followed by three booster sessions.

3. Project Northland: https://www.hazelden.org/web/public/projectnorthland.page

    Project Northland is a multi-component substance abuse prevention program delivered over 3 years, starting in grade 6. The program is based on a combined social influence and social competence model and involves parent, peer, and community participation.

Secondary Prevention Programs

1. Preventure: https://positivechoices.org.au/teachers/preventure

    Preventure is a school-based program delivered by trained teachers or mental health practitioners. It is a secondary prevention program that uses cognitive-behavioral skills training with high-risk teens. Teens are identified based on personality profiles typically associated with high-risk behaviors and taught specialized coping skills matched to the high-risk personality profile. The intervention is delivered over two 90-minute sessions.

2. Project Towards No Drug Abuse: tnd.usc.edu

    Project Towards No Drug Abuse consists of 12 classroom sessions delivered by trained teachers or health education specialists. The curriculum was originally developed for high-risk students in alternative school classrooms. All sessions are highly interactive and explore multiple aspects of substance abuse. The program content covers factors from both social influence and social competence models.

Sample Computer-Based Programs

1. Climate Schools: https://www.climateschools.com
   Climate schools is an online curriculum that targets alcohol, cannabis, and psychostimulus education. The modules were developed for students in grades 8–10 and include online cartoon scenarios and activities that can be selected by teachers to reinforce information presented in the cartoons.
2. Thinking Not Drinking: https://www.childtrends.org/programs/thinking-not-drinking
   Thinking Not Drinking is a computer-based alcohol prevention program developed for urban youth (ages 10–12 years old) and their parents. Based on social learning theory, the program targets modeling, changing normative perceptions, increasing self-efficacy, and goal setting and includes a parent component.

Note

1. Rates vary across provinces and states. See www.canada.ca/en/health-canada/services/canadian-student-tobacco-alcohol-drugs-survey/2014-2015-summary.html; www.cdc.gov/healthyyouth/data/yrbs/pdf/2015/ss6506_updated.pdf

References

American Psychiatric Association. (2013). *Diagnostic and statistical manual of mental disorders (DSM-5®)*. Washington, DC: American Psychiatric Pub.

Bandura, A. (1977). *Social learning theory*. Princeton, NJ: Englewood Cliff.

Boden, J. M., & Fergusson, D. M. (2011). The short and long term consequences of adolescent alcohol use. *Young People and Alcohol: Impact, Policy, Prevention and Treatment, 32*–46.

Botvin, G. J. (2000). Preventing drug abuse in schools: Social and competence enhancement approaches targeting individual-level etiologic factors. *Addictive Behaviors, 25*(6), 887–897.

Botvin, G. J., & Botvin, E. M. (1992). Adolescent tobacco, alcohol, and drug abuse: Prevention strategies, empirical findings, and assessment issues. *Journal of Developmental and Behavioral Pediatrics, 13*, 290–301.

Botvin, G. J., & Griffin, K. W. (2003). Drug abuse prevention curricula in schools. In Z. Sloboda & W. J. Bukoski (Eds.), *Handbook of drug abuse prevention: Theory, science, and practice* (pp. 45–74). New York, NY: Kluwer Academic/Plenum Publishers.

Botvin, G. J., & Griffin, K. W. (2004). Life skills training: Empirical findings and future directions. *Journal of Primary Prevention, 25*, 211–232.

Botvin, G. J., & Griffin, K. W. (2007). School-based programmes to prevent alcohol, tobacco and other drug use. *International Review of Psychiatry, 19*(6), 607–615.

Brooks-Russell, A., Simons-Morton, B., Haynie, D., Farhat, T., & Wang, J. (2014). Longitudinal relationship between drinking with peers, descriptive norms, and adolescent alcohol use. *Prevention Science, 15*(4), 497–505.

Brown, S. A., McGue, M., Maggs, J., Schulenberg, J., Hingson, R., Swartzwelder, S., . . . Winters, K. C. (2008). A developmental perspective on alcohol and youths 16 to 20 years of age. *Pediatrics, 121*(Supplement 4), S290–S310.

Brown, S. A., McGue, M., Maggs, J., Schulenberg, J., Hingson, R., Swartzwelder, S., . . . Murphy, S. (2009). Underage alcohol use: Summary of developmental processes and mechanisms: Ages 16-20. *Alcohol Research & Health, 32*, 41–52.

Butt, P., Beirness, D., Gliksman, L., Paradis, C., & Stockwell, T. (2011). *Alcohol and health in Canada: A summary of evidence and guidelines for low-risk drinking.* Ottawa, ON: Canadian Centre on Substance Abuse.

Canadian Centre on Substance Abuse (CCSA). (2010). *Building on our strengths: Canadian standards for school-based youth substance abuse prevention* (version 2.0). Ottawa, ON: Canadian Centre on Substance Abuse.

Casey, B. J., Jones, R. M., & Hare, T. A. (2008). The adolescent brain. *Annals of the New York Academy of Sciences, 1124*(1), 111–126.

Center for Behavioral Health Statistics and Quality. (2016). *2015 National survey on drug use and health: Methodological summary and definitions.* Rockville, MD: Substance Abuse and Mental Health Services Administration.

Champion, K. E., Newton, N. C., Barrett, E. L., & Teesson, M. (2013). A systematic review of school-based alcohol and other drug prevention programs facilitated by computers or the Internet. *Drug and Alcohol Review, 32*(2), 115–123.

Clapp, J. D., & McDonnell, A. L. (2000). The relationship of perceptions of alcohol promotion and peer drinking norms to alcohol problems reported by college students. *Journal of College Student Development, 41*(1), 19–26. doi: 10.1037/0893-164X.18.3.203

Colby, M., Hecht, M. L., Miller-Day, M., Krieger, J. L., Syvertsen, A. K., Graham, J. W., & Pettigrew, J. (2013). Adapting school-based substance use prevention curriculum through cultural grounding: A review and exemplar of adaptation processes for rural schools. *American Journal of Community Psychology, 51*(1–2), 190–205.

Committee on Substance Abuse. (2010). Alcohol use by youth and adolescents: A pediatric concern. *Pediatrics, 125*(5), 1078–1087. doi:10.1542/peds.2010–0438

Conway, K. P., Vullo, G. C., Nichter, B., Wang, J., Compton, W. M., Iannotti, R. J., & Simons-Morton, B. (2013). Prevalence and patterns of polysubstance use in a nationally representative sample of 10th graders in the United States. *Journal of Adolescent Health, 52*, 716-723. doi: 10.1016/j.jadohealth.2012.12.006.

Cuijpers, P. (2002). Effective ingredients of school-based drug prevention programs: A systematic review. *Addictive Behaviors, 27*(6), 1009–1023.

Christie, D., & Viner, R. (2005). ABC of adolescence: Adolescent development. *BMJ: British Medical Journal, 330*(7486), 301.

D'Amico, E. J., Tucker, J. S., Miles, J. N., Zhou, A. J., Shih, R. A., & Green, H. D. (2012). Preventing alcohol use with a voluntary after-school program for middle school students: Results from a cluster randomized controlled trial of CHOICE. *Prevention Science, 13*(4), 415–425.

Elliott, D. S., Huizinga, D., & Menard, S. (2012). *Multiple problem youth: Delinquency, substance use, and mental health problems*. New York, NY: Springer Science & Business Media.

Ennett, S. T., Foshee, V. A., Bauman, K. E., Hussong, A., Cai, L., Reyes, H. L. M., ... DuRant, R. (2008). The social ecology of adolescent alcohol misuse. *Child Development*, *79*(6), 1777–1791.

Faggiano, F., Minozzi, S., Versino, E., & Buscemi, D. (2014). Universal school-based prevention for illicit drug use. *The Cochrane Library*, *12*, 1–167.

Fergusson, D. M., & Boden, J. M. (2008). Cannabis use and later life outcomes. *Addiction*, *103*(6), 969–976. doi:10.1111/j.1360-0443.2008.02221.x

Fischer, B., Russell, C., Sabioni, P., van den Brink, W., Le Foll, B., Hall, W., Rehm, . . . Room, R. (2017). Lower-Risk Cannabis Use Guidelines (LRCUG): An evidence-based update. *American Journal of Public Health*, *107*(8). doi:10.2105/AJPH.2017.303818

Flay, B. R. (2000). Approaches to substance use prevention utilizing school curriculum plus social environment change. *Addictive Behaviors*, *25*(6), 861–885.

Freeman, J., King, M., & Pickett, W. (2016). *Health behaviour in school-aged children (HBSC) in Canada: Focus on relationships*. Ottawa, ON: Public Health Agency of Canada.

George, T., & Vaccarino, F. (Eds.). (2015). *Substance abuse in Canada: The effects of cannabis use during adolescence*. Ottawa, ON: Canadian Centre on Substance Abuse.

Gottfredson, D. C., & Wilson, D. B. (2003). Characteristics of effective school-based substance abuse prevention. *Prevention Science*, *4*(1), 27–38.

Griffin, K. W., Bang, H., & Botvin, G. J. (2010). Age of alcohol and marijuana use onset predicts weekly substance use and related psychosocial problems during young adulthood. *Journal of Substance Use*, *15*(3), 174–183.

Hall, W. (2015). What has research over the past two decades revealed about the adverse health effects of recreational cannabis use? *Addiction*, *110*(1), 19–35.

Hall, W. D., & Pacula, R. (2010). *Cannabis use and dependence: Public health and public policy*. Cambridge: Cambridge University Press.

Health Canada. (2015). *Canadian tobacco, alcohol and drugs survey 2013*. Canada: Statistics Canada.

Health Canada. (2016). *Canadian student tobacco, alcohol and drugs survey 2014–15*. Canada: Statistics Canada.

Herman, K. C., Reinke, W. M., Frey, A., & Shepard, S. (2013). *Motivational interviewing in schools: Strategies for engaging parents, teachers, and students*. New York, NY: Springer Publishing Company.

Hingson, R. W., & Zha, W. (2009). Age of drinking onset, alcohol use disorders, frequent heavy drinking, and unintentionally injuring oneself and others after drinking. *Pediatrics*, *123*(6), 1477–1484.

Homel, J., Thompson, K., & Leadbeater, B. (2014). Trajectories of marijuana use in youth ages 15–25: Implications for postsecondary education experiences. *Journal of Studies on Alcohol and Drugs*, *75*(4), 674–683.

Hopfer, S., Shin, Y., Davis, D., Elek, E., Kam, J. A., & Hecht, M. L. (2010). A review of elementary school-based substance use prevention programs: Identifying program attributes. *Journal of Drug Education*, *40*(1), 11–36.

Jacobus, J., & Tapert, S. F. (2013). Neurotoxic effects of alcohol in adolescence. *Annual Review of Clinical Psychology*, *9*, 703–721.

Jessor, R., & Jessor, S. L. (1977). *Problem behavior and psychosocial development: A longitudinal study of youth*. Cambridge, MA: Academic Press.

Jester, J. M., Wong, M. M., Cranford, J. A., Buu, A., Fitzgerald, H. E., & Zucker, R. A. (2015). Alcohol expectancies in childhood: Change with the onset of drinking and ability to predict adolescent drunkenness and binge drinking. *Addiction, 110*(1), 71–79.

Kann, L., McMannus, T., Harris, W., . . . Zaza, S. (2016). Youth risk behavior surveillance—United States, 2015. *MMWR Surveill Summ, 65*(No. SS-6), 1–180.

Kim, M. J., Mason, W. A., Herrenkohl, T. I., Catalano, R. F., Toumbourou, J. W., & Hemphill, S. A. (2017). Influence of early onset of alcohol use on the development of adolescent alcohol problems: A longitudinal binational study. *Prevention Science, 18*(1), 1–11.

Kuntsche, E., Gabhainn, S. N., Roberts, C., Windlin, B., Vieno, A., Bendtsen, P., . . . , Wicki, M. (2014). Drinking motives and links to alcohol use in 13 European countries. *Journal of Studies on Alcohol and Drugs, 75*, 428–437.

Lemstra, M., Bennett, N., Nannapaneni, U., Neudorf, C., Warren, L., Kershaw, T., & Scott, C. (2010). A systematic review of school-based marijuana and alcohol prevention programs targeting adolescents aged 10–15. *Addiction Research & Theory, 18*(1), 84–96.

Li, Y., & Learner, R. M. (2011). Trajectories of school engagement during adolescence: Implications for grades, depression, delinquency, and substance use. *Developmental Psychology, 47*(1), 233–247. doi: 10.1037/a0021307

Lisdahl, K. M., Gilbart, E. R., Wright, N. E., & Shollenbarger, S. (2013). Dare to delay? The impacts of adolescent alcohol and marijuana use onset on cognition, brain structure, and function. *Frontiers in Psychiatry, 4.*

MacArthur, G. J., Harrison, S., Caldwell, D. M., Hickman, M., & Campbell, R. (2016). Peer-led interventions to prevent tobacco, alcohol and/or drug use among young people aged 11–21 years: A systematic review and meta-analysis. *Addiction, 111*, 391–407.

McGuire, W. J. (1964). Inducing resistance to persuasion: Some contemporary approaches. In L. Berkowitz (Ed.), *Advances in experimental social psychology* (pp. 192–227). New York, NY: Academic Press.

McKetin, R., Coen, A., & Kaye, S. (2015). A comprehensive review of the effects of mixing caffeinated energy drinks with alcohol. *Drug and Alcohol Dependence, 151*, 15–30.

McKiernan, A., & Fleming, K. (2017). *Canadian youth perceptions on Cannabis.* Ottawa, ON: Canadian Centre on Substance Abuse.

Midford, R. (2010). Drug prevention programmes for young people: Where have we been and where should we be going?. *Addiction, 105*(10), 1688–1695.

Midford, R., Munro, G., McBride, N., Snow, P., & Ladzinski, U. (2002). Principles that underpin effective school-based drug education. *Journal of Drug Education, 32*(4), 363–386.

Miech, R. A., Johnston, L. D., O'Malley, P. M., Bachman, J. G., & Schulenberg, J. E. (2016). *Monitoring the Future national survey results on drug use, 1975–2015: Volume I, Secondary school students.* Ann Arbor: Institute for Social Research, The University of Michigan.

Minaker, L. M., Bonham, A., Elton-Marshall, T., Leos-Toro, C., Wild, T. C., & Hammond, D. (2017). Under the influence: Examination of prevalence and correlates of alcohol and marijuana consumption in relation to youth driving and passenger behaviours in Canada. A cross-sectional study. *CMAJ Open, 5*(2), E386-E394.

Moss, H. B., Chen, C. M., & Yi, H. Y. (2014). Early adolescent patterns of alcohol, cigarettes, and marijuana polysubstance use and young adult substance use outcomes in a nationally representative sample. *Drug and Alcohol Dependence, 136*, 51–62.

Nelson, S. E., Van Ryzin, M. J., & Dishion, T. J. (2015). Alcohol, marijuana, and tobacco use trajectories from age 12 to 24 years: Demographic correlates and young adult substance use problems. *Development and Psychopathology, 27*(1), 253–277.

Newton, N. C., Conrod, P., Teesson, M., & Faggiano, F. (2012). School-based alcohol and other drug prevention. In *Drug abuse and addiction in medical illness* (pp. 545–560). New York, NY: Springer.

Newton, N. C., Teesson, M., Vogl, L. E., & Andrews, G. (2010). Internet-based prevention for alcohol and cannabis use: Final results of the Climate Schools course. *Addiction, 105*, 749–759.

O'Brennan, L. M., & Furlong, M. J. (2010). Relations between students' perceptions of school connectedness and peer victimization. *Journal of School Violence, 9*(4), 375–391.

Onrust, S. A., Otten, R., Lammers, J., & Smit, F. (2016). School-based programmes to reduce and prevent substance use in different age groups: What works for whom? Systematic review and meta-regression analysis. *Clinical Psychology Review, 44*, 45–59.

Patrick, M. E., Bray, B. C., & Berglund, P. A. (2016). Reasons for marijuana use among young adults and long-term associations with marijuana use and problems. *Journal of Studies on Alcohol and Drugs, 77*(6), 881–888.

Patrick, M. E., Kloska, D. D., Terry-McElrath, Y. M., Lee, C. M., O'Malley, P. M., & Johnston, L. D. (2017). Patterns of simultaneous and concurrent alcohol and marijuana use among adolescents. *The American Journal of Drug and Alcohol Abuse*, 1–11.

Patte, K. A., Qian, W., & Leatherdale, S. T. (2017). Is Binge drinking onset timing related to academic performance, engagement, and aspirations among youth in the COMPASS study? *Substance Use & Misuse*, 1–6.

Peacock, A., Pennay, A., Droste, N., Bruno, R., & Lubman, D. I. (2014). 'High' risk? A systematic review of the acute outcomes of mixing alcohol with energy drinks. *Addiction, 109*(10), 1612–1633.

Pearson, C., Janz, T., & Ali, J. (2013). *Mental and substance use disorders in Canada*. Ottawa, ON: Statistics Canada.

Perkins, H. W., & Craig, D. W. (2003). The imaginary lives of peers: Patterns of substance use and misperceptions of norms among secondary school students. In H. W. Perkins (Ed). *The social norms approach to preventing school and college age substance abuse: A handbook for educators, counselors, and clinicians* (pp. 209–223). San Francisco, CA: John Wiley & Sons.

Porath-Waller, A. J., Beasley, E., & Beirness, D. J. (2010). A meta-analytic review of school-based prevention for cannabis use. *Health Education & Behavior, 37*(5), 709–723.

Ringwalt, C. L., Ennett, S., Johnson, R., Rohrbach, L. A., Simons-Rudolph, A., Vincus, A., & Thorne, J. (2003). Factors associated with fidelity to substance use prevention curriculum guides in the nation's middle schools. *Health Education & Behavior, 30*(3), 375–391.

Roditis, M. L., & Halpern-Felsher, B. (2015). Adolescents' perceptions of risks and benefits of conventional cigarettes, e-cigarettes, and marijuana: A qualitative analysis. *Journal of Adolescent Health, 57*(2), 179–185.

Rosenbaum, M. (2016). New perspectives on drug education/prevention. *Journal of Psychoactive Drugs, 48*(1), 28–30.

Sawyer, S. M., Afifi, R. A., Bearinger, L. H., Blakemore, S. J., Dick, B., Ezeh, A. C., & Patton, G. C. (2012). Adolescence: A foundation for future health. *Lancet, 379*(9826), 1630–1640. doi: 10.1016/S0140-6736(12)60072-5

Shin C. (2001). A review of school-based drug prevention program evaluations in the 1990's. *American Journal of Health Education, 32, 3*, 139–147.

Sitnick, S. L., Shaw, D. S., & Hyde, L. W. (2014). Precursors of adolescent substance use from early childhood and early adolescence: Testing a developmental cascade model. *Development and Psychopathology, 26*(1), 125–140.

Stigler, M. H., Neusel, E., & Perry, C. L. (2011). School-based programs to prevent and reduce alcohol use among youth. *Alcohol Research & Health, 34*, 157.

Stockwell, T., Zhao, J., Panwar, S., Roemer, A., Naimi, T., & Chikritzhs, T. (2016). Do "moderate" drinkers have reduced mortality risk? A systematic review and meta-analysis of alcohol consumption and all-cause mortality. *Journal of Studies on Alcohol and Drugs, 77*(2), 185–198.

Subbaraman, M. S., & Kerr, W. C. (2015). Simultaneous versus concurrent use of alcohol and cannabis in the national alcohol survey. *Alcoholism: Clinical and Experimental Research, 39*(5), 872–879.

Taylor, G. (2016). *The Chief Public Health Officer's Report on the State of Public Health in Canada 2015: Alcohol Consumption in Canada.* Ottawa, ON: Public Health Agency of Canada, 13–17, 19.

Terry-McElrath, Y. M., O'Malley, P. M., & Johnston, L. D. (2013). Simultaneous alcohol and marijuana use among US high school seniors from 1976 to 2011: Trends, reasons, and situations. *Drug and Alcohol Dependence, 133*(1), 71–79.

Thompson, K., Leadbeater, B., & Ames, M. (2015). Reciprocal effects of internalizing and oppositional defiance symptoms on heavy drinking and alcohol-related harms in young adulthood. *Substance Abuse: Research and Treatment, 9*(S1), 21–31. doi:10.4137/SART.S33928.

Thompson, K., Leadbeater, B., Ames, M., & Merrin, G. J. (2018). Associations between marijuana use trajectories and educational and occupational success in young adulthood. *Prevention Science*, 1–13.

Thompson, K., Merrin, G. J., Ames, M., & Leadbeater, B. (2018). Marijuana trajectories in Canadian youth: Associations with substance use and mental health. *Canadian Journal of Behavioural Science, 50*, 17–28. doi:10.1037/cbs0000090.

Trenz, R. C., Dunne, E. M., Zur, J., & Latimer, W. W. (2015). An investigation of school-related variables as risk and protective factors associated with problematic substance use among vulnerable urban adolescents. *Vulnerable Children and Youth Studies, 10*(2), 131–140.

Trucco, E. M., Colder, C. R., Wieczorek, W. F., Lengua, L. J., & Hawk, L. W. (2014). Early adolescent alcohol use in context: How neighborhoods, parents, and peers impact youth. *Development and Psychopathology, 26*(2), 425–436.

Volkow, N. D., Baler, R. D., Compton, W. M., & Weiss, S. R. (2014). Adverse health effects of marijuana use. *New England Journal of Medicine, 370*(23), 2219–2227.

Wang, M., & Fredricks, J. (2014). The reciprocal links between school engagement, youth problem behaviours, and school dropout during adolescence. *Child Development, 85*(2), 722–737. doi: 10.1111/cdev.12138

White, A. M., Hingson, R. W., Pan, I. J., & Yi, H. Y. (2011). Hospitalizations for alcohol and drug overdoses in young adults ages 18–24 in the United States, 1999–2008: Results from the Nationwide Inpatient Sample. *Journal of Studies on Alcohol and Drugs, 72*(5), 774–786.

Wood, S. K., Eckley, L., Hughes, K., Hardcastle, K. A., Bellis, M. A., Schrooten, J., . . . Voorham, L. (2014). Computer-based programmes for the prevention and management of illicit recreational drug use: A systematic review. *Addictive Behaviors, 39*(1), 30–38.

World Health Organization. (2014). *Health for the worlds adolescent's. A second change in the second decade*. Retrieved from http://apps.who.int/adolescent/second-decade/

World Health Organization. (2014b). *Global status report on alcohol and health*. Retrieved from http://apps.who.int/iris/bitstream/10665/112736/1/9789240692763_eng.pdf

World Health Organization. (1994). *Lexicon of alcohol and drug terms*. Geneva, Switzerland: World Health Organization.

Yurasek, A. M., Aston, E. R., & Metrik, J. (2017). Co-use of alcohol and Cannabis: A review. *Current Addiction Reports, 4*(2), 184–193.

Zaharakis, N., Mason, M. J., Mennis, J., Light, J., Rusby, J. C., Westling, E., . . . Way, T. (2017). School, friends, and substance use: Gender differences on the influence of attitudes toward school and close friend networks on Cannabis involvement. *Prevention Science*, 1–9.

Talking to Young Children About Sexual Abuse Prevention

3

Sandy K. Wurtele and
Maureen C. Kenny

Child sexual abuse (CSA) has been defined as "A type of maltreatment that refers to the involvement of the child in sexual activity to provide sexual gratification or financial benefit to the perpetrator, including contacts for sexual purposes, molestation, statutory rape, prostitution, pornography, exposure, incest, or other sexually exploitative activities" (U.S. Department of Health & Human Services, Administration for Children and Families, Children's Bureau, 2018, p. 110). CSA can include experiences of physical contact between a perpetrator and victim (e.g., fondling, intercourse) and also "interactions" in which physical contact may be limited or absent (e.g., voyeurism, photographing or videotaping a child in sexual poses or actions). Although estimates vary depending on the type of sample and definition of sexual abuse used, recent meta-analyses demonstrated that the global prevalence of CSA is alarmingly high, with about 20% of women and 8% of men reporting being sexually abused during childhood (Pereda, Guilera, Forns, & Gómez-Benito, 2009; Stoltenborgh, van IJzendoorn, Euser, & Bakermans-Kranenburg, 2011). In the United States, the most recent *Child Maltreatment* report found there were an estimated 57,460 confirmed cases of sexual abuse in 2016 (U.S. Department of Health & Human Services, Administration for Children and Families, Children's Bureau, 2018). According to results from three administrations of the National Survey of Children's Exposure to Violence, Finkelhor, Shattuck, Turner, and Hamby (2014) reported an estimated prevalence of 27% for females and 5% for males, or approximately 1 in 4 girls and 1 in 20 boys. With this many victims, it is inevitable that teachers will have a child in their classroom who is a victim of CSA. It is therefore imperative that educators be trained in victim identification so they can accurately identify sexual abuse cases and intervene to terminate the abuse and protect child victims. This chapter describes CSA prevention programs for young children (ages 3 through 10) and provides a list of commonly used school-based programs. It is intended to assist educators in selecting and implementing a program for young children.

A Teacher's Role

Early identification and reporting can lead to a better outcome for victims. To effectively identify victims, teachers need to know specific signs and symptoms of CSA. Resources are available to describe possible physical, emotional, and behavioral indicators of sexual abuse and the ages at which these symptoms may occur (e.g., Kenny & Wurtele, 2009). Sometimes, young children act out their abuse in the classroom setting by exhibiting sexual behaviors, giving an astute teacher the opportunity to intervene. Discriminating between typical and atypical sexual behaviors is critical to recognizing whether a child has been sexually abused (Wurtele & Kenny, 2011). Beyond recognizing behaviors, childhood educators may feel ill-equipped to address children's sexual questions or behaviors in the classroom. Although they received training in childhood development, sexual development is rarely given the attention it deserves. However, there are resources to assist teachers with responding to children's sexual questions, comments, and behaviors (e.g., Kenny, Dinehart, & Wurtele, 2015; Kenny & Wurtele, 2009; Wurtele & Kenny, 2011).

Discussion of sexual matters in general is typically met with reluctance on the part of educators, many of whom are unsure of how to initiate such discussions or believe parents are better suited to educate their children on these topics. Granted, parents play a key role in promoting healthy sexual development by discussing sexuality with their children and they acknowledge it is their responsibility to engage in such conversations. However, there are many barriers to parent-child sexuality communication. Parents have difficulty acknowledging their children's sexuality, have an inadequate base of information, are affected by cultural pressures to not discuss sexuality, and some feel uncomfortable or embarrassed being sexuality educators (El-Shaieb & Wurtele, 2009; Flores & Barroso, 2017; Kenny & Wurtele, 2013). Given their discomfort, no wonder parents often prefer that sexuality education, including sexual abuse prevention, be taught in elementary schools (Fisher, Telljohann, Price, Dake, & Glassman, 2015). In addition, research has shown that parents lack crucial information about CSA and often endorse common myths (Babatsikos & Miles, 2015; Wurtele & Kenny, 2010). For example, despite the fact that most sexual abuse is carried out by someone known to the child and their family, the majority of parents (80–95%) focus their CSA-prevention discussions on "stranger-danger" warnings (Deblinger, Thakkar-Kolar, Berry, & Schroeder, 2010; Wurtele, Kvaternick, & Franklin, 1992).

Schools evolved as the logical location to teach children about personal safety, given that their primary function is to meet children's educational, emotional, and behavioral needs, and also because of their ability to reach large numbers of diverse children in a relatively cost-efficient fashion. The importance of providing children with sexual abuse prevention education has led to school-based programs or curricula becoming accepted and common within schools (Lynas & Hawkins, 2017; Wurtele & Kenny, 2012). A universal primary prevention approach of this nature also eliminates the stigma of identifying specific children or families as being at risk for sexual abuse, and thus avoids costly and intrusive interventions into family privacy. In addition, violence in its many forms, including CSA, is increasingly being viewed as a major health issue that can be addressed by schools. Schools are often a safe setting for children to learn about CSA, and with proper training and skills, school personnel can be trusted adults to whom children can disclose abuse.

School-based CSA prevention programs were created and widely disseminated in both the US and Canada during the 1980s and 1990s. Analyses of the effectiveness of these programs have been published (based on studies conducted mostly in the US, but also Canada, the UK, Ireland, Australia, and China). Reviews consistently conclude that children benefit from participating in these programs. Specifically, program participants have demonstrated increased knowledge of sexual abuse and self-protective behaviors (Daro, 1994; Davis & Gidycz, 2000; Fryda & Hulme, 2015; Kenny & Wurtele, 2010; MacMillan et al., 2009; Mikton & Butchart, 2009; Topping & Barron, 2009; Walsh, Zwi, Woolfenden, & Shlonsky, 2015; Wurtele, 1987, 2002; Wurtele & Kenny, 2010, 2012; Zwi et al., 2007). Studies also find that programs increase participants' willingness to disclose abuse, enhance positive feelings about their bodies, teach correct genital terminology, and help children learn that it is not their fault if abuse occurs (Kenny & Wurtele, 2009; Wurtele & Owens, 1997). Reviews also conclude that child-focused educational programs can build children's knowledge and self-protective skills without producing negative side-effects (e.g., elevated anxiety, making false allegations, overgeneralizing to appropriate touches) and may actually produce positive effects (e.g., increased parent-child communication) (Fryda & Hulme, 2015; Wurtele, 2009). However, studies are inconclusive about whether these programs actually *prevent* CSA.

Only one study has attempted to determine whether participation in personal safety programs might prevent sexual victimization. In 2000, Gibson and Leitenberg asked 825 undergraduate women in the US to report their past histories of CSA as well as their participation in school-based prevention programs. Women who had not participated in a prevention program in childhood were about twice as likely to have experienced CSA as those who had participated in a program. Even though this study used a relatively weak, non-experimental design, it provides tentative support for the assertion that, at least for women, school-based CSA prevention programs are associated with a decreased occurrence of sexual abuse. In his review of child-focused educational programs, childhood victimization expert Finkelhor (2007) concluded that "the weight of currently available evidence shows that it is worth providing children with high-quality prevention-education programs" (p. 644).

Characteristics of High-Quality CSA Prevention Programs

School personnel (teachers, counselors) can recommend high-quality CSA prevention programs for young children. Several characteristics of "high-quality" personal safety programs have been identified and are reviewed next to assist with program selection. Table 3.1 provides information about commonly used CSA prevention programs. In addition, the California Evidence-Based Clearinghouse for Child Welfare (https://www.cebc4cw.org) describes evidence-based prevention programs, including three listed in Table 3.1 (i.e., *Body Safety Training Workbook; Safe Child Program;* and *Who Do You Tell?*). Brassard and Fiorvanti (2015) present the pros and cons of several of the programs (i.e., *Stay Safe; Body Safety Training Workbook;* and *Safe Child Program*). The National Center for Missing and Exploited Children (1999) published guidelines for high-quality CSA prevention programs (available at www.ncmec. org) and the Child Welfare Information Gateway also lists tools, curricula, and programs designed to raise awareness and reduce risk factors related to child sexual abuse (https://www.childwelfare.gov/topics/preventing/prevention-programs/sexualabuse/). In 2006, the National Sexual Violence Resource Center (www.nsvrc.org) produced a directory of CSA prevention programs and initiatives (*Preventing Child Sexual Abuse: A National Resource Directory and Handbook*). The book *Off Limits* (Wurtele & Berkower, 2010), a parent's and professional's guide to keeping kids safe from sexual abuse, also contains a detailed listing of resources (including books, websites, and programs).

Content Considerations

Most educational initiatives for young children share common goals, including the *five R's*: (1) helping children *recognize* potentially abusive situations or potential abusers, (2) encouraging children to *refuse* sexual requests by saying "No", (3) teaching children to *resist* by getting away from the perpetrator, (4) encouraging children to *report* previous or ongoing abuse to a trusted authority figure, and (5) explaining that secret or inappropriate touching is never the child's *responsibility* (Wurtele, 2008). Programs also attempt to enhance children's knowledge about CSA by teaching various concepts (e.g., that boys and girls can be victims; that perpetrators can be both strangers and people they know; that sexual abuse is never the victim's fault). Some programs also teach children the correct terminology for the genitals, so they can effectively communicate experiences of inappropriate touching. Common objectives often include the following:

1. Help children distinguish between appropriate and inappropriate requests to touch or look at their private parts or someone else's.
2. Describe perpetrators (examples should include authority figures, babysitters, family members, and strangers).
3. Help children identify the private parts of their bodies using correct genital terminology;
4. Describe potential victims (examples should include both males and females of all races, ages, sizes, and physical abilities/limitations).
5. Teach children self-protective skills to avoid abuse (say "no", try to get away).
6. Stress body ownership, personal space, and self-pride.
7. Build positive skills including confidence, self-esteem, assertiveness, and problem-solving skills.
8. Help children differentiate between good and bad secrets, and teach them not to keep secrets about touches.
9. Promote disclosure by instructing children to tell an adult (even if sworn to secrecy) and to keep on telling until the touching stops.
10. Emphasize that abuse is never the fault of the child.

Table 3.1 Selected Child Sexual Abuse Prevention Programs for Children

Program/ Organization Name	Audience	Materials	Duration	Contact Person	School or Parent	Languages
Body Safety Training Workbook	Preschool Elementary (3- to 8-year-olds)	Script Pictures Role plays Token reward system Take-home materials	10 lessons	Sandy Wurtele, Ph.D. University of Colorado at Colorado Springs Phone: 719-255-4150 swurtele@uccs.edu www.sandywurtele.com	School, Parents	English Spanish Turkish Chinese
Child Assault Prevention (CAP) Project	Preschool Elementary Middle school Adolescents Special needs	Role plays Group discussions	1 hour classroom workshops (elementary); 40- to 45-minute program on 3 sequential days (teen)	National Center for Assault Protection Sewell, NJ Toll Free: 800-258-3189 www.njcap.org	School, Parents	English Spanish French Japanese Russian Slovenian
Child Lures	Elementary Middle school	Role plays Videos Take-home materials	7 Cornerstone lessons 10–11 Lures lessons	Child Lures Prevention Shelburne, VT Phone: 802-985-8458 www.childlures.org	School, Parents	English, Parent in Spanish

Program	Audience	Components	Duration/Format	Source	Setting	Language
Child Safety Matters	Elementary Grades K–6	Script Videos Interactive activities Take-home worksheets for parents and children Lesson plans and curriculum Rewards for children Intro for parents and school staff	Two lessons for the child program; Three lessons for the teen program	Child Safety Matters Jacksonville, Florida 904.642.0210 www.mbfchildsafetymatters.org	School Parents and staff introduction	English Spanish Portuguese Creole
Feeling Yes, Feeling No	Elementary Middle school	Videos Group discussions Role plays	15–18 Classroom hours	National Film Board of Canada Montreal, Quebec, Canada Toll Free: 800-542-2164 https://www.nfb.ca/	School	English
No-Go-Tell!	Preschool Elementary Special needs	Lesson pictures, teaching dolls	76 Illustrated teaching panels	James Stanfield Publishing Santa Barbara, CA Toll Free: 800-421-6534 www.stanfield.com	School	English
Risk Reduction: Child Abuse Prevention	Elementary Middle school Adolescents Faith based	Faith-based curriculum Videos Role plays Discussions	10 Sessions (ages 5–8) 13 sessions (ages 9–12)	Faith Trust Institute Seattle, WA Toll Free: 877-860-2255 www.faithtrustinstitute.org	School, Parents	English Parent materials: Spanish Korean

(Continued)

Table 3.1 (Continued)

Program/ Organization Name	Audience	Materials	Duration	Contact Person	School or Parent	Languages
Red Flag, Green Flag© People	Preschool Elementary Special Needs	Videos Work Book Role Plays Discussions	2 Sessions (45 minutes each) 2nd grade 30 minutes for K	Red Flag Green Flag Resources Fargo, ND Toll Free: 800-627-3675 https://www.raccfm.com/education/elementary	School, Parents	English Spanish French
Safe Child Program	Preschool Elementary (Pre–3rd grade)	Videos Lesson plans Games Role Plays	5–10 Lessons per grade level	Coalition for Children Denver, CO Toll Free: 800-320-1717 www.safechild.org	School, Parents	English, Spanish, Creole, French
Safe TOUCH	Elementary	Films Songs Role Plays Activities	5-Day lessons	Migima Designs Portland, OR Phone: 503-244-0044 www.migima.com	School	English
Stay Safe Program	Preschool Elementary (K–6) Special Needs	Lessons Posters Role Play Stories Games Discussion	10–12 thirty-minute sessions, varies by grade level	Child Abuse Prevention Program Dublin, Ireland Available online: http://www.staysafe.ie	School, Parents	English

Program	Age	Materials	Duration	Source	Audience	Language
Second Step Child Protection Unit	Preschool Elementary (K–5)	Lesson binder Take-home materials Discussion Poster Videos Role plays Songs	6 Weekly lessons per grade level	Committee for Children Seattle, WA Toll Free: 800-634-4449 www.secondstep.org	School, Parents	English, Spanish
Three Kinds of Touches	Preschool Special needs	Classroom presentations Book Take-home materials		Pennsylvania Coalition Against Rape Enola, PA Toll Free: 800-692-7445 www.pcar.org	School, Parents	English, Braille, Spanish
Who Do You Tell?	Elementary (K–6)	Videos Pictures Discussion Role plays	Two 60-minute sessions	Communities Against Sexual Assault Calgary, AB CANADA Phone: 403- 237-6905 www.calgarycasa.com	School, Parents	English
Yellow Dyno	Preschool Elementary	Curriculum Videos Songs	Twelve 35-minute lessons	Yellow Dyno Austin, TX Phone: 512-288-2882, ext. 100 www.yellodyno.com	School, Parents	English, Spanish

Source: From Kenny, M. C., & Wurtele, S. K. (2010). Child sexual abuse prevention: Choosing, implementing, and evaluating a personal safety program for young children. In K. L. Kaufman (Ed.), *The prevention of sexual violence: A practitioner's sourcebook* (pp. 303–317). Holyoke, MA: NEARI Press.

The importance of the first objective cannot be underestimated—warnings can only be effective if children have a clear idea of what it is they are being warned about. Unfortunately, many programs fail in meeting this first objective, by either using abstract definitions or developmentally inappropriate ways to teach children to recognize abuse (such as telling them to "trust their feelings" or using the "good touch/bad touch" teaching approach). Wurtele and Berkower (2010) recommend teaching young children a rule to protect their private parts using "OK" and "not OK" terms instead of teaching children the difference between "good touches" and "bad touches". The problem with the "good touch/bad touch" approach is that some touches that feel bad (like getting a shot) are actually "OK", and some touches that feel good may be "not OK". For example, when a child's genitals are fondled, it can feel good even though it is "not OK". The "good touch/bad touch" approach has been shown to be confusing, especially for young children (Wurtele, Kast, Miller-Perrin, & Kondrick, 1989). Young children also get confused about "bad" touches coming from "good" people. Prior to participating in a personal safety program, Kenny and Wurtele (2010) found that very few young children correctly understood that a "good" person (i.e., someone described as good, kind, or nice) could be a potential abuser. At pre-testing, only 38% of the sample correctly recognized the inappropriateness of a "good" person's request to touch their private parts, compared with 50% of the sample who correctly recognized the inappropriateness of a "bad" person's request. Consistent with the preoperational stage of cognitive development, children in this study appeared to center on the "good/bad" descriptor and judged an inappropriate touching request as "OK" when it came from a "good" person.

Educational programs vary in how they help children recognize potentially abusive situations or potential perpetrators. The *Body Safety Training Workbook* (BST; Wurtele, 2007) is a rules-based program that teaches children a concrete rule to protect their "private parts" and encourages children to use this rule to discriminate between "OK" and "not OK" touches. Research on this program found that after completion, preschool-aged children were able to identify potentially abusive situations and differentiate between appropriate and inappropriate touches of the genitals (Wurtele & Owens, 1997). Other programs (e.g., Second Step's *Child Protection Unit; Safe TOUCH*) teach children the difference between "safe" and "unsafe" touches.

The second teaching objective is also challenging, given what parents have told their children about sexual abusers. Parents report talking to their children about sexual abuse but their descriptions of perpetrators are often inaccurate. They describe child molesters as "dirty old men" (Morison & Greene, 1992) or, most frequently, as dangerous "strangers" (Berrick, 1988; Calvert &

Munsie-Benson, 1999; Chen & Chen, 2005; Deblinger et al., 2010; Tutty, 1997; Wurtele, Moreno, & Kenny, 2008). Few parents include family members, relatives, teenagers, siblings, or trusted acquaintances in the list of potential perpetrators, despite the fact that these are the most likely perpetrators of sexual abuse (Finkelhor, 2008). Instead, children are taught to watch out for "bad" people, especially strangers (Kraizer, 1996). Thus, parents may not be teaching their children to be aware of potential perpetrators who are familiar to them and believed to be "good" people. As Kenny and Wurtele's (2010) study demonstrated, helping children to understand that no one (whether "good" or "bad") has a right to touch their private parts is a critical objective of effective personal safety programs. As noted by Tobin and Kessner (2002), "well-intentioned parents warn their children about strangers, yet are often at a loss when it comes to protecting them from people they know and trust" (p. 8). Including multiple examples of perpetrators familiar to the child and considered "good" engaging in inappropriate touching will help children understand that these types of touches are never acceptable. This concept of a "good" person (someone known and possibly loved by the child) committing a "bad" touch may remain confusing for children and thus constant repetition of the concept is necessary.

There are many advantages to teaching children correct genital terminology—the third objective. First, teaching children the correct names for all the parts of their bodies, including their genitals, helps children develop a healthy, more positive body image. In contrast, using nicknames for genitals can give children the idea that there is something shameful or bad about their genitals. This knowledge also gives children the correct language for understanding their bodies and for asking questions about their sexual development. Although almost all preschool children know the correct terms for their non-genital body parts, very few know the correct names for genitals (Kenny & Wurtele, 2008; Wurtele, 1993; Wurtele, Melzer, & Kast, 1992). Second, without proper terminology, children have a hard time telling someone about sexual touching. For example, children who make disclosures using incorrect and idiosyncratic terminology (e.g., "He touched my muffin") may not be understood and, consequently, may not receive a positive, supportive response. As a result, adults may be less likely to report abuse and child protection agencies may be reluctant to investigate reports perceived as difficult to substantiate. The most compelling evidence for teaching children correct genital terminology comes from the sex offender literature. Some sex offenders do not target children who know the correct names for their genitals, as this knowledge implies to them that these children have been educated about body safety and sexuality, and that there is open communication between the parent and child (Elliot, Browne, & Kilcoyne, 1995; Sprengelmeyer & Vaughan, 2000). Some programs suggest that children be taught correct terms, but recognize that not all settings will allow for this. Second Step's *Child Protection Unit* (Committee for Children, n.d.), for example, recommends that correct terms be used for genitals, but acknowledges that certain communities may not be receptive to having children learn correct genital terminology. Likewise, the *Body Safety Training Workbook* encourages teachers and parents to teach children the correct names for the genitals. For ease of discussion, genitals are then referred to as "private parts".

When selecting a CSA prevention program, it should be examined to ensure it addresses the remaining objectives. All children are potential targets for sex offenders, and programs should be offered universally to all children. As discussed next, some children, such as those with disabilities, may be at a higher risk, and need programming as well. Teaching children self-protective skills and body ownership are important components of a program. For example, the *Body Safety Training* program teaches children to "say no" and get help as well as the idea that they are the "boss of their body". Because CSA occurs in private and many offenders operate by having the child keep it a secret, the concept of not keeping a secret is critical to any CSA prevention program. Second Step's *Child Protection Unit* program teaches children that you should never keep secrets about touching and you should keep on telling until the touching stops. Finally, given that many victims develop feelings of shame and guilt subsequent to CSA, teaching children that abuse is never their fault needs to be emphasized across the curriculum.

Teaching Considerations

Young children can learn personal safety skills if they are taught concrete concepts in a clear, developmentally appropriate way, and are given adequate time for learning across multiple sessions using skill-building exercises. Reviews have consistently concluded that programs that incorporate modeling (i.e., demonstrating the skill to be learned) and rehearsal (e.g., role plays) are more effective than programs that primarily rely on individual study or passive exposure (Davis & Gidycz, 2000; Topping & Barron, 2009; Walsh, Zwi, Woolfenden, & Shlonsky, 2015; Wurtele, 1990, 2008, 2009; Wurtele & Kenny, 2010, 2012; Wurtele & Owens, 1997; Zwi et al., 2007). Wurtele, Marrs, and Miller-Perrin (1987) confirmed that behavioral skills training is critical by comparing a participant modeling condition, in which children observed a skill and then practiced it, and a symbolic modeling condition, in which students simply observed the skill; results were significantly better for the participant modeling condition. The US General Accounting Office's (1996) summary of CSA educational programs concluded that concepts and skills are better grasped when taught with active participation (e.g., modeling, role-playing, or behavioral rehearsal techniques) compared with more passive methods (e.g., viewing a film or hearing a lecture). A similar conclusion was reached by Finkelhor, Asdigian, and Dziuba-Leatherman (1995), who asked 2,000 youth about their experiences with and responses to actual or threatened sexual assaults. Children were more likely to use self-protection strategies if they had received comprehensive prevention instruction, which included opportunities to practice the skills in class. Likewise, Roberts and Miltenberger (1999) concluded that "a behavioral skills training approach to prevention results in the greatest improvement in sexual abuse knowledge and prevention skills relative to approaches involving plays, films, lecture/discussion, and written materials" (p. 85). In their meta-analysis, Rispens, Aleman, and Goudena (1997) found that resistance skill scores were higher when children participated in active-learning programs that provided multiple opportunities for children to practice the skills during the program. In another meta-analysis, Davis and Gidycz (2000) concluded that "programs that allowed physically active participation and made use of behavioral skills training such as modeling, rehearsal, and reinforcement produced the largest changes in performance level" (pp. 261–262).

In addition, programs for young children (ages 3–10 years) are more effective if they are longer in duration (four or more sessions) and repeat important concepts across spaced sessions rather than massed presentation (Davis & Gidycz, 2000; Kenny & Wurtele, 2010; MacIntyre & Carr, 2000; Topping & Barron, 2009; Wurtele & Owens, 1997). It is helpful for children to be re-exposed to concepts each year, as the repetition helps them master the skills. Second Step's *Child Protection Unit* curriculum, for example, provides developmentally appropriate lessons across multiple grades without excessive repetition.

Diversity Considerations

Given the emerging diversity of the US, program selection should also include a consideration of the needs of participants who are culturally and linguistically diverse. Very few programs make significant reference to modifying materials to meet the demands of culturally diverse people. In her 2001 review of prevention programs, Plummer found that only 17% of the

87 prevention programs surveyed were aimed at culturally specific groups, thus indicating a need for greater sensitivity on this topic. Topping and Barron's (2009) review of school-based CSA prevention programs found they were unlikely to address culturally or ethnically diverse student populations. Tobin and Kessner (2002) advise that programs include culturally appropriate materials (dolls) and culturally relevant names in role plays with children. For example, the *Body Safety Training Workbook*'s pictures include both boys and girls of different ethnicities. Clearly, having program materials translated into other languages is a minimum criterion to ensure children's comfort and comprehension. As seen in Table 3.1, several programs have materials available in languages other than English.

In many cultures (including Hispanic and Asian), discussion of sexual matters appears to be taboo, particularly discussions with children about sex (Futa, Hsu, & Hansen, 2001; Kenny & McEachern, 2000; Lira, Koss, & Russo, 1999; Russell, 2004). Fontes (2005, 2007) describes how many Latinos are raised to avoid "talking dirty" and many Latina women have not been taught the correct words to describe sexual acts. Latina women in general are raised not to discuss their sexual feelings, which may impede the negotiation of safe sex and increase their vulnerability to sexual abuse (Van Oss Marín, 2003; Werner-Wilson, 1998).

Understanding the cultural values and mores of a particular group is essential to implementing a successful program. It may be necessary to modify materials and curriculum when working with specific cultural groups. In our previous study comparing Spanish- and English-speaking children's knowledge of genital terminology (Kenny & Wurtele, 2008), we found that none of the Spanish-speaking children knew the correct terms for *breasts*, *penis*, or *vulva*, suggesting a void in sexuality education in Spanish-speaking homes. Kenny, Wurtele, and Alonso (2012) found that the knowledge Latino children acquired in the CSA prevention program was maintained at the 3-month follow up, but they no longer remembered the correct names for genitals. This may indicate parents' reluctance to review or use these terms even after training. As suggested in some programs (e.g., *Body Safety Training; Child Protection Unit*), the use of the general term "private parts" may be preferable for Latino families, after teaching the correct names.

Other issues relate to the ability of some children from certain cultural backgrounds (e.g., Asian) to assert themselves and say "no" to a family member (Boyle & Lutzker, 2005). Furthermore, Latino culture emphasizes *"verguenza"* (shame) for the victim (and potential victim blaming) that may hinder the disclosure of sexual abuse on the part of the child (and parents) (Fontes, 2007). Program presenters need to emphasize that abuse is never the child's fault to combat potential messages in the Latino culture that female victims are responsible for the abuse. Many African-American families typically have extended family members (e.g., grandparents) living in the household, so involving those caretakers may be critical to program success (Hines & Boyd Franklin, 2005). Program staff can facilitate discussions with diverse caregivers geared towards understanding their cultural background and ways parents can stay "loyal" to their culture while also supporting the goals of the program.

Although culture is beginning to be addressed by some programs, other issues of diversity, particularly disabilities, seem largely ignored. Yet children with disabilities are at an increased risk for CSA. For example, among a school-based population, Sullivan and Knutson (2000) found that children with disabilities were over three times more likely to be sexually abused than children without disabilities. Young people who live with intellectual and mental health disabilities are 4.6 times more likely to be sexually abused than children without disabilities (Lund & Vaughn-Jensen, 2012). Risk for sexual abuse is also higher if the disability impairs the child's perceived credibility or ability to resist (e.g., blindness, deafness, intellectual disability) or if the disability impedes disclosure. For example, deaf children are less likely to report the abuse (e.g., only 6% of victims who were deaf at the time reported their abuse to the school or other authorities in Kvam, 2004). Children who are hard of hearing may be unable to report their abuse unless there are adults who are able to communicate in sign language. In addition, they appear to be at higher risk due to lack of knowledge. Yu et al. (2017) found that Chinese students with hearing loss had lower levels of CSA prevention knowledge and self-protection skills compared to their peers with normal hearing. These researchers suggested that "students with hearing loss should learn how to refuse inappropriate requests, how to recognize and deal with dangerous situations, and which person they can tell if sexual abuse occurred" (p. 348).

Limited research has been done on CSA prevention programs with individuals with developmental disabilities (Lee & Tang, 1998; Lumley, Miltenberger, Long, Rapp, & Roberts, 1998). Hawkins and Briggs (1997) emphasize the need for programs for children who are particularly vulnerable to abuse, such as those with intellectual and physical disabilities. Unique instructional strategies need to be developed to ensure learning for these populations. Research on young adults with autism spectrum disorder (ASD) found that behavioral skills training averaging nine sessions was enough to help them learn basic conversational skills (Ryan, Brady, Holloway, & Lydon, 2017). Small-group instruction appeared to assist in skill acquisition through observation of peers during practice and feedback. These results could be used to inform programming for CSA prevention. Encouragingly, five of the programs listed in Table 3.1 include special-needs children as potential audiences. For example, the *Body Safety Training Workbook* has been used by educators working with intellectually challenged youth (Lee & Tang, 1998) and with a child with ASD (Kenny, Bennet, Dougery, & Steele, 2013).

Instructor Characteristics

CSA prevention programs can be taught successfully by teachers or other school personnel. In fact, the qualification/occupation of facilitators was not found to be a significant variable in several studies, with teachers, parents, mental health professionals, and law enforcement officers effectively teaching students (Davis & Gidycz, 2000; MacIntyre & Carr, 2000).

However, classroom teachers offer many advantages as instructors. Teachers are trained in educational instruction and are able to present material in developmentally sensitive ways. They can also use "teachable moments" to make it easier to talk about sexual issues with their students (Wurtele & Berkower, 2010). For example, if students use a slang term for genitals, they can correct them and use that opportunity to discuss the importance of correct terminology. Kenny and Wurtele (2013) recommend using a television show, movie, or recent news event to bring up sexual topics. Teachers can integrate safety topics into other parts of the educational curriculum (e.g., studying health or general safety) and can continue to have students practice lessons or use classroom time for skill reinforcement.

Another advantage of having teachers implement programs is they remain present in the classroom to support children after the curriculum is delivered. Children may disclose to teachers because they trust them and see them every day. For Latino children, who may be reluctant to ask their parents questions about sexuality, teachers may be seen as more approachable adults (Kenny & Wurtele, 2013). Teachers will also be available to respond to parent concerns during or after programming. When teachers provide instruction, it is viewed as part of school programming and not an external voluntary program, making it less likely for parents to "opt out". Teachers can follow up on disclosures made during program presentation, involve appropriate school personnel, and make reports to the state child abuse hotline (as mandatory reporters) (Pulido et al., 2015).

Whoever implements abuse prevention curricula must be trained and supported, and teachers should be given the option of having someone else present the program if (perhaps because of personal beliefs and experiences) they do not feel they are able to deliver the curriculum appropriately. Topping and Barron (2009) report that although teachers have pedagogical competence, they may possess little content knowledge, possible personal sensitivities, or lack confidence in delivery. Instructors should feel comfortable and confident conveying the curricular concepts. Kenny et al. (2013) recommend that educators examine their judgments of different abusive situations, and explore those judgments so they can begin to confront their own attitudes. Training on the curriculum as provided by the developers as well as a thorough review of materials may assist teachers in their comfort level. Finally, fluency in the preferred language of the children (and if the curriculum is translated) is a necessary criterion for anyone delivering a program.

Partnering with Parents

Gaining parent and administrative support for programming is a critical first step. Prior to implementation in schools, program leaders may want to host an introductory session for parents to gain their cooperation and address potential cultural concerns. Given the reluctance of some cultures to discuss sexuality education, educating parents about the content and need for such education is critical for program success. *Child Safety Matters* (Monique Burr Foundation for Children, n.d.), for example, includes both staff and parent orientations. Some programs provide materials for parents that are sent home prior to and during program implementation.

Effective programs use repeated presentation of material, with both teachers and parents reinforcing the messages. Although many programs target only children, the active participation of parents contributes to the success of CSA educational programs (Babatsikos, 2010; Mendelson & Letourneau, 2015; Wurtele & Kenny, 2010). Simultaneous education of children and parents about personal safety allows for increased communication between them, which may potentially decrease the chance of a child keeping the abuse secret (Fieldman & Crespi, 2002). Offering training for parents to improve their confidence in delivering sexual abuse prevention messages at home is a good step. Parents who are skilled, comfortable, and confident in their knowledge about sexuality issues are more likely to communicate with their children frequently and effectively (Kenny et al., 2012). Their children receive repeated exposure to prevention information in their natural environment, thus providing booster sessions to supplement classroom presentations.

Another advantage of targeting parents is that parents can make the home environment safer for their children and they also have the ability to limit the access of potential perpetrators to their children. Involving the family in the educational process may help reduce the secrecy surrounding the topic of CSA and can stimulate parent-child discussions about sexuality in general. Parents should be seen as complementary, not alternative, educators of their children, with parent-focused CSA prevention integrated with school-focused initiatives to augment their impact (Mendelson & Letourneau, 2015; Walsh & Brandon, 2012).

Implementation

In addition to considerations around diversity, which we previously discussed, the choice of a particular program may be affected by many factors, including available funding, cost of the program, number and length of sessions, availability of presenters, and school administrator and parental support (Payne, Gottfredson, & Gottfredson, 2006). Programs vary according to types of presentations (e.g., video, theatrical presentation, use of puppets) and duration, ranging from single-contact programs ("one-time") to multi-lesson programs. Research has consistently demonstrated that programs employing repeated exposure to material are more effective than those taught on one occasion (Davis & Gidycz, 2000; National Center for Missing and Exploited Children, 1999). We therefore recommend that programs be multi-session and provide booster sessions for repeated material exposure. Topping and Barron (2009), in their meta-analysis, report that effective school-based CSA prevention programs incorporate modeling, discussion, and skill rehearsal; are at least 4–5 sessions long; have the capacity to be delivered by a range of personnel; and involve active parent participation.

Most programs utilize a range of materials, including videos, photo cards, coloring books, story books, puppets, guided discussions, and audio material (songs). Videos are often used to educate, prompt discussion, and model problem-solving and decision-making skills. Another technique that can be used is storytelling, in which the teacher begins telling a story and a child finishes it. Puppets can also be used to demonstrate situations. Teachers will act out an appropriate or inappropriate touch and then have children identify the type of touch and show (through the use of puppets or dolls) what action they might take in that situation. Second Step's *Child Protection Unit* program uses photo cards showing safety situations as visual stimuli for children during a lesson. Referring to the picture, the teacher can ask questions to prompt critical thinking such as, "What is happening in this picture? What can he do?" Techniques such as these allow young children to discuss their own thoughts, ideas, and feelings through displacement rather than directly (Webb, 1991). Programs that encourage active participation of children (e.g., through modeling or role-playing techniques) have been shown to be more effective than programs using more passive methods (e.g., watching videos or plays) (Davis & Gidycz, 2000; Wurtele, 2008; Wurtele et al., 1987).

Program Recommendations

Although school-based prevention programs can effectively teach young children to recognize, resist, and report abuse, it is necessary to expand the content of these programs if CSA is ever to be eradicated (Wurtele, 2009). For example, this information could be incorporated into a curriculum promoting healthy sexuality across the lifespan. In addition, CSA-specific information could be embedded into programs that focus on helping children and youth develop healthy relationship skills, including communication, social skills, conflict resolution, and assertiveness skills, and content should address their emotional and social needs. An advantage of this integrated approach is that it would tie together many stand-alone programs that focus on unhealthy relationships (e.g., CSA, bullying, sexual harassment, dating violence) to help schools avoid what Adelman and Taylor (2014) call "projectitis" (p. 162). Instead of schools implementing primary prevention projects focused on specific problems such as bullying, sexual harassment, or CSA, these authors argue that information about specific problems be embedded into a continuum of efforts to promote positive development of all students and "create a caring and safe learning environment" (p. 166). This recommendation is consistent with a whole-school approach (building a safe school environment in which all staff are trained to recognize the signs of abuse and handle disclosures). We have advocated for an ecological approach to CSA prevention, which can be done by educating children, their parents, professionals, and the general public about CSA and changing policies, laws, and social norms to foster a zero-tolerance attitude towards CSA (Kenny & Wurtele, 2012).

Conclusion

When children are the targets of offenders, the result is childhood sexual abuse, which has a devastating impact on the victims, their families, and communities (Pereda et al., 2009). Because children spend a good deal of time in schools, teachers are well poised to provide prevention programs in this area.

The goal of such programming is to arm children with the knowledge and skills to resist inappropriate touching or to report if abuse has occurred. Finkelhor (2009) reports that although children should not be given sole responsibility for prevention, it may also be considered reckless not to equip them with effective actions to recognize and report sexual abuse. Prevention of sexual abuse requires a multi-faceted approach, and children who are knowledgeable about this risk and know safety and touching rules will be better armed to avoid abuse. Informed adults, including teachers and parents, can also be prepared to identify victims and handle their potential disclosures. With an increased awareness of the problem of CSA and visibility of prevention programming at schools, we can begin to eliminate this pervasive public health issue.

Key Messages

What you need to know about childhood sexual abuse:

1. It is often perpetrated by someone known to the child.
2. Children rarely disclose sexual abuse to others.
3. Education and prevention programs can begin in preschool and kindergarten.
4. Child sexual abuse programs have positive outcomes for children.
5. Repetition and practice of material is key to student learning.
6. Involvement and support of parents/caregivers are essential to successful program implementation.

References

Adelman, H. S., & Taylor, L. (2014). Addressing student and schooling problems: Not another project! *Child Abuse & Neglect, 38,* 160–169.

Babatsikos, G. (2010). Parents' knowledge, attitudes and practices about preventing child sexual abuse: A literature review. *Child Abuse Review, 19*(2), 107–129.

Babatsikos, G., & Miles, D. (2015). How parents manage the risk of child sexual abuse: A grounded theory. *Journal of Child Sexual Abuse, 24,* 55–76.

Berrick, J. D. (1988). Parental involvement in child abuse prevention training: What do they learn? *Child Abuse & Neglect, 12,* 543–553.

Boyle, C. L., & Lutzker, J. R. (2005). Teaching young children to discriminate abusive from nonabusive situations using multiple exemplars in a modified discrete trial teaching format. *Journal of Family Violence, 20*(2), 55–69.

Brassard, M. R., & Fiorvanti, C. M. (2015). School-based child abuse prevention programs. *Psychology in the Schools, 52*(1), 40–60.

California Evidence-Based Clearinghouse for Child Welfare. Retrieved from www.cebc4cw.org/

Calvert, J. F., Jr., & Munsie-Benson, M. (1999). Public opinion and knowledge about childhood sexual abuse in a rural community. *Child Abuse & Neglect, 23,* 671–682.

Chen, J. Q., & Chen, D. G. (2005). Awareness of child sexual abuse prevention education among parents of Grade 3 elementary school pupils in Fuxin City, China. *Health Education Research, 20*(5), 540–547.

Child Welfare Information Gateway. (n.d.). In *U.S. Department of Health and Human Services Administration for children and families*. Retrieved August 8, 2014, from www.childwelfare.gov

Committee for Children. (n.d.). *Second Step child protection unit*. Retrieved from www.secondstep.org/child-protection

Daro, D. A. (1994). Prevention of child sexual abuse. *Future of Children, 4*(2), 198–223.

Davis, M. K., & Gidycz, C. A. (2000). Child sexual abuse prevention programs: A meta-analysis. *Journal of Clinical Child Psychology, 29*(2), 257–265.

Deblinger, E., Thakkar-Kolar, R. R., Berry, E. J., & Schroeder, C. M. (2010). Caregivers' efforts to educate their children about child sexual abuse: A replication study. *Child Maltreatment, 15*(1), 91–100.

El-Shaieb, M., & Wurtele, S. K. (2009). Parents' plans to discuss sexuality with their young children. *American Journal of Sexuality Education, 4*(2), 103–115.

Elliott, M., Browne, K., & Kilcoyne, J. (1995). Child sexual abuse prevention: What offenders tell us. *Child Abuse & Neglect, 19*(5), 579–594.

Fieldman, J. P., & Crespi, T. D. (2002). Child sexual abuse: Offenders, disclosure, and school-based initiatives. *Adolescence, 37,* 151–160.

Finkelhor, D. (2007). Prevention of sexual abuse through educational programs directed toward children. *Pediatrics, 120*(3), 640–645.

Finkelhor, D. (2008). *Childhood victimization: Violence, crime, and abuse in the lives of young people.* New York, NY: Oxford University Press.

Finkelhor, D. (2009). The prevention of childhood sexual abuse. *The Future of Children, 19*(2), 169–194.

Finkelhor, D., Asdigian, N., & Dziuba-Leatherman, J. (1995). The effectiveness of victimization prevention instruction: An evaluation of children's responses to actual threats and assaults. *Child Abuse & Neglect, 19*, 141–153.

Finkelhor, D., Shattuck, A., Turner, H. A., & Hamby, S. L. (2014). The lifetime prevalence of child sexual abuse and sexual assault assessed in late adolescence. *Journal of Adolescent Health, 55(3)*, 329–333.

Fisher, C. M., Telljohann, S. K., Price, J. H., Dake, J. A., & Glassman, T. (2015). Perceptions of elementary school children's parents regarding sexuality education. *American Journal of Sexuality Education, 10*(1), 1–20.

Flores, D., & Barroso, J. (2017). 21st century parent-child sex communication in the United States: A process review. *The Journal of Sex Research 43*(4–5), 532–548.

Fontes, L. A. (2005). *Child abuse and culture: Working with diverse families.* New York, NY: Guilford Press.

Fontes, L. (2007) Sin vergüenza: Addressing shame with Latino victims of child sexual abuse and their families. *Journal of Child Sexual Abuse, 16*, 61–83.

Fryda, C. M., & Hulme, P. A. (2015). School-based childhood sexual abuse prevention programs: An integrative review. *Journal of School Nursing, 31*(3), 167–182.

Futa, K. T., Hsu, E., & Hansen, D. J. (2001). Child sexual abuse in Asian American families: An examination of cultural factors that influence prevalence, identification, and treatment. *Clinical Psychology: Science and Practice, 8*(2), 189–209.

Gibson, L. E., & Leitenberg, H. (2000). Child sexual abuse prevention programs: Do they decrease the occurrence of child sexual abuse? *Child Abuse & Neglect, 24*, 1115–1125.

Hawkins, R. M. F., & Briggs, F. (1997). The institutionalized abuse of children in Australia: Past and present. *Early Child Development and Care, 133*, 41–55.

Hines, P. M., & Boyd-Franklin, N. (2005). African American families. In M. McGoldrick, J. Giordano, & N. Garcia-Preto (Eds.), *Ethnicity and family therapy* (3rd ed., pp. 87–100). New York, NY: Guilford Press.

Kenny, M. C., & McEachern, A. G. (2000). Racial, ethnic, and cultural factors of childhood sexual abuse: A selected review of the literature. *Clinical Psychology Review, 20*(7), 905–922.

Kenny, M. C., Bennett, K., Dougery, J., & Steele, F. (2013). Teaching general safety and body safety training skills to a Latino preschool male with Autism. *Journal of Child and Family Studies, 22*(8), 1092–1102.

Kenny, M. C., Dinehart, L. H., & Wurtele, S. K. (2015). Recognizing and responding to young children's sexual behaviors in the classroom. *Young Exceptional Children, 18*(1), 17–29.

Kenny, M., & Wurtele, S. (2008, April). *Toward prevention of childhood sexual abuse: Preschoolers' knowledge of genital body parts.* Paper presented at the College of Education Research Conference, Miami, FL.

Kenny, M. C., & Wurtele, S. K. (2009). A counselor's guide to preventing childhood sexual abuse. *Counseling and Human Development, 42*(1), 1–14.

Kenny, M. C., & Wurtele, S. K. (2010). Child sexual abuse prevention: Choosing, implementing, and evaluating a personal safety program for young children. In K. L. Kaufman (Ed.), *The prevention of sexual violence: A practitioner's sourcebook* (pp. 303–317). Holyoke, MA: NEARI Press.

Kenny, M. C., & Wurtele, S. (2012). Preventing childhood sexual abuse: An ecological approach. *Journal of Child Sexual Abuse, 21*(4), 361–367.

Kenny, M. C., & Wurtele, S. K. (2013). Latino parents' plans to communicate about sexuality with their children. *Journal of Health Communication, 18*(8), 931–942.

Kenny, M. C., Wurtele, S. K., & Alonso, L. (2012). Evaluation of a personal safety program with Latino preschoolers. *Journal of Child Sexual Abuse, 21*(4), 368–385.

Kraizer, S. (1996). *The safe child book: A commonsense approach to protecting children and teaching children to protect themselves.* New York, NY: Fireside.

Kvam, M. H. (2004). Sexual abuse of deaf children: A retrospective analysis of the prevalence and characteristics of childhood sexual abuse among deaf adults in Norway. *Child Abuse & Neglect, 28,* 241–251.

Lee, Y. K., & Tang, C. S. (1998). Evaluation of sexual abuse prevention program for female Chinese adolescents with mild mental retardation. *American Journal on Mental Retardation, 103*(2), 105–116.

Lira, L. R., Koss, M. P., & Russo, N. F. (1999). Mexican American women's definitions of rape and sexual abuse. *Hispanic Journal of Behavioral Sciences, 21*(3), 236–265.

Lumley, V. A., Miltenberger, R. G., Long, E. S., Rapp, J. T., & Roberts, J. A. (1998). Evaluation of a sexual abuse prevention program for adults with mental retardation. *Journal of Applied Behavior Analysis, 31*(1), 91–101.

Lund, E. M., & Vaughn-Jensen, J. E. (2012). Victimisation of children with disabilities. *Lancet, 380*(9845), 867–869.

Lynas, J., & Hawkins, R. (2017). Fidelity in school-based child sexual abuse prevention programs: A systematic review. *Child Abuse & Neglect, 72,* 10–21.

MacIntyre, D., & Carr, A. (2000). Prevention of child sexual abuse: Implications of programme evaluation research. *Child Abuse Review, 9,* 183–199.

Macmillan, H. L., Wathen, C. N., Barlow, J., Fergusson, D. M., Leventhal, J. M., & Taussig, H. N. (2009). Interventions to prevent child maltreatment and associated impairment. *Lancet, 373*(9659), 250–266.

Mendelson, T., & Letourneau, E. J. (2015). Parent-focused prevention of child sexual abuse. *Prevention Science, 16,* 844–852.

Mikton, C., & Butchart, A. (2009). Child maltreatment prevention: A systematic review of reviews. *Bulletin of the World Health Organization, 87,* 353–361.

Monique Burr Foundation for Children. (n.d.). *MBF Child Safety Matters.* Retrieved from https://mbfchildsafetymatters.org/

Morison, S., & Greene, E. (1992). Juror and expert knowledge of child sexual abuse. *Child Abuse & Neglect, 16,* 595–613.

National Center for Missing and Exploited Children. (1999). *Guidelines for programs to reduce child victimization: A resource for communities when choosing a program to teach personal safety to children.* Alexandria, VA: Author.

National Sexual Violence Resource Center. (2006). *Preventing child sexual abuse: A national resource directory and handbook.* Retrieved from www.nsvrc.org/

Payne, A. A., Gottfredson, D. C., & Gottfredson, G. D. (2006). School predictors of the intensity of implementation of school-based prevention programs: Results from a national study. *Prevention Science, 7*(2), 225–237.

Pereda, N., Guilera, G., Forns, M., & Gómez-Benito, J. (2009). The prevalence of child sexual abuse in community and student samples: A meta-analysis. *Clinical Psychology Review, 29*(4), 328–338.

Plummer, C. A. (2001). Prevention of child sexual abuse: A survey of 87 programs. *Violence and Victims, 16*(5), 575–588.

Pulido, M., Dauber, S., Tully, B., Hamilton, P., Smith, M., & Freeman, K. (2015). Knowledge gains following a child sexual abuse prevention program among urban students: A cluster-randomized evaluation. *American Journal of Public Health, 105*, 1344–1350.

Rispens, J., Aleman, A., & Goudena, P. P. (1997). Prevention of child sexual abuse victimization: A meta-analysis of school programs. *Child Abuse & Neglect, 21*, 975–987.

Roberts, J. A., & Miltenberger, R. G. (1999). Emerging issues in the research on child sexual abuse prevention. *Education & Treatment of Children, 22*, 84–102.

Russell, S. (2004). Practitioners' perspectives on effective practices for Hispanic teenage pregnancy prevention. *Perspectives in Sexual and Reproductive Health, 36*, 142–149.

Ryan, G., Brady, S., Holloway, J., & Lydon, H. (2017). Increasing appropriate conversation skills using a behavioral skills training package for adults with intellectual disability and autism spectrum disorder. *Journal of Intellectual Disabilities*, 1–14.

Sprengelmeyer, M. E., & Vaughan, K. (2000, October 8). *Stalking children. Imprisoned molesters reveal dark secrets, tell Colorado's parents how to protect their children*. Denver Rocky Mountain News, pp. 5a, 41–45a. Retrieved from www.highbeam.com/doc/1G1-81071310.html

Stoltenborgh, M., van IJzendoorn, M. H., Euser, E. M., & Bakermans-Kranenburg, M. (2011). A global perspective on child sexual abuse: Meta-analysis of prevalence around the world. *Child Maltreatment, 16*(2), 79–101.

Sullivan, P. M., & Knutson, J. F. (2000). Maltreatment and disabilities: A population-based epidemiological study. *Child Abuse & Neglect, 24*(10), 1257–1273.

Tobin, P., & Kessner, S. (2002). *Keeping kids safe: Child sexual abuse prevention manual*. Alameda, CA: Hunter House.

Topping, K., & Barron, I. (2009). School-based child sexual abuse prevention programs: A review of effectiveness. *Review of Educational Research, 79*, 431–463.

Tutty, L. (1997). Child sexual abuse prevention programs: Evaluating "Who Do You Tell." *Child Abuse & Neglect, 21*, 869–881.

US Department of Health & Human Services, Administration for Children and Families, Children's Bureau. (2018). *Child Maltreatment 2016*. Retrieved from https://www.acf.hhs.gov/cb/resource/child-maltreatment-2016

U.S. General Accounting Office. (1996). *Preventing child sexual abuse: Research inconclusive about effectiveness of child education programs*. Washington, DC: U. S. Government Printing Office.

Van Oss Marín, B. (2003). HIV prevention in the Hispanic community: Sex, culture, and empowerment. *Journal of Transcultural Nursing, 14*(3), 186–192. doi:10.1177/1043659603014003005

Walsh, K., & Brandon, L. (2012). Their children's first educators: Parents' views about child sexual abuse prevention education. *Journal of Child and Family Studies, 21*, 734–746.

Walsh, K., Zwi, K., Woolfenden, S., & Shlonsky, A. (2015). School-based education programmes for the prevention of child sexual abuse. *Cochrane Database of Systematic Reviews*, 2015(4). Retrieved from http://dx.doi.org/10.1002/14651858.CD004380.pub3 [Art. No.: CD004380].

Webb, N. (1991). Play therapy crisis intervention with children. In N. B. Webb (Ed.), *Play therapy with children in crisis* (pp. 26–42) New York, NY: Guilford Press.

Werner-Wilson, R. J. (1998). Gender differences in adolescent sexual attitudes: The influence of individual and family factors. *Adolescence, 33*(131), 519–531.

Wurtele, S. K. (1987). School-based sexual abuse prevention programs: A review. *Child Abuse & Neglect, 11*(4), 483–495.

Wurtele, S. K. (1990). Teaching personal safety skills to four-year-old children. *Behavior Therapy, 21*, 32–45.

Wurtele, S. K. (1993). Enhancing children's sexual development through child sexual abuse prevention programs. *Journal of Sex Education & Therapy, 19*(1), 37–46.

Wurtele, S. K. (2002). School-based child sexual abuse prevention. In P. A. Schewe (Ed.), *Preventing violence in relationships* (pp. 9–25). Washington, DC: American Psychological Association.

Wurtele, S. K. (2007). *The body safety training workbook: A personal safety program for parents to teach their children.* Retrieved from www.sandywurtele.com

Wurtele, S. K. (2008). Behavioral approaches to educating young children and their parents about child sexual abuse prevention. *The Journal of Behavior Analysis of Offender and Victim Treatment and Prevention, 1*(1), 52–64.

Wurtele, S. K. (2009). Preventing sexual abuse of children in the 21st century: Preparing for challenges and opportunities. *Journal of Child Sexual Abuse, 18*, 1–18.

Wurtele, S. K., & Berkower, F. (2010). *Off limits: A parent's guide to keeping kids safe from sexual abuse.* Brandon, VT: Safer Society Press.

Wurtele, S. K., & Kenny, M. C. (2010). Partnering with parents to prevent childhood sexual abuse. *Child Abuse Review, 19*, 130–152.

Wurtele, S. K., & Kenny, M. C. (2011). Normative sexuality development in childhood: Implications for developmental guidance and prevention of childhood sexual abuse. *Counseling and Human Development, 43*(9), 1–24.

Wurtele, S. K., & Kenny, M. C. (2012). Preventing child sexual abuse: An ecological approach. In P. Goodyear-Brown (Ed.), *Handbook of child sexual abuse: Identification, assessment and treatment* (pp. 531–565). Hoboken, NJ: John Wiley & Sons, Inc.

Wurtele, S. K., & Owens, J. S. (1997). Teaching personal safety skills to young children: An investigation of age and gender across five studies. *Child Abuse & Neglect, 21*(8), 805–814.

Wurtele, S. K., Kvaternick, M., & Franklin, C. F. (1992). Sexual abuse prevention for preschoolers: A survey of parents' behaviors, attitudes, and beliefs. *Journal of Child Sexual Abuse, 1*, 113–128.

Wurtele, S. K., Marrs, S. R., & Miller-Perrin, C. L. (1987). Practice makes perfect? The role of participant modeling in sexual abuse prevention programs. *Journal of Consulting and Clinical Psychology, 55*(4), 599–602.

Wurtele, S. K., Melzer, A. M., & Kast, L. C. (1992b). Preschoolers' knowledge of and ability to learn genital terminology. *Journal of Sex Education & Therapy, 18*(2), 115–122.

Wurtele, S., Moreno, T., & Kenny, M. C. (2008). Evaluation of a sexual abuse prevention workshop for parents of young children. *Journal of Child & Adolescent Trauma, 1*(4), 331–340.

Wurtele, S. K., Kast, L. C., Miller-Perrin, C. L., & Kondrick, P. A. (1989). A comparison of programs for teaching personal safety skills to preschoolers. *Journal of Consulting and Clinical Psychology, 57*, 505–511.

Yu, B., Chen, J., Jin, Y., Zhang, W., Feng, Y., & Zhao, X. (2017). The knowledge and skills related to sexual abuse prevention among Chinese children with hearing loss in Beijing. *Disability and Health Journal, 10*, 344–349.

Zwi, K. J., Woolfenden, S. R., Wheeler, D. M., O'Brien, T. A., Tait, P., & Williams, K. W. (2007). School-based education programmes for the prevention of child sexual abuse. *Cochrane Database of Systematic Reviews*, 2007(3). Retrieved from http://dx.doi.org/10.1002/14651858 [Art. No.: CD004380. Pub2].

Talking About Mental Illness in Classrooms and Communities

4

Julie A. Gocey and Shanda R. Wells

Mental illness is one of the most common health issues faced by students. For example, 1 in 5 children will be diagnosed with a mental illness between the ages of 4–17, and 1 in 10 children experiences mental illness that severely impairs daily functioning (Merikangas et al., 2010). Additionally, approximately 70% of chronic mental health problems begin to develop during childhood (Costello, He, Sampson, Kessler, & Merikangas, 2014; Stewart & Hirdes, 2015), and a history of mental illness has been found in 59–70% of adolescent suicide attempts (Holland, Vivolo-Kantor, Logan, & Leemis, 2017; King, Arango, & Foster, 2018). The acute and chronic consequences of mental illness have resulted in increased demands for mental health treatments for children and adolescents in schools (Center for Behavioral Health Statistics and Quality, 2016).

Educators, therefore, face a dilemma. In addition to teaching the curriculum, they are increasingly expected to monitor and address mental health needs in classrooms (Rothì, Leavey, & Best, 2013). Balancing academic instruction with providing adequate emotional support to struggling students remains challenging (Ko et al., 2008; Reinke, Stormont, Herman, Puri, & Goel, 2011). Despite strong evidence for approaching student emotional and behavioral concerns using a multi-tiered system of support, individual educators have reported feeling inadequately prepared to address student mental health needs, and staff with specialized training in addressing mental illnesses report barriers to partnering with community mental health providers (Stephan, Sugai, Lever, & Connors, 2015).

Having a mental illness increases a student's risk for poor academic, emotional, and physical health outcomes, and exposure to a parent's mental illness may be traumatic enough to exacerbate mental health problems of children and adolescents (Felitti et al., 1998; Shonkoff et al., 2012). Nearly 13% of parents report some degree of mental illness in any given year, and 3.8% of parents live with a serious mental illness (Stambaugh et al., 2017). Thus, mental illness and traumatic experiences caused by a parent's mental illness impact students, schools, and communities.

This chapter provides an overview of mental illness, including the causes, stressors, risks, and consequences of mental illness and related traumatic experiences. Important components of evidence-based practices for supporting kids with mental illness, including the impact of myths and stigma, will be discussed. Additional resources for individual, small-group, or school-wide interventions aimed at addressing potential trauma related to mental illness exposures are listed in Appendix 4.

Establishing Common Definitions for Discussing Mental Illness

1. *Mental illness* is a disorder by definition, meaning it falls outside the range of normal development. In a general sense, mental illness involves problems in thinking, mood, or behavior (Perou, Bitsko, Blumberg, et al., 2013). Medically speaking, the term mental illness refers to disorders diagnosed by a qualified health provider based on criteria for symptoms and impairment as defined in the DSM-5, the *Diagnostic and Statistical Manual of Mental Disorders, 5th edition* (American Psychiatric Association, 2013). Examples include major depressive disorder (MDD), generalized anxiety disorder (GAD), attention deficit/hyperactivity disorder (ADHD), and post-traumatic stress disorder (PTSD).

2. *Mental health*, in contrast, is more than the absence of mental illness. Rather, mental health is a state of well-being in which a person fully realizes their potential, copes with normal stresses in life, works productively, and contributes to the community (Galderisi et al., 2015).

3. *Typical development* involves physical, emotional, and cognitive growth over time, and it is best supported by a responsive environment of nurturing relationships that enhances learning and helps kids develop

adaptive capacities that promote well-regulated stress-response systems (Sege & Linkenbach, 2014).

4. *Stress* is a general term used to describe the body's physical and emotional responses to challenges or experiences in the environment, with some amount of stress in life being considered normal and necessary (American Academy of Pediatrics, 2014). According to the American Academy of Pediatrics (2014), stress may be positive (e.g., brief increases in heart rate or mild elevations in stress hormone levels), tolerable (e.g., serious but temporary stress responses buffered by supportive relationships), or toxic (see next item).

5. *Toxic stress* is a persistent, harmful physiologic activation of the body's stress-response systems caused by strong, frequent, or prolonged adversity in the absence of safe nurturing relationships to buffer the negative physical reaction (Garner & Shonkoff, 2012; Shonkoff et al., 2012).

6. *Adverse childhood experiences (ACEs)* are a group of traumatic childhood experiences that, in the absence of adequate adult support, are linked to chronic physical and mental illnesses throughout life. The original 1998 study of ACEs by Felliti and colleagues found negative effects from the following childhood experiences: physical, sexual, or emotional abuse; emotional or physical neglect; exposure to violence; household substance abuse; household mental illness; chronic financial hardship; or parental separation due to divorce, death, or incarceration (Felitti, 1998).

7. *Post-traumatic stress disorder (PTSD)* is a diagnosis reserved for severe, persistent, and maladaptive responses to traumatic experiences that interfere with daily functioning in response to witnessing or living through trauma. Symptoms include a combination of avoidance and hyperarousal. *Avoidance* can involve difficulty thinking about the trauma, memory lapses, or feeling numb, whereas *hyperarousal* causes a person to feel on edge and overly aroused to such a degree that difficulty sleeping, irritability, overreacting to sounds, or reminders of the trauma are frequently experienced (American Psychiatric Association, 2013).

8. *Stigma* is defined as a negative reaction due to perceptions of mental illness that results in feeling ashamed or different (Corrigan & Watson, 2002, Milin, Kutcher, & Lewis et al., 2016).

9. *Suicide* is a potential consequence of mental illness that is fatal, caused by "self-directed injurious behavior with an intent to die" (Crosby, Ortega, & Melanson, 2011, p. 23).

10. *Resilience* is the ability to adapt to difficult situations, such as "trauma, threats, or significant sources of stress" (American Psychological Association Help Center, 2018). Resiliency can be promoted by safe, nurturing relationships, and is shown to ameliorate negative outcomes of adversity to some degree.

Understanding the Causes of Mental Illness

Mental illnesses are complex, with biology, environment, and human experience all determining a person's mental health or illness. It is important to point out that living with a mental illness does not necessarily result in dangerous or traumatic exposures for all students. As will be explained later, many factors such as the severity of the illness, environmental circumstances, availability of resources, and protective support interact to determine the impact of having or living with a mental illness. The complex nature of mental illnesses often warrants using a multimodal, multisystem approach when seeking to understand, prevent, and/or intervene with students in school settings.

One model that accounts for the complex interactions between individual risks and mental illness outcomes is the *diathesis-stress model* (Goldstein & Naglieri, 2011). This model illustrates how genetically predetermined biological sensitivities, such as genetic predisposition to mental illness, interact with other factors to influence how well an individual can respond to life stresses. Specific stressors, genetic vulnerabilities, coping skills, and availability of social and community resources interact to influence an individual's ability to deal with their unique circumstances (Goldstein & Naglieri, 2011).

In this model, a child with many life stressors could become mentally ill despite having a strongly protective genetic background and a highly supportive environment. Likewise, another person with a high level of biological risk for mental illness might fare quite well if they experience tolerable levels of stress while living in a supportive environment. Therefore, it is extremely important for children to have access to supportive adults, and parents to have access to community support in the form of safe housing, transportation, healthcare, and other services.

Forms of support in the child's environment, often referred to as protective factors, can significantly lessen the potential harm caused by trauma (Bruner, 2017).

Consequences of Mental Illness on Parenting and Child Health Outcomes

The reasons for adverse outcomes in the social, emotional, academic, and physical well-being of some children with mentally ill parents are highly complex and factors are often interrelated (Manning & Gregoire, 2009). Children may experience trauma from having a mentally ill parent or instead may experience their own illness (e.g., anxiety, depression, inattention, self-harm, or suicidal behaviors) according to Kessler et al. (2005). The problems associated with childhood mental illness are potentially compounded if the parent's ability to provide support to the distressed child is limited by mental illness. Keep in mind that traumatic exposures due to family mental illness can involve single, acute events or sustained neglect or stress over time, according to research summarized by the American Academy of Pediatrics (2014). It is important to reiterate that not all parents with mental health problems struggle to parent effectively.

Children living with a mentally ill *biological* parent are born with higher genetic and prenatal risks for developing a mental disorder during childhood or adolescence (Uher, 2014). For example, biological offspring may have also been exposed in utero to physiological stresses experienced during pregnancy, or parental mental disorders may interfere with self-care (e.g., adequate nutrition) during pregnancy. These biological factors occur in addition to the increased likelihood of experiencing traumatic interactions on a day-to-day basis, according to Manning and Gregoire (2009). Parents who have experienced their own trauma may also respond to their children's needs in maladaptive ways, in part due to physiological changes to their own stress-response systems (American Academy of Pediatrics, 2014).

The Impact of Adverse Childhood Experiences (ACEs) on Child Health and Development

Nearly 20 years ago, a groundbreaking report involving over 17,000 adults from middle-class backgrounds revealed that chronic exposure to adverse childhood experiences, termed ACEs, increases the risk of developing numerous serious chronic health issues during the school years and throughout adulthood (Felitti et al., 1998). In the study, participants were asked about ten specific ACEs that were sorted into three groups: abuse, neglect, and household challenges. Abuse was reported as emotional (11%), physical (28%), or sexual (21%), and neglect as emotional (15%) or physical (10%). Household challenges included the mother being treated violently (13%), substance abuse (27%), mental illness (19%), separation/divorce (23%), or an incarcerated household member (5%). A majority of participants (67%) reported at least one ACE, and 87% of those participants had experienced two or more ACEs by 18 years of age (Felitti et al., 1998). The same study also found that, as the number of ACEs increased, so did the risk for serious health issues, with many participants reporting co-occurring traumatic experiences.

The original ACE questionnaire specifically queried exposure to mental illness by asking, "Was a household member depressed or mentally ill, or did a household member attempt suicide?" Nearly 1 in 5 participants reported exposure to a household mental illness during childhood. Not surprisingly, exposure to family mental illness or a suicide attempt was associated with higher risk for mental illness in adulthood. Results indicated that exposure to one or more ACE before 18 years of age also increased the risk for suicide, drug use, poverty, poor academic achievement, and other chronic health problems such as diabetes, obesity, and other leading causes of death in adults (Felitti et al., 1998).

A more recent study from Bethell, Newacheck, Hawes, and Halfon (2014) found that children with two or more ACEs had more than 2.5 times the risk of repeating a grade in school, compared to children without any ACEs in their lives. Kindergarten children with three or more ACEs were found to have higher odds of language and literacy delay, as well as behavior problems (Jimenez, Wade, Lin, Morrow, & Reichman, 2016). It should also be noted that ACEs have been shown to affect students of all races, economic backgrounds, and geographic regions, but children and adolescents growing up in poverty have a much higher chance of facing multiple ACEs (Bruner, 2017; Evans & Kim, 2013).

Acute Responses to Traumatic Exposures

Children are at an increased risk of developing a mental illness after experiencing either an acute trauma exposure or chronic traumatic stress; however, only a small minority of children develop an acute mental illness such as PTSD or MDD (American Psychiatric Association, 2008). Between 39% and 85% of children are, at minimum, witnesses to violence in their community (American Psychiatric Association, 2008). Some of the most common reactions to trauma, divided by age and developmental stage, are included in Table 4.1.

During the days and weeks following acute trauma, children may struggle in school in a variety of ways. Academic performance can suffer following a stressful event if concentration is compromised, impairing learning and memory, and students may miss more school than usual or act out behaviorally (National Child Traumatic Stress Network, 2008). Although these behaviors may not stem from traumatic experiences, awareness is important for monitoring student safety. Keep in mind that a somewhat adaptive response used during specific, short-term circumstances can become unhealthy and disruptive to the student over time.

When a child may have experienced adverse or dangerous events, it is crucial to determine whether there is reason to suspect child abuse or neglect.

Table 4.1   Typical Responses Associated with Exposure to Trauma Based on Age

Age	Physical Responses	Emotional Responses
1–3 years	Sleep difficulties, poor appetite, weight loss, more crying, developmental regression (increase in thumb sucking, bedwetting, baby-talk)	Re-enacting trauma during play, fearfulness, sadness, becoming withdrawn, more attention-seeking, acting out, reacting in anger
4–7 years	Nightmares, sleep difficulties, appetite changes, regression in toileting skills, lethargy, increased general physical symptoms such as headaches, stomach aches, fatigue, etc.	Feeling helpless, uncertainty about their safety, more fearful, reassurance-seeking, regressing emotionally, extreme clinginess, traumatic play related to events
8–12 years	Nightmares, sleep difficulties, lethargy, problems concentrating, increased physical symptoms such as headaches, stomach aches, fatigue	Worrying about safety for themselves and others, preoccupation with talking about the event, aggression or acting-out behaviors
13–18 years	Nightmares, sleep difficulties, irritability, lethargy, being easily startled, problems with concentrating, physical symptoms	Fearfulness, detachment, social withdrawal, feeling vulnerable, shame, guilt, aggression, self-destructive behaviors, reliving the event

Adapted from the National Child Traumatic Stress Network (2010) and Substance Abuse and Mental Health Service Administration (November 2012).

> *As mandated reporters of suspected child abuse or neglect, school professionals are required to document and report suspicions to law enforcement or child protection authorities but are not expected to fully investigate or make a definitive determination before contacting authorities.*
>
> (Child Welfare Information Gateway, 2016)

Each individual educator is responsible for following state and local regulations, but a team approach that includes consultation with other school professionals with additional training and experience with assessment and referral may be helpful (Dowd, 2014).

Responding to Acute Stress From Traumatic Experiences

Adults can provide basic responses to trauma to help students cope shortly after a traumatic event. The National Child Traumatic Stress Network (NCTSN) Toolkit for Educators (2014) suggests offering young children (1–7 years old) comfort and reassurance, being patient with moodiness and developmental regression. It is not uncommon for young children to revert to previous developmental milestones, such as having difficulty with previously mastered eating or toileting skills. Typically, this passes after a few weeks. It is also helpful to allow children to act out the trauma as needed through drawing, play, or telling stories. Allowing children opportunities to express their feelings by replaying what happened is important as they try to cope after a traumatic experience (Siegal & Bryson, 2012).

For children in elementary or middle school (5–14 years old), allowing them to talk about their experiences and worries helps in processing them. The goal is for supportive adults to provide reassurance, acknowledge student fears, and help them understand that others tend to have similar thoughts and emotions after a scary event (National Child Traumatic Stress Network, 2014).

For older teens, it is important to encourage them to discuss the trauma once they are ready. Try to frame any acting-out behaviors in the context of the trauma and discuss this with the youth. Let teens know that you understand acting-out behaviors may relate to the traumatic experiences, but there is an expectation that they will work to develop coping skills and find alternative ways to deal with stress. Help them problem-solve a different way of letting others know they are upset and normalize that feeling for them. Encourage them to take breaks as needed to help avoid these issues (National Child Traumatic Stress Network, 2008).

Fortunately, with appropriate buffers such as adult support and protective environmental factors, stress and trauma may exert a positive influence on development by promoting resiliency. By guiding children through difficult situations, adults may ultimately help build a student's confidence. (American Academy of Pediatrics, 2014).

When Acute Symptoms Persist

As discussed previously, many children temporarily show signs of distress in the days and weeks following trauma, and a subset of those students will show some degree of acute traumatic stress without fully meeting the diagnostic criteria for a disorder as outlined in the DSM-5 (American Psychiatric Association, 2013). The behaviors listed in Table 4.1, such as difficulties concentrating, sleep problems, or developmental regression, typically become worrisome when they persist and are severe enough to interfere with routine daily functioning for more than 1 month. Several factors may indicate that a child has developed a bona fide mental illness, including problem symptoms of long duration, negative effects on day-to-day life, and impaired social relationships, academics, or physical health (e.g., sleep, appetite, irritability). If a child's behavior or emotions negatively affect multiple areas of function, further assessment by a qualified professional is needed.

Long-Term Consequences of Mental Illness and Trauma

For many children living with chronic traumatic stresses (e.g., homelessness, losing a parent, or having a chronically ill parent), those experiences began at an early age. As discussed previously, it is often the dose, or amount, of trauma that increases a child's likelihood of adverse reactions and mental illness. For example, children exposed to higher number of ACEs have significantly increased chances of developmental delays, as shown in Figure 4.1.

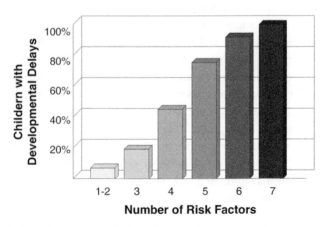

Figure 4.1 Significant Adversity Impairs Development in First Three Years

Developmental delays are often considered to result primarily from biology and genetics; however, the ACE study demonstrated that toxic stress also interrupts normal, healthy development to the point of increasing the risk for delays. The trend shown in Figure 4.1 holds true for a variety of other issues, such as disability, unemployment, alcohol and drug abuse, and mental health disorders such as depression and suicidality (Center on the Developing Child, 2007). Effects are more harmful when the adverse exposure is chronic, unpredictable, without positive support, or part of multiple negative events that compound to increase the maladaptive physiological response (Dowd, 2014). ACE research has shown that the consequences of cumulative, toxic stress include chronic mental and physical health issues, including increased risk of diabetes, alcohol or substance abuse, mental illness, and suicide (Dowd, 2014).

Examples of Evidence-Based Interventions

Fortunately, there are programs designed to ameliorate some of the stresses related to trauma, and there are different ways to help students deal with challenges they may face after being exposed to the trauma. For example, the American Psychological Association (APA) developed an intervention—the ACT (Adults & Children Together) Raising Kids Safe Program—with early childhood development in mind to teach caregivers how to effectively support child development during times of traumatic stress (Knox & Burkhart, 2014). The program focuses on teaching parents and advocates about child development, understanding adult responses, discipline techniques that support positive behavior, and other knowledge and skills, with the goal of preventing the traumas of abuse or neglect (Knox & Burkhart, 2014).

Three evidence-based intervention programs are presented below as examples of well-studied methods that may be considered for use in schools as a part of school-wide approach to providing positive social and emotional support. *Cognitive Behavioral Intervention for Trauma in School (CBITS)* was specifically designed to reduce symptoms of post-traumatic stress disorder (PTSD), depression, and psycho-social problems in a school setting in children who have witnessed or experienced trauma (Stein et al., 2003). *CBITS* is implemented by mental health providers through a series of ten sessions that focus on coping skills, linking thoughts to feelings, combating negative thinking styles, understanding traumatic experiences, and social problem solving (Stein et al., 2003). For instance, a group session may help children link their worries about safety to how their bodies feel in that moment and provide them tools such as relaxation techniques for calming down. Children who have completed the program showed vast mental health improvement (e.g., fewer self-reported symptoms of PTSD or depression, less parent-reported psycho-social dysfunction) that lasted at least 6 months after program completion (Stein et al., 2003).

Strengthening Families was developed by the Center for the Study of Social Policy, and adaptations with various ages, cultures and communities have shown benefits for improving child functioning in the face of adversity (Kumpfer, Pinyuchon, de Melo, & Whiteside, 2008; Kumpfer & Summerhays, 2007). The program has been shown to reduce the risk of traumatic experiences such as child abuse and neglect, by providing action steps for professionals who work directly with preschool-aged children and their families. The program that was developed with modules for working with children of different age groups, has been shown to reduce child maltreatment, children's problem behaviors, delinquency, aggression, and adolescent alcohol and drug abuse, as well as improve social competencies and school performance (Kumpfer, Whiteside, Greene, & Allen, 2010). Resiliency for parents and kids is promoted using the following program strategies:

1. Facilitate friendships and mutual support.
2. Strengthen parenting skills.
3. Respond to family crises.
4. Link families to services and opportunities.
5. Value and support parents.
6. Facilitate children's social and emotional development.
7. Observe and respond to early warning signs of abuse and neglect.

By focusing on enhancing known protective factors (e.g., nurturing relationships, community connectedness), the program helps children and families tap into their strengths. The approach helps build parental resilience by enhancing a school's relationship with parents, using family support workers, and learning to identify the early signs of family stress. It supports social connections and knowledge of parenting and child development by making space for family fellowship, providing classes for families, and offering special outreach to engage families. Providing concrete support in times of need is integrated into the program through partnerships with local community resources. According to a 2007 scientific review by the National Registry of Evidence-based Programs and Practices (NREPP), *Strengthening Families* is unique in that it involves the entire family in training sessions with opportunities for working together to practice new skills that enhance family relationships.

A third approach, the Family Check-up (FCU), has been studied extensively and shows long-term benefits in preventing problem behaviors through increasing the positve supports given by parents and caregivers (Sitnick, Shaw, & Gill, et al., 2015; Dishion, Connell, Weaver, Shaw, Gardner, & Wilson, 2008). The FCU focuses on improving negative parenting interactions and is typically administered with three types of meetings: initial contact, assessment and feedback. There is a strong evidence that this individual family assessment and feedback is effective as a prevention or as an intervention strategy. The details of the process are outside the scope of the chapter; however, additional information may be found in the Appendix.

Implementation

Mental health is integral to a child's learning experience and development. Given the strong link between academic achievement and social-emotional and behavioral functioning, the school environment provides a unique opportunity for assessing and supporting the mental health needs of students (Stephan, Sugai, Lever, & Connors, 2015). One strategy for dealing with the issues of mental health and trauma in schools is to have on-site mental health providers such as counselors, psychologists, and social workers that can help address these issues. However, these professionals may be faced with competing administrative responsibilities that limit their scope of practice. A multi-tiered system of support has been shown to be a feasible approach in schools seeking to provide targeted help to improve a child's mental health and, in turn, improve their academic experience.

The Response to Intervention (RtI) framework is such a multi-tiered system that supports adjusting the level of intervention to meet the academic needs of the individual student. As a parallel model to RtI, the Positive Behavior Interventions & Supports (PBIS) model is used to support emotional and behavioral health for all students and enable educators to individualize the type and level of emotional and behavioral support based on the needs of students (Stephan, Sugai, Lever, & Connors, 2015):

> Within an RtI framework, all students receive high-quality instruction in the general education classroom, and struggling learners are identified and provided with additional interventions to accelerate their rate of learning. Similarly, all students should be supported with universal behavioral and emotional supports (such as positive behavior support strategies and social emotional competencies), and those with

emotional or behavioral challenges would then be offered additional support services. Services are often delivered within a 3-tiered framework of intensive, targeted, and universal supports.

(p. 215)

In this type of multi-tiered support system, Tier 1 PBIS is intended to offer sufficient support to promote pro-social behaviors, emotional well-being, skill development, and positive mental health to the entire school population through classroom support and systematic reinforcement for appropriate behaviors. Tier 1 support is expected to meet the needs of approximately 80–85% of students. Teaching all students to recognize feelings, thoughts, and behaviors associated with stress can be a useful foundation for talking about mental health and illness (Kame'enui, 2007).

Roughly, 10–15% of students are expected to require further support in addition to ongoing universal forms of support due to mental health problems, inappropriate social interactions, or negative classroom behaviors. Students referred for consideration by an intervention team will be monitored more closely and may be provided with small-group interventions, additional reminders, or individualized positive reinforcements.

For the 5% of students who need more intensive help, Tier 3 includes additional services and monitoring. Additional assessments and referrals for interventions outside of school may be required. This could include individual therapy, crisis teams, or a student support room (Stephan, Sugai, Lever, & Connors, 2015). During the process of evaluating and implementing targeted support mechanisms, families are viewed as experts and can provide valuable input on the cultural and ecological variables.

Collaboration among families, teachers, and professionals is essential to developing support mechanisms that meet the needs of individual students in the contex of unique and complex family systems (Eagle, Dowd-Eagle, & Garbacz, 2016). The intensive Tier 2 and Tier 3 interventions have been found to result in more significant benefits for students with behavioral and emotional problems compared to the effects seen with Tier 1 support mechanisms, according to a recent meta-analysis (Sanchez et al., 2018).

Conclusion

Mental illness is prevalent in the lives of children/families, impacting life at home, at school, and in the community. Adverse childhood experiences (ACEs), including mental illness, can have long-lasting effects and interfere with multiple aspects of health and development. Protective factors, such as having a safe, supportive, and nurturing relationship with an adult, developing positive appraisal styles in children, and teaching parents the importance of good self-care skills and consistent household routines (Traub & Boynton-Jarrett, 2017) can buffer the negative effects of toxic stress. Resilience was shown to mitigate the impact of adverse childhood experiences on grade repetition and school engagement (Bethell, Newacheck, Hawes, and Halfon, 2014). In the same study, students with other healthcare needs as well as a history of two or more adverse experiences who showed aspects of resilience were 1.5 times more likely to be engaged in school compared to peers who did not exhibit resilience. Fortunately, resilience can be facilitated, and supportive adult relationships (parents and teachers) can make a positive difference. Therefore, evidence that adverse experiences during childhood do not necessarily dictate the future of the child is considered hopeful (Sege et al., 2017).

Prevention starts with increased appreciation of the prevalence of mental illness and the risks to children and families. Learning about mental illnesses and being prepared to address warning signs of potential traumatic experiences are critical for helping prevent or ameliorate the impact of mental illness. The importance of knowledge and preparation stem, in part, from negative stereotypes attributed to mental illness. According to DeFosset, Gase, Ijadi-Maghsoodi, and Kuo (2017), myths and confusion about mental illnesses can strengthen negative stereotypes leading to anxiousness and stigma.

Children and families dealing with serious mental illness are often doubly challenged: the disabling symptoms of their disorder and the prejudices that result from misconceptions about mental illness are both obstacles to overcome (Corrigan and Watson, 2002). Therefore, prevention efforts require school teams to commit to a "trauma-sensitive" approach, emphasizing that teachers cannot be expected to take on the role of therapist, but instead receive professional development regarding how to monitor students and promote student resiliency as part of a team-based multi-tiered approach.

Intervention must be implemented using a coordinated, team-based approach, with some students requiring treatment through community mental health professionals. School efforts must focus on developmentally appropriate education about mental health, with targeted individual or group mental health treatments determined by a team of professionals in a particular school. Additional universal support mechanisms for students who need intensive interventions include optimizing parenting skills and behavior management, teaching safety skills, promoting advocacy, and coordinating services within the school and larger community.

Key Messages

1. Development of mental illness is determined by complex interactions among genetics, social interactions, psychological traits, and environmental factors.
2. Adverse childhood experiences (ACEs), including exposure to mental illness, are associated with higher risks for multiple short- and long-term health problems.
3. Emotional regulation skills need to be taught explicitly.
4. Maintaining adaptive routines is important for all kids, especially during or after traumatic experiences.
5. Providing accurate information about mental health and illness is critical for refuting myths and lessening the stigma of mental illness.
6. A "trauma-sensitive" approach emphasizes that educators are not expected to take on the role of therapists, but instead monitor interactions and promote student resiliency through team-based support.
7. Decisions about appropriate levels and types of support are team-based and determined by the needs of individual students and families.

Appendix 4

Resource Materials for Parents, Teachers, School Administrators, Pediatricians and Others Who Work with Youth

1. AACAP. (2017). *Facts for families: Talking to kids about mental illness.* Handout. Retrieved from https://www.aacap.org/aacap/families_and_youth/facts_for_families/FFF-Guide/Talking-To-Kids-About-Mental-Illnesses-084.aspx

2. AACAP (2013). *Improving lives, avoiding tragedies.* Fact sheet. Retrieved from https://www.aacap.org/App_Themes/AACAP/docs/Advocacy/policy_resources/Children's_Mental_Health_Fact_Sheet_FINAL.pdf

3. American Academy of Pediatrics and Dave Thomas Foundation for Adoption. (2016). *Parenting after trauma: Understanding your child's needs. A guide for foster and adoptive parents.* Handout. Retrieved from https://www.aap.org/en-us/advocacy-and-policy/aap-health-initiatives/healthy-foster-care-america/Documents/FamilyHandout.pdf

4. American Academy of Pediatrics. (2014). Handout. *Bring out the best in your children.* Retrieved from https://www.aap.org/en-us/Documents/ttb_bring_out_best.pdf/

5. Child Health and Development Institute of Connecticut, Inc. (2017). *Supporting young children who experience trauma: The Early Childhood Trauma Collaborative.* Retrieved from https://www.chdi.org/index.php/publications/issue-briefs/supporting-young-children-who-experience-trauma

6. Dishion, T. J., Stormshak, E.(2007). *Intervening in children's lives: An ecological, family-centered approach to mental health care.* Washington, DC: APA Books.

7. National Child Traumatic Stress Network. (2003). *Complex trauma in children and adolescents.* White paper from the National Child Traumatic Stress Network Complex Trauma Task Force. Los Angeles, CA, and Durham, NC: National Center for Child Traumatic Stress. Retrieved from http://www.nctsnet.org/nctsn_assets/pdfs/edu_materials/ComplexTrauma_All.pdf

8. National Scientific Council on the Developing Child. (2010). *Persistent fear and anxiety can affect young children's learning and development.* Working paper no. 9. Retrieved from https://developingchild.harvard.edu/science/key-concepts/

9. National Scientific Council on the Developing Child (2005/2014). *Excessive stress disrupts the architecture of the developing brain*. Working paper no. 3. Updated edition. Retrieved from https://developingchild.harvard.edu/science/key-concepts/toxic-stress/

10. Family Voices (2013). Improving Maternal Child Health Programs and Policies so All Children Thrive (IMPACT). A project that focuses on promoting holistic, culturally relevant health and wellness for all families and children including those with special healthcare needs and disabilities. Mental health resources. Retrieved from http://fv-impact.org/health-wellness-themes/mental-health/

11. National Child Traumatic Stress Network. (n.d). Handout discussing expected reactions to trauma based on age and how to deal with them. Retrieved from https://www.nctsn.org/resources/age-related-reactions-traumatic-event.

12. National Child Traumatic Stress Network. (n.d.). *Child trauma toolkit for educators*. Retrieved from https://www.nctsn.org/resources/child-trauma-toolkit-educators

13. Child Welfare Information Gateway. (2016). *Mandatory reporters of child abuse and neglect*. Mandated reporting resource with state-specific guidelines on reporting suspected abuse. Retrieved from https://www.childwelfare.gov/topics/systemwide/laws-policies/statutes/manda

14. Substance Abuse and Mental Health Service Administration (n.d). *How to talk to children of different ages following a traumatic event*. Handout. Retrieved from https://store.samhsa.gov/shin/content/SMA12-4732/SMA12-4732.pdf.

Books for Preschool to Grade 2 (to be read with an adult)

15. Holmes, M. M. (2000). *A terrible thing happened: A story for children who have witnessed violence or trauma*. Washington, DC: Magination Press.

    Sherman the raccoon witnesses something terrible (not described further) and begins to have intrusive thoughts, trouble sleeping, somatic complaints, anxiety, anger, and sadness. After he begins to get into trouble at school, he goes to see Ms. Maple to help him process his feelings and feels much better.

16. Kraulis, J. (2013). *Whimsy's heavy things*. Toronto, ON: Tundra Books.

    A sweet story about Whimsy who learns she can change the things that weigh us down into the things that lift us up.

17. Mulcahy, W. (2014). *Zach gets frustrated*. Minneapolis, MN: Free Spirit Publishing.

A useful story to help children understand how to handle frustration by using the frustration triangle: (1) Name It, (2) Tame It, and (3) Reframe It.
18. Papageorge, T. (2014). *My yellow balloon.* San Francisco, CA: Minoan Moon Publishing.

   A tale of love, loss, and letting go that can serve as a powerful tool for parents, teachers, librarians, and healing professionals.

Books for Elementary School (to be read independently by some children)

19. Jesse. (2001). *Please tell! A child's story about sexual abuse.* Center City, MN: Hazeldon Publishing.

   A book by a 9-year-old survivor of sexual abuse by her uncle at age 4 ½. She explains how she felt as a result of the abuse and what helped her get through it.
20. Straus, S. F. (2013). *Healing days: A guide for kids who have experienced trauma.* Washington, DC: Magination Press.

   This story covers the feelings, thoughts, and behaviors of kids, who have experienced bad or scary events with sensitivity.
21. Levine, P. A., & Kline, M. (2006). *Trauma through a child's eyes: Awakening the ordinary miracle of healing, infancy through adolescence.* Berkeley, CA: North Atlantic Book.
22. Perry, B. (2002). *Stress, trauma and posttraumatic stress disorders in children. Caregiver education series.* Houston, TX: Child Trauma Academy.

Books for Teens and Adults

23. Lezine, D., & Brent, D. (2007). *Eight stories up: An adolescent chooses hope over suicide.* New York, NY: Oxford University Press.

   This is the story of DeQuincy Lezine written in the first person. He describes his deteriorating mental state and how he fought to manage his suicidal thoughts.
24. Rappaport, N. (2009). *In her wake: A child psychiatrist explores the mystery of her mother's suicide.* New York, NY: Basic Books.

   A prominent child psychiatrist who was 4 years old when her mother committed suicide explores her mother's life and death in a search for meaning and understanding.

Websites and Videos for Kids

25. Sesame Street's website with resources on traumatic childhood experiences. https://sesamestreetincommunities.org/topics/traumatic-experiences/

26. Kid's Health website with resources on feelings. https://kidshealth.org/en/kids/feeling/?WT.ac=k-nav-feeling

Websites for Educators and Parents

27. Center for the Study of Social Policy. (n.d). *The protective factors framework.* Retrieved from https://www.cssp.org/reform/strengthening-families/the- basics/protective-factors/
28. Centers for Disease Control & Prevention. (n.d.) *Essentials for childhood: Steps to create safe, stable, and nurturing relationships and environments for all children.* Retrieved from https://www.cdc.gov/ViolencePrevention/childmaltreatment/essentials/index.html.

Links to Model Programs Addressing Trauma and Mental Health

29. *Center for Youth Wellness.* A center for pediatric primary care with a multidisciplinary team that allows for on-site mental health referrals and access to community support services. This practice serves a neighborhood in San Francisco that struggles with high rates of poverty and violence. https://centerforyouthwellness.org/
30. *Chicago Youth Programs.* A long-standing wellness project that serves high-risk children living in Chicago's public housing projects and other distressed neighborhoods. The program began with supportive services and programs for the neighborhood children and grew to include the primary care clinic that now provides multidisciplinary services, including mental health supportive services. https://chicagoyouthprograms.org
31. *Health Center at Lincoln.* A school-based health center in rural Walla Walla, Washington, that focuses on teens with high ACE scores, but works with parents with high ACE scores, as well. The school and health center work in partnership to provide an approach to medical care and school discipline that incorporates the science of toxic stress and resiliency, resulting in more effective methods that improve student behavior and health outcomes. http://thehealthcenterww.org
32. *Project DULCE: Developmental Understanding and Legal Collaboration for Everyone.* A project designed to implement the *Strengthening Families* approach within the patient-centered medical home. Families meet with a DULCE family specialist at all routine visits, as well as home visits and telephone check-ins depending on the needs of the family. http://bmc.org/Project-DULCE.htm/

References

American Academy of Child and Adolescent Psychiatry (AACAP). (2015). *Facts for Families: Mental Illness in Families, 39*. Retrieved from https://www.aacap.org/AACAP/Families_and_Youth/Facts_for_Families/FFF-Guide/Children-Of-Parents-With-Mental-Illness-039.aspx

American Academy of Pediatrics. (2014). *Trauma guide: Adverse childhood experiences and the lifelong consequences of trauma*. Elk Grove Village, IL: AAP.

American Psychiatric Association (APA). (2008). *Children and trauma: Update for mental health professionals*. Retrieved from www.apa.org/pi/families/resources/children-trauma-update.aspx.

American Psychiatric Association (APA). (2013). *Diagnostic and statistical manual of mental disorders* (5th ed.). Arlington, VA: American Psychiatric Publishing.

American Psychological Association Help Center. (2018). *The road to resilience*. Retrieved from www.apa.org/helpcenter/road-resilience.aspx

Bethell, C. D., Newacheck, P., Hawes, E., & Halfon, N. (2014). Adverse childhood experiences: Assessing the impact on health and school engagement and the mitigating role of resilience. *Health Affairs, 33*(12), 2106–2115.

Center on the Developing Child. (2007). *The impact of early adversity on child development*. [In Brief]. Retrieved from www.developingchild.harvard.edu/

Bruner, C. (2017). ACE, place, race and poverty: Building hope for children. *Academic Pediatrics, 17*, S123–S129.

Center for Behavioral Health Statistics and Quality. (2016). *Key substance use and mental health indicators in the United States: Results From the 2015 National Survey on Drug Use and Health* (HAS Publication No. SAM 16–4984, SADHU Series H-51). Retrieved from www.samhsa.gov/data/

Centers for Disease Control and Prevention (CDC). (2015). *Web-based Injury Statistics Query and Reporting System (WISQARS™)*. Retrieved from www.cdc.gov/injury/images/lc-charts/leading_causes_of_death_age_group_2015_1050w740h.gif

Child Welfare Information Gateway. (2016). *Mandatory reporters of child abuse and neglect*. Washington, DC: U.S. Department of Health and Human Services, Children's Bureau.

Corrigan, P. W., & Watson, A. C. (2002). Understanding the impact of stigma on people with mental illness. *World Psychiatry, 1*(1), 16–20.

Costello, E. J., He, J., Sampson, N. A., Kessler, R. C., & Merikangas, K. R. (2014). Services for adolescent psychiatric disorders: 12-month data from the national comorbidity survey-adolescent. *Psychiatric Services, 65*(3), 359–366.

Crosby, A. E., Ortega, L., & Melanson, C. (2011). *Self-directed violence surveillance: Uniform definitions and recommended data elements, Version 1.0*. Atlanta (GA): Centers for Disease Control and Prevention, National Center for Injury Prevention and Control.

DeFosset, A. R., Gase, L. N., Ijadi-Maghsoodi, R., & Kuo, T. (2017). Youth descriptions of mental health needs and experiences with school-based services: Identifying ways to meet the needs of underserved adolescents. *Journal of Health Care for the Poor and Underserved, 28*(3), 1191–1207. doi: 10.1353/hpu.2017.0105

Dishion, T. J., Connell, A., Weaver, C., Shaw, D., Gardner, F., & Wilson, M. (2008). The family check-up with high-risk indigent families: Preventing problem behavior by increasing parents' positive behavior support in early childhood. *Child Development, 79*(5), 1395–1414. doi: 10.1111/j.1467-8624.2008.01195.x

Dowd, M. D. (Ed.). (2014). *AAP trauma toolbox for primary care*. Retrieved from www.aap. org/en-us/advocacy-and-policy/aap-health-initiatives/healthy-foster-care-america/ Pages/Trauma-Guide.aspx

Eagle, J. W., Dowd-Eagle, S. E., & Garbacz, S. A. (2016). The role of family and cross-setting supports to reduce impairment and promote success. In S. Goldstein & J. A. Naglieri (Eds.), *Assessing impairment: From theory to practice* (pp. 17–44). New York, NY: Springer.

Evans, G. W., & Kim, P. (2013). Childhood poverty, chronic stress, self-regulation, and coping. *Child Development Perspectives, 7*, 43–48.

Felitti, V. J., Anda, R. F., Nordenberg, D., Williamson, D. F., Spitz, A. M., Edwards, V., & Koss, M. P. (1998). Relationship of childhood abuse and household dysfunction to many of the leading causes of death in adults: The Adverse Childhood Experiences (ACE) Study. *American Journal of Preventive Medicine, 14*(4), 245–258.

Galderisi, S., Heinz, A., Kastrup, M., Beezhold, J., & Sartorius, N. (2015). Toward a new definition of mental health. *World Psychiatry, 14*(2), 231–233. doi: 10.1002/wps.20231

Garner, A. S., & Shonkoff, J. P. (2012). Early childhood adversity, toxic stress, and the role of the pediatrician: Translating developmental science into lifelong health. Committee on psychosocial aspects of child and family health, committee on early childhood, adoption, and dependent care, and section on developmental and behavioral pediatrics. *Pediatrics, 129*(1), e224–e231.

Goldstein, S., & Naglieri, J. (2011). *Encyclopedia of child behavior and development*. New York, NY: Springer.

Holland, K. M., Vivolo-Kantor, A. M., Logan, J. E., Leemis, R. W. (2017). Antecedents of suicide among youth aged 11–15: A multistate mixed methods analysis. *Journal of Youth & Adolescence, 46*, 1598–1610. doi: 10.1007/s10964-016-0610-3

Jimenez, M. E., Wade, R., Lin, Y., Morrow, L. M., & Reichman, N. E. (2016). Adverse experiences in early childhood and kindergarten outcomes. *Pediatrics, 137*(2), e20151839.

Kame'enui, E. J. (2007). A new paradigm: Responsiveness to intervention. *Teaching Exceptional Children, 39*(5), 6–7.

Kessler, R. C., Berglund, P., Demler, O., Jin, R., Merikangas, K. R., & Walters, E. E. (2005). Lifetime prevalence and age-of-onset distribution of DSM-IV disorders in the national co-morbidity survey replication. *Archives of General Psychiatry, 62*, 593–602.

King, C. A., Arango, A., & Foster, C. E. (2018). Emerging trends in adolescent suicide prevention research. *Current Opinion in Psychology, 22*, 89–94. doi:10.1016/j.copsyc.2017.08.037

Knox, M., & Burkhart, K. (2014). A multi-site study of the ACT raising kids safe program: Predictors of outcomes and attrition. *Children and Youth Services Review, 39*, 20–24.

Ko, S. J., Ford, J. D., Kassam-Adams, N., Berkowitz, S. J., Wilson, C., Wong, M., . . . Layne, C. M. (2008). Creating trauma-informed systems: Child welfare, education, first responders, healthcare, juvenile justice. *Professional Psychology: Research and Practice, 39*(4), 396–404.

Kumpfer, K. L., Pinyuchon, M., de Melo, A., & Whiteside, H. (2008). Cultural adaptation process for international dissemination of the strengthening families program. *Evaluation and Health Professions, 33*(2), 226–239.

Kumpfer, K. L., & Summerhays, J. F. (2007). Prevention approaches to enhance resilience among high-risk youth. *Annals of the New York Academy of Sciences, 1094*, 151–163. doi: 10.1196/annals.1376.014

Kumpfer, K. L., Whiteside, H. O., Greene, J. A., & Allen, K. C. (2010). Effectiveness outcomes of four age versions of the strengthening families program in statewide field sites. *Group Dynamics: Theory, Research, and Practice, 14*(3), 211–229.

Manning, C., & Gregoire, A. (2009). Effects of parental mental illness on children. *World Psychiatry, 8*(1), 7–9.

Merikangas, K. R., He, J. P., Burstein, M., Swanson, S. A., Avenevoli, S., Cui, L., . . . Swendsen, J. (2010). Lifetime prevalence of mental disorders in U.S. adolescents: Results from the National Comorbidity Survey Replication--Adolescent Supplement (NCS-A). *Journal of the American Academy of Child and Adolescent Psychiatry, 49*(10), 980–989.

Milin, R., Kutcher, S., Lewis, S. P., Walker, S., Wei, Y., Ferrill, N., & Armstrong, M.A. (2016). Impact of a Mental Health Curriculum on Knowledge and Stigma Among High School Students: A Randomized Controlled Trial. *Journal of the American Academy of Child & Adolescent Psychiatry, 45*(5), 383–391. doi:10.1016/j.jaac.2016.02.018

National Child Traumatic Stress Network. (2010). *Age-related reactions to a traumatic event.* Retrieved from www.nctsn.org/resources/age-related-reactions-traumatic-event

National Child Traumatic Stress Network. (2014). *Complex trauma: Facts for educators.* Los Angeles, CA & Durham, NC: National Center for Child Traumatic Stress.

National Registry of Evidence-based Programs and Practices. (2007). *Intervention summary: Strengthening families program.* Retrieved from www.nrepp.samhsa.gov/

Perou, R., Bitsko, R. H., Blumberg, S. J., Pastor, P., Ghandour, R. M., Gfroerer, J. C., . . . Huang, L. N. (2013). *Mental health surveillance among children—United States, 2005–2011, Morbidity and Mortality Weekly Report_Surveillance Summary, 62*(2), 1–35.

Reinke, W. M., Stormont, M., Herman, K. C., Puri, R., & Goel, N. (2011). Supporting children's mental health in schools: Teacher perceptions of needs, roles, and barriers. *School Psychology Quarterly, 26,* 1–13. doi:10.1037/a0022714

Rothì, D. M., Leavey, G., & Best, R. (2013). On the front-line: Teachers as active observers of pupils' mental health. *Teaching and Teacher Education, 24*(5), 1217–1231.

Sanchez, A. L., Cornacchio, D., Poznanski, B., Golik, A. M., Chou, T., & Comer, J. S. (2018). The effectiveness of school-based mental health services for elementary-aged children: A meta-analysis. *Journal of American Academy of Child Adolescent Psychiatry, 57*(3), 153–165.

Sege, R., Bethell, C., Linkenbach, J., Jones, J., Klika, B., & Pecora, P. J. (2017). *Balancing adverse childhood experiences with HOPE: New insights into the role of positive experience on child and family development.* Boston, MA: The Medical Foundation. Retrieved from www.cssp.org/

Sege, R., & Linkenbach, J. (2014). Essentials for childhood: Promoting healthy outcomes from positive experiences. *Pediatrics, 133*(6), e1489–1491.

Shonkoff, J. P., Garner, A. S., The Committee on Psychosocial Aspects of Child and Family Health, Committee on Early Childhood, Adoption, And Dependent Care, and Section On Developmental And Behavioral Pediatrics, Siegel, B. S., Dobbins, M. I., Earls, M. F., . . . Wood, D. (2012). The lifelong effects of early childhood adversity and toxic stress. *Pediatrics, 129*(1), e232–e246.

Siegal, D., & Bryson, T. P. (2012). *The whole brain child.* New York, NY: Bantam Books.

Stambaugh, L. F., Forman-Hoffman, V., Williams, J., Pemberton, M. R., Ringeisen, H., Hedden, S. L., & Bose, J. (2017). Prevalence of serious mental illness among parents in the United States: Results from the National Survey of Drug Use and Health, 2008–2014. *Annals of Epidemiology, 27*(3), 222–224.

Stein, B. D., Jaycox, L. H., Kataoka, S. H., Wong, M., Tu, W., Elliott, M. N., & Fink, A. A. (2003). Mental health intervention for schoolchildren exposed to violence: A randomized controlled trial. *Journal of the American Medical Association, 290*(5), 603–611.

Stephan, S. H., Sugai, G., Lever, N., & Connors, E. (2015). Strategies for integrating mental health into schools via a multi-tiered system of support. *Child and Adolescent Psychiatric Clinics of North America, 24*, 211–231. doi:10.1016/j.chc.2014.12.002

Stewart, S. L., & Hirdes, J. P. (2015). Identifying mental health symptoms in children and youth in residential and in-patient care settings. *Healthcare Management Forum, 25*(4), 150–156.

Sitnick, S. L., Shaw, D. S., Gill, A., Dishion, T., Winter, C., Waller, R., . . ., Wilson, M. (2015). Parenting and the family check-up: Changes in observed parent-child interaction following early childhood intervention. *Journal of Clinical Child and Adolescent Psychology, 44*(6), 970–984. doi: 10.1080/15374416.2014.940623

Substance Abuse and Mental Health Service Administration. (November 2012). *Tips for talking with and helping children and youth cope after a disaster or traumatic event.* Retrieved from https://store.samhsa.gov/shin/content/SMA12-4732/SMA12-4732.pdf

Traub, F., & Boynton-Jarrett, R. (2017). Modifiable resilience factors to childhood adversity for clinical pediatric practice. *Pediatrics, 139*(5), e20162569.

Uher, R. (2014). Gene-environment interactions and severe mental illness. *Frontiers in Psychiatry, 5*(48). doi:10.3389/fpsyt.2014.00048

Promoting Safety for LGBTQ+ Kids in School Communities

5

Brittany J. Allen and Sherie Hohs

Lesbian, gay, bisexual, transgender, queer, and questioning (LGBTQ+) students have, through history and in present day, experienced increased rates of discrimination, school violence, and trauma compared to their peers (Earnshaw, Bogart, Poteat, Reisner, & Schuster, 2016; Kosciw, Greytak, Giga, Villenas, & Danischewski, 2016). Indeed, a recent nation-wide study of LGBTQ students in the United States showed that more than half (57.6%) felt unsafe at school due to their sexual orientation and nearly half (43.3%) due to their gender expression (Kosciw et al., 2016). Negative experiences of LGBTQ+ students may be often multifaceted, including overt threats and violence as well as feelings of isolation in a culture that elevates heterosexual orientations and cisgender identities as the norm. Historically, LGBTQ+ students have been unable to see people like themselves represented in their educational curricula and may have had difficulty identifying either student or teacher allies as sources of support (Elia & Eliason, 2010; Kosciw et al., 2016). As we outline in this chapter, LGBTQ+ students experience threats to safety in many forms, including homophobic comments from peers, teachers, and administrators; discriminatory school and district policies; and threats and experiences of harassment and assault. Despite these challenges, many LGBTQ students are able to thrive in school, and there are steps that educators can take that have been shown to prevent trauma and support this resilience. In this chapter, we explore means of developing structures that empower LGBTQ+ students to create affirming environments to counter these personal and community histories of trauma.

Who Are LGBTQ+ Students?

As detailed in Table 5.1, LGBTQ+ students identify with a sexual orientation or gender identity outside the heterosexual, cisgender identity considered the norm in mainstream society. Data from Youth Risk Behavior Surveys performed on state and national levels in the United States show that 1–2% of 13–18 year olds identify as gay or lesbian, 3–6% identify as bisexual, and 2–3% answer that they are unsure or questioning with regards to their sexual orientation (Kann et al., 2016; Mustanski et al., 2014). Data measuring the prevalence of transgender students are limited, but the Williams Institute estimates there are 150,000 transgender youth in the US (Flores, Herman, Gates, & Brown, 2016). One study of nearly 300,000 college students found that 0.17% (1 in 588) identified as transgender (Diemer, Grant, Munn-Chernoff, Patterson, & Duncan, 2015). In school-based surveys in specific geographic populations in the US, 1.3–1.5% of middle (Shields et al., 2013) and high school (Dane County Youth Commission, 2015) students identified as transgender. As global data on LGBTQ+ youth are limited, UNESCO (2016) recently acknowledged the need for more research on and action to support LGBTQ students worldwide. Educators everywhere encounter LGBTQ+ students in their communities, whether they are aware of these identities or not.

Like all students, LGBTQ+ students have more facets to their identity than their sexual orientation or gender identity. *Intersectionality* is the concept that social justice problems—like racism, ableism, sexism, and homophobia—often overlap, creating multiple levels of social injustice, particularly for people that experience multiple minority identities (Crenshaw, 2016). As we will discuss, it is important to consider that students that identify as LGBTQ+ also simultaneously experience other aspects of their identities, including but not limited to race, class, physical abilities, and religion, and may experience oppression and discrimination—and strength, resilience, and support—related to different aspects of identity.

Experiences of LGBTQ+ Students in Schools

Research has consistently shown that LGBTQ+ students experience less safe school environments than their heterosexual and cisgender peers. Whereas verbal, physical, and online harassment, including bias-based bullying, constitute the majority of threats to safety that students experience in their day to

Table 5.1 Definitions: Who are LGBTQ+ Students?

LGBTQ+ is an acronym used to describe sexual orientation and gender identities that are not heterosexual or cisgender; some describe these as sexual and gender minority identities.

Sexual Orientation

Describes a person's emotional, romantic or sexual attraction to other people. Some examples of sexual orientations are gay, lesbian, bisexual, asexual, and pansexual.

Gender Identity

An internal, deeply felt sense of being male, female, a blend of both, nonbinary, or neither – how individuals perceive themselves and what they call themselves. One's gender identity can be the same as or different from their sex assigned at birth.

Sex

A person's biological and physical attributes used to assign a sex category (most often male or female) at birth. These attributes can include external genitalia, sex chromosomes, hormone levels, and internal reproductive structures.

Gender Expression

How a person outwardly expresses their gender through appearance and behavior. This may include, but is not limited to, clothing, hairstyle, body language, interests, and mannerisms.

Lesbian: A person who identifies as a woman who is emotionally, romantically, and/or sexually attracted to other women.

Gay: A term that describes a person who is emotionally, romantically, and/or sexually attracted to members of the same gender.

Bisexual: A term that describes a person who is emotionally, romantically, and/or sexually attracted to people of more than one sex, gender, or gender identity.

Transgender: A term that describes people whose gender identity and/or expression differs from the sex they were assigned at birth. This can include people identities that are masculine, feminine, both, nonbinary, and without gender.

Cisgender: In contrast to transgender, a term that describes people whose gender identity and gender expression align with the sex they were assigned at birth.

Nonbinary: An umbrella term for people who transcend commonly held concepts of gender through their own expression and identities. Other terms for this might include gender expansive, gender creative, or genderqueer. Some nonbinary people also identify as transgender.

Queer: A term some people use to identify themselves with a flexible and inclusive view of gender and/or sexuality. Historically, queer has been used as a negative term for LGBTQ people. Some people still find the term offensive, whereas some embrace the term as an identity.

(Continued)

Table 5.1   (Continued)

Intersex: The term used by some to describe people who are born with naturally occurring variations in chromosomes, hormones, genitalia, and other sex characteristics. In medicine, these variations are also called differences of sex development. **Asexual:** A term that describes a person who does not experience sexual attraction or desire for other people. **Ally:** A term that describes a person who speaks out or takes actions on behalf of someone else or for a group they are not a part of. **Pansexual:** A person who can be attracted to any sex, gender, or gender identity.

Note: This is not a comprehensive list.

Adapted from Human Rights Campaign's *Welcoming Schools*, 2017.

day, LGBTQ+ youth often also move through environments that fail to affirm their identities in a larger social context. Many consider this environmental discrimination more insidious, having real impact on students, and creating feelings of isolation and lack of perceived social support that can negatively affect mental and physical health.

Bias-Based Harassment, Bullying, and Other In-Person Threats to Safety

Bias-based bullying is not solely experienced by LGBTQ+ students, but does constitute a significant negative experience in the lives of youth that identify as LGBTQ+. Bias-based bullying is defined as bullying in which the target is harassed based on a real or perceived aspect of their identity, including— but not limited to—race, gender, sexual orientation, gender identity, national origin, religion, or ability. Results from the California Healthy Kids Survey showed that 75–80% of students that are harassed are targeted based on their identity or perception of their identity, including race/ethnicity, religion,

Table 5.2   Verbal Harassment, Physical Harassment, and Physical Assault Experienced in School by LGBTQ+ Students

	Targeted Based on Any Identity Characteristic	Targeted Based on Any Sexual Orientation	Targeted Based on Any Gender Expression
Verbal Harassment	85.2%	70.8%	54.5%
Physical Harassment (pushing, shoving)	34.7%	27%	20.7%
Physical Assault (punched, kicked, or injured with a weapon)	15.5%	13%	9.4%

Source: J. G. Kosciw et al., 2016.

gender, sexual orientation, and physical or mental disability (Austin, Polik, Hanson, & Zheng, 2016).

LGBTQ+ students report significant rates of bias-based harassment and bullying. When surveyed, 85.2% of LGBTQ+ students state that they had been verbally harassed in the last year based on any identity characteristic and the majority had experienced verbal harassment related to sexual orientation or gender expression (Table 5.2) (Kosciw et al., 2016). Similarly, more than 1 in 5 LGBTQ+ students had experienced physical harassment based on gender expression or sexual orientation (Table 5.2), with 6–7% of students reporting physical harassment that occurred "often" or "frequently" (Kosciw et al., 2016). Data from the Teen Health and Technology and Healthy Passages studies also show that sexual minority youth experience higher rates of general/peer victimization, bullying, and sexual harassment compared to heterosexual peers (Schuster & Bogart, 2015; Ybarra, Mitchell, Palmer, & Reisner, 2015). Schuster et al. (2015) report in their longitudinal study that these experiences of harassment may even predate a youth's coming out: youth that eventually identified as lesbian, gay, or bisexual in grade 10 reported high levels of bullying and victimization 5 years earlier in grade 5, an age at which not all youth would be aware of or likely to have disclosed their sexual orientation.

Transgender or gender expansive students experience particularly high rates of threats to safety. A striking 75.1% of transgender students report feeling unsafe in school due to their gender/gender expression, which is higher than rates reported by students that identify as genderqueer (61.6%) or other gender identities (61.2%), all of which were, in turn, higher than rates reported by students that were cisgender sexual minority students (cisgender females, 22.5%; cisgender males, 32.2%) (Kosciw et al., 2016).

In addition to physical and verbal harassment and bullying, LGBTQ+ youth also experience higher rates of other threats to safety in school environments. For example, over one-third of LGBTQ+ youth reported that they had property stolen or damaged in the previous 12 months, and this occurred often or frequently for 7.5% of LGBTQ+ youth (Kosciw et al., 2016). In comparison to heterosexual youth, sexual minority youth are more likely to skip school because they do not feel safe (Russell, Everett, Rosario, & Birkett, 2014).

Intersections of different aspects of students' identities also may impact whether or how they experience harassment or bullying. Kosciw, Greytak, and Diaz's (2009) analysis of the 2007 National School Climate Survey data examined how gender identity correlated with differences in experiences among LGBTQ students and showed that cisgender female students were less likely than cisgender males or transgender students to report victimization based on either sexual orientation or gender expression. Similarly, differences in the increased rates of threats to safety and victimization between sexual minority males and sexual minority females have been attributed primarily to higher risk in males who were identified as bisexual or had male and female sexual partners, suggesting that bisexual males may be at particularly high risk (Russell et al. (2014).

Differences in experiences of victimization also can be found based on race/ethnicity, geographic and economic characteristics, and age of youth surveyed. Among LGBTQ+ youth responding to the 2016 National School Climate Survey, students that were Arab/Middle Eastern or Hispanic/Latino reported the highest rates of verbal harassment, physical harassment, and physical assault based on sexual orientation. LGBTQ+ Arab/Middle Eastern students also reported the highest rates of harassment and assault based on race across these three categories (Kosciw et al., 2016). Interestingly, Kosciw et al. (2009) found that black students were actually *less* likely than white students to report victimization based on sexual orientation, but the two groups experienced similar rates of victimization related to gender expression. Additionally, although sexual minority students experience disproportionate victimization and bullying at every grade level when compared to heterosexual peers (Russell et al., 2014), younger LGBTQ students reported higher rates of harassment and victimization related to both sexual orientation and gender expression than older LGBTQ students, a trend that mirrors general population trends in bullying (Dake, Price, & Telljohann, 2003). Interestingly, although more students reported victimization related to sexual orientation and gender identity in the Midwest and South of the United States compared to New England, much of this can be attributed to community-level socio-economic characteristics, with higher reports of victimization in rural and high-poverty communities (Kosciw et al., 2009).

Cyberbullying

Cyberbullying, defined as bullying that occurs via technology, affects the lives of many LGBTQ+ youth. The 2015 National School Climate Survey showed that almost half (48.6%) of surveyed youth had experienced electronic harassment in the year previous to the survey, and 15% reported that this occurred often or frequently (Kosciw et al., 2016). The Teen Health and Technology Survey found that, although online bullying did not occur as frequently as in-person bullying, LGBTQ+ youth were much more likely to experience online peer victimization, including cyberbullying, with nearly half (47.2%) of gay, lesbian, and queer youth and 54% of transgender youth reporting online peer victimization compared with 15.7% of heterosexual youth and 25% of cisgender youth, respectively (Ybarra et al., 2015).

Perception of LGBTQ+ Identity

Because LGBTQ+ identities are a personal identification, these identities cannot be accurately assessed based on external characteristics of a student, which means that bias-related bullying can occur based on *perceived* rather than actual identity. It is notable that bias-based bullying related to perceived sexual orientation has been associated with more negative effects than bullying that occurs for other reasons. Indeed, Swearer, Turner, and Givens (2008) found that students at an all-male school that were bullied because they were perceived to be LGBTQ+—whether or not they identified as such— had higher rates of depression and anxiety, experienced more frequent verbal and physical bullying, and perceived school climate to be more negative than those that were bullied for other reasons.

Other Aspects of Hostile School Environment

Representation in Curricula and Resources

In addition to specific acts of harassment, LGBTQ+ youth experience additional daily reminders of the heteronormative, cisgender societal norm in their school environment. LGBTQ+ persons, including their history and achievements, have often gone unrecognized or undiscussed in curricula.

According to the 2015 National School Climate Survey, only 22.4% of LGBTQ students were taught representations of LGBT people, history, or events that were positive in their school; a similar proportion (17.9%) had been taught negative content about LGBT topics (Kosciw et al., 2016). Less than half of the students surveyed (42.4%) reported being able to access information about LGBTQ-related topics in their library (Kosciw et al., 2016). Specifically, sex and sexuality education are often limited to descriptions of heterosexual relationships and sexual activity (Elia & Eliason, 2010). This erasure of same-sex relationships and transgender bodies means that LGBTQ+ youth may lack not only the knowledge of how to protect themselves in sexual activity, but also any acknowledgment that LGBTQ+ people are able to have healthy, fulfilling relationships and sexual experiences. School policies also do not universally include sexual orientation or gender identity in anti-bullying or non-discrimination work, and many completely lack policies related to supporting youth during gender transition.

Access to Safe Spaces

Even accessing safe spaces for day-to-day activities can be an issue for LGBTQ+ youth. Whereas Canada has included gender identity and expression as protected aspects of identity at the federal level in the Canadian Human Rights Act (Canadian Human Rights Act, 2009), there are only 17 states in the US that specifically outline protection in schools based on gender identity and expression and sexual orientation, and two with protections only based on sexual orientation (Human Rights Campaign, 2017b). Additionally, as of the writing of this chapter, although only North Carolina has passed (and then repealed) a "bathroom bill" limiting bathroom use to those whose sex assigned at birth matches the "sex" designated by the facility, similar laws have been introduced or are being discussed in other states in the US (National Conference of State Legislatures & Kralik, n.d.). Previous guidance from the US Department of Education (2016) had stipulated that transgender students should have access to safe and affirming school environments under Title IX, but this specific federal support was subsequently withdrawn (Somashekhar et al., 2017). And although Gender and Sexuality Alliances (GSAs) can be affirming and protective spaces for LGBTQ+ youth, most youth do not have access to this resource. According to the National School Climate Survey (Kosciw et al., 2016), less than one quarter (22%) of all LGBTQ+ and non-LGBTQ students report that their school has a GSA or another type of student club that addresses LGBTQ+ students' issues. Issues of intersectionality further confound access to safe spaces: African-American students, students in rural areas, and students in the US South report less access to a GSA than their white, urban, and non-Southern peers (Kosciw et al., 2016).

Microaggressions

The effect of lack of appropriate, affirming policies means that youth may experience daily microaggressions, such as homophobic or transphobic remarks, even if not directed at that particular youth. More than 95% (95.8%) of respondents in the National School Climate Survey had heard homophobic remarks at school and 85.7% had heard remarks that were specifically transphobic. Moreover, greater than half (58.8%) and more than 40% (40.8%) heard homophobic and transphobic comments, respectively, frequently or often (Kosciw et al., 2016). This differs based on intersectional aspects of identity as well as environmental characteristics. In a past National School Climate Survey (Kosciw et al., 2009), it was noted that African American/Black and Asian/Pacific Islander students were less likely to hear such homophobic comments than white students. That same study showed that, not surprisingly, youth were more likely to hear "gay" used as a derogatory remark in schools that had higher ratios of students to teachers and that younger students and students in rural communities were also more likely to hear homophobic remarks. Interestingly, although there were higher rates of victimization for LGBTQ+ students in communities with high poverty rates, youth in such communities reported lower rates of hearing homophobic remarks (Kosciw et al., 2009).

Identity Suppression

Inadequate school protections also may mean that students are punished for expression of their identity. More than half (50.9%) of transgender students report that they have not been able to use their preferred name or pronoun in the school setting and 1 in 5 (22.2%) have been stopped from wearing clothing considered inappropriate based on their sex assigned at birth (Kosciw et al., 2016). Similarly, about 1 in 6 LGBTQ students (15.6%) report that they have been prevented from attending a dance or similar event with someone of the same gender and nearly one-third (29.8%) have been disciplined for affectionate displays with same-sex partners (Kosciw et al., 2016). These experiences send a repetitive, damaging message that sexual and gender minority identities are "against the rules" and that the identities themselves are deserving of punishment. A transgender student in Wisconsin outlined this well in describing an experience with a school administrator:

> Our principal did not respect me, did not respect my pronouns. My guidance counselor sent him multiple emails about my coming out. Once my Dad kind of [asked] "why aren't you respecting him", his excuse was out. He was waiting for me to legally change my name which costs a

few hundred bucks, and that was three months after I came out to the school. I don't know. He would purposefully say my name every single day, my legal name, and I did not feel comfortable speaking up to a person in power.

(Gattis & McKinnon, 2015)

Short- and Long-Term Impact on LGBTQ+ Students

Of Harassment and Bullying

As noted in Chapter 2 ("Talking About Bullying in the Classroom and Beyond"), students that are the targets of bullying have been shown to have more concerns related to mental and physical health as well as poor school performance and school avoidance. This is confirmed for LGBTQ+ students in multiple National School Climate Surveys over the years, which illustrate that LGBTQ students that reported higher levels of victimization were also more likely to have low levels of self-esteem and school belonging, increased levels of depression, and poor school attendance and performance (Kosciw et al., 2016; Kosciw, Palmer, Kull, & Greytak, 2013). Sexual and gender minority youth are also more likely than their heterosexual peers to feel unsafe ("somewhat or extremely") in their school environment (Ybarra et al., 2015), and victimization has been shown to mediate lower grades and increase truancy rates in lesbian, gay, bisexual, and unsure high school students (Birkett, Russell, & Corliss, 2014). Victimization can also affect educational and career goals: LGBTQ+ students that experienced victimization at high levels were less likely to pursue post-secondary education and, when LGBTQ+ students reported that they did not plan to finish high school, almost half (42.5%) said that plans to dropout were related to the harassment experienced at school (Kosciw et al., 2016). With regard to physical health, students that experienced bias-based harassment had increased rates of drug and alcohol use, depression, and suicidality compared to those that experienced harassment not reported to be related to bias (Russell, Sinclair, Poteat, & Koenig, 2012). Rates of victimization also specifically mediate differences in increased rates of substance use and sexual risk behaviors of LGBQ compared to heterosexual students (Rosario et al., 2014). Based on these reports, it is likely an escalation of factors that contribute to negative educational outcomes for LGBTQ+ students: victimization, bullying, and harassment lead to school avoidance and increased discipline problems, risk behaviors, and lower school engagement that cumulatively affect school performance and post-secondary planning and options. In a qualitative study of school experience, one trans-gender student described how they navigated unsafe school environments:

> So, like, I always kept something noisy like a necklace or a bracelet so that people knew that I was coming and I always averted populated areas and, at one point it got so bad that I didn't even go to the lunch-room to eat lunch. I quickly grabbed my food and sat in the hallways and stuff and talked to the facilitator . . . who just happened to be the GSA advisor.
>
> (Gattis & McKinnon, 2015)

Of a Hostile School Environment

For LGBTQ+ students in hostile school environments, there is evidence that school climate—whether negative or supportive—may have a significant impact on students' experiences and health. Analysis of more than 21,000 gay, lesbian, and bisexual youth in California showed lower rates of alcohol, cigarette, marijuana, inhalant, and opioid use in students with more school connectedness and adult support (De Pedro, Esqueda, & Gilreath, 2017). Bidell's (2014) study of LGBT homeless youth showed higher levels of psy-chological distress among high school graduates compared with those that dropped out of high school, and the authors posit that spending more time in negative home and school environments may contribute to this. In the 2015 National School Climate Survey, LGBTQ+ students that experienced institu-tional discrimination showed lower educational achievement, higher rates of school discipline, and were more than three times more likely to report miss-ing school in the last month (Kosciw et al., 2016). Students that experienced institutional discrimination also were less likely to report a sense of school belonging, which has been tied to academic achievement, and reported lower levels of psychological well-being, even when accounting for experiences of victimization (Kosciw et al., 2016).

A number of studies have examined population-level data to determine the impact of environment hostility or acceptance on LGBTQ+ students. Hat-zenbuehler and Keyes (2013) examined counties in Oregon with higher and lower numbers of districts with inclusive anti-bullying policies and found that rates of self-reported suicide attempts in the previous 12 months were 2.25 times higher in lesbian, gay, and bisexual students that lived in counties with few inclusive anti-bullying policies. Hatzenbuehler, Birkett, Van Wagenen, and Meyer (2014) also examined rates of suicide thoughts, plans, and attempts among LGB youth from Youth Risk Behavior Survey (YRBS) data and compared this to measures of protective school climates. They found that students in protective school climates had lower levels of suicidality overall and that the disparity between LGB students and heterosexual peers was nearly eliminated in cities and states with highly protective school climates. The presence of GSAs in high schools—which are an often used marker of school climate—has been associated with improved young adult psychological well-being and self-esteem, even if that individual did not participate in the GSA, suggesting that the effect on school climate extends to the school community beyond the members of these organizations (Toomey, Ryan, Diaz, & Russell, 2011).

Hostile environments extend, of course, beyond schools and can occur in communities and families. These are notably connected: rates of in-person and online bullying were higher in LGB youth that resided in Boston neighborhoods with higher rates of hate crimes against LGBT people (Hatzenbuehler, Duncan, & Johnson, 2015). Although school environments can be protective, creating comprehensive improvement in school climates involves school, district, and community engagement.

Strategies to Create Safe, Affirming Schools

Research clearly shows that there is a compelling need for schools to improve the outcomes for LGBTQ+ youth, but many schools struggle to identify where to begin. The Gay, Lesbian & Straight Education Network (GLSEN) has been a leader in this area, conducting nation-wide surveys of LGBTQ youth in the US from which they have derived clear, evidence-based recommendations (Kosciw et al., 2016). In considering recommendations from GLSEN and other organizations focused on addressing disparities faced by LGBTQ+ youth in school settings, we outline a concrete, comprehensive approach that positively impacts school climates and creates supportive, affirming school learning environments for LGBTQ+ youth. A summary of these strategies is shown in Figure 5.1.

Proactive Strategy #1: Develop Enumerated Policies Inclusive of LGBTQ+ Youth

A critical step in creating safe, supportive schools for LGBTQ+ youth is to establish and implement comprehensive anti-bullying and non-discrimination policies so that bullying and harassment will not be tolerated. Enumerated

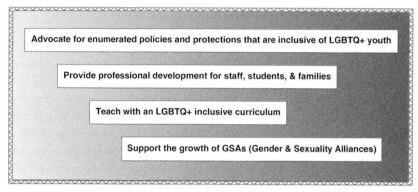

Figure 5.1   Proactive Strategies to Build Safe, Inclusive School Communities for LGBTQ+ Youth Based on Recommendations from GLSEN's 2015 National School Climate Survey (J. G. Kosciw et al., 2016)

policies are those that require the listing of specific identity categories most often subjected to bullying and harassment, such as race, color, national origin, sex, sexual orientation, gender identity or expression, disability, and religion (GLSEN, 2017), and explicitly address bias-based bullying as particularly harmful.

Rationale for Enumerated Policies

When policies are enumerated, they protect the entire school community, not just the students with marginalized identities who are most subjected to bias-based bullying. Students from schools with enumerated policies inclusive of LGBTQ+ youth report hearing less biased remarks around gender and sexual orientation, experience less victimization, and miss school half as often as those from schools without enumerated policies (GLSEN, 2017). As a specific example, LGBTQ students with a comprehensive policy were less likely to hear "gay" used in a negative way often or frequently (51.7%) than students in schools with a generic policy (73.6%) or no policy (80.2%) (Kosciw et al., 2016). There is also clear evidence that LGBTQ+ students in schools with enumerated policies report more safety and less bullying or harassment (Kosciw et al., 2016). Additionally, fewer suicide attempts were reported by LGBT youth in districts with comprehensive anti-bullying policies (Hatzenbuehler & Keyes, 2013).

Enumerated policies also mandate the implementation of anti-bullying and non-discrimination policies, empowering administrators and educators with strong rationale and resources to prevent and address bias-based bullying and harassment. Comprehensive policies send a clear message to school staff, students, and families about values regarding appropriate behavior. Once adopted, clearly articulated language exists as a reference, requiring educators to recognize that anti-LGBTQ bullying and harassment is unacceptable and that these policies must be enforced, which makes the duty not to discriminate concrete. In fact, students in schools with enumerated policies reported that teachers intervened in potential bullying incidents more than twice as often compared to students in schools with generic anti-bullying policies, and more than three times as often compared to students in schools with no policy at all (Kosciw et al., 2016).

Despite the strong rationale and documented effectiveness of enumerated policies inclusive of gender identity and sexual orientation, many school districts have not taken the initiative to implement them. The 2015 GLSEN National School Climate Survey documents that of the 83.6% of students who report having an anti-bullying policy in their school, only 10.2% of students reported that their policy was enumerated to include sexual orientation, gender identity, and gender expression (Kosciw et al., 2016). This is the case despite wide support for enumeration among educational organizations, politicians, and the general public as part of the effort to stop bullying (GLSEN, 2017; National Center for HIV/AIDS, Viral Hepatitis, STD, and TB Prevention, Division of Adolescent and School Health, 2016). Students, families, educators, and community members should draw on this knowledge as they advocate within their school districts to implement comprehensive policies inclusive of LGBTQ+ youth.

Best Practices for Implementation

Effective advocacy efforts for enumerated policies involve gathering relevant data, providing promising practices from other school districts, mobilizing stakeholders, presenting to school board members, and sharing personal stories that demonstrate the benefits of enumerated policies. Once a school district adopts comprehensive policies that specifically enumerate gender identity, gender expression, and sexual orientation, it is critical that they are implemented effectively and clearly understood by all school personnel. Steps to help facilitate this process are outlined in Box 5.1.

Enumerated policies are a critical framework on which to build safe, affirming schools and can serve as a basis for best practice-based guidance to ensure that all students are safe, included, and respected in school.

Box 5.1 Steps to Ensure Your District's Comprehensive Policies are Implemented Consistently

Districts should provide professional development to all staff so they fully understand these policies and their district guidance for implementation.

1. Schools should have clear processes and procedures that delineate how policies will be enforced, by whom, and how they will be monitored.
2. Schools should establish reporting procedures for bullying incidents, in which reports of potential bullying or harassment are documented and investigated in a timely manner.
3. All school staff should be trained to recognize and stop bias-based bullying and harassment, including harassment based on actual or perceived sexual orientation, gender identity, and gender expression.
4. Staff members, students, and families should be provided ongoing education and communication about these policies using multiple channels of communication, such as website and social media updates, newsletters, Parent-Teacher Organization updates, and handouts at registration.
5. Schools and staff members should use comprehensive policies inclusive of gender identity and expression to create specific guidance— including resources and best practices—to support transgender, non-binary, and gender expansive youth.

Adapted from Burdge, Snapp, Laub, Russell, and Moody (2013); GLSEN (2017); Human Rights Watch (2001); and National Center for HIV/AIDS, Viral Hepatitis, STD, and TB Prevention, Division of Adolescent and School Health (2016).

Proactive Strategy #2: Provide Professional Development for Staff to Become Allies

To build safe, affirming school environments in which LGBTQ+ youth thrive, we must equip educators with the necessary language, tools, and professional development to become true allies.

Rationale for Professional Development

Increased LGBTQ Visibility
Because of the historical absence of professional development and pre-service training around gender and sexual orientation, many educators feel

ill-equipped to have classroom dialogues around topics of identity and are reluctant to incorporate LGBTQ+ narratives into curriculum. This has resulted in the invisibility of queer identities in teacher language, books and other learning resources, school events, and curriculum. Many staff members are uncomfortable addressing issues of sexual orientation and gender identity in the classroom. Some educators have never talked about LGBTQ+ topics before, in their own community or in the classroom. Others may have concerns that LGBTQ+ topics are controversial or that there may be pushback from students' families. But having the language and comfort to increase LGBTQ+ visibility matters: in an evaluation of the *Welcoming Schools* program, focused professional development around LGBTQ+ inclusive schools was linked to more a positive school climate, educators with increased LGBTQ+ community knowledge and reduced fears around pushback, and a change in attitude regarding the importance of teaching LGBTQ+ topics (Human Rights Campaign, 2017a). With ongoing professional learning, high-quality resources and material, and authentic practice, educators can develop the skills necessary to increase LGBTQ+ visibility and create the affirming learning environments that their LGBTQ+ students need.

Improved Safety and Support

When schools prioritize professional development around LGBTQ+ youth, there are many positive effects on school climate. Training around the needs of LGBTQ+ youth has resulted in increased school safety and a reduction in bullying behaviors in schools (Sawyer, Porter, Lehman, Anderson, & Anderson, 2006). When schools provide quality professional development, educators have a stronger understanding of school policies and procedures that support LGBTQ+ youth, intervene more around incidents of bullying and harassment, and are more supportive of LGBTQ+ students (GLSEN, 2016).

Growth of Ally Support

We can never discount the power that one trusted adult can have on the life of an LGBTQ+ student, and school staff can be powerful allies for students. When schools commit to ongoing professional learning, educators gain the knowledge, skills, and desire to become committed allies who affirm LGBTQ+ identities. As previously noted, LGBTQ visibility matters and is connected to fostering allies: students at schools with inclusive curricula, for example, were more likely to feel comfortable discussing LGBTQ issues with a teacher (Kosciw et al., 2016). Allyship, in turn, is powerful: compared to LGBTQ students with no supportive school staff, those with many (11 or more) supportive staff were less likely to feel unsafe, felt more connected to their school community, and were less likely to miss school because they felt unsafe or uncomfortable (Kosciw et al., 2016). These supported students also had higher grade point averages (GPAs) and were less likely to report that they might not graduate or pursue post-secondary education (Kosciw et al., 2016).

Best Practices for Implementation

Educators need to be strategic to effectively advocate for dedicated professional development around LGBTQ+ identities with their administrators and school leadership teams, as obtaining professional learning time is a challenge in our schools. Often, we are competing for scarce resources and must have strong justification for LGBTQ+ inclusion to be a priority. Next are some helpful tips to strengthen your advocacy efforts.

Be Prepared to Justify the Need for Safe, Welcoming Schools

Finding data relevant to your community—in addition to anecdotal experiences of children and families—lays the groundwork to demonstrate the need for investment in professional development. If you have school-based data or specific student experiences that demonstrate the impact of bullying by identity groups, this can highlight the specific need in your school. There are also excellent data sources (such as Youth Risk Behavior Surveys, GLSEN National School Climate Surveys, or other county- or city-level youth assessments) that illuminate the impact of bullying and harassment on LGBTQ+ youth in schools; data from these sources can often be accessed at the state or city level. For instance, if a school or city's climate data illustrates that 75% of students have been bullied or harassed because of their gender expression, an educator can draw on this to emphasize the need for school-wide intervention and training. Standardizing documentation of harassment and bullying can also serve as a means of collecting information about each incident that can be compiled into data for advocacy. Bringing relevant data to the table that links school safety to academic achievement also strengthens the need and can be referenced in advocating within a specific school or district.

Create In-Depth and Ongoing Professional Learning

Many times, we are given a small amount of time for "diversity" work, which is commonly referred to as the "good ol' one and done": one or two hours of education is provided to "check a box" without ongoing assessment or engagement. This is not sufficient for school-wide culture change and LGBTQ+ inclusion. This work is layered, complex, and requires ongoing practice. LGBTQ+ inclusive schools are open and affirming of family structures, promote gender equity, address the bias in bullying, and embrace the many diverse identities that exist in their school community to ensure safety and respect. Educators need ongoing professional development and support to learn vocabulary, practice using inclusive language, challenge their misconceptions, experience responding to questions about LGBTQ+ topics, and learn strategies to incorporate LGBTQ+ identities into curriculum.

Connect LGBTQ+ Inclusion with Other School Efforts

It is critical to connect this work to many of the other important school initiatives already in place. If it is seen as a separate entity, it will likely not be prioritized. LGBTQ+ inclusion work directly connects with social-emotional learning, equity, school culture and climate, bullying prevention, Core Curriculum (literacy, social studies, etc.), mental health, physical health, and family involvement work. Examine the priorities of your school's professional development plan and find natural connections to demonstrate your case.

Find Allies in the Work

Look to fellow advocates in your school building, district, and community for allyship. This complex work often starts with a champion dedicated to LGBTQ+ safety and inclusion, but needs systematic teamwork and schoolwide commitment to survive. Bring together a diverse group of leaders who possess the skill and the will to change the culture and climate of your school to be welcoming of LGBTQ+ youth and families, as well as the youth and families of all identities. Healthcare providers and community leaders doing anti-oppression work of any kind can be powerful partners. If these allies do not exist in your building, seek out resources in your community and beyond to find experts on professional learning to create safe, affirming school environments for LGBTQ+ youth. Welcoming Schools, GSA Network, Gender Spectrum, GLSEN, and Minus 18 are all leading organizations in the US with extensive professional training resources (see Appendix 5 for details). While on this journey, look to promising practices and success stories in other schools and districts to increase efficiency and avoid recreating the wheel.

Use Student Voice and the Power of Stories to Motivate Your Staff

Sometimes, it takes the power of someone's truth to illustrate just how essential professional learning is around the safety and inclusion of LGBTQ+ youth. Someone might be able to explain away the data or minimize the needs of LGBTQ+ students in your building, but it is much more difficult to deny someone's personal story. The emotional impact resonates and compels many educators to improve their teaching practices to embrace and affirm queer youth. There are a variety of effective strategies to involve student voices: student panels, student performance (spoken word, poetry, art, etc.), student-led professional development, student-run assemblies, and more. Our youth are ahead of the curve when it comes to their knowledge of LGBTQ+ topics and their desire to engage in layered discussions around multiple aspects of identity. Although LGBTQ+ youth should not be required to educate their teachers, many times they are eager and willing to be a part of professional development so that their school can be LGBTQ+ affirming. Separate—but related—spaces can be created for panels with family members of LGBTQ+ youth and panels of students with other diverse identities and are also forums to give voice to compelling experiences that elevate this equity work.

Proactive Strategy #3: Teach with an LGBTQ+ Inclusive Curriculum

> *When someone with the authority of a teacher, say, describes the world and you are not in it, there is a moment of psychic disequilibrium, as if you looked into a mirror and saw nothing.*
>
> —Adrienne Rich (1994)

All students deserve to have a school experience that positively reflects their identities. Unfortunately, most students do not receive an LGBTQ+-inclusive curriculum, and many queer students suffer the adverse effects of invisibility and systematic discrimination. By increasing access to inclusive books and curricula that include accurate representations of LGBTQ+ people, history, and events, educators can play a critical role in reducing bias and creating safer learning environments.

Rationale for LGBTQ+ Inclusive Curriculum

There is compelling evidence that teaching with a curriculum inclusive and affirming of LGBTQ+ people and experiences contributes to a safer, affirming learning environment for LGBTQ+ youth. According to youth focus groups in GSA Network's 2013 study, students believe that a LGBTQ-inclusive curriculum has the potential to improve safety, engagement, learning, academic achievement, self-esteem, and success in school and beyond (Burdge et al., 2013). The GLSEN 2015 National School Climate Survey confirms this fact, reporting that 75.2% of LGBTQ+ students in schools with an inclusive curriculum said their peers were accepting of LGBTQ+ people, compared to 39.6%

of those without an inclusive curriculum (Kosciw et al., 2016). Additionally, in a previous survey, LGBTQ+ students who learned about LGBTQ+ topics in school reported fewer homophobic slurs, less homophobic victimization, more feelings of safety, and more supportive conversations with teachers at school (Kosciw, Greytak, Palmer, & Boesen, 2014).

Best Practices for Implementation

Start Early

Contrary to some misconceptions, we must talk about LGBTQ+ topics in early childhood education and elementary school. This is a critical time in the lives of young people to teach respect and acceptance for diverse identities, inclusive of LGBTQ+ people, in a developmentally appropriate way. Although many believe that younger children do not form stereotypes, research has actually shown that these biases form at very young ages and that intervention can make a difference in future experiences. Children are internalizing harmful stereotypes about gender by age 3 (Spears, Brown, & Bigler, 2005). By age 4 or 5, they use gender and race to infer relationships between others (Shutts, Pemberton, & Spelke, 2013) and reinforce "gender-appropriate behavior" (defined by cultural norms) without the intervention of adults (Spears et al., 2005). Espelage, Basile, De La Rue, and Hamburger (2015) found that boys that engaged in bullying and use homophobic verbal harassment in early middle school were more likely to engage in sexual harassment 2 years later, suggesting that interventions that address bias-based bullying may reduce sexual harassment later.

Examine your implicit biases, along with your books, posters, language, and materials. It might be time for a curriculum makeover! People in non-dominant groups often look for clues to determine whether or not an educator is an active ally. You might start your journey with some self-reflection, and then determine the need for more inclusive options for your curriculum. Begin by asking yourself some questions:

- Whose identities are visually represented, highlighted, and welcomed in your classroom and school community?
- Whose narratives are most present in your classroom readings?
- Are your lessons inclusive of diverse gender identities, family structures, cultures, abilities, etc.?
- What language about families do you use in forms, permission slips, family newsletters, etc.?

- Do you unknowingly reinforce gender stereotypes, binary-gendered language, dominant cultures, and heteronormative family structures and identities?
- Do you feel comfortable disrupting harmful stereotypes around diverse identities that may lead to bias?

This self-assessment will likely lead to some natural next steps for LGBTQ+ inclusion, and may point to some other representation gaps as well.

Find Reputable LGBTQ+-Inclusive Resources and Integrate Them Into Curriculum

An example of a premier elementary school program committed to LGBTQ+ visibility is *Welcoming Schools* (Human Rights Campaign, 2018), an educational program of the Human Rights Campaign. The *Welcoming Schools* program provides lessons, professional development resources, and book lists in an effort to "create safe, inclusive learning environments that: welcome all children and their families; promote gender equity, reject rigid gender stereotypes and support transgender and non-binary students; proactively work to prevent and address bias-based bullying; and promote understanding and respect for all people" (Human Rights Campaign, n.d.). Through picture books, lessons, teachable moments, and experiential activities, programs like *Welcoming Schools* provide educators the resources to teach students the language, skills, and understanding to become respectful allies in their school communities. These lessons can be easily integrated with social-emotional learning, literacy, and social studies, and are aligned with Common Core standards. Other leaders in LGBTQ+ inclusive curriculum include GLSEN (Gay, Lesbian & Straight Education Network), GSA Network, Teaching Tolerance, Gender Spectrum, and the Anti-Defamation League.

Engage School-Wide Messaging and Action as a Powerful Tool

Schools must be consistent in their messaging around inclusion and respect. Connect and integrate curriculum with other inclusive practices, such as school policies, social-emotional learning, bullying intervention, and school events. Although there are different approaches to LGBTQ+ inclusion, students report feeling safer and more supported when LGBTQ+-inclusive curriculum is institutionalized versus isolated in a stand-alone lesson (Burdge et al., 2013). Many schools engage in school-wide events such as Ally Weeks, Mix-it-up Lunches, Kindness Campaigns, Day of Silence, and LGBTQ+ book readings to integrate this social justice work with a school culture of respect and inclusion.

Advocate for School District Support of Educators

Advocating for an inclusive school might begin with a champion or a group of allies, but to systematize the teaching of LGBTQ+-inclusive curriculum, school leadership and administration must prioritize the work. Research performed by the GSA Network and the Francis McClelland Institute for Youth demonstrates the importance of training, planning time, practice, and instructional resources—as well as district support—in integrating quality, age-appropriate, accurate, and culturally relevant information about LGBTQ+ people and history into instruction (Burdge et al., 2013). Engage school board members using data and personal stories and ask for ongoing commitment at the district level.

Proactive Strategy #4: Support the Growth of GSAs (Gender and Sexuality Alliances)

Another proven strategy to advance safety and acceptance of LGBTQ+ youth is to advocate for Gender and Sexuality Alliances (GSAs) in schools. GSAs are school clubs for queer and allied youth to support one another, educate their school community, and engage in advocacy efforts on behalf of LGBTQ+ and other social justice movements. In addition to covering hallways with rainbow posters, GSA students often lead the charge around LGBTQ+ inclusion and equity in their classrooms, with their peers, and with the educators in their building. It is not uncommon for GSA students to teach about LGBTQ+ identities in health class, lead a student assembly for "Words Hurt" week, or train their teachers during professional development on the difference between gender identity and sexual orientation. As noted previously, the majority of LGBTQ+ students and allies do not have access to a GSA in their school.

Rationale for Supporting the Growth of GSAs

GSA clubs not only provide an accepting, brave space for LGBTQ+ youth to exist in a nonjudgmental way—their mere existence has been shown to increase school safety for both LGBTQ+ and heterosexual students (Szalacha, 2003). Students in schools with GSAs report hearing less homophobic language compared to schools without a GSA (57% compared to 75%) and are less likely to miss school for safety reasons compared to other students (Kosciw et al., 2016). Other studies suggest the presence of GSAs reduce prejudice around sexual orientation for heterosexual students (Horn & Szalacha,

2009), lessen mental health concerns (Toomey et al., 2011), and lower risks of health-risk behaviors such as tobacco, alcohol abuse, and risky sexual behaviors (Poteat, Sinclair, DiGiovanni, Koenig, & Russell, 2013). Through the presence of a GSA, students are often able to identify staff allies in their building. This not only improves their school connectedness and academic achievement, but helps LGBTQ+ students identify trusted adults they can turn to in times of need or if bullying and/or harassment occur (GLSEN, 2007). GSAs normalize affirmation of LGBTQ+ identities within the school structure and support the message (outlined in a school's enumerated policies, we hope!) that bias-based harassment will not be tolerated.

Best Practices for Implementation

If Your School Does Not Have a GSA, Consider Starting One

You now know the impact Gender and Sexuality Alliances (GSAs) can have on LGBTQ+ youth and on a school community. If your school is lacking this vital resource, it is not very challenging to create one. Start by gathering stakeholders—including staff members, students, and community members—to characterize the need, begin the brainstorming process, and identify logistical considerations. Your GSA will need 1–2 advisors who are committed to planning and leading meetings, along with the leadership of GSA students. Many advisors find this role one of the most rewarding of their careers: it allows them to build authentic relationships with queer youth, advocate for equity and social justice, and make significant changes in their school culture and climate. GSA advisors do not have to identify as queer; allies can be powerful GSA advisors with appropriate reflection and intentionality. In the absence of queer leadership, it becomes necessary to be intentional about inviting LGBTQ+ guest speakers into the club and involving your GSA in LGBTQ+ affirming events and activities. If GSA advisors are in need of some direction for leading their group, there are many supportive resources from GLSEN and the GSA Network.

Although some may encounter barriers in advocating for a GSA, students in public schools in the US have the power to form a GSA club. Just like a chess club or math club, it is an extracurricular club, and by law, they cannot be discriminated against (American Civil Liberties Union, n.d.; GLSEN, 2007). Despite this, sometimes non-accepting schools create barriers to impede the progress of GSAs. As allies to LGBTQ+ youth, ensure students know their rights and help them advocate with school administration to reduce obstacles. In the US, the local chapter of the American Civil Liberties Union may be a helpful resource if legal advocacy is needed to support your GSA.

Use the GSA as a Vehicle for Big Picture Change

GSAs are often full of very motivated groups of queer and allied youth that will dedicate themselves to equity work and social change. Take advantage! Your GSA club can be the vehicle to change your school climate and culture. Empower GSA leaders to lead student assemblies, survey their peers, and educate in homerooms or over student announcements. Focus your GSA on larger projects that connect with school curriculum and themes. GLSEN has resources for GSAs to lead school-wide movements such as Ally Week, LGBTQ+ History Month, and Day of Silence. GSA members have the potential to transform their school community in these efforts, and school administration is often pleased to report an improved school climate. Encourage your GSA to write grants for books that can be integrated across curriculum. Assist student leaders in hosting social activities that bring joy and awareness, such as bake sales, school dances, and spirit weeks. The opportunities for GSA leadership and activism are endless; this proactive inclusion work has a profound impact on school communities.

Embrace Coalition-Building and Intersectionality in Your GSA's Work

We want Gender and Sexuality Alliances (GSAs) that are open and welcoming to all students, including students of all races, genders, sexualities, abilities, socio-economic backgrounds, and religions. If not intentional, your GSA might be very supportive to queer students, but might leave out others. Historically, many transgender people and people of color have been rendered invisible in the LGBTQ+ Rights movement, despite their leadership and heroism. We must ensure that our GSAs do not repeat this history. As outlined in Box 5.2, engaging other leadership groups can also strengthen both your GSA and your school community's anti-oppression efforts overall. As noted in the GSA Network's description of the importance of creating inclusive GSAs:

> Multi-issue organizing is a strong and powerful way to incorporate all aspects of a community and the people it is made up of. The LGBTQ youth movement cannot survive unless it includes people of color and addresses issues of sexism, racism, classism, ageism, and environmental injustice. We must link ourselves together to create a multi issue social justice movement which incorporates the needs and rights of multiple communities.
>
> (Genders & Sexualities Alliance Network, n.d.)

Box 5.2 Best Practices for Inclusive GSAs

- Highlight and celebrate the activism and history of people of color and transgender people in the fight for equality. Look to historical movements, current events, community organizations, and guest speakers.
- Reach out to other social justice groups in your school, such as equity clubs or Black and Latinx Student Unions, and build coalitions for justice. Make sure you do not have competing meeting times, compelling queer youth of color to choose between clubs. Connect in shared organizing efforts and join forces for school-wide change.
- Strive towards social justice for all identity groups. For example, anti-racist GSAs engage in anti-oppression education, participate in "Black Lives Matter" movements, and focus advocacy efforts in an intersectional fashion, involving the experiences of multiple identity groups.
- Address potential barriers for accessing the GSA. Ensure materials are in multiple languages and reach out to bilingual advisors and educational assistants so that all students are welcome and can participate in the GSA. If your GSA is lacking the diversity of your school population, be intentional in your outreach to student groups, listen to their rationale for non-participation, and make a concerted effort to become more inclusive.

Adapted from the GSA Network and GLSEN (Genders & Sexualities Alliance Network, n.d.)

Continue to Grow Student Leaders

GSAs empower students to learn advocacy and leadership skills that can transform their education experience and lives. As they become champions for social justice, often there will be great energy and excitement. There is a tendency for some voices to overpower others. To sustain a strong, effective GSA, remember to ensure equal power and opportunity for all members and identities. Be intentional around growing your younger students into future leaders. Find creative ways to utilize all the talents GSA group members bring to the table, and find safe ways for students to rise and grow.

Conclusion

The experiences of LGBTQ+ students are diverse and vary based on multiple factors, including intersecting aspects of identity and environmental characteristics. In acknowledging that diversity, it is also clear that LGBTQ+ students as a whole are at risk of negative school experiences that can impact their school engagement and educational goals as well as day-to-day safety and mental health. However, concrete changes in the school community, curriculum, and physical space can create an environment that counters this violence and fosters resilience, engagement, and social justice. Working towards better environments for LGBTQ+ students is critical not just for those with sexual and gender minority identities, but for all students, as this engages the entire school community in facilitating inclusion and celebrating diversity.

Key Messages

1. LGBTQ+ students experience disproportionate in-person, online, and structural harassment and violence compared to their heterosexual peers.
2. Improving safety for all students, including LGBTQ+ students, involves comprehensive, ongoing, multi-faceted interventions to address harassment and support diversity of identities and encourage school engagement and resilience.
3. Many of these interventions are evidence-based and associated with improved outcomes, including reduced suicidality and increased school performance and engagement for LGBTQ+ students.

Appendix 5

Resources to Improve School Climates for LGBTQ+ Youth

Welcoming Schools

Mission: The Human Rights Campaign's *Welcoming Schools* program is a national professional development program in the United States with a mission of creating safe and welcoming schools for all children and families. *Welcoming Schools* provides "training and resources to elementary school educators to welcome diverse families, create LGBTQ and gender inclusive schools, prevent bias-based bullying, and support transgender and non-binary students".
Website: www.welcomingschools.org/
Address: Welcoming Schools, c/o Human Rights Campaign, 1640 Rhode Island Ave. N.W., Washington, DC 20036–3278, USA.

GSA Network

Mission: GSA Network is a "next-generation LGBTQ racial and gender justice organization in the United States that empowers and trains queer, trans and allied youth leaders to advocate, organize, and mobilize an inter-sectional movement for safer schools and healthier communities".
Website: https://gsanetwork.org/
Phone: 415–552–4229; Fax: 415–552–4729 (US phone numbers; country code +1)
Email address: info@gsanetwork.org
Located in Oakland, CA, USA.

Gender Spectrum

Mission: Gender Spectrum "helps to create gender sensitive and inclusive environments for all children and teens". To accomplish this, Gender Spectrum provides in-person and online training, support, and education to help families, organizations, and institutions increase understanding of gender, gender identity, and expression.
Website: https://www.genderspectrum.org/
Phone: 510–788–4412 (US phone number; country code +1)
Email address: info@genderspectrum.org

GLSEN (Gay, Lesbian and Straight Education Network)

Mission: GLSEN is a national organization in the US dedicated to creating safe and affirming schools for all, regardless of sexual orientation, gender identity, or gender expression. GLSEN accomplishes this mission through research, including the National School Climate Survey, as well as professional development for educators and legislative advocacy related to school safety. GLSEN has partnered with UNESCO to elevate an international dialogue around "homophobic and transphobic prejudice and violence in schools".
Website: https://www.glsen.org/
Phone: 212–727–0135 (US phone number; country code +1)
Email address: info@glsen.org
Address: 110 William Street, 30th Floor, New York, NY 10038, USA.

Minus 18

Mission: Minus 18 is "Australia's Youth Driven Network for LGBTIQ Youth". Minus 18 aims to improve experiences of LGBTIQ youth by creating safe events and support spaces, offering workshops for educators and youth, and advocating for LGBTIQ visibility.
Website: https://www.minus18.org.au/
Phone: (03) 9427 7702 (Australian phone number; country code +61)
Address: 8–10/892 Bourke St, Docklands VIC 3008, Australia

Teaching Tolerance

Mission: "To reduce prejudice, improve intergroup relations and support equitable school experiences for our nation's children". Teaching Tolerance uses an anti-bias and social justice approach in the free resources they provide for educators, including professional development opportunities and classroom resources. Teaching Tolerances is a project of the Southern Poverty Law Center in the United States.
Website: https://www.tolerance.org/

Anti-Defamation League

Mission: ADL's mission is "to stop the defamation of the Jewish people, and to secure justice and fair treatment to all". ADL's educational programs provide training and resources for grades PreK–12 and college/university settings. ADL's anti-bias and bullying prevention programs assist educators and students in understanding and challenging bias and building ally behaviors.

Website: https://www.adl.org/
Phone: 212–885–7700 (US phone number; country code +1)
Address: The Anti-Defamation League has offices throughout the United States and also has an office in Israel.

References

American Civil Liberties Union (ACLU). (n.d.). *Know your rights! A guide for LGBT high school students.* Retrieved December 17, 2017, from www.aclu.org/know-your-rights/know-your-rights-guide-lgbt-high-school-students

Austin, G., Polik, J., Hanson, T., & Zheng, C. (2016). *School climate, substance use, and student well-being in California, 2013–2015. Results of the fifteenth Biennial Statewide Student Survey, Grades 7, 9, and 11.* San Francisco, CA: WestEd Health & Human Development Program.

Bidell, M. P. (2014). Is there an emotional cost of completing high school? Ecological factors and psychological distress among LGBT homeless youth. *Journal of Homosexuality, 61,* 366–381.

Birkett, M., Russell, S. T., & Corliss, H. L. (2014). Sexual-orientation disparities in school: The mediational role of indicators of victimization in achievement and truancy because of feeling unsafe. *American Journal of Public Health, 104*(6), 1124–1128.

Burdge, H., Snapp, S., Laub, C., Russell, S. T., & Moody, R. (2013). *Implementing lessons that matter: The impact of LGBTQ-inclusive curriculum on student safety, well-being, and achievement.* San Francisco, CA: Gay-Straight Alliance Network and Tucson, AZ: Frances McClelland Institute for Children, Youth, and Families at the University of Arizona.

Canadian Human Rights Act, Pub. L. No. R.S.C., 1985, c. H-6. (2009). Retrieved from http://laws-lois.justice.gc.ca/PDF/H-6.pdf

Crenshaw, K. (2016). The urgency of intersectionality. *Filmed October.* Retrieved from www.ted.com/talks/kimberle_crenshaw_the_urgency_of_intersectionality/transcript

Dake, J. A., Price, J. H., & Telljohann, S. K. (2003). The nature and extent of bullying at school. *The Journal of School Health, 73,* 173–180.

Dane County Youth Commission. (2015). *Dane County Youth Assessment 2015.* Retrieved from https://danecountyhumanservices.org/yth/dox/asmt_survey/2015/2015_hs.pdf

De Pedro, K. T., Esqueda, M. C., & Gilreath, T. D. (2017). School protective factors and substance use among lesbian, gay, and bisexual adolescents in California public schools. *LGBT Health, 4,* 210–216.

Diemer, E. W., Grant, J. D., Munn-Chernoff, M. A., Patterson, D. A., & Duncan, A. E. (2015). Gender identity, sexual orientation, and eating-related pathology in a national sample of college students. *The Journal of Adolescent Health: Official Publication of the Society for Adolescent Medicine, 57,* 144–149.

Earnshaw, V. A., Bogart, L. M., Poteat, V. P., Reisner, S. L., & Schuster, M. A. (2016). Bullying among lesbian, gay, bisexual, and transgender youth. *Pediatric Clinics of North America, 63,* 999–1010.

Elia, J. P., & Eliason, M. (2010). Discourses of exclusion: Sexuality education's silencing of sexual others. *Journal of LGBT Youth, 7*(1), 29–48.

Espelage, D. L., Basile, K. C., De La Rue, L., & Hamburger, M. E. (2015). Longitudinal associations among bullying, homophobic teasing, and sexual violence perpetration among middle school students. *Journal of Interpersonal Violence, 30*(14), 2541–2561.

Flores, A. R., Herman, J. L., Gates, G. J., & Brown, T. N. T. (2016). *How many adults identify as transgender in the United States?* Los Angeles, CA: The Williams Institute.

Gattis, M. N., & McKinnon, S. L. (2015). *School experiences of transgender and gender non-conforming students in Wisconsin.* Madison, WI: GSAFE.

Genders & Sexualities Alliance Network. (n.d.). *Creating inclusive GSAs.* Retrieved December 17, 2017, from https://gsanetwork.org/resources/creating-inclusive-gsas

GLSEN. (2007). *Gay-straight alliances: Creating safer schools for LGBT students and their allies (GLSEN Research Brief).* New York, NY: Gay, Lesbian and Straight Education Network.

GLSEN. (2016). *GLSEN 2015 National School Climate Survey (NSCS) executive summary: The experiences of lesbian, gay, bisexual, transgender, and queer youth in our nation's schools.* Retrieved from www.glsen.org/sites/default/files/GLSEN%202015%20National%20School%20Climate%20Survey%20%28NSCS%29%20-%20Executive%20Summary.pdf

GLSEN. (2017). *Enumeration.* Retrieved December 17, 2017, from www.glsen.org/sites/default/files/Enumeration_0.pdf

Hatzenbuehler, M. L., Birkett, M., Van Wagenen, A., & Meyer, I. H. (2014). Protective school climates and reduced risk for suicide ideation in sexual minority youths. *American Journal of Public Health, 104*(2), 279–286.

Hatzenbuehler, M. L., Duncan, D., & Johnson, R. (2015). Neighborhood-level LGBT hate crimes and bullying among sexual minority youths: A geospatial analysis. *Violence and Victims, 30,* 663–675.

Hatzenbuehler, M. L., & Keyes, K. M. (2013). Inclusive anti-bullying policies and reduced risk of suicide attempts in lesbian and gay youth. *The Journal of Adolescent Health: Official Publication of the Society for Adolescent Medicine, 53*(1 Suppl), S21–S26.

Horn, S. S., & Szalacha, L. A. (2009). School differences in heterosexual students' attitudes about homosexuality and prejudice based on sexual orientation. *European Journal of Developmental Science, 3*(1), 64–79.

Human Rights Campaign. (2017a). *Case study: Piloting HRC welcoming schools.* Retrieved December 22, 2017, from www.welcomingschools.org/research/case-study-piloting-welcoming-schools/

Human Rights Campaign. (2017b, December 1). *State maps of laws & policies.* Retrieved December 17, 2017, from www.hrc.org/state-maps/education

Human Rights Campaign. (n.d.). *What is an LGBTQ-inclusive school? | Welcoming schools.* Retrieved December 17, 2017, from www.welcomingschools.org/resources/school-tips/lgbtq-inclusive-schools-what/

Human Rights Campaign (Producer). (2018). *Welcoming schools.* Retrieved February 5, 2018, from www.welcomingschools.org.

Human Rights Watch. (2001). *Hatred in the hallways: Violence and discrimination against lesbian, gay, bisexual, and transgender students in U.S. schools.* New York/Washington/London/Brussels: Human Rights Watch. Retrieved from www.hrw.org/legacy/reports/2001/uslgbt/toc.htm

Kann, L., O'Malley Olsen, E., McManus, T., Harris, W. A., Shanklin, S. L., & Flint, K. H. (2016). Sexual identity, sex of sexual contacts, and health-related behaviors among students in grades 9–12 — United States and selected sites, 2015. *Morbidity and Mortality Weekly Report. Surveillance Summaries, 65,* 1–202.

Kosciw, J. G., Greytak, E. A., & Diaz, E. M. (2009). Who, what, where, when, and why: Demographic and ecological factors contributing to hostile school climate for lesbian, gay, bisexual, and transgender youth. *Journal of Youth and Adolescence, 38*, 976–988.

Kosciw, J. G., Greytak, E. A., Giga, N. M., Villenas, C., & Danischewski, D. J. (2016). *The 2015 National School Climate Survey: The experiences of lesbian, gay, bisexual, transgender, and queer youth in our nation's schools.* New York, NY: GLSEN.

Kosciw, J. G., Greytak, E. A., Palmer, N. A., & Boesen, M. J. (2014). *The 2013 National School Climate Survey: The experiences of lesbian, gay, bisexual and transgender youth in our nation's schools.* New York, NY: GLSEN.

Kosciw, J. G., Palmer, N. A., Kull, R. M., & Greytak, E. A. (2013). The effect of negative school climate on academic outcomes for LGBT youth and the role of in-school supports. *Journal of School Violence, 12*, 45–63.

Mustanski, B., Birkett, M., Greene, G. J., Rosario, M., Bostwick, W., & Everett, B. G. (2014). The association between sexual orientation identity and behavior across race/ethnicity, sex, and age in a probability sample of high school students. *American Journal of Public Health, 104*, 237–244.

National Center for HIV/AIDS, Viral Hepatitis, STD, and TB Prevention, Division of Adolescent and School Health. (2016). *Anti-bullying policies and enumeration: An info-brief for local education agencies* (No. CS261182). CDC. Retrieved from www.cdc.gov/healthyyouth/health_and_academics/pdf/anti_bullying_policies_infobrief.pdf

National Conference of State Legislatures & Kralik, J. (n.d.). *"Bathroom bill" legislative tracking.* Retrieved November 27, 2017, from www.ncsl.org/research/education/-bathroom-bill-legislative-tracking635951130.aspx

Poteat, V. P., Sinclair, K. O., DiGiovanni, C. D., Koenig, B. W., & Russell, S. T. (2013). Gay-straight alliances are associated with student health: A multischool comparison of LGBTQ and heterosexual youth. *Journal of Research on Adolescence: The Official Journal of the Society for Research on Adolescence, 23*, 319–330.

Rich, A. (1994). *Blood, bread, and poetry: Selected prose 1979–1985.* New York, NY: W. W. Norton & Company.

Rosario, M., Corliss, H. L., Everett, B. G., Russell, S. T., Buchting, F. O., & Birkett, M. A. (2014). Mediation by peer violence victimization of sexual orientation disparities in cancer-related tobacco, alcohol, and sexual risk behaviors: Pooled youth risk behavior surveys. *American Journal of Public Health, 104*(6), 1113–1123.

Russell, S. T., Everett, B. G., Rosario, M., & Birkett, M. (2014). Indicators of victimization and sexual orientation among adolescents: Analyses from youth risk behavior surveys. *American Journal of Public Health, 104*, 255–261.

Russell, S. T., Sinclair, K. O., Poteat, V. P., & Koenig, B. W. (2012). Adolescent health and harassment based on discriminatory bias. *American Journal of Public Health, 102*, 493–495.

Sawyer, R. J., Porter, J. D., Lehman, T. C., Anderson, C., & Anderson, K. M. (2006). Education and training needs of school staff relevant to preventing risk behaviors and promoting health behaviors among gay, lesbian, bisexual, and questioning youth. *Journal of HIV/AIDS Prevention in Children & Youth, 7*(1), 37–53.

Schuster, M. A., & Bogart, L. M. (2015). A longitudinal study of bullying of sexual-minority youth. *The New England Journal of Medicine, 372*, 1872–1874.

Shields, J. P., Cohen, R., Glassman, J. R., Whitaker, K., Franks, H., & Bertolini, I. (2013). Estimating population size and demographic characteristics of lesbian, gay, bisexual, and transgender youth in middle school. *The Journal of Adolescent Health: Official Publication of the Society for Adolescent Medicine, 52*, 248–250.

Shutts, K., Pemberton, C. K., & Spelke. E. S. (2013). Children's use of social categories in thinking about people and social relationships. *Journal of Cognition and Development: Official Journal of the Cognitive Development Society, 14* (1), 35–62.

Somashekhar, S., Brown, E., Balingit, M., Somashekhar, S., Brown, E., & Balingit, M. (2017, February 22). Trump administration rolls back protections for transgender students. *The Washington Post.* Retrieved from www.washingtonpost.com/local/education/trump-administration-rolls-back-protections-for-transgender-students/2017/02/22/550a83b4-f913-11e6-bf01-d47f8cf9b643_story.html

Spears Brown, C., & Bigler, R. S. (2005). Children's perceptions of discrimination: A developmental model. *Child Development, 76* (3), 533–553.

Swearer, S. M., Turner, R. K., & Givens, J. E. (2008). "You're so gay!": Do different forms of bullying matter for adolescent males? *School Psychology Review, 37*(2), 160–173.

Szalacha, L. (2003). Safer sexual diversity climates: Lessons learned from an evaluation of Massachusetts safe schools program for gay and lesbian students. *American Journal of Education, 110*, 58–88.

Toomey, R. B., Ryan, C., Diaz, R. M., & Russell, S. T. (2011). High school gay-straight alliances (GSAs) and young adult well-being: An examination of GSA presence, participation, and perceived effectiveness. *Applied Developmental Science, 15*, 175–185.

UNESCO. (2016, April 26). *Homophobic and transphobic violence in education.* Retrieved December 19, 2017, from https://en.unesco.org/themes/school-violence-and-bullying/homophobic-transphobic-violence

US Department of Education. (2016, May 13). *U.S. Departments of Education and Justice release joint guidance to help schools ensure the civil rights of transgender students.* Retrieved November 27, 2017, from www.ed.gov/news/press-releases/us-departments-education-and-justice-release-joint-guidance-help-schools-ensure-civil-rights-transgender-students

Ybarra, M. L., Mitchell, K. J., Palmer, N. A., & Reisner, S. L. (2015). Online social support as a buffer against online and offline peer and sexual victimization among U.S. LGBT and non-LGBT youth. *Child Abuse & Neglect, 39*, 123–136.

Reframing Stranger Danger   **6**

Online Child Sexual Exploitation

Roberta Sinclair, Kristin Duval, and Mauranne Ste-Marie

Child protection, particularly from child sexual exploitation, has been and continues to be a priority for many countries, especially Canada and the United States. Although child sexual exploitation is unfortunately not a new phenomenon, the nature of this threat in terms of the ways in which it is facilitated has changed significantly (Public Safety Canada, 2015). A key factor contributing to the sexual exploitation of children in today's society is the Internet. Although technological advances have brought forth many positive aspects, this chapter examines some of the negative impacts of the Internet in regard to online child sexual exploitation, and more specifically, the need to reframe *who* poses a risk to youth and children within this context. The anonymity afforded by the Internet, its wide accessibility, and its associated lack of accountability (Cooper, 1998) all work together to create a social environment conducive to online child sexual exploitation; this online reality needs to inform our approaches to child protection broadly, and education and awareness efforts more specifically. An important factor that needs to be re-examined are the ways in which we teach youth and children about online and offline safety, and how we conceptualize offenders within child sexual exploitation education and awareness initiatives.

In this chapter, the issue of online child sexual exploitation is examined in light of the impacts of technology, and some of the resources available to youth, parents, and school personnel will be highlighted. Understanding *how* child sex offenses are committed and facilitated via the use of various technologies, in both online and offline contexts, is critical to being able to engage in constructive and informed dialogues with youth. Although conversations about age appropriateness, technology, and sexual exploitation can be difficult, educating oneself about these issues is one of the most effective methods to developing holistic response strategies.

As technological advancements have evolved, so have child sex offenders—they are now taking advantage of the Internet and new communication technologies to gain access to children, develop relationships with them, and potentially lure them into inappropriate communication or sexual interactions, therefore reframing the notion of "stranger danger". The nature of the Internet has changed the ways in which these relationships develop. It is not surprising to hear young people speak of their several hundred friends on social media. Many youth consider these relationships to be similar to their offline ones—even though they may not have met some of these "friends" in person. What is most problematic, however, is that they may eventually meet these individuals offline. For example, in a 2014 study, over 5,000 Canadian students were surveyed on their online habits, and the report noted that at least 15% of them met (in-person) with someone they had initially met in a chat room (Media Awareness Net, 2000). Similarly, the Pew Research Center found that of the American teenagers surveyed[1] who had met people online, one-third of them followed up with an in-person meeting (Lenhart, 2015).

The "stranger danger" theory has also become an outdated approach to protect children from victimization from online child sexual exploitation. Previous education and awareness efforts in the area of child protection have focused on the danger posed by strangers. Recent discourse now acknowledges that the majority of sexual offenses against children (on- and off-line) are committed by someone who the child knows. For example, a study on child sex offenders found that 94% of offenders abused their own children or a child they knew (Smallbone & Wortley, 2011). In Canada, in the 2012 police-reported sexual offenses against youth, it was determined that about 88% of all sexual offenses were committed by an individual known to the victim (Cotter & Beaupré, 2014). Similarly, an American study found that only about 10% of perpetrators of child sexual abuse are strangers to the victims (Truman, Langton, & Planty, 2013). Offenders who sexually abuse children may also record the abuse and distribute it online, contributing an additional layer of victimization for the child. Victims of these "dual offenders" (i.e., offenders who commit both contact sexual abuse and online offenses) are typically individuals who know the victim. To demonstrate, the National Center for Missing and Exploited Children in the United States reported that, of the victims identified by police, 79% were victimized by an adult they knew and trusted (Collins, 2012).

In light of these realities, we must re-examine our understanding of who is to be considered a "danger" in terms of child sexual exploitation and how we educate youth within this context. Online child sexual exploitation is a societal issue that needs the support and involvement of all sectors, in particular educators who play a significant role in child and youth development. Drawing on the historical reference cited back to Sir William Curtis[2] (reading, writing, and arithmetic), we suggest that to provide a holistic response to online child sexual exploitation as educators, we need to focus on the three E's:

Educate. By educating yourself and reading this resource, you are increasing your ability to be a resource for youth.

Engage. By engaging others (especially youth) and sharing your knowledge, you are promoting safety, awareness, and prevention.

Empower. By engaging and educating, you are empowering yourself and others to be part of a positive and collective response strategy to child sexual exploitation.

Background

Canada was one of the first countries to recognize the severity of the threat posed by online child sexual exploitation and to take action through the adoption of a national strategy dedicated to protecting children online. The *National Strategy for the Protection of Children from Sexual Exploitation on the Internet* (referred to as *National Strategy*) was launched in 2004 as a horizontal initiative that brings the Royal Canadian Mounted Police (RCMP), Public Safety Canada (PS), the Department of Justice (DOJ), and the Canadian Centre for Child Protection (C3P) together to provide a comprehensive, coordinated approach to enhance Canada's efforts against online child sexual exploitation (CSE).[3] As can be expected, the technological landscape has changed considerably since the *National Strategy* was developed in 2004. Canadians now have access to the Internet across multiple devices and platforms and from virtually anywhere in the world. The same is true within the youth population.

Specifically for the United States, the PROTECT Our Children Act of 2008 required that the Attorney General develop and implement a *National Strategy for Child Exploitation Prevention and Interdiction* (also referred to as *National Strategy*). The first *National Strategy* was published in 2010 and renewed in 2016. The strategy provides a comprehensive threat assessment of the nature and scope of the current dangers facing American children, including child pornography offenses, sextortion, live-streaming of child sexual abuse, child sex trafficking, transnational child sex offenses, and sex offense registry violations. It also analyzes the work of federal law enforcement agencies and prosecutors, as well as other agencies and offices that play important roles by supporting victims, providing grants to state, local, and tribal governments and non-profit partners, and educating the public about the dangers of child exploitation (Department of Justice, 2016).

Teens are more connected than ever, and they rely heavily on technology and the Internet for entertainment, school work, communicating with their friends and family, and sharing media. Youth frequent social media websites and applications for entertainment, competition, boredom, and attention among other reasons (Ipsos Reid, 2012; Steeves, 2014). Within their peer groups, there is strong pressure to maintain an online social media presence and the sharing of images is part of that culture. Behavior can be inhibited when using technology and the Internet (Media Awareness Net, 2000). As such, teens are not passive users, but rather content producers and will share images as part of a need to fit in and be accepted by their peers—sharing photos is not an isolated event but a routine part of teen life (Johnson, Steeves, Shade, & Foran, 2017). The perception of anonymity and privacy online can impact a youth's willingness to share personal information, putting them at higher risk for potential manipulation by others. Their need for acceptance and belonging strongly drives their decisions. The digital realm also allows them to experiment in ways they typically might not engage in if they were face-to-face, including who they talk to and what they talk about. Further, electronic communication is increasingly considered to be as accepted as face-to-face encounters. For instance, youth often make no distinction between their online and offline sense of self; the relationship between the virtual and physical world is becoming seamless or merged (Maczewski, 2002).

Establishing Common Definitions and Terminology

A discussion surrounding terminology is a critical component when reframing stranger danger. To begin, the term stranger danger is short, simple, and even rhymes; however, is it really the most effective prevention lesson for youth within our society today in terms of online child sexual exploitation? The origins of this term can be traced back to the 1960s, when stories of horrific crimes against children, such as abductions, sexual assaults, and murder perpetrated by individuals unknown to the victims' families, made the headlines in many newspapers. Suddenly, stranger danger became a real threat, and parents used this expression to teach their children about safety. Moreover, the expression was used in the United States in various safety advertisements and campaigns that later spread to other parts of the world, including Canada (Martin, 2017). As a result of these past threats, the term "stranger" has often been associated with "bad", "mean", or "ugly" (Canadian Centre for Child Protection, 2012a). These misconceptions can misguide children, as not all strangers are bad or dangerous. Children will observe their parents speaking with "strangers" rather frequently (which may confuse them), and there may be times when children will be required to approach a stranger for help (e.g., a police officer). The notion of "stranger danger" also implies that acquaintances or people who we "know" are all safe, and yet we know this is not always the case. We therefore need to teach youth how to recognize behavior and situations that present risk rather than focus on an individual's character and who that individual is in relation to the youth.

Who and what the term stranger encompasses must also be considered within an online context, as the development of relationships has been altered through the increased use of the Internet and communication technologies. A frequent worry about youth using social media is that they will be in contact with strangers; however, not all people who they know only online are considered to be "strangers" in their eyes. In Johnson et al.'s (2017) study, participants described how many people on their friends list (who have access to their photos/videos) are friend's friends or youth their age who requested their friendship on a specific platform. One participant stated, "there is definitely quite a lot of people I've never like had a conversation with or met . . . unless it's some old man I don't know, but generally people who request to follow me are kids my age". Another participant stated, "I feel like if people from other schools . . . follow me, it's fine". These examples demonstrate that although youth are selecting their online friends based on location and age, they are still accepting requests from individuals whom they have never met or conversed with before. Some of these "profiles" may be deceitful and created specifically for the purpose of targeting local youth. Alternatively, some youth may also befriend other youth in their area for ulterior motives, such as sexually exploiting them via social media platforms, cyberbullying, and other reasons. It is important to note that even though they do not have many of these contacts offline, in many cases, they consider these contacts to be "friends" rather than strangers.

It is also important that we establish a definition of child/youth.[4] Although this can be different based on country, for the purpose of this chapter, the definition of child is drawn from the Convention on the Rights of the Child (CRC).[5] According to the CRC, Article 1, "[f]or the purposes of the present Convention, a child means every human being below the age of eighteen years unless under the law applicable to the child, majority is attained earlier". However, drawing on the guidelines on terminology developed in 2016, "while emphasising the importance of ensuring all persons under the age of 18 are considered children and granted the rights and protection that come with this status, it should also be acknowledged that older children in their adolescent years are commonly referred to (especially in non-legal contexts) as 'adolescents' or 'teenagers'" (Greijer & Doek, 2016, p. 6).

There is growing concern among academics, nongovernmental organizations (NGOs), and law enforcement agencies regarding the appropriateness of commonly used terms related to online child sexual exploitation. Terminology significantly impacts the way members of the policing community, judiciary, and public understand and view online child sexual exploitation—the way agencies perceive victims, offenders, and other aspects of these crimes. Certain words can themselves convey power, authority, or weaknesses. As a result, terminology can also be used as a way of empowering people through the normalization and justification of various actions.

For instance, the terms "child pornography", "kiddie porn", and "child modeling" are frequently used to define material that, in reality, involves the depiction of child sexual exploitation and abuse. The aforementioned terms normalize child sexual exploitation and can allow people to think that it is somehow acceptable and appropriate, like other forms of legal pornography. Further, these terms imply consent, which, legally, children cannot provide. Thus, by definition, child pornography is abusive and coercive (Cohen-Almagor, 2013). Although "child pornography" remains the term used within the legal literature, child sexual abuse material or child sexual exploitation material is considered more appropriate terminology, as it accurately reflects the reality of the material (Interpol, 2015; Sinclair, Serapiglia, Wittreich, Murphy, & Goyette, 2010; Sinclair & Sugar, 2005; United Nations Office on Drugs and Crime, 2015). In addition, parents and educators should refrain from using terms such as "horrific images" or "dirty pictures" to describe child sexual exploitation material. This may discourage children and youth from disclosing the abuse, out of fear of being shamed or judged. Hence, for the purposes of this chapter, the term "online child sexual exploitation" will be the used.

Additionally, the term "child sexual offender" is often used interchangeably with the term "pedophile". In several media outlets, the terms "pedophile" and "monsters" are often used to describe individuals who sexually exploit children. However, "pedophilia" is a diagnostic term that refers to those who have persistent and recurrent sexual interest, fantasies, or behaviors towards children and not necessarily those who take action based on this sexual interest (Healy, 2004). It must be noted that pedophilia is considered a mental disorder[6] by the American Psychiatric Association's *Diagnostic and Statistical Manual of Mental Disorders, 5th edition* (DSM-5), and is not a criminal act (American Psychiatric Association, 2013). Therefore, members of law enforcement, the public, and educators are encouraged to use terms such as "child sexual offender" or "child sex abuser" to refer to those who are engaged in the sexual exploitation of children as well as "online child sex offender or abuser" for those who sexually exploit children online.

Similarly, "monster" is occasionally used by the media and the public to typify, among others, child sexual offenders. Referring to these individuals as "monsters", gives the impression that they appear evil or monster-like, when in reality, child sexual offenders are similar in many ways to non-child sex offenders. There is no typical "appearance"—they vary in physical appearance, socio-economic status, ethnicity, gender, education, and employment status. As a result, children, parents, and educators may let their guard down around individuals who are rather attractive, who seem pleasant, and appear trustworthy. Therefore, we should be mindful of the terminology employed when speaking about these individuals (Sinclair & Sugar, 2005; Sinclair et al., 2010).[7]

As defined in the Criminal Code of Canada, there are several online child sexual exploitation offenses prosecutable in Canada that are related to the online context. The focuses in this chapter are child pornography (s.163.1)[8] and child luring (s.172.1). Luring a child (otherwise known as the "enticement of a child") is defined in the Criminal Code of Canada as the use of telecommunication (i.e., digital technology, including the Internet and mobile phones) to communicate with a child for the purpose of facilitating a sexual offense. For more information on each of these offenses, please refer to the Criminal Code of Canada.

In the United States, child sexual exploitation falls under US Federal Law and includes the following offenses: sexual exploitation of children (i.e., production of child pornography;[9] 18 USC § 2251); selling and buying of children (18 USC § 2251A); certain activities relating to material involving the sexual exploitation of minors (i.e., possession, distribution, and receipt of child pornography; 18 USC § 2252); certain activities relating to material constituting or containing child pornography (18 USC § 2252A); and the production of sexually explicit depictions of a minor for importation into the United States (18 USC § 2260). It is important to note that an offender can be prosecuted under state child pornography laws in addition to, or instead of, federal law. For more information, please refer to the Code of Laws of the United States of America (or the United States Code).

The Nature of Child Sexual Exploitation

Child Sexual Exploitation on the Internet

Although violent crime in Canada has decreased overall in recent years, Statistics Canada indicates that sexual violations against children were among the few violent crimes that increased[10] with 6,917 reports in 2016,[11] a 30% increase since 2015.[12] In addition, the number and rate of child pornography incidents continued to rise in 2016, up 41% from 2015 (4,380 incidents) to 2016 (6,245 incidents; Keighley, 2017). UNICEF also recently reported that 92% of all child sexual abuse URLs are hosted in five countries (i.e., Canada, the Netherlands, the United States, France, and the Russian Federation) (United Nations Children's Fund, 2017).

Cybertip.ca, Canada tipline for reporting online child sexual exploitation offenses, has observed an increase in public reporting, particularly of child sexual exploitation images and videos on the Internet. In 2016–2017, Cybertip.ca received 40,251 reports from the public regarding concerns involving the online sexual exploitation of children—a 365% increase since 2010–2011. Similarly, in 2016, the National Child Exploitation Coordination Centre (NCECC) received 27,300 complaints, reports, and requests for assistance, a 349% increase since 2011. As of October 2017, the NCECC had already received nearly 28,000 reports. The NCECC receives approximately 28% of its reports from within Canada (either from Cybertip.ca or from other law enforcement agencies), and approximately 72% from abroad. A large portion of international reports are received from the National Center for Missing and Exploited Children (NCMEC) in the United States—18,903 in 2016, up from 10,673 reports in 2015.

In the United States, NCMEC's CyberTipline received 4,403,657 reports from the public in 2015, representing a 298% increase since 2014. Of those reports, 99% were about incidents of apparent child exploitation offences (National Center for Missing and Exploited Children, 2015). An average of 25 million images are reviewed by NCMEC annually. In addition, for the past 5 years, NCMEC has reported a growth in self-produced content (14%) and content stemming from online enticement (18%) (Thorn, 2014). In a 2017 report, the Bureau of Justice Statistics announced that the annual number of persons prosecuted for the commercial sexual exploitation of children[13] in the United States nearly doubled (54% increase) from 2004 to 2013, and suspects reported for possession, receipt, or distribution of child pornography accounted for 72% of the offenders.

Many offenders are knowledgeable and technologically advanced (United Nations Office on Drugs and Crime, 2015). The accessibility, affordability, and assumed anonymity of the Internet have turned it into a virtual hunting ground for child sexual offenders. It provides them with a means to gain access to children, and to contact them, allowing them the ability to "groom" and manipulate their victims through a virtual presence without having to leave their homes (McGuire & Dowling, 2013; Sinclair, 2005; Williams, 2013). Despite the limited research on online sexual grooming, it has been defined as "a process by which a person prepares a child, significant adults and the environment for the abuse of this child" (Craven, Brown, & Gilchrist, 2006, p. 297). It is also a "patterned behaviour designed to increase opportunities for sexual assault, minimize victim resistance or withdrawal, and reduce disclosure or belief" (Tanner & Brake, 2013, p. 1). It is suggested that all acts of sexual exploitation involve grooming in some form, and at some point in time, although the actual elements of grooming varies across victims (e.g., depending on age) and the length of the grooming period (Tanner & Brake, 2013).

The literature in this area seems to agree on a certain process of online grooming, whereby the offender gradually escalates from casual conversations, to sexually explicit online interactions, to wanting to arrange an offline meeting for the purpose of sexually abusing the child. Studies suggest that once the sexual offender has made initial contact with a child, the grooming process starts (Williams, 2013). Usually it begins with the offender trying to gain insight into the child's life, assessing aspects of the child's circumstances that may make them vulnerable (i.e., relationships with parents, friends, school, etc.). The information is then used for the purpose of being able to relate to the child. Offenders will present themselves as being similar to their victim to break the age barrier between them and build a friendship or relationship based on "pretend" common interests (Sinclair & Sugar, 2005; Williams, 2013). Offenders will aim to establish themselves as a confidante with whom the child can talk to about any problems without being judged to form a special bond—more than just online strangers (William, 2013). They will seek to create a mature friendship or relationship based on friendliness, empathy, affection, understanding, and guidance. For the most part, offenders will appear harmless, responsible, caring, playful, having good intentions, polite, and sensitive (Sinclair & Sugar, 2005; Tanner & Brake, 2013; Williams, 2013). This approach is more typically used to groom girl victims, as the offender fills an emotional need, whereas with boys (less prevalent), the relationship and dependency revolves mostly around the use of gifts, gift certificates, money, drugs, and alcohol (Sinclair & Sugar, 2005; Tanner & Brake, 2013).

Although initial communication with a victim may start on more public forums, offenders may eventually invite their victims to join a private chat area, or exchange email addresses and/or phone numbers (for text messaging; Sinclair & Sugar, 2005; Wolak, Finkelhor, Mitchell, & Ybarra, 2008). Offenders will try to create a sense of exclusivity between them as well as isolate the victim from their family environment. At that moment, once the child has an emotional attachment and the offender feels that s/he has gained his/her trust, the offender may start introducing sexual themes and references to their conversations. It then becomes hard for the child to avoid uncomfortable questions, as they have become close friends or perceived "lovers". The offender will continue to gently and subtly push boundaries, and incorporate more overtly explicit themes to normalize sexual language and behaviors (McGuire & Dowling, 2013). Offenders will provide sexual advice, question the child on their past sexual activities, and make him/her understand that sexuality is part of growing up (Williams, 2013). Often, the offender engages the child as if they were older, thus making the child feel special (Tanner & Brake, 2013).

The offender may also introduce the child to sexual abuse images with the intent of lowering inhibitions. The offender might use nude pictures of other children and/or sexual activities with adults that depicts them smiling to turn these acts into "normal" and acceptable behavior for their age, given that other children do it and are perceived to be enjoying it (Sinclair & Sugar, 2005). This is how victims can often be persuaded to engage in behaviors they would otherwise reject (Tanner & Brake, 2013). The child's response to sexual content lowers the threshold needed to engage the child in sexual interaction and establishes the special (sexual) relationship between them (Tanner & Brake, 2013). The offender might send pictures/videos of him/her and request the same from the child. In some cases, because the offender has already gained the child's trust, the offender may no longer act in a compassionate and sensitive manner. As a result, s/he might start using more forceful techniques to coerce the child into participating in sexual activities (Williams, 2013). The offender may convince the child that viewing the pictures or videos is illegal and that s/he has therefore done something wrong to force them into keeping the abuse a secret. They might capitalize on the child's fears, embarrassment, and guilt, confusing the victim into feeling responsible for the abuse (Department of Children and Families, 2014). By doing so, the offender may keep the child in the victimizing role for a long period of time (Tanner & Brake, 2013). Finally, the grooming process frequently terminates with the proposition of an offline meeting for the purpose of sexually abusing the child. As various studies have demonstrated, there is a strong overlap between online grooming and offline contact sexual abuse (e.g., see Media Awareness Net, 2000; Williams, Elliott, & Beech, 2013).[14]

The frequency, intensity, and duration of the grooming process vary across assault types (Tanner & Brake, 2013). Whether it takes days or years, "the planning, organization, and financial investments that a sex offender will use within the grooming process conveys how determined they are to obtain their desired outcome" (Williams et al., 2013, p. 138). The grooming process is often not an uncontainable or irresistible urge but rather a controlled, persistent, and vigilant process. Given the similarities between the online grooming process and the general process of forming a friendship or relationship online, this can make identification of a crime particularly hard for victims and law enforcement. Victims may believe they are friends with the offender or have a romantic relationship; the offender may use a fake identity to portray themselves as similarly aged peers to trick victims into sending self-generated indecent imagery, blurring the line between consensual cybersex and crime (Lorenzo-Dus & Izura, 2017; Quayle, Allegro, Hutton, Sheath, & Lööf, 2014; Tanner & Brake, 2013; Williams et al., 2013). Also, recent studies suggest that offenders generally spend small amounts of time with large numbers of potential victims rather than devoting large quantities of time to a small number of victims (e.g., McGuire & Dowling, 2013). They will assess which child is more vulnerable and more susceptible to agree to the offender's ultimate goal, which could include an offline meeting or sextortion (described in more detail following).

The term self-exploitation, also known as sexting, is often used to refer to the creating and/or sending sexually explicit messages, images, and/or videos via the Internet or electronic devices (Cybertip.ca, n.d.). It is very common among young people, and implies some form of consent between both parties. The broader sharing of these images without the originator's consent is a form of sexual exploitation and, like other forms of sexual exploitation, it re-victimizes the child or youth in the photo each time it is shared. The social stakes are very high, as once an image is shared, it does not only impact the youth's day-to-day life and interactions with peers but, in extreme cases, may result in teens taking their own lives. As a result of recently passed legislation in Canada under the Protecting Canadians from Online Child Crime Act,[15] the distribution of intimate images without consent has become a criminal act. This new offense offers prosecutors an alternative when dealing with young people who have disseminated intimate images of other youth. In the past, youth were prosecuted under the existing child pornography provision,[16] which is more severe in penalty and the stigma that comes with this offense can be much more damaging. Similarly, in the United States (as of 2017), more than 30 states and the District of Columbia have laws against the nonconsensual disclosure of sexually explicit images and videos, as compared to only three states in 2013. The rules and penalties vary by state, and for this reason, advocacy groups have been pushing for a nation-wide law (Hanna, 2017).

Another emerging form of online child sexual exploitation is sextortion. In sextortion cases, the offender makes contact with the victim through social media or other platforms and obtains sexualized material, often by posing as a youth of similar age. The offender then threatens to send the image to other people to make the victim fulfill a specific request, or for revenge or humiliation purposes. Findings from Wolak and Finkelhor's (2016) study on sextortion determined that the offender's main goals were to obtain additional sexual photographs (often scripted by the offender; 51% of the cases), for the victim to stay in or return to a relationship with the perpetrator (42%), to instruct the victim how to look or what to do in the material (28%), to meet in person (26%), to meet the victim online for sexual activity (24%), to tell them to hurt themselves (10%), for money (9%), and to make the victim take sexual images of someone else (7%).

In these exchanges, the offender exerts the power s/he holds over the victim. A common mistake made by youth is believing that if they give in just once, the requests for additional material will end—which is rarely, if ever, the case (Canadian Centre for Child Protection, 2017a). The abuse continues, which can seem never-ending to a victim. It is said that the increased use of mobile devices has also increased the volume of these crimes (Global Alliance Against Child Sexual Abuse Online, 2015). Notably, the number of reports submitted to Cybertip.ca involving youth being targeted through sextortion has increased over the years. Based on reports submitted to Cybertip.ca between January 1, 2015, and December 15, 2017, Cybertip.ca has received more than 240 reports related to sextortion incidents involving youth. Of these reports, 68% of incidents involved a female victim. The average age of victims was 15 years (L. Lobb, Canadian Centre for Child Protection, personal communication, December 21, 2017). The United States has also observed a significant increase in sextortion cases—up 150% within the first several months of 2016 compared to the number of reports in that same time frame in 2014. It was recorded that 78% of the reports involved female victims, and similar to Canada, the average age was 15 years old (National Center for Missing and Exploited Children, 2016).

There are many factors that contribute to the risks that youth face online. Offenders are technologically savvy, know where and how to access potential victims, and have insight into youth's behaviour—these factors all work to facilitate the grooming process. Young people may feel a great deal of pressure to maintain an online social media presence and have a large network. As a result, their online identity and relationships are very important to them, including with those who they do not know or have never met. To demonstrate, 43% of school-aged Canadians converse with people whom they have only met online and 29% of this demographic post their contact information online for others to see (Steeves, 2014). Similarly, a study conducted by McAfee[17] on online habits and interests of preteens and teens found that many teens post personal information without their parents' knowledge or awareness. For example, 50% of the surveyed teens share their personal email address and personal activities (31%). In addition, about 22% of the participants admitted using their mobile devices to hide activity from their parents (McAfee, 2013). There is little hesitation to share information, pictures, and videos in an effort to meet the expectations of their audience and establish and defend their online identities (Johnson et al., 2017). Teen social media users readily post personal information on their sites, such as photos of themselves (91%), videos of themselves (24%), school name (71%), town/city in which they reside (71%), and email addresses (53%) (Madden et al., 2013). The need to educate youth on the risks of welcoming an unfamiliar person into their network is critical, but we must be cognizant of their reality and reframe "stranger danger" in a way that is sensitive to how youth operate online and how they perceive their relationships.

Puberty increases experimentation, sexual curiosity, and sexual arousal. It is important for parents and educators to have conversations with youth about the risks associated with using technology to experiment sexually and the potential risk of blackmail/sextortion (Canadian Centre for Child Protection, 2017a). The University of New Hampshire Crimes Against Children Research Center, in partnership with Thorn, completed an exploratory study on the phenomena of sextortion, involving 1,631 participants ages 18–25 (Wolak & Finkelhor, 2016). The following findings demonstrate the various risks posed to children and youth:

- Similar to online child sexual exploitation, the perpetrator was not a stranger. Sixty percent of the participants knew the perpetrator offline prior to victimization.
- In 55% of the cases, the perpetrators lied about who they were or otherwise gave a false impression, such as wanting a romantic relationship (42% of those who lied), their age (39%), their gender (17%), being someone they knew (13%), or something else (21%).
- In about 70% of the cases, the victim knowingly provided a sexual image to the perpetrator for the following reported reasons: they were in a relationship (72%), they felt pressured or were made to feel bad (51%), they were tricked (15%), they were threatened or forced (13%), they expected to be paid for them (2%), or they thought the images would be used for modeling (2%).

- In 45% of the cases, images were acquired by the perpetrators without the knowledge or consent of the victim. In 18% of cases, webcam images were recorded. In 9%, they were taken without permission from a mobile phone. In 8%, they were fake or photoshopped. In 5%, they were accessed by hacking into the computer or mobile device of the target.
- In 45% of the cases, the perpetrator carried out the threats. Among other outcomes, the perpetrators stalked the victim with repeated, unwanted online and cell phone contact (71% of the cases), sent the sexual images to the victim's friends and family (45%), stalked or harassed (or attempted to) the victim in person (41%), and posted the sexual images online (40%).

Child Sexual Abuse: Realities Offline

In the context of child sexual abuse in the offline world, we have seen that "stranger danger" is no longer the right approach for teaching our children about safety and prevention. Although for many years it was believed that sexual abuse was more likely to be committed by a stranger, the reality is that, nowadays, it is more likely to be carried out by someone who the child knows (Collins, 2012; Smallbone & Wortley, 2011). Often, the offender is a family member, but it can also be someone who the victim knows and trusts from outside the home, such as a teacher or coach (Canadian Centre for Child Protection, 2012b). Not only do these offenders sexually abuse their victims, but some record the abuse and create a permanent record of the victimization, in many cases sharing or posting these images on the Internet. These "dual offenders" also typically know their victims personally. For example, in a 2017 international study by the Canadian Centre for Child Protection, it was reported that only 4% of offenders in cases in which a single offender sexually abused one or more victims and recorded the abuse/distributed it online was a stranger to the victim. The offender was more likely to be a parent or relative (50%); an acquaintance of either the victim or victim's family (23%); a person in a position of trust, such as a teacher, clergy member, counselor, or babysitter (19%); or a neighbor (4%). In cases in which multiple offenders were involved in the abuse and recording/distribution, 82% of primary offenders (i.e., the most active/prominent in the abuse out of all those involved) were a parent or part of the child's extended family. Approximately 16% of primary offenders were either family friends or acquaintances, persons in a position of trust, or neighbors. Only 2% of primary offenders were strangers to the victim or his/her family (Canadian Centre for Child Protection, 2017b). Various studies in the United States also suggest that sexual abuse perpetrated by a stranger is least likely (ranging from 7% to 25%), compared to family members or acquaintances (Douglas & Finkelhor, 2005).

Some child sex offenders will deliberately seek access to children to facilitate the commission of an offense, and to find the right victim. For example, some offenders may become active within a child-serving organization, such as a school or recreational program.[18] These types of environments allow offenders to maintain a position of trust and authority over children, which offers them the opportunity to gain their trust while appearing dedicated and caring. As with online child sexual exploitation, grooming occurs offline as well, and offenders will take very similar steps to build trust and comfort, and desensitize the child to the offender's advances. The offender may even go so far as to befriend the victim's family to gain their sense of comfort and trust, so they would be comfortable allowing their child to spend time alone with the offender. As a result, it is very important that we are aware of behavior that is sexually inappropriate or demonstrates a violation of boundaries so intervention can happen as soon as possible. It is equally important for us to teach our children about healthy relationships between adults and children—teach them to identify and respond to threatening situations rather than warning them about certain types of people (Craven et al., 2006; Knoll, 2010; Canadian Centre for Child Protection, 2012b).

Short- and Long-Term Consequences

The Impacts of Child Sexual Abuse

Victims of child sexual abuse can be impacted in various ways and to different extents, as it is often linked to the nature, duration, and severity of abuse, and the victim's relationship to the offender, among other factors (Hindman, 1999). Some impacts present themselves immediately and while the abuse is taking place, whereas others may only surface later on in life after the abuse has stopped. Either way, research indicates that child sexual abuse victims often have life-long struggles with trauma-related impacts and disorders (Salter & Richters, 2012).

In terms of the impact of sexual abuse on children, there are four suggested trauma-causing factors as described by Finkelhor and Browne (1985), which are frequently cited in other research and reference material (e.g., Canadian Centre for Child Protection, 2017b): betrayal, powerlessness, stigmatization, and traumatic sexualization. Each factor is discussed in more detail in the following sections, and the consequences of each are presented.

Betrayal

As discussed earlier, victims of child sexual abuse often know the offender. When the offender is someone who they view as a person in a position of trust, such as a parent or figure of authority, the victim may feel a sense of betrayal. The same principle applies in the online world, wherein offenders will often take great measures to show affection and love towards their victims. As the relationship develops between the offender and victim, so does the level of trust. It can be devastating to suffer abuse from someone who was perceived to be trustworthy. This betrayal can result in reduced confidence and trust in authority figures in general, and can generate a lack of respect for rules. Victims are vulnerable to being re-victimized because they have lost the ability to judge who they can or cannot trust. The victim may experience relationship issues, even as an adult, as it can be difficult to get close to people. Friendships may be superficial and parenting may be impacted (e.g., hypervigilance with children, not able to parent or delay becoming a parent).

Powerlessness

Throughout the grooming process, offenders manipulate their victims and gain control over them. Victims will often not recognize that grooming is taking place, and become "cooperative" participants. Once they do realize what is happening, they may feel like they have lost control over many different aspects of their lives. This sense of powerlessness can be more prominent when the abuse is repetitive, force or threats are used, and the child feels that there is no escaping the situation. In cases of sextortion, victims may feel particularly powerless as they lose control over what happens to their intimate images, and feel compelled to respond to offenders' additional demands. That sense of powerlessness can cause panic attacks, nightmares, and flashbacks. Victims may also feel the need to regain control in their life, but may do so with extreme measures (e.g., through obsessions and compulsions, or through aggression). Eating problems and the feeling of always being on the run may also result.

Stigmatization

Offenders take advantage of children's trusting and innocent nature, and manipulate them into believing they are active participants in the abuse, and are responsible for what happened, or that they themselves have done something wrong. The stigmatization that results from the offender's behavior and actions is also reinforced by other people in the victim's environment or from general views, perceptions, and attitudes within society (e.g., use of inappropriate terminology, "taboo" subject). Negative connotations surrounding the abuse, such as worthlessness, shame, guilt, and being "dirty", can be communicated to the child, which then get incorporated into the victim's self-image. Consequently, the victim may resort to various coping mechanisms, such as substance abuse (depending on age), may suffer from depression or anxiety, have suicidal ideations or attempts/self-harm, and have low self-esteem. The victim may also feel that life is empty and meaningless.

Traumatic Sexualization

During the grooming process, an offender will attempt to normalize sexualized behavior (particularly between adults and children) by giving the victim incorrect information about sex, sexuality, and intimacy. This can cause the victim's sexual feelings and attitudes to be shaped in a developmentally inappropriate way. As a result of this trauma, victims of child sexual abuse may develop a fear of intimacy, confusion about sexual identity, may have intrusive images or flashbacks during sex later on in life, and may engage in sexual promiscuity.

The Impact of Technology-Facilitated Child Sexual Abuse

Children and youth who were sexually exploited online experience rather unique impacts. Having the abuse recorded (and potentially distributed) can add an additional and extraordinary layer of trauma for victims due to the accessibility and anonymity of the Internet, and the ease in which child sexual exploitation material can be shared. Once content has been uploaded, there is a loss of control over what happens to it and who it is shared with. Victims can experience feelings of shame and humiliation, and may feel as though they are being abused over and over. They often recognize the permanence of this record of abuse and feel powerless, as they cannot stop the circulation of the images. This loss of control exacerbates the fear and guilt that victims may feel, as they fear that the images could be seen by other people they know. In fact, in a study by the Canadian Centre for Child Protection (2017b),[19] 69% of survey respondents who were victims of online child sexual exploitation indicated that they constantly worry about being recognized by someone who has seen the abusive material. Alarmingly, 30% of victims reported that they had been identified by someone who had viewed the images.

Further contributing to this fear is how the child believes s/he is portrayed in the content. Offenders will often instruct their victims to behave/look a certain way when the images or videos are being taken (e.g., tell their victims to smile). This normalizes the behavior and makes it appear as though the child is "enjoying the abuse" and is a "willing" participant. Victims are manipulated into believing that anyone viewing the images will hold that same perception—that they "wanted" the abuse to happen.

In cases of sextortion, the personal and psychological consequences are also serious. In Wolak and Finkelhor's (2016) survey, 24% of the respondents had seen medical or mental health practitioners and 12% had to move as a result of the sextortion experienced. In addition, 41% lost a relationship with a friend, family member, or partner because of the incident. Considering the particular impact that online child sexual exploitation, including sextortion, has on victims, research indicates a clear need for distinct preventive and awareness initiatives, ones that would take into account the online aspect of the crime (Europol, 2017).

These impacts are important to be aware of and should inform our approach in terms of education and awareness strategies with youth.

Effective Response Strategies to Minimize the Impacts

Education and awareness is critical to our response strategies to child sexual exploitation. Not only is it important to be able to recognize signs of inappropriate behavior or child sexual exploitation and to teach those signs to our children, it is also important to know how to react and respond to a child who discloses abuse. As educators, parents, and caretakers of youth, it is important to be aware of the issues that youth may come to us to discuss. Often, if we are not aware of the intricacies of an issue, our reaction may be somewhat critical or appear to be unsupportive of the youth, and research has demonstrated that this can have a detrimental impact on victims. For example, in a study examining the effects of disclosing childhood sexual abuse, the researcher found that this experience was a strong contributor to adult psychopathology. Those who received a negative reaction from their family after disclosing the abuse had a worse score on general trauma symptoms, post-traumatic stress disorder symptoms, and dissociation (Roesler, 1994). The findings were echoed by Gries et al. (2000), who found that children who received full support from their parents or foster parents after disclosing sexual abuse showed significantly lower depression scores, and exhibited less externalizing behavior problems. These studies demonstrate that our reactions to disclosure are key to how the healing process progresses. It is critical that our first response to the issue is open and supportive for the child.

It is very difficult for many victims to reach out to someone and disclose that they have been / are being sexually abused. In fact, some may never report their abuse. Many factors play into this, including the power and control the offenders have over the victim. Victims often feel ashamed or embarrassed, are scared, or feel they will not be believed (Canadian Centre for Child Protection, 2014; Denov, 2003; Shoop, 2003). However, a victim is more likely to report sexual abuse if s/he feels that the safe adult is capable of managing the sensitive information and will respond in a way that the victim needs. We must control our reactions (i.e., do not over- or underreact) and praise the child for reporting. Never raise the questions, "Why didn't you tell me sooner?" or "How could this happen?", as this can unintentionally intensify feelings of blame. The offender is solely responsible for the sexual abuse (Canadian Centre for Child Protection, 2014).

To foster a more positive and supportive experience, we also need to be careful of the language and terminology that we use (refer to terminology section) and avoid correcting the child's language. It is also important that we avoid making promises we do not have control over (e.g., the offender will be convicted) and, of course, report the abuse to law enforcement and child welfare immediately. Be prepared to listen and pay close attention—disclosures may not always be obvious, especially when the victim is very young. Empathize with the child's feelings to demonstrate acceptance and validate that you are listening. We cannot minimize the seriousness of the situation (Cooper, 2005; Gil, 1988).

Child sexual abuse can be a difficult and uncomfortable topic to discuss but we can learn to become more comfortable in addressing this subject. Discussing the issue with other adults can help normalize the issue. Role-playing can be an effective way to help us familiarize ourselves with potential scenarios of disclosure. How would you respond to a youth who discloses that s/he has shared intimate images with someone s/he only knows online? Or how would you respond when a youth discloses that s/he is in a relationship with someone who is much older and they are having intimate relations via webcam? It is important that these scenarios become part of our repertoire when thinking about dealing with disclosures. Although we might not have all the answers, our response to a disclosure needs to be supportive to begin the healing process of a sexual abuse victim. Educating ourselves on the signs, terminology, and various scenarios that might come up in a discussion with youth is the best preparation. This will help us to react in a way that does not stigmatize the youth or his/her experience.

Prevention and Intervention Strategies

Adults bear the responsibility for safeguarding and protecting children from sexual exploitation on- and offline. As an educator, there are proactive steps that can be taken to help reduce the risk of a child being sexually exploited.[20] It is important to understand what child sexual exploitation is, to recognize signs of misconduct, and to know how to help a victim should they disclose abuse to avoid further exploitation and minimize the impacts. There are many resources available to school personnel, parents, and legal guardians to not only inform them on these issues, but help them engage with young people in an age-appropriate way, and in a manner that recognizes the importance of online presence among youth. Some of these resources are outlined next.

Education is a key component in keeping children and youth safe from online sexual exploitation. To complement what may already be taught in schools, organizations have developed campaigns to enhance awareness of personal safety for children on the Internet. For example, *Kids in the Know* (offered through C3P) is a national interactive education program for increasing the personal safety of children and reducing their risk of victimization online and offline (www.kidsintheknow.ca). Designed for children from kindergarten to high school, it focuses on building self-esteem through teaching critical problem-solving skills. The program includes a comprehensive curriculum, program training for teachers, school counselors, and parents, downloadable home activities for families, and supplemental material for communities. The program is used in thousands of schools across Canada and the 2006 version of the program received the nationally recognized Curriculum Services of Canada seal of approval. Lessons are matched to outcomes mandated by Departments of Education in jurisdictions across Canada.

In the United States, the *NetSmartz* educational outreach program (offered through NCMEC) offers educators, parents and guardians, law enforcement, teens, and kids a wide variety of interactive resources to promote online safety (e.g., presentations, videos, activity cards, and much more). The program's goals are to educate children, engage children and adults in conversation about online risks, and empower children to report victimization (www.netsmartz.org). Also offered by NCMEC, Kidsmartz.org is specifically designed for children under the age of 12 to encourage them to practice safer behaviors (e.g., preventing abduction and empowering children).

The *Commit to Kids* (offered through C3P) program is a step-by-step plan to help child-serving organizations (including schools) reduce the risk of child sexual abuse and create safer environments for the children in their care (www.commit2kids.ca). The *Commit to Kids* program works directly with organizations to prevent child sexual abuse through: increased awareness and education; teaching employees and volunteers the difference between appropriate and inappropriate behavior; providing specific strategies on how to prevent abuse; and ensuring that allegations of child sexual abuse are handled in a sensitive, timely, and effective manner.

Many resources also exist to provide youth with appropriate information on remaining safe in the context of child sexual abuse, reporting abuse online, and dealing with the impacts of having been a victim of child sexual exploitation. For example, the NeedHelpNow.ca website (offered through C3P) is designed to provide youth (ages 13–17) with practical steps to regain control over situations that they may be faced with relating to online child sexual exploitation. This includes information about contacting websites or online services to request that an intimate picture or video be removed and dealing with peers who may have seen or shared the content.

Cybertip.ca is Canada's national tipline for the public to report suspected cases of online sexual exploitation of children—predominantly involving child sexual abuse images and videos. The tipline, operated by C3P, focuses on facilitating public reporting surrounding crimes against children. The website also offers a mechanism for Internet service providers to report an IP address or URL that may have been involved in sharing or posting child sexual exploitation material. The Cybertip.ca website also provides the public with a broad range of education and awareness materials for children, youth, educators, and parents, as well as support and referral services.

Much of Cybertip.ca's services for children and youth involve providing support for one of two scenarios: (1) cases involving pre-pubescent children who have been sexually abused, where abuse has been recorded, uploaded, and shared online; and (2) youth cases that often involve extortion, online luring, and sexting. These different types of online child sexual abuse scenarios have distinct response strategies based on the needs of the victims in both types of scenarios. The response strategies will differ based on the pathway to victimization, age of the child, guardianship and safety of the child, and potential remedies required (for example, cases of youth who have been extorted may require different strategies than a youth who has shared an image with a trusted person who subsequently distributed that image without consent).

Launched in 1998, NCMEC's CyberTipline is a US national tipline that provides public and electronic service providers (ESPs) the ability to report online or via telephone incidents of online child sexual exploitation.[21] NCMEC reviews the reports for potential imminent danger and prioritization and then shares information and reports with the appropriate law enforcement agency. In addition, NCMEC uses the information submitted to the CyberTipline to create and update safety and prevention publications that are provided to educators, parents and guardians, and the public to help prevent future victimization (https://www.report.cybertip.org/).

MediaSmarts is a Canadian not-for-profit charitable organization that has been developing digital and media literacy programs and resources for Canadian homes, schools, and communities since 1996. Its vision is that children and youth have the critical thinking skills to engage with media as active and informed digital citizens. To achieve this goal, MediaSmarts develops and delivers high-quality Canadian-based resources; provides leadership in advancing digital and media literacy in Canadian schools, homes, and communities; and contributes to the development of informed public policy on issues related to media. The MediaSmarts website includes some specific resources with respect to online sexual exploitation including online sexual offenders (however, this is not their primary focus), safety tips, and resources for parents and teachers.[22]

Canada also has a well-entrenched Kids Help Phone service, which provides free 24/7 phone and web counseling to children and youth ages 20 and under. It provides an anonymous, confidential, and non-judgmental environment in which children and youth can talk about any issues affecting them, including online child sexual exploitation and abuse.[23] In addition, the Childhelp National Child Abuse Hotline is available to both American and Canadian children in 170 languages, and offers crisis intervention, information, and referrals to social services and support resources.[24]

Implementation

How Might You Engage with This Issue In Your Classroom, School, or Youth Setting?

Although it is important to educate youth on the issue of online child sexual exploitation, we also need to actively engage and empower them. Youth need to be a part of the solution. It is not about giving them a list of "what not to do" but, rather, encourage them to become involved in the education process, to develop their own response strategies, and get them thinking and talking about these issues.

The Internet is an important source of information, and youth/children should be encouraged to use it for research, entertainment, and school work, among other activities. Spending time on the Internet with children and showing them educational resources at their disposal means they can explore its potential in a safe and controlled way. Having open and honest discussions with children about the risks of sexual exploitation on the Internet, the problems that might arise from sharing intimate images/videos online, the high prevalence of deceiving identities online, and the dangers of building friendships with strangers in the virtual world may help reduce incidents. For instance, educators could practice "what if" scenarios with their students, using stories from the media to talk about real-life situations and generate options for getting out of or avoiding these situations. Youth have a strong need and desire to be socially present and active online; therefore, the most effective approach is to teach them how to use the Internet safely, and promote open conversations about possible incidents. Simply denying their online access or use of technology could be detrimental to them.

As a parent or educator, try integrating questions about online safety and activities into everyday conversations. This will set the stage for open dialogue, and will show an interest in their hobbies. Consider asking questions such as:

- What are some of your favorite applications? How do they work?
- Who do you video chat with online?
- Who are your friends on social media and how do you know them?
- Have you ever been asked for information/content that made you feel uncomfortable?
- Have any of your friends talked about a difficult situation they faced on the Internet? What are your views around what happened? How could you help them?
- What are the most common things you share with your friends and others you are connected to?
- What are the most unusual requests you have received online? How did you handle the situation(s)?
- Have you activated any of the privacy settings or other controls on your accounts?
- Do you know how to protect yourself online?
- What would you do if you found yourself in a situation in which someone pressured you to share intimate images of yourself?

How Can Youth Engage in the Online World More Safely?

Children and youth are also responsible for creating personal safety strategies that are current and effective in keeping them safe in both the online and offline world. Youth should activate any privacy settings or other controls on their social media application accounts. In addition, youth should review the personal information entered into their social network profiles—many services require certain fields to be completed, but this information does not need to be truthful. Chat options should also be restricted to those on their contact or "friends" list rather than being open to all users of the service.

Many social networking sites and applications have a reporting mechanism that can be used to report an abusive user's activities. Youth should be aware of these features and encouraged to use them when needed. If none are readily available, Cybertip.ca and NCMEC's CyberTipline for youth located in the United States remain the primary resources to report any abuse occurring online.

Overall, when it comes to any sexual activity, even if strictly online, consent is key. Consent is not limited to simply saying "yes". Both parties have to be willingly and freely consensual from beginning to end to all sexually explicit interactions, and if sexually explicit pictures or videos are shared, this consent is required for sharing the material with other individuals as well. Consent and healthy sexual relationships are important topics that should be discussed with youth regarding both online and offline contexts. Without a clear understanding of what constitutes a healthy relationship, young people are more likely to tolerate relationships that put them at increased risk.

Conclusion

Most media cases of online child sexual abuse involve male perpetrators and female victims (Martello, Nehring, & Taylor, 2010)—which does not reflect official Canadian and American statistics. There has also been a misconception that most child sex offenders are strangers rather than someone who is in a position of trust or authority. Education programs are encouraged to provide clear language about what behaviors are considered sexually abusive, coercive, or exploitive rather than just focusing on the sex of the perpetrator or victim, or the fact that the offender was a stranger met online. This is simply not a reality for youth today. Nowadays, young males are as victimized as young females and, often, the perpetrator is known to the victim (Canadian Centre for Child Protection, 2017b). It is important that we promote gender-neutral education about sexual abuse and sex offenders. Defining these behaviors as those being perpetrated by both males and females may help children understand healthy boundaries and reduce the likelihood of their own victimization. Educating youth and children that sex offenders can be male or female, old or young, and strangers or acquaintances may help them recognize and report any abuse they experience.

Many victims of child sexual abuse do not report their abuse until they are much older, if ever. Building awareness around the unique services provided by the Canadian and American helplines is needed. Furthermore, raising public knowledge of the importance of reporting online child sexual exploitation, and helping all members of society to be adequately prepared to respond to such disclosures to minimize the impact on the victim, is critical. This will help to create favorable conditions and a positive environment to encourage disclosure, making victims more comfortable, and more likely to seek help.

Online child sexual exploitation continues to expand both domestically and internationally, putting more youth and children at risk of being victimized. Online child sexual exploitation crimes transcend traditional boundaries and pose significant challenges for government, law enforcement, nongovernment organizations, and victim service providers. As technology continues to evolve, offenders engage in the online sexual exploitation of children via various means, utilizing techniques that help them evade police detection. Offenders rely on the interconnectedness of the Internet, encryption, and large data storage to facilitate their crimes. Keeping pace with the technological skills and resources necessary to fight online child sexual exploitation requires new measures that place renewed emphasis on cooperative action and information sharing. Understanding and reframing the notion of "stranger danger" is essential to protecting Canadian youth and children from sexual exploitation. All of us, including educators, need to continue to engage with the complexities of online child sexual exploitation, educate ourselves on positive response strategies, and empower ourselves and youth / children to address online child sexual exploitation.

Key Messages

What you need to know before you can talk to children and youth about online child sexual exploitation:

1. Online child sexual exploitation is not a new issue—it is still sexual exploitation, but the methods and mediums through which it occurs are different.
2. Educate. Knowledge is power in this area—the more you know, the better equipped you will be to help your students/youth. Becoming familiar and comfortable with speaking about this issue can enhance a child's learning experience.
3. Engage. This is an ever-changing issue and you need to be open to continually learning more.
4. Empower. If you empower yourselves and others, this will infiltrate into your classrooms. Help students to be knowledgeable and critical users of the Internet as well.
5. Prevention. Draw on national resources and products, and involve peer-to-peer strategies.

Appendix 6

Resource Materials for Teachers, School Administrators, Pediatricians, Parents, and Others Who Work with Youth

Educational Pamphlets

1. Many educational resources on online safety and cyberbullying are available for all ages on the C3P website, which can be either downloaded or ordered online. https://www.protectchildren.ca/app/en/order
2. Cybertip.ca: *Internet Safety Information for Youth* (12 years and older). https://www.cybertip.ca/app/en/internet_safety-for_youth
3. Cybertip.ca: *Internet Safety Information for Children* (5–11 years old). https://www.cybertip.ca/app/en/internet_safety-for_children
4. Cybertip.ca: *Self/Peer Exploitation* resource guide. https://www.cybertip.ca/app/en/internet_safety-self_peer_exploitation
5. Cybertip.ca: Cyberbullying activity books. www.cybertip.ca/app/en/internet_safety-cyberbullying
6. *Teatree Tells: A Child Sexual Abuse Prevention Kit* (preschool to grade 1). https://www.teatreetells.ca/app/en/
7. *Billy Brings his Buddies* (grade 1). https://www.billybuddy.ca/app/en/
8. *Zoe and Molly Online* (grades 3 and 4). https://www.zoeandmolly.ca/app/en/
9. *Be Smart, Strong & Safe* (grades 5 and 6). https://www.smartstrongsafe.ca/app/en/
10. C3P, *Parenting Tweens and Teens in the Digital World.* https://www.protectchildren.ca/pdfs/C3P_ParentingintheDigitalWorld_en.pdf
11. C3P, *Child Sexual Abuse: It Is Your Business.* https://www.protectchildren.ca/app/en/overview
12. Self/peer exploitation: NeedHelpNow.ca
    Resources for youth: https://needhelpnow.ca/app/en/downloadable_resources-youth
    Resources for adults: https://needhelpnow.ca/app/en/downloadable_resources-adults
13. NCMEC, *Helping Schools & Communities Prevent Child Sexual Exploitation.* https://www.missingkids.org/ourwork/publications/exploitation/exploitationcommunities

14. NCMEC, *Helping Families Prevent Child Sexual Exploitation*. https://www.missingkids.org/ourwork/publications/exploitation/exploitationfamilies

15. NCMEC, *Safe to Compete: Best Practices*. https://www.missingkids.org/ourwork/publications/safety/pdf24a

16. NCMEC, *What You Need to Know About Sex Offenders in Your Community*. https://www.missingkids.org/ourwork/publications/exploitation/copsp220

17. NCMEC, *Sex Offender Tracking Map* (US only). https://www.missingkids.org/ourwork/publications/exploitation/so-map

18. KidSmartz teaching tools for educators and/or law enforcement. https://www.kidsmartz.org/TeachingTools

Websites

1. Cybertip.ca, by C3P, is Canada's tipline for reporting the online sexual exploitation of children. Please visit the following website for definitions, additional information, and to report any abuse online. https://www.cybertip.ca/app/en/

2. *Kids in the Know* is a national interactive safety education program for increasing the personal safety of children and reducing their risk of victimization online and in the offline world. https://www.protectchildren.ca/app/en/overview_kidsintheknow

3. The *Commit to Kids* program is a step-by-step plan to help child-serving organizations reduce the risk of child sexual abuse and create safer environments for the children in their care. https://www.protectchildren.ca/app/en/overview_commit2kids

4. Need Help Now.ca helps teens stop the spread of sexual pictures or videos and provides support along the way (grades 7 and up). https://needhelpnow.ca/app/en/

5. Protect Kids Online.ca helps parents/guardians stay on top of the digital world that their children are engaging in. http://protectkidsonline.ca/app/en/

6. The International Association of Internet Hotlines (INHOPE) is an active and collaborative global network of hotlines, dealing with illegal content online and committed to stamping out child sexual abuse from the Internet. https://www.inhope.org/gns/home.aspx

7. *NetSmartz Workshop* is an interactive, educational program that provides age-appropriate resources to promote youth online safety. https://www.netsmartz.org

8. NetSmartz411 is designed for parents and guardians to answer questions about Internet safety, computers, and the web. http://www.netsmartz411.org/NetSmartz411/AboutNetsmartz.aspx

9. KidSmartz is a child safety program that educates families and children under the age of 12 to practice safer behaviors. https://www.kidsmartz.org/About

Presentations

1. C3P has created electronic resources and engaging presentation material to supplement their *Kids in the Know* program. Available for all age groups. https://www.kidsintheknow.ca/app/en/program-electronic_resources

2. NetSmartz offers free, multimedia Internet safety presentations tailored for specific audiences—parents and communities, tweens, teens, and younger children. https://www.netsmartz.org/Presentations

3. KidSmartz offers presentations for children under the age of 12 years old. https://www.kidsmartz.org/TeachingTools/Presentation

Research

1. In 2016, C3P conducted a study titled "Child Sexual Abuse Images on the Internet: A Cybertip.ca Analysis", which provides an overview of the information received through reports to the tipline over the last 8 years, with a particular focus on child sexual abuse images. The report can be accessed at: https://www.protectchildren.ca/app/en/csa_imagery

2. In 2016/2017, C3P conducted an international survivors' survey to better understand the impacts of online child sexual exploitation. The results can be viewed at: https://protectchildren.ca/app/en/csa_imagery#csa_imagery-survey_results

3. In 2010, NCMEC published the fifth edition of "Child Molesters: For Professionals Investigating the Sexual Exploitation of Children" by K. Lanning, a former supervisory special agent at the Federal Bureau of Investigation (FBI). https://www.missingkids.org/content/dam/ncmec/en_us/desktop/publications/nc70.pdf

4. In 2016, Wolak and Finkelhor published the findings from a survey of 1,631 victims of sextortion. This research was conducted in partnership with Thorn and the Crimes Against Children Research Center. https://www.missingkids.org/content/dam/ncmec/en_us/documents/2016crimes-againstchildrenresearchcentersextortionresearch.PDF

5. NCMEC conducted a study on hotlines around the world combating Internet-facilitated child sexual abuse material. https://www.missingkids.org/supportus/partners/grp

Notes

1. The survey was administered online in English and Spanish to a nationally representative sample of over 1,600 teens ages 13–17.
2. Sir William Curtis was a member of parliament in approximately 1825 who apparently referenced the three R's in a speech to the board of education (www.wikipedia.org).
3. Under the *National Strategy*, each partner serves a different but complementary function. Public Safety coordinates and oversees the Strategy's implementation, which includes ongoing policy development, coordinating research and reporting, and monitoring current and proposed legislation. The RCMP's National Child Exploitation Coordination Centre (NCECC) is a central point of contact for investigations related to the online sexual exploitation of children in Canada, and those international investigations involving Canadian victims or offenders, and also provides a number of services to domestic and international law enforcement. As a registered charitable organization, C3P operates Cybertip.ca for the public to report suspected cases of online child sexual exploitation, through which it examines and triages reports to appropriate law enforcement officials, and provides public awareness and education programming. The DOJ rounds out these efforts by developing and reviewing legislation and providing training, legal advice, and support to federal Strategy partners.
4. For the purpose of this paper, the terms youth/child will be used interchangeably.
5. The United Nations Convention on the Rights of the Child is a human rights treaty that outlines the rights of children, including civil, political, social, economic, and cultural rights. Please see www.ohchr.org/EN/ProfessionalInterest/Pages/CRC.aspx for more information.
6. According to the DSM-5, pedophilia is a disorder in which an adult's primary sexual attraction is to pre-pubescent children (American Psychiatric Association, 2015).
7. Taken from the Internet Facilitated Sexual Exploitation of Children and Youth Environmental Scan, Canadian Police Centre for Missing and Exploited Children 2016.
8. "Child pornography" is defined in accordance with the Criminal Code of Canada (s. 163.1), wherein child pornography is:
   (a) a photographic, film, video or other visual representation, whether or not it was made by electronic or mechanical means,
   (i) that shows a person who is or is depicted as being under the age of 18 years and is engaged in or is depicted as engaged in explicit sexual activity, or
   (ii) the dominant characteristic of which is the depiction, for a sexual purpose, of a sexual organ or the anal region of a person under the age of 18 years;
   (b) any written material, visual representation, or audio recording that advocates or counsels sexual activity with a person under the age of 18 years that would be an offense under this Act;
   (c) any written material whose dominant characteristic is the description, for a sexual purpose, of sexual activity with a person under the age of 18 years that would be an offense under this Act; or
   (d) any audio recording that has as its dominant characteristic the description, presentation, or representation, for a sexual purpose, of sexual activity with a person under the age of 18 years that would be an offense under this Act.
9. Section 2256 of Title 18, United States Code, defines child pornography as any visual depiction of sexually explicit conduct involving a minor (someone under the age of 18).

Visual depictions include photographs, videos, digital or computer-generated images indistinguishable from an actual minor, and images created, adapted, or modified but appearing to depict an identifiable, actual minor. The legal definition of sexually explicit conduct does not require that an image depict a child engaging in sexual activity. A picture of a naked child may constitute illegal child pornography if it is sufficiently sexually suggestive (Office of Law Revision Counsel of the US House of Representatives, 2017). See the *Citizen's Guide to U.S. Federal Law on Child Pornography* for more information.

10. The greatest increase was reported for incidents of sexual interference, which is the act of touching any person under the age of 16 for sexual purposes.

11. Statistics Canada does not delineate between online child pornography and offline child pornography.

12. The increase in the rate of sexual violations against children may be partly attributable to the effects on data classification of the July 2015 implementation of Bill C-26. The Tougher Penalties for Child Predators Act increased the maximum penalties for most types of sexual violations against children. As crime statistics are reported based on the most serious offense as determined by the maximum penalty, legislative changes such as Bill C-26, which increase maximum penalties, can contribute to an increase in official statistics for violations affected.

13. Commercial sexual exploitation of children involves crimes of a sexual nature committed against a child victim for financial or other economic reasons (Development Services Group, Inc., 2014).

14. In Williams, Elliott, and Beech's (2013) study, the authors explain how the grooming process is often used to lower a child's inhibitions with the ultimate goal of meeting offline and sexually abusing them.

15. Please refer to S.C. 2014, c.31, for more information.

16. In the past, youth could be charged and convicted for accessing, production, possession, and distribution of child pornography, as the law applies to "every person", not limited to adults only.

17. The researchers conducted a total of 2,474 online interviews in the US with youth ages 10–23. To participate in the study, respondents were required to use the Internet for a minimum of 1 hour a day.

18. To mitigate the risk within your child-serving organization, please refer to the Commit to Kids program (available through the Canadian Centre for Child Protection), which is a step-by-step plan to help prevent sexual abuse (additional details available in the Prevention and Intervention Strategies section).

19. In January 2016, the Canadian Centre for Child Protection launched an international survey for adult survivors whose child sexual abuse was recorded and was, or may have been, distributed online. One hundred and fifty survivors participated in the survey (85% female). For 87% of the survivors, the abuse began at the age of 11 or younger, and 56% between the ages of 0 and 4. In terms of the origins of the respondents, 48% were from the Netherlands, 17% from Germany, 11% from Canada, 11% from the United States, and 10% were from other countries in Europe.

20. It is important to always remember that this does not mean that victims could have done anything in particular to avoid being victimized. Children and youth are never to be blamed for their victimization.

21. Offenses include online enticement of children for sexual acts, extra-familial child sexual molestation, child pornography, transnational child sex offenses, child sex trafficking, unsolicited obscene materials sent to a child, misleading domain names, and misleading words or digital images on the Internet.
22. http://mediasmarts.ca/digital-media-literacy/digital-issues/sexual-exploitation
23. See www.kidshelpphone.ca/Teens/InfoBooth/Violence-and-Abuse/online-sexual-exploitation-abuse.aspx for more information or call a counselor at 1–800–668–6868.
24. See www.childhelp.org/hotline/ for more information or call a counselor at 1–800–422–4453.

References

American Psychiatric Association. (2013). *Diagnostic and statistical manual of mental disorders: DSM-V* (5th ed.). Arlington, VA: American Psychiatric Association.

Canadian Centre for Child Protection. (2012a). *The changing face of safety education*. Retrieved November 30, 2017, from www.kidsintheknow.ca/pdfs/KIK_StrangerDanger_en.pdf

Canadian Centre for Child Protection. (2012b). *Parent guide: Commit to kids*. Winnipeg, Canada: Canadian Centre for Child Protection.

Canadian Centre for Child Protection. (2014). *Child sexual abuse—It's your business*. Winnipeg, Canada: Canadian Centre for Child Protection.

Canadian Centre for Child Protection. (2017a). *How to talk to youth about sextortion: Safety sheet*. Winnipeg, Canada: Canadian Centre for Child Protection.

Canadian Centre for Child Protection. (2017b). *Survivor's survey full report 2017*. Winnipeg, Canada: Canadian Centre for Child Protection.

Cohen-Almagor, R. (2013). Online child sex offenders: Challenges and counter-measures. *The Howard Journal of Criminal Justice, 52(2)*, 190–215.

Collins, M. (2012). *Testimony of Michelle Collins (National Center for Missing & Exploited Children) before the U.S. Sentencing Commission*. February 15, 2012. Retrieved from www.ussc.gov/sites/default/files/pdf/amendment-process/public-hearings-and-meetings/20120215-16/Testimony_15_Collins.pdf

Cooper, A. (1998). Sexuality and the Internet: Surfing into the new millennium. *CyberPsychology and Behaviour, 1(2)*, 181–187.

Cooper, S. W., Estes, R. J., Giardino, A. P., Kellog, N. D., & Vieth, V. I. (2005). *Medical, legal & social science aspects of child sexual exploitation: A comprehensive review of pornography, prostitution and Internet crimes*. St. Louis, MO: G.W. Medical Publishing Inc.

Cotter, A., & Beaupré, P. (2014). Police-reported sexual offences against children and youth in Canada, 2012. Component of Statistics Canada catalogue no. 85-002-X, Juristat, ISSN 1209-6393.

Craven, S., Brown, S., & Gilchrist, E. (2006). Sexual grooming of children: Review of literature and theoretical considerations. *Journal of Sexual Aggression, 12(3)*, 287–299.

Cybertip.ca. (n.d.). *Self/Peer exploitation*. Retrieved November 23, 2017, from www.cybertip.ca/app/en/internet_safety-self_peer_exploitation

Denov, M. (2003). The myth of innocence: Sexual scripts and the recognition of child sexual abuse by female perpetrators. *The Journal of Sex Research, 40*, 303–328.

Department of Children and Families. (2014). *The grooming process.* Agency of Human Services. Retrieved October 2, 2015, from www.dcf.vermont.gov

Department of Justice. (2016). *Department of Justice Releases the 2016 National Strategy for child exploitation prevention and interdiction.* Retrieved January 21, 2017, from www.justice.gov/opa/pr/department-justice-releases-2016-national-strategy-child-exploitation-prevention-and

Department of Justice. (2017). *Citizen's guide to U.S. federal law on child pornography.* Retrieved January 21, 2017, from www.justice.gov/criminal-ceos/citizens-guide-us-federal-law-child-pornography

Development Services Group, Inc. (2014). *Commercial sexual exploitation of children/sex trafficking. Literature review.* Washington, DC: Office of Juvenile Justice and Delinquency Prevention.

Douglas, E. M., & Finkelhor, D. (2005). *Childhood sexual abuse fact sheet May 2005.* Durham, NC: Crimes against Children Research Center, University of New Hampshire.

Europol. (2017). *Online sexual coercion and extortion as a form of crime affecting children: Law enforcement perspective.* The Hague, the Netherlands: European Union Agency for Law Enforcement Cooperation.

Finkelhor, D., & Browne, A. (1985). The traumatic impact of child sexual abuse: A conceptualization. *American Journal of Orthopsychiatry, 55*(4), 530–541.

Gil, E. (1988). *Treatment of adult survivors of childhood abuse.* Walnut Creek, CA: Launch Press.

Global Alliance Secretariat. (2015). *Global Alliance against child sexual abuse online: Threat assessment report.* Retrieved from https://ec.europa.eu/home-affairs/sites/homeaffairs/files/what-we-do/policies/organized-crime-and-human-trafficking/global-alliance-against-child-abuse/docs/global_alliance_threat_assessment.pdf

Greijer, S., & Doek, J. (2016). *Terminology guidelines for the protection of children from sexual exploitation and sexual abuse.* Adopted by the Interagency Working Group in Luxembourg, 28 January 2016, ECPAT Luxembourg, Bangkok, Thailand.

Gries, L., Goh, D., Andrews, M., Gilbert, J., Praver, F., & Stelzer, D. (2000). Positive reaction to disclosure and recovery from child sexual abuse. *Journal of Child Sexual Abuse, 9,* 29–51.

Hanna, J. (March 12, 2017). *What can you do if someone posts an explicit images of you online.* Retrieved from www.cnn.com/2017/03/12/us/nonconsensual-or-revenge-porn-recourse-trnd/index.html

Healy, M. (2004). Child pornography: An international perspective. *Computer Crime Research Centre.* Retrieved from www.crime-research.org/articles/536/4

Hindman, J. (1999). *Just before dawn: From the shadows of tradition to new reflections in trauma assessment and treatment of sexual victimization.* Ontario, Oregon: AlexAndria Associates.

Interpol. (2015). *Appropriate terminology.* Retrieved October 10, 2015, from www.interpol.int/Crime-areas/Crimes-against-children/Appropriate-terminology

Ipsos Reid. (2012). *The Ipsos Canadian Inter@ctive Reid Report 2012 fact guide: The definitive resource on Canadians and the Internet.* Toronto, ON: Ipsos.

Johnson, M., Steeves, V., Shade, L., & Foran, G. (2017). *To share of not to share: How teens make privacy decisions about photos on social media.* Ottawa, ON: MediaSmarts.

Keighley, K. (2017). *Police-reported crime statistics in Canada, 2016.* Ottawa, ON: Canadian Centre for Justice Statistics. Juristat, ISSN 1209–6393.

Knoll, J. (2010). Teacher sexual misconduct: Grooming patterns and female offenders. *Journal of Child Sexual Abuse, 19,* 371–386.

Lenhart, A. (2015). *Teens, social media and technology overview.* Washington, DC: Pew Research Center.

Lorenzo-Dus, N., & Izura, C. (2017). " Cause ur special " : Understanding trust and complimenting behaviour in online grooming discourse. *Journal of Pragmatics, 112,* 68–82.

Maczewski, M. (2002). Exploring identities through the internet: Youth experiences online. *Child & Youth Care Forum, 31*(2), 111–129.

Madden, M., Lenhart, A., Cortesi, S., Gasser, U., Duggan, M., & Smith, A. (2013). *Teens, social media and privacy.* Washington, DC: Pew Internet and American Life Project.

Martin, G. (2017). *Stranger danger.* Retrieved from www.phrases.org.uk/meanings/stranger-danger.html

Martellozzo, E., Nehring, D., & Taylor, H. (2010). Online child sexual abuse by female offenders: An Exploratory study. *International Journal of Cyber Criminology (IJCC). Jan-July 2010, July-December 2010 (Combined Issue), 4*(1–2), 592–609.

McAfee. (2013). *Digital deception: Exploring the online disconnect between parents and kids.* Retrieved from www.businesswire.com/news/home/20130604005125/en/America's-Youth-Admit-Surprising-Online-Behaviour-Change

McGuire, M., & Dowling, S. (2013). Cybercrime: A review of the evidence. *Home Office Research Report 75.* Retrieved October 10, 2015, from www.gov.uk/government/uploads/system/uploads/attachment_data/file/246749/horr75-summary.pdf

Media Awareness Net. (2000). *Canada's children in a wired world: The parent's view.* Retrieved September 29, 2014, from www.media-awareness.ca

National Center for Missing and Exploited Children. (2015). *Annual report.* Retrieved from www.missingkids.com/content/dam/ncmec/en_us/publications/ncmec2015.pdf

National Center for Missing and Exploited Children. (2016). *Sextortion fact sheet.* Retrieved from www.missingkids.com/content/dam/ncmec/en_us/documents/sextortionfactsheet.pdf

Office of Law Revision Counsel of the US House of Representatives. (2017). *United States Code.*

Public Safety Canada. (2015). *2013–2014 Evaluation of the national strategy for the protection of children from sexual exploitation on the internet: Final report.* Retrieved from https://www.publicsafety.gc.ca/cnt/rsrcs/vltn-prtctn-chldrn-2013-14/vltn-prtctn-chldrn-2013-14-eng.pdf

Quayle, E., Allegro, S., Hutton, L., Sheath, M., & Lööf, L. (2014). Rapid skill acquisition and online sexual grooming of children. *Computers in Human Behaviour, 39,* 368–375.

Roesler, T. (1994). Reactions to disclosure of childhood sexual abuse: The effect on adult symptoms. *The Journal of Nervous and Mental Disease, 182,* 618–624.

Salter, M., & Richters, J. (2012). Organised abuse: A neglected category of sexual abuse with significant lifetime mental healthcare sequelae. *Journal of Mental Health, 21*(5), 499–508.

Shoop, R. (2003). *Sexual exploitation in schools: How to spot it and stop it.* Thousand Oaks, CA: Corwin Press.

Sinclair, R., & Sugar, D. (2005). *Internet based sexual exploitation of children and youth. Environmental scan.* Ottawa, ON: The National Child Exploitation Coordination Centre.

Sinclair, R., Serapiglia, M., Wittreich, A., Murphy, L., & Goyette, R. (2010). *IT-enabled sexual exploitation of children and youth. Environmental Scan.* Ottawa, ON: Canadian Police Centre for Missing and Exploited Children.

Smallbone, S., & Wortley, L. (2011). Victim resistance in child sexual abuse: A look into the efficacy of self-protection strategies based on the offender's experience. *Journal of Interpersonal Violence, 26*(9), 1868–1883.

Steeves, V. (2014). *Young Canadians in a wired world, Phase III: Online privacy, online publicity.* Ottawa, ON: MediaSmarts.

Tanner, J., & Brake, S. (2013). *Exploring sex offender grooming.* Retrieved September 5, 2015, from www.kbsolutions.com/Grooming.pdf

Thorn. (2014). *Redefining "child pornography".* Retrieved from https:www.wearethorn.org/blog/redefining-child-pornography/

Truman, J., Langton, L., & Planty, M. (2013). *Criminal victimization 2012.* Washington, DC: US Department of Justice. Office of Justice Programs Bureau of Justice Statistics.

United Nations Children's Fund. (2017). *Children in a digital world.* Retrieved from https://www.unicef.org/publications/files/SOWC_2017_ENG_WEB.pdf

United Nations Office on Drugs and Crime. (2015). *Study on the effects of new information technologies on the abuse and exploitation of children.* Retrieved October 13, 2015, from www.unodc.org/documents/commissions/CCPCJ/CCPCJSessions/CCPCJ_23/E-CN15-2014-CRP1_E.pdf

Williams, T. (2013). *Social media: An investigative and criminal tool.* Sacramento, CA: Western States Information Network.

Williams, T., Elliott, I., & Beech, A. (2013). Identifying sexual grooming themes used by Internet sex offenders. *Deviant Behaviour, 34*(2), 135–152.

Wolak, J., Finkelhor, D., Mitchell, K., & Ybarra, M. (2008). Online predators and their victims: Myths, realities, and implications for prevention and treatment. *American Psychologist, 63*(2), 111–128.

Wolak, J., & Finkelhor, D. (2016). *Sextortion: Findings from a survey of 1,631 victims.* Crimes Against Children Research Center, in partnership with Thorn. Durham, NH: University of New Hampshire.

Using a Trauma-Informed Lens to Understand and Implement Evidence-Based Practices with Children Experiencing Disruptive Behavior in School and Beyond

7

Leena Augimeri, Erin Rajca, Monique Verpoort, Andrea Blackman, and Margaret Walsh

> *When people look at me, they see a liar. A troublemaker. A lost cause. They see my outbursts. My dirty looks. My frustration. People see the girl who gets sent home from school.*
>
> *And the girl you wouldn't leave alone with your purse. People see a mean sister. The way I swear at my mom. And the kid who leaves her mom crying in the parking lot. People see all these things. But they don't see me. My name is Maria. And I can be more than this.*
>
> (Child Development Institute, 2016)

We need to pay attention to our children, especially children like Maria who are experiencing disruptive behavior problems. Such issues can impact the individual child, their parents/caregivers, family, school, and community. If left undetected or unnoticed, it can lead to serious consequences and, in some cases, death. Over the years, there have been more accounts of school violence and victimization, and the traumatic impact it is having on students, educators, families, and the community. Often, in the aftermath, we hear such statements as, "We knew he/she was a problem since elementary school". So it behooves us to think about processes and support mechanisms for schools and educators to ensure our children are kept safe in school and out of trouble.

Today, educators need to be both knowledgeable and skilled in risk identification and behavior management. It is not that disruptive behaviors, such as aggression, are new to the school culture—rather, it is the intensity, severity, and variety of methods used (e.g., cyberbullying, assault, and gun violence) that are of major concern (Augimeri & Walsh, 2013); such behaviors often have an incubation period. Research shows us there are 7 years of warning before a young child age 7 becomes a serious violent and chronic offender at age 14 ½ (Loeber, Farrington, & Petechuk, 2003).

Our own research and clinical experience has demonstrated the importance of building strong and healthy relationships and support systems for all children, especially those classified as being high risk (Augimeri, Jiang, Koegl, & Carey, 2006; Augimeri, Pepler, Walsh, & Kivlenieks, 2017). For many children, the school system may be the only place and means to access services (Hoagwood, Burns, Kiser, Ringeisen, & Schoenwald, 2001). For these children, having even one adult in their lives who cares can be the most important factor in determining what the future will hold, and in many cases, this is their teacher (Sabol & Pianta, 2012).

Applying early prevention principles/approaches is required. We need to recognize, acknowledge and act on the early warning signs and ensure that schools are equipped with the right resources and strategies to deal effectively with mental health issues, serious disruptive behavior problems, and trauma. This chapter discusses serious disruptive behavior problems and the trauma associated with escalating violence.

Establishing a Common Definition of Disruptive Behavior Problems

What constitutes a childhood "disruptive behavior problem"? Disruptive behaviors are an often widespread issue across settings, including home and school (Fergusson, Boden, & Horwood, 2009; Little, Hudson, & Wilks, 2000). Oppositional, aggressive, antisocial, and delinquent behaviors all represent categories of disruptive behaviors (Matthys & Lochman, 2016). Some forms of these, such as disobedience (Kalb & Loeber, 2003), arise at various points in time with many children as part of a typical developmental process. As caregivers, educators, and others working closely with children, it is obvious that not every undesirable behavior can be pathologized. As Matthys and Lochman (2016, p. 18) point out, "All children sometimes refuse to comply. And a lot of children occasionally get involved in fights".

There has been a strong push for programming to support educators and provide the necessary tools and strategies for managing these behaviors effectively within the classroom (Marlow et al., 2015). In some cases, however, it may be necessary to identify when a particular student is in need of additional support both within and outside of school. Research has identified that rates of trauma are significant in families of children with an early history of disruptive behavior problems (Cohen, Berliner, & Mannarino, 2010; Thomas & Guskin, 2001; Vachon, Krueger, Rogosch, & Cicchetti, 2015). Often, this type of behavior represents a chronic failure of the self-regulatory system, including difficulty regulating emotions (e.g., persistent irritability, moodiness, or frustration; Cavanagh, Quinn, Duncan, Graham, & Balbuena, 2017), and/or the inability to practice effortful control (e.g., shifting attention from negative to neutral or positive thoughts or inhibiting inappropriate behavior; Eisenberg, Spinrad, & Eggum, 2010). Distinguishing between concerning behavioral patterns that include the effects of trauma and those that occur as a natural part of social and emotional development, and responding effectively, is important for reasons we explore throughout this chapter.

Oppositional Defiant Disorder and Conduct Disorder

In defining what constitutes a disruptive behavior problem in children, it is important to include discussion of the two most frequently associated disorders: oppositional defiant disorder (ODD) and conduct disorder (CD). As you will see, a great deal of what we know about disruptive behavior problems comes from research with children and adolescents who have been classified as having either ODD or CD.

ODD typically appears earlier than CD, and is characterized by a persistent pattern of angry/irritable mood, argumentative/defiant behavior, or vindictiveness (American Psychiatric Association, 2013). Within the classroom, this can manifest as frequent arguments with or challenges to teachers and other authority figures, rule-breaking, or an excessive temper. In some children, there is a progression from ODD to CD (Rowe, Costello, Angold,

Copeland, & Maughan, 2010). CD is characterized by more extreme behaviors and tends to be antisocial in nature (Scott, 2015). For this reason, it is less common in younger children, although it does sometimes occur, and in these instances, should be a red flag for a particularly troubling trajectory (Moffitt et al., 2008). CD is underscored by repeated transgressions with respect to the rules, rights of others, or basic social norms. This includes aggression to people and animals, destruction of property, deceitfulness and theft, and serious violations of rules (American Psychiatric Association, 2013). Within the context of the classroom, engaging in frequent cruelty, bullying, or meanness towards others is a particularly important warning sign that should not be ignored (Jiang, Walsh, & Augimeri, 2011).

ODD and CD present as a pattern of behavior that violates the rights of others or results in significant conflict with societal norms or authority figures (American Psychiatric Association, 2013). Together, they represent one of the most pervasive issues in children's mental health (Hinshaw & Lee, 2003). Based on data from international samples, prevalence rates are estimated to fall between 5% and 8%, with boys outnumbering girls (this is at least partially due to the criteria used to diagnose these disorders; Scott, 2015). Their effects can and often do permeate nearly every aspect of an affected child's life, perhaps none more so than within the realm of interactions and relationships with others. This assures that the burden of these problems will be felt by families, teachers, and broader communities.

What IS and Is NOT a Disruptive Behavior Problem?

The term "disruptive behavior problem" was chosen intentionally for the purposes of this chapter, rather than the disorders it typifies. More often than not, those of us working closely with affected children do so in the absence of a diagnosis. More important than labeling is the ability to recognize warning signs that place a child at risk, especially those who have also experienced trauma, and in turn know what to do about them.

In determining the severity of a disruptive behavior problem (namely, whether it poses a substantial risk to the child and therefore warrants intervention), the frequency, intensity, and duration of the problem are good indicators (Charach, Bélanger, McLennan, & Nixon, 2017; Frick & Nigg, 2012). These factors can help distinguish behavior that is part of normative development from a more serious problem. Some disruptive behaviors emerge from a young age, as early as preschool, and remain relatively stable (Scott, Augimeri, & Fifield, 2017). Some researchers argue that pervasiveness across settings can be an additional red flag; children who exhibit problematic behaviors across contexts may be susceptible to higher levels of maladjustment (Frick & Nigg, 2012).

When the behavior lasts for 6 months or longer, exceeds what would be expected for that child's age, gender, and culture, and causes distress to the child or others, or interferes with academic or social functioning, this would be considered problematic through a diagnostic lens (American Psychiatric Association, 2013). As you will see in the section that follows, when behavior falls outside of what would be expected from a typically developing child, the reasons for this can be quite complex.

The Nature of Disruptive Behavior Problems

Early Risk Factors

There is still much to learn about the factors contributing to disruptive behavior problems in children. A great deal of research has been dedicated to this topic; however, there remains a strong need to separate factors that actually cause these problems from those merely associated with them (Murray & Farrington, 2010). For example, the effects of poverty, a well-known correlate, seem to act indirectly by affecting parenting practices, which in turn influence child behavior (Murray & Farrington, 2010). With respect to this, parenting styles and practices appear to be major influences in the development and maintenance of these problems, and are a strong focus of intervention programs aimed at addressing them. Studies investigating this association typically highlight problems with parent-child attachment, harsh and inconsistent discipline practices, and lack of parental warmth (reviewed in Matthys & Lochman, 2016; Scott, 2015). There is also strong support for the existence of a coercive cycle, (others may refer to as a reinforcement trap), between parent and child, whereby the child's behavior elicits negative reactions from the parent, and these reactions in turn perpetuate further unwanted behaviors (Patterson, 1982). Other implicated environmental factors include maltreatment and exposure to adverse events/trauma (Carliner, Gary, McLaughlin, & Keyes, 2017), which we discuss later in this section.

Although not an exhaustive list, together these environmental factors may strongly influence any temperamental and genetic elements, such that the combination is much more likely to produce disruptive behavior problems than genes or temperament alone (reviewed in Scott et al., 2015). Critically, it appears there is also a cumulative effect of risk factors, meaning that the more risks experienced by the child, the worse the prognosis (van der Laan, Veenstra, Bogaerts, Verhulst, & Ormel, 2010).

School Factors

There are a myriad of school factors that can exert perception of and influence over problem behaviors. For one, there seems to be a significant link between overall school climate and problem behaviors (Gottfredson, Gottfredson, Payne, & Gottfredson, 2005; Reaves, McMahon, Duffy, & Ruiz, 2018). Classroom atmosphere (namely, the level of disruption during academic time, use of problem solving during conflicts, adherence to rules, teacher responsiveness to students' needs and feelings, and level of teacher criticism versus supportiveness) has been shown to hold significant influence over aggressive and disruptive behaviors within the classroom (Thomas, Bierman, Thompson, Powers, & The Conduct Problems Prevention Research Group 2008). With respect to the impact of teachers, it appears that positive relationships with students can help mitigate the risks associated with disruptive behaviors. Teachers who reduce their use of negative remarks, for example, can help their students increase on-task behavior and decrease talking out (Leflot, van Lier, Onghena, & Colpin, 2010). When teachers are trained to support their students with social-emotional learning, these pupils demonstrate more positive social behavior, fewer problem and conduct behaviors, and better overall academic performance (Durlak, Weissberg, Dymnicki, Taylor, & Schellinger, 2011). An example of this would be a student who is coached to become aware of the triggers, body cues, feelings, and unhelpful thoughts that lead to poor choices. Being made aware of the early indicators that suggest this student is becoming emotionally aroused (e.g., clenched jaw, red face) can serve to remind the child that options to stay calm are available (see Appendix 7.1, SNAP Learning Log, for details).

Links to Trauma

As stated earlier, for children with a history of problematic and persistent behavioral issues, trauma is a significant factor (Cohen et al., 2010; Thomas & Guskin, 2001; Vachon et al., 2015), although prevalence differs depending on the definition of trauma used. As part of a recent initiative to create a unified concept and guidelines for trauma-informed care, the Substance Abuse and Mental Health Services Administration (SAMHSA), a branch of the US

Department of Health and Human Services, established the following defi-nition: "Individual trauma results from an event, series of events, or set of circumstances that is experienced by an individual as physically or emotion-ally harmful or life threatening and that has lasting adverse effects on the individual's functioning and mental, physical, social, emotional, or spiritual well-being" (Huang et al., 2014, p. 7). Key to this definition are the "three E's": the *event*, which is the threat of, or exposure to, physical or psychologi-cal harm; the *experience*, which can differ between individuals exposed to the same event; and the lasting adverse *effects* (Huang et al., 2014, p. 8).

Adverse Childhood Experiences

One of our best sources regarding the impact of childhood trauma on mental health, including disruptive behavior problems, comes from a long-term US research study known as the Adverse Childhood Experiences (ACE) study. More than 17,000 participants were recruited and reported on three categories of past childhood trauma exposure: abuse, serious family dysfunction, and neglect (Felitti et al., 1998). Importantly, this study established a graded rela-tionship between early adverse experiences and later outcomes. This means that for each additional experience of early trauma, the risks for later prob-lems increased significantly. In the ACE study, those who had experienced four or more early adversities were up to 12 times more likely to experience later physical and mental health problems than those who had experienced none (Felitti et al., 1998). The results have confirmed a robust connection between early traumatic exposure and a multitude of significant, life-long impacts. Subsequent studies examining early adverse experiences have linked these to behavior difficulties and disorders, mood and anxiety problems and disorders, and academic difficulties (Carr, Martins, Stingel, Lemgruber, & Juruena, 2013; Fergusson et al., 2009; Porche, Fortuna, Lin, & Alegria, 2011). Moreover, there is a strong connection between ACE scores and serious, violent, and chronic offending (Fox et al., 2015).

Post-Traumatic Stress Disorder

Post-traumatic stress disorder (PTSD), which represents the most common measure of dysfunctional trauma response and the only one formerly rec-ognized, is identified at a much higher rate in individuals with CD (Bern-hard, Martinelli, Ackermann, Saure, & Freitag, 2018). Maltreatment, which is one form of traumatic exposure linked to PTSD, has been shown to confer significant odds of developing maladaptive behaviors congruent with ODD and CD, including rule-breaking, aggression, and disruptive behaviors (Jaffee et al., 2005; Vachon et al., 2015) and with developing CD itself (Bernhard et al., 2018). Moreover, exposure to various forms of potentially traumatic events known to cause PTSD, in particular interpersonal violence (Carliner et al., 2017) and polyvictimization (wherein the individual is the victim of more than one form of trauma; Ford & Blaustein, 2013), have been strongly associated with later behavioral problems.

Complex Trauma

Still, there are some researchers who feel that the early traumatic experiences often endured by children with disruptive behavior problems do not get considered under the definition of PTSD (Cook et al., 2005; D'Andrea, Ford, Stolbach, Spinazzola, & van der Kolk, 2012; van der Kolk, 2005). In an effort to more broadly address the multitude of traumatic experiences (Cook et al., 2005; van der Kolk, 2005) for children, the term "complex trauma" was coined, which includes "multiple, chronic, and prolonged, developmentally adverse traumatic events, most often of an interpersonal nature and early-life onset" (van der Kolk, 2005, p. 402).

This is important because in the view of complex trauma, many of the established risk factors for disruptive behavior problems have the potential to be indicative of trauma or are likely to increase risk for traumatization. Complex trauma often involves a breakdown of the caregiving system relied upon by the child, wherein the caretaker is either unable to support the child in the demands of coping with overwhelming traumatic stress, or is in fact the source of that stress (van der Kolk, 2005). Harsh and inconsistent parenting has been consistently linked to elevated risk of developing a disruptive behavior problem (Murray & Farrington, 2010; Scott, 2015). Critically, it has also been associated with a breakdown in the capacity for self-regulation (Bridgett, Burt, Edwards, & Deater-Deckard, 2015), a core construct underlying both complex trauma (van der Kolk, 2005) and disruptive behavior problems (Woltering & Shi, 2016).

Self-Regulation

Poor self-regulation is thought to be a core construct underlying antisocial and disruptive behaviors (Rocque, Posick, & Piquero, 2016), and is strongly influenced by chronic, unmodulated stress during childhood (Blair, 2010; Felitti & Anda, 2010; Kim & Cicchetti, 2010; Thompson, 2014). Generally, there is a lack of consensus regarding a clear definition of self-regulation, with various disciplines (e.g., psychology, criminology) operationalizing the term in many different ways or using it interchangeably with self-control (McClelland et al., 2018; Shanker, 2010). Recognizing the importance of a functional definition of self-regulation for teachers and researchers alike, Shanker (2010, p. 4) suggests that it can be thought of simply as the "ability to stay calmly focused and alert", and although this includes self-control, it cannot be boiled down to this element alone. There is general agreement that self-regulation includes a number of functional components, including self-control and emotion regulation (Bridgett et al., 2015; Eisenberg et al., 2010; McClelland et al., 2018), and can be thought of as an "umbrella" construct. Critically, self-regulation capacity can largely determine the way in which a child integrates information and behaves. Self-control, for example, plays a considerable role in decision-making and behavior, and has been largely implicated in research on delinquency and criminality, wherein a deficit is thought to underlie many criminal careers (Gottfredson & Hirschi, 1990). In children, impulsive aggression, hyperactivity, lack of persistence, low-frustration tolerance, inattention, and impulsivity are all indicators of poor self-regulation/control (Moffitt et al., 2011); these traits have been found to predict adult outcomes such as poorer overall health, reduced wealth, and crime (Moffitt et al., 2011).

The behaviors and practices of caregivers appear in many cases to account for variations in children's abilities to self-regulate (Bridgett et al., 2015). This is in addition to many other factors within the overall child rearing environment that can either facilitate or hinder the potential development of self-regulation skills, including dysfunctional or chaotic relationships within the home and low socio-economic status (Bridgett et al., 2015). According to Duckworth and colleagues (2014), the capacity for self-regulation does not develop by chance. Rather, it is the modeling and support of well-regulated adults—including parents and teachers—that allow for adaptive self-regulation to emerge.

In children with disruptive behavior problems, there is unfortunately a strong tendency towards dysregulation that often results in "fight, flight, or freeze" reactions when dealing with seemingly innocuous or non-threatening situations (Woltering & Lewis, 2013). Although these reactions may seem unelicited or unprovoked to observers, it is important to understand that in cases in which there has been excessive exposure to overwhelming stress and trauma, these reactions may represent attempts to cope, and must be reframed this way to address them effectively (Fallot & Bebout, 2012). Programs aimed at addressing deficits in self-regulation/control in children with disruptive behavior problems have demonstrated considerable success (e.g., The Incredible Years, Triple P Parenting, and Nurse Family Partnerships—Piquero et al., 2016; Stop Now And Plan [SNAP®]—Augimeri, Walsh, Donato, Blackman, Piquero, 2017).

Short- and Long-Term Consequences of Disruptive Behavior Problems

The importance of addressing disruptive behavior problems, and doing so as early as possible, cannot be overstated. For some children, these problems may appear as early as preschool and demonstrate considerable stability over time (Scott, Augimeri, & Fifield, 2017). Early onset tends to signal a particularly troubling trajectory, with pervasive negative effects on overall quality of life lasting well into adolescence and early adulthood (Erskine et al., 2016; Fergusson, Horwood, & Ridder, 2005; Kretschmer et al., 2014; Odgers et al., 2008; Wertz et al., 2018). Although it may sometimes seem like there are few options but to wait until these behaviors resolve themselves or are "outgrown", decades of research on the subject has taught us that the consequences of doing so make this a seriously ill-advised approach.

Within the context of the classroom, these behaviors can compromise the quality of education and take a substantial toll on teachers, representing a significant source of distress and burnout. In some cases, educators may feel they have no option but to resort to discipline measures such as detention, suspension, and expulsion, resulting in even more lost instructional time (Reaves, McMahon, Duffy, & Ruiz, 2018). Often, the challenge of providing support to these children must be reconciled with an absence of adequate assistance or training (Lang, Marlow, Goodman, Meltzer, & Ford, 2013).

A New Zealand study involving over 1,200 young children (ages 7–9) who exhibited serious conduct problems showed that those who ranked in the top 5% according to severity were up to ten times more likely to be involved with crime and deviance in young adulthood (up to age 25). These individuals had significantly elevated patterns of violent offenses, arrests / convictions, and imprisonment (Fergusson et al., 2005). This helps to explain the large overrepresentation of individuals who meet criteria for disruptive behavior disorders within the criminal justice system (Teplin, Abram, McClelland, Dulcan, & Mericle, 2002; Underwood & Washington, 2016), many of whom have complex trauma histories (Ford, Chapman, Connor, & Cruise, 2012), and represents a massive cost to society (Cohen & Piquero, 2009).

Of no less importance, however, is the long list of consequences facing these individuals beyond the realm of delinquency. In terms of associated mental health outcomes, longitudinal evidence from children identified as having either ODD or CD has linked these to a variety of later life disorders, including substance use, depression, and anxiety (Kim-Cohen et al., 2003). A recent study found that children with moderate to severe conduct problems were at risk for poor functioning at age 18 across every measured outcome; these included everything from education/employment to weight, smoking, heavy drinking, suicide attempts, social isolation, and overall life satisfaction (Wertz et al., 2018). All of these outcomes were partially explained by the behavior itself, but were also found to be largely associated with exposure to familial risk factors (Wertz et al., 2018). This highlights once again the importance of strategies that not only address the problem behavior, but also take into account the number of complex factors that contribute to the emergence of these problems, including childhood adversity and trauma exposure.

Prevention and Intervention Strategies

Stop Now And Plan (SNAP®)

SNAP is an evidence-based children's mental health model designed for middle years children (ages 6–11) with serious disruptive behavior problems focusing on emotion regulation, self-control, and problem solving. The model is embedded within an eco-systemic framework, informed by five core theories (Cognitive Behavioral Theory, Feminist Theory, Social-Interactional Learning Theory, Attachment Theory, and Systems Theory), and delivered through a developmental lens (Rajca, Sewell, Levene, & Augimeri, 2018). The goal of SNAP is to teach children to stop and think before they act and make better choices "in the moment". Developed more than 3 decades ago (Augimeri, Pepler, Walsh, & Kivlenieks, 2017), SNAP is a multi-modal, gender-sensitive model grounded in the scientist-practitioner framework (Augimeri, Walsh, Levene, Sewell, & Rajca, 2014).

The SNAP approach/model promotes the importance of working with these children, their families, peers, and schools during the middle years, a critical developmental stage. Core and additional program components include a child cognitive/behavioral group, a concurrent parent group, individual child counseling/mentoring, family counseling, community connections, school advocacy, and teacher consultation. These are provided based on an individual assessment of the child and family's risk and needs. For each of these SNAP components, the focus is to reinforce the SNAP strategy skills across a variety of settings, increasing generalization.

The SNAP model was initiated in 1985 to fill a gap in services when Canada raised the age of criminal responsibility from 7 to 12 in 1984 with the introduction of the Young Offenders Act. During this period of time, social skills training programs for children with conduct problems were being instituted (e.g., McGinnis, Goldstein, Sprafkin, & Gershaw, 1984). SNAP took a multi-faceted approach to intervention that included a self-regulation and problem-solving skills group for children and their families in which the group leaders modeled cognition-based strategies for emotion regulation, self-control, and effective problem solving (see Hrynkiw-Augimeri, 1986; Hrynkiw-Augimeri, Pepler, & Goldberg, 1993). The cornerstone of the SNAP model is the SNAP technique that was originated from the Child Development Institute (CDI; formerly, Earlscourt Child and Family Centre) day treatment classroom for children with behavioral problems. In the classroom, the student support worker would "snap her fingers" to cue the students to begin regulating their emotions and begin the SNAP self-control process. This technique and subsequent model was formalized with the creation and publication of the original program manuals (e.g., Earlscourt Child and Family Centre, 1986a, 1986b, 1996a, 1996b; Child Development Institute, 2018a, 2018b) and was trademarked in 1998.

Since 1985, the SNAP program has had numerous internal and external evaluations that showed positive short- and long-term treatment effects (Augimeri, Farrington, Koegl, & Day, 2007; Burke & Loeber, 2015, 2016; Hrynkiw-Augimeri, 1986; Lipman et al., 2008; Pepler et al., 2010). SNAP reduces children's disruptive behavior (e.g., in terms of aggression, rule-breaking, conduct, and oppositional behavior) as well as depression and anxiety. In a recent large-scale randomized controlled trial, Burke and Loeber (2015, 2016) found that SNAP outperformed standard community services (STND; families in this condition were provided with wrap-around-services), and SNAP children showed increased social competencies and emotional regulation skills. Emotion regulation skills also predicted reduced anxious/depressed behaviors (Burke & Loeber, 2016). Further results indicated improved academic success, coping abilities, and community engagement; more effective parent management strategies; and more positive support systems (reviewed in Augimeri et al., 2014). In addition, neuroscience research has found that SNAP "improved ability to regulate task-focused behavior . . . perhaps because they are better able to stay on task in the face of frustration" (Woltering et al., 2011 p. 877) and reduce emotional arousal (Lewis et al., 2008). On a larger scale, participation in SNAP reduces police contact and involvement in the criminal justice system (Augimeri et al., 2006; Augimeri, Pepler, Walsh, Jiang, & Dassinger, 2010). A cost-benefit analysis (Farrington & Koegl, 2015) revealed that up to $31.77 is saved for every $1.00 spent on the SNAP program.

As noted in the SNAP program manuals, there are a number of steps to the SNAP technique that have been mapped onto the image of a stoplight—red light (STOP), yellow light (NOW AND), and green light (PLAN). These steps are used to teach children to regulate their emotions by first helping them deal with their body cues (e.g., by taking deep breaths, taking a step back, and/or counting to ten) (STOP); replace "hard thoughts with cool thoughts", which are realistic coping statements/cognitive restructuring to challenge negative and/or unrealistic thinking to help them remain calm (e.g., "this is hard but I can do this") (NOW AND); and generate effective solutions that meet these three criteria: (1) make their problems smaller instead of bigger; (2) feel okay about how they handled the situation; and (3) not hurt anyone, anything, or themselves (PLAN).

Due to the complexity of the presenting problems, SNAP has always maintained a holistic treatment approach, underscored by the importance of how self-regulation/control fit into a broader context of individual risk and protective factors (e.g., supportive school environment, nurturing and caring parents, positive peers; Augimeri et al., 2017). Treatment planning incorporates assessed risk and need and is anchored by the Early Assessment Risk Lists (EARL; EARL-20B for Boys—Augimeri, Koegl, Webster, & Levene, 2001; EARL-21G for Girls—Levene et al., 2001). Typically, the first step is to complete the EARL Pre-Checklist (EARL-PC; Augimeri, Walsh, Koegl, & Logue, 2013, a "concern" screener; see Appendix 7.2). The EARL-PC was specifically designed for educators and police to help ascertain if the child is in need of prevention/intervention programming. If the child is referred/recommended for mental health services, a more comprehensive structured professional judgment risk assessment using the Early Assessment Risk Lists should occur.

Currently, SNAP is replicated in 69 communities worldwide including Florida (11 cities state-wide through the Florida Network of Youth and Family Services), Pittsburgh, the Netherlands, Scotland, and the Cayman Islands. SNAP is now embarking on a cross-Canada expansion plan to reach over 100 communities, including schools. The SNAP National Implementation Strategy offers three options for service delivery. Level 1 is for the SNAP Boys and SNAP Girls full clinical program delivery that incorporates a continued-care model, working with the child and family up to the age of 18. Level 2 is a time-limited service delivery model that works with the child and family for 4–6 months, and Level 3 is a universal prevention model, SNAP in Schools. This program is delivered in classrooms to all children using the SNAP for Schools manual and/or app. This includes 13 classroom sessions facilitated by a designated trained staff—these are typically from an outside organization and/or a member of the school support team.

Next is a case example, "Maria", that demonstrates how the EARL-PC and SNAP strategies, using a trauma-informed lens and resources (e.g., SNAP Learning Log and SNAP Wheel of Self-Control and Plan), can be implemented in the classroom.

Maria

Maria is an 8-year-old girl who lives at home with her mother, sisters, and maternal grandparents. Mom reports that Maria's behavioral issues first became apparent when she was 7 (e.g., viewed as oppositional by her teacher and aggressive towards her mother and siblings). Maria's school attendance is a significant concern; on average, she attends two out of five school days a week. Most mornings, Maria becomes physically aggressive when her mother asks her to get ready. Maria says she does not like her teacher (Mr. B.), who yells at her when she does not do her work or follow class rules. Maria often runs out of the classroom to the school secretary. Mr. B. reports Maria's capacity to manage frustration and anger is lacking as evidenced by her stomping her feet, crying, and throwing objects. He further reports that she has difficulty making and maintaining friends due to her sporadic attendance. Mr. B. says peers avoid Maria because of her outbursts. He also describes her as immature—she sucks her thumb and whines when she does not get her own way. School administration has indicated that if Maria does not attend school regularly, they will contact Child Protection Services. Mom describes Maria as moody, has a hard time enjoying herself, and believes her daughter has poor self-esteem. She was recently diagnosed with attention deficit/hyperactivity disorder (ADHD) and has witnessed family violence. Mom left Maria's father when she was 3 years old. He has supervised access every second weekend, which can often be preceded by Maria having nightmares and difficulty sleeping.

Maria and her family live with her maternal grandparents in which there are different parenting styles. Grandparents endorse an authoritarian style (e.g., expect immediate compliance with little to no reward or praise, quick to punish for misbehavior), whereas Mom has more of a lenient and inconsistent parenting style. Mom reports feeling overwhelmed and lacking confidence. She sees the school (Mr. B. and administration) as a source of chronic stress. Mom says she feels resentful towards her daughter, as she cannot maintain a full-time job due to Maria's truancy; when Maria does attend school, Mom is often called to pick her up.

Assessment

As educators play a critical role in the early identification of at-risk children, the EARL-PC can help structure information and ascertain a level of "concern" to determine if a child like Maria and her family should be referred to children's mental health and/or community-based services. Even though it is recommended that Maria and her family access services, there are effective strategies that can be implemented in the classroom and school to support her, the teacher, and her peers.

Intervention Strategies in the School

The principles of trauma-informed practice (e.g., creating safety, fostering connection, managing emotion, and maximizing opportunities for choice and control) can be implemented in a school environment to guide how educators and administrators view, interact with, and ultimately respond to students.

Principle 1: Creating Safety

Students who have experienced trauma can exhibit a state of hypervigilance, and tend to scan their environments for potential threats. As in Maria's case, a loud noise, disapproving facial expression, raised voice, or any other aspect that is sensory in nature can act as "triggers". These triggers often elicit a fight-flight-freeze response, which may not be evident to other people in their midst and can leave educators wondering, "What is wrong with this child?"

A trauma-informed approach requires adopting a perspective in which Maria's behaviors are viewed as a coping mechanism to keep her safe from others (e.g., other students, teachers, administrators). Establishing safety in the classroom and nurturing the teacher-student relationship is key.

Safety in the Classroom

A consistent (e.g., clear routines and expectations), predictable (e.g., communicating with students about transitions), and nurturing (e.g., accepting, understanding, and supportive) environment can best support Maria and other students struggling to feel safe in the classroom and school community. Students and teachers can work together to identify a "safe place" where children can retreat to self-regulate, soothe, or comfort themselves.

Safety in the Student-Teacher Relationship

Given many children who struggle with self-regulation in a classroom environment may have experienced varying degrees of trauma, the question then becomes, "What happened to you?" rather than "What is wrong with you?" Reframing Maria's intent when she misbehaves is critical to enhancing trust and safety. When Maria leaves the classroom, is she attention-seeking, or is this a "flight" reaction in response to her teacher's raised voice? This increased empathy/enhanced perspective shifts the thinking from "this child is scary" to "this child is scared". This reframe can make all the difference in how an educator responds to a child, who may otherwise be viewed as "unlikeable" or "difficult".

Building trust also involves educators being aware of their assumptions and biases regarding the child's potential or lack thereof. For example, students who experience racialized trauma such as microaggressions may act out in response. These aggressions are defined as "brief, commonplace, and daily, verbal, behavioural, and environmental slights and indignities directed at members of Black communities, often automatically and unintentionally" (Sue, Capodilupo, & Holder, 2008, p. 329). Educators need to consider the possibility that children may have been scapegoated or targeted as a result of their race and/or culture (Sue et al., 2008).

Principle 2: Fostering Connections

Relationship building can be facilitated in a variety of ways. Meeting with the child and primary caregiver before the start of the school year to gauge the child's likes and dislikes can serve to humanize the teacher and minimize anxiety from the start. Asking caregiver(s) to identify strengths and needs of the child, and establish an open line of communication, can impart the message that both teacher and caregiver are on the same team.

Principle 3: Manage Emotions

Children who have been impacted by trauma often have difficulty effectively processing emotion, tolerating stress, and self-regulating. These children need assistance to help manage their emotions, which can be achieved by using SNAP emotion regulation strategies and coaching the child to self-regulate. In SNAP, this would involve engaging the child in a STOP skill, such as deep breathing. Educators may also choose to model and demonstrate the SNAP technique to encourage the child's skill-practice by using soothing tones and allowing for personal space.

Another area for consideration is being aware of the child's needs related to promoting self-regulation. Wherever possible, offering choices (e.g., opportunities for physical exertion and/or calming activities/environments) may also maximize the child's sense of control, something that is compromised when trauma is experienced.

Equally important is the acknowledgment that educators also need to manage their own emotions and prioritize self-care. This is where the SNAP strategy can be highly effective in helping educators increase their self-awareness and practice emotion regulation and self-control strategies. When teachers can identify their own triggers (e.g., noise level, interruptions), feelings (e.g., annoyance, irritation), body cues (e.g., red face, raised voice, increased heartbeat), and "hard thoughts" (e.g., "she's manipulative"; "he's attention seeking"), they are then in a better position to self-regulate, tolerate the child's difficult behaviors, and effectively engage a child in distress.

The use of the SNAP Learning Log and Wheels of Self-Control and Plans (Child Development Institute, 2017) are excellent tools to be used with teachers and students alike to promote self-reflection (see Appendix 7.3). The SNAP Learning Log was adapted from the Hassle Log (Glick & Goldstein, 1987) to help users begin to understand the link between a trigger, one's thoughts, feelings, and actions. The SNAP Learning Log can be used by an educator, student, classroom, parent/caregiver, or administrator. Assisting a student or themselves with self-reflection in a particular situation that led to a poor choice is an effective way for an educator to build self-awareness.

Implementation: How Might You Establish This in Your School or Youth Setting?

Implementing strategies for dealing with problem behaviors involves mobilization of resources at a multitude of levels, both within and outside of the classroom, ranging from the support and education of individual teachers to collaboration with community organizations and key government stakeholders (Augimeri, Pepler, et al., 2017). This is characterized by a systems approach, whereby teachers, administrators, and government work together to ensure resources meet children's needs (Augimeri & Walsh, 2013).

At the level of educators, it is critical to ensure that adequate training and resources are provided. Insufficient support is a common problem, despite the fact that these individuals are often expected to cope with disruptive behavior problems, and sets the stage for increased teacher stress, less effective classroom management strategies, increased potential for problematic behaviors, and teacher burnout (Brouwers & Tomic, 2000; Hastings & Bham, 2003; Skaalvik & Skaalvik, 2007; Webster-Stratton, Reid, & Hammond, 2001). Psychoeducation for teachers and administration around the impact of trauma on emotional, cognitive, social, and behavioral development needs to be a starting point. Teacher training also needs to be sustainable to enhance the support network for students and staff. Educators need to feel supported as well. Establishing a peer support network in which educators can access training, consultation, and self-care resources is encouraged.

Effective tools and strategies for behavior management training are essential, and have been shown to improve the behavior of students (Korpershoek, Harms, de Boer, van Kuijk, & Doolaard, 2016; Oliver, Wehby, & Reschly, 2011). Programs like SNAP for Schools may help teachers learn to recognize overlapping symptoms of traumatic stress as well as behavior difficulties (e.g., compromised emotion regulation, problematic parent-child relationships, peer relationships, physical problems, cognitive/academic difficulties). These typically take a universal prevention approach, targeting all students in the classroom versus only those who exhibit the most disruptive or extreme behaviors, and have four main targets to reach: (1) promotion of positive behaviors such as compliance and following established classroom rules and procedures; (2) prevention of problem behaviors such as talking at inappropriate times and fighting with peers; (3) teaching social and emotional skills such as conflict resolution, self-control, and problem solving; and (4) prevention of escalated angry behavior and acting out (Scott et al., 2017).

Moreover, the practice of risk identification and referral protocols should be strongly encouraged and specific training around this for teachers needs to occur. Risk/need assessments such as the EARLs help educators identify the level of concern/risk and what services are needed that exceeds a school's or educator's capabilities; in these instances, a student and their family can be connected with more intensive services, such as those offered by the clinical level of SNAP programs. A number of tools exist to support teachers in this endeavor and can be implemented in a school setting, including the EARL-PC, which has been previously discussed and demonstrated as an adapted tool for use in schools (Augimeri et al., 2013). This is meant to ensure that children with the highest level of risk and need who require services the most gain access through a formalized process, reducing the possibility of a child "slipping through the cracks".

Conclusion

In this chapter, we provided an overview of the impact of disruptive behavior and its relationship to trauma. Additionally, we offered a few "nuggets" that can be used within schools to help identify, manage, and, if needed, refer elementary school-aged children with serious and concerning disruptive behavior.

It has been recently reported that, "Every school shooter since 1990 had either mental health issues, suicidal thoughts, or extreme family problems" (Weinschenker, 2018). Therefore, we need to ensure that we can recognize the early warning signs so we can be proactive and help get these children to the doors of effective services to prevent serious violence, such as school shootings. Furthermore, schools need to have access to the right resources and strategies to deal effectively with mental health issues and serious disruptive behavior problems.

Applying early prevention principles / approaches are essential. Investing in sustainable programs that have proven to be effective, such as SNAP, as part of universal programming to the school curriculum can create a caring school culture by improving emotion regulation, self-control, and problem solving. Using evidence-based programming / strategies offers a means of eradicating aggression and violence and, most importantly, keeping our children safe, in school, and out of trouble. For this to work, we need to saturate schools with resources, support, specialized programs, and professionals trained to deal with the variety of complex issues such as trauma plaguing our children, families, and schools. It is important that we invest in school-based sustainable and promising programs targeting self-regulation and problem-solving skills that can enhance emotion regulation and self-control. Developing community partnerships (e.g., mental health centers, child welfare, police departments, recreation) will also help create a healthy and caring school culture whereby schools become the "heart and mind" of a community (Augimeri & Walsh, 2013).

Key Messages

What you need to know about children experiencing disruptive behavior problems from a trauma-informed lens:

1. Disruptive behavior detected and treated early can prevent serious consequences.
2. Self-regulation programs are highly effective for children with disruptive behavior problems.
3. Trauma is often a factor in families of children with disruptive behavior problems.
4. Positive relationships with students can help mitigate the risks.
5. Trauma-informed practices are transferable to a school environment.
6. Investing in sustainable proven programs can create a caring school culture.
7. Schools need resources, support, and training to deal with the complex issues.

Appendix 7.1

SNAP Learning Log

NAME _Maria_   DATE _April 9, 2018_

WHAT HAPPENED (EVENT)? _Maria ran out of the classroom_

WHEN WAS IT?	☒ Morning	☐ Afternoon	☐ Evening
WHERE WERE YOU?	☐ Home	☐ Work	☒ School ⊗ Classroom
	☐ Other _____		○ Recess
			○ Bus
WHO WAS INVOLVED?	☒ Child	☐ Partner	☐ My Parent
	☐ Teacher	☐ Boss	☐ Friend
	☐ Other _____		

TRIGGER (What set you off?)   _Teacher's loud voice; Being singled out_

I can't handle this/I am not okay/I can handle this/I am okay/other

WHAT WAS I THINKING?   _"Mr. Belaney hates me"_

Heart pounding/churning stomach/hot/tears/headache/fists/other

BODY CUES   _Red face; Heart pounding; Stomp feet_

Scared/angry/sad/tired/frustrated/confused/worried/other   *How strong was your feeling? 10 – 1*

FEELINGS   _Scared; Embarrassed_

Actions: negative or positive

WHAT DID I DO?   _Threw my lunch bag; Ran out of class_

On a scale of 1 (negative) to 10 (positive), how did I do? ● 1 — 2 — ③ — 4 — 5 — 6 — 7 — 8 — 9 — 10 ●

The Wheel of Self-Control and Plans can help you come up with STOPS, COOL THOUGHTS and PLANS to help keep your problem small.

Appendix 7.2

EARL-PC Form

CH✦LD
DEVELOPMENT
INSTITUTE

EARL-PC Form
Early Assessment Risk List – Pre Checklist
(Augimeri, Walsh, Jiang, Koegl, & Logue, 2013)
Development of the EARL-PC was funded in part by the Ontario Ministry of Public

---

Instructions

The EARL-PC is a general checklist designed specifically for those working with young children (under 12 years of age) to determine potential risk/concern for disruptive behaviour problems. Identifying high-risk children early and connecting them to appropriate services within their own community is imperative in improving their life chances. Given that police officers and or school personnel may often be a first point of contact for high risk children, their role is similar to that of a triage nurse in an emergency room. Key to such a process is the ability to do a quick assessment that determines level of risk, severity and need. To ensure effective response rates and positive crime prevention outcomes is how we see the proposed EARL-PC being utilized.

The EARL-PC guides users to exercise their best judgment in assessing areas of concern. When assessing the evidence, it is important to give the most weight to those circumstances which have had the greatest effect on the child (e.g., child's living situation improved substantially in the last year, however, previous to this, it was drastically unstable); therefore, users are encouraged to take into account the *totality* of impact on the family/child. Overall, the purpose of the EARL-PC is to determine appropriate community based services for these most at risk children.

The EARL-PC comprises of 18 items divided into two domains (Family and Child). Users evaluate and document the existence of each item as "Y" for *Yes*, which indicates that there is evidence for concern; "N" for *No*, the risk/concern is absent or "?" for unsure (not enough information). At the end of the Form, there is an opportunity for users to assign an overall level of risk concern: "low", "moderate" or "high". Use of the EARL-PC requires the gathering and documenting of sensitive information. Every effort should be made to keep confidential any information that could jeopardize the safety of the child. An accompanying EARL-PC Guide is available.

Please Note: The EARL-PC was adopted from the Early Assessment Risk Lists (EARL-20B for boys and the EARL-21G for girls). Those interested in conducting a thorough clinical risk assessment should use these original tools. The EARLs have been in use since 2001 by organizations that provide early intervention services for children with conduct problems (and their families), and schools/other organizations interested in assessing risk in young children.

Identifying Information

Child's Name: *Maria*	**Date of Completion:** *March 28, 2018*

ID/CASE #:	**Gender:** *Female*	**Date of Birth:** (mm/dd/yyyy) *23/01/2010*	**Age:** *8*

Completed By: *Jennifer S.*	**Signature:**

Presenting Issues (e.g., stealing, vandalism, aggression, assault):

Information Sources (check all that apply):	**Police Contact:**
☐ Interview with Child	☐ Yes ☐ No
☐ Interview with Parent/Caregiver	If yes, please indicate:
☐ Interview with _____	When _____
☐ Review of Police Records	Reason_____
☐ Other:	**Other authority contact:** (e.g., school officials, fire service, security)
	☐ Yes ☐ No
	If yes, explain:

CH LD
DEVELOPMENT
INSTITUTE

EARL-PC Form
Early Assessment Risk List – Pre Checklist
(Augimeri, Walsh, Jiang, Koegl, & Logue, 2013)
* Development of the EARL-PC was funded in part by the Ontario Ministry of Public

Section I: Family Concerns *This section includes risk concerns related to the child's family environment that may be problematic. Key indicators are listed to help guide the user in identifying whether any of these items are of concern.*	**Evidence** *Y = Yes; N = No;* *? = Unsure*
1. **The family is experiencing financial difficulties and/or living in inadequate housing.** *Key indicators: family has an assisted income; income at or below poverty line; lives in a household described as decrepit, unsanitary, and/or crowded*	☐ Y ☐ N ☒ ?
2. **The relationship between child and parent(s)/caregiver(s) is or has been unstable.** *Key Indicators: child has had many caregiver(s); experienced disruptions/separation from significant caregiver(s); lived away from his/her caregiver for an extended period of time*	☐ Y ☒ N ☐ ?
3. **The family lacks positive social supports.** *Key Indicators: no access to community resources (e.g., family doctor, mental services, recreation, religious); family is isolated (e.g., no friends/extended family); has negative supports*	☐ Y ☐ N ☒ ?
4. **The child's parent(s) uses ineffective parenting/discipline strategies.** *Key Indicators: parenting is lax, inconsistent, permissive; punitive; unreasonable expectations in relation to the child's age; poor monitoring; harsh parenting (e.g., child maltreatment, harsh disciplinary practices)*	☒ Y ☐ N ☐ ?
5. **The parents/other family members engage/engaged in antisocial behaviour.** *Key Indicators: family member(s) have they been incarcerate; endorse antisocial values and thinking (e.g., violence, illegal drug use, education not valued)*	☒ Y ☐ N ☐ ?
6. **The child lives in a disadvantaged neighbourhood.** *Key Indicators: crime; high unemployment; gangs; weapons; drugs; prostitution; unsafe; lacks positive structured social outlets and supports; child is exposed to drugs within the neighbourhood; neighbourhood displays a positive attitude towards drugs*	☐ Y ☐ N ☒ ?
7. **The family is experiencing major stress.** *Key indicators: marital discord/divorce; job stress; mental and physical health issues; serious sibling rivalry; lack of family cohesion*	☒ Y ☐ N ☐ ?
8. **The family is unwilling/disinterested in getting help.** *Key Indicators: child's parents have not engaged in treatment/service; not interested in making changes; parents don't see themselves as part of the problem (i.e., "it's the child's problem only")*	☐ Y ☐ N ☒ ?

If needed, please use this space to indicate other related concerns and/or strengths (e.g., the family is or is not actively engaged in their child's schooling):

CHILD
DEVELOPMENT
INSTITUTE

EARL-PC Form
Early Assessment Risk List – Pre Checklist
(Augimeri, Walsh, Jiang, Koegl, & Logue, 2013)
* Development of the EARL-PC was funded in part by the Ontario Ministry of Public

Section II: Child Concerns *This section includes risk concerns directly related to the child that may be problematic. Key indicators are listed to help guide the user in identifying whether any of these items are of concern.* ***Extra consideration should be given to underlined key indicators.***	**Evidence** *Y = Yes; N = No;* *? = Unsure*
9. There is evidence or suspicion of abuse, neglect or trauma. *Key Indicators: documented or well-substantiated evidence of the child having experienced past or current physical, sexual, or emotional abuse; severe neglect; a traumatic event (e.g., physical injury or profound loss of a relative or friend); has witnessed violence*	☒ Y ☐ N ☐ ?
10. Adults (parents, teachers, neighbours, others) find it difficult to like this child. *Key Indicators: child lacks social skills; hard to please; unpleasant demeanour (e.g., moody, uncooperative, needy)*	☒ Y ☐ N ☐ ?
11. The child has inappropriate peer relationships. *Key Indicators: child has negative/delinquent peers who engage in antisocial behaviours (e.g., substance use); is bullied or rejected; isolated; hangs out with older/younger children*	☒ Y ☐ N ☐ ?
12. The child is experiencing academic problems. *Key indicators: identified learning disability; in a specialized learning program; needs extra academic support; below grade level*	☒ Y ☐ N ☐ ?
13. The child exhibits inappropriate sexual behaviour or interests. *Key Indicators: age inappropriate sexualized behaviour (e.g., sexualized language, mimics sexual acts); early physical maturity*	☐ Y ☒ N ☐ ?
14. The child displays negative attitudes/values. *Key Indicators: child does not distinguish between right and wrong; does not take responsibility for actions; misplaced sense of entitlement; thinking errors; (e.g., "stealing is okay, it doesn't hurt anyone"); positive attitude towards antisocial behaviour (e.g., values drugs, delinquency); anti-authority, social criticism; negative school attitudes and motivation*	☒ Y ☐ N ☐ ?
15. The child has poor self-control and/or is impulsive. *Key Indicators: attention problems; difficulty focusing; doesn't think before they act; reactive; reckless; impulsive*	☒ Y ☐ N ☐ ?
16. The child displays antisocial behaviours. *Key Indicators: child behavioural problems (e.g., lying, acting out, general conduct problems, substance use, violence, aggression)*	☒ Y ☐ N ☐ ?
17. The child has had problems with authority contact. *Key Indicators: child has had contact for their own misbehavior with those in authority (e.g., police, security guards, principals, teachers, fire service)*	☒ Y ☐ N ☐ ?
18. The child shows indications of internalizing behavioral problems. *Key Indicators: anxiety, withdrawal, irritability, depression, low self-esteem, suicide ideation, coping issues*	☒ Y ☐ N ☐ ?

**OVERALL RISK CONCERN FOR FUTURE ANTISOCIAL BEHAVIOUR
BASED ON THE EARL-PC APPRAISAL**
Using your professional discretion assign a risk concern rating of "low", "moderate", or "high"

☐ LOW   ☐ MODERATE   ☒ HIGH

Notes:

CH LD
DEVELOPMENT
INSTITUTE

EARL-PC Form
Early Assessment Risk List – Pre Checklist
(Augimeri, Walsh, Jiang, Koegl, & Logue, 2013)
* Development of the EARL-PC was funded in part by the Ontario Ministry of Public

Suggested Risk Management Strategies Based on the EARL-PC Appraisal
(Users are encouraged to use the list below to recommend risk management strategies based on their review of the child/family's needs/concerns. Please note: This should be done independent of services that may or may not be available in the community; as this will help to identify potential gaps/needs.)

CHILD:

- [X] ANGER MANAGEMENT
- [X] MENTORING PROGRAM
- [X] STRUCTURED RECREATION ACTIVITIES (e.g., after school, summer)
- [ ] SOCIAL SKILLS TRAINING
- [X] SCHOOL SUPPORT
- [X] SPECIALIZED MENTAL HEALTH SERVICES (e.g., conduct problems, trauma, substance abuse, age inappropriate sexual behaviour)
- [ ] CHILD WELFARE INVOLVEMENT
- [ ] OFFENCE SPECIFIC PROGRAMS (e.g., fire safety, stop stealing, sexual assault)
- [ ] OTHER:

PARENT/FAMILY:

- [X] PARENT SKILLS TRAINING
- [ ] ANGER MANAGEMENT
- [X] SPECIALIZED MENTAL HEALTH SERVICES (e.g., family violence, trauma, substance abuse)
- [X] PARENT COUNSELLING
- [ ] PARENT SUPPORT (e.g., housing, financial, outreach services)
- [ ] OTHER:

PLANNING
(Based on the recommendations noted above, please indicate a community service that may be able to assist this child/family)

IS THE CHILD/FAMILY ALREADY INVOLVED IN SERVICE(S) (if yes, please provide details):

- [ ] Yes   [X] No

IS A FULL RISK ASSESSMENT WARRANTED? (if yes, please provide details):

- [X] Yes   [ ] No

CURRENT SERVICE RECOMMENDATIONS

NEAREST INTERSECTION TO CHILD'S HOME:	CLOSEST APPROPRIATE SERVICE PROVIDER(S):	
Dufferin St. & St. Clair Ave. West		
AGENCY REFERRED TO: *Child Development Institute*		**DATE:**

DESIGNATED PROGRAM (e.g., SNAP® for children in conflict with the law, TAPP-C for fire setters):
SNAP Girls

CONTACT PERSON: *Jennifer S.*	**TITLE:** *Child & Family Worker*
PHONE NUMBER: *416-641-3256 ext. 5021*	**EMAIL ADDRESS:** *JenniferS@cdi.org*

AGENCY ADDRESS: *423 Dundas St. West*

NOTES:

Appendix 7.3

Wheels of Self-Control and Plans

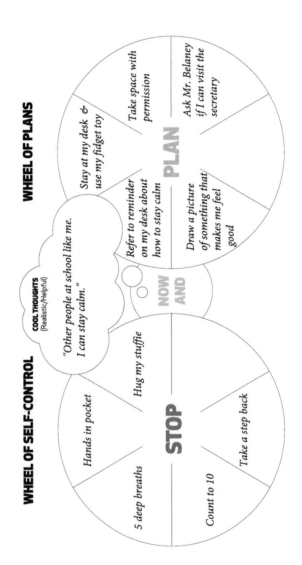

WHEEL OF SELF-CONTROL

WHEEL OF PLANS

COOL THOUGHTS
(Realistic/Helpful)

"Other people at school like me. I can stay calm."

5 deep breaths

Hands in pocket

Hug my stuffie

Count to 10

Take a step back

STOP

NOW AND

Refer to reminder on my desk about how to stay calm

Stay at my desk & use my fidget toy

Take space with permission

Draw a picture of something that makes me feel good

PLAN

Ask Mr. Belaney if I can visit the secretary

Circle the STOPS and the PLAN you would try first.

References

American Psychiatric Association. (2013). *Diagnostic and statistical manual of mental disorders* (5th ed.). Arlington, VA: American Psychiatric Publishing.

Augimeri, L. K., Farrington, D. P., Koegl, C. J., & Day, D. M. (2007). The Under 12 Outreach Project: Effects of a community based program for children with conduct problems. *Journal of Child and Family Studies, 16*(6), 799–807.

Augimeri, L. K., Jiang, D., Koegl, C. J., & Carey, J. (2006). *Differential effects of the SNAP® Under 12 Outreach Project (SNAP® ORP) Associated with Client Risk & Treatment Intensity. Program Evaluation Report Submitted to the Centre of Excellence for Child and Youth Mental Health at CHEO.* Toronto, ON: Centre for Children Committing Offences (CCCO).

Augimeri, L. K., Koegl, C. J., Webster, C., & Levene, K. (2001). *Early assessment risk list for boys: EARL-20B* (Version 2). Toronto, ON: Earlscourt Child and Family Centre.

Augimeri, L. K., Pepler, D., Walsh, M. M., Jiang, D., & Dassinger, C. R. (2010). *Aggressive and antisocial young children: Risk prediction, assessment and clinical risk management.* Submitted to The Provincial Centre of Excellence for Child and Youth Mental Health at Children's Hospital of Eastern Ontario, Child Development Institute, Toronto, ON.

Augimeri, L. K., Pepler, D., Walsh, M., & Kivlenieks, M. (2017). Addressing children's disruptive behavior problems: A thirty-year journey with SNAP (Stop Now And Plan). In P. Sturmey (Ed.), *Handbook of violence and aggression: Assessment, prevention, and treatment of individuals* (Vol. 2). Hoboken, NJ: Wiley-Blackwell. Augimeri, L., & Walsh, M. (2013). School-based interventions: Commentary. In D. Pepler & B. Ferguson (Eds.), *Understanding and addressing girls' aggressive behavior problems: A focus on relationships* (pp. 135–142). Waterloo, ON: Wilfrid Laurier University Press.

Augimeri, L. K., Walsh, M., Donato, A., Blackman, A., & Piquero, A. (2017). SNAP (Stop-Now-And-Plan): Helping children improve their self-control and externalizing behavior problems. *Journal of Criminal Justice, 56*, 43–49.

Augimeri, L. K., Walsh, M., Koegl, C., & Logue, L. (2013). *Early assessment risk list: Pre checklist.* Toronto, ON: Child Development Institute.

Augimeri, L. K., Walsh, M., Levene, K., Sewell, K., & Rajca, E. (2014). *Stop Now And Plan (SNAP) Model. Encyclopedia of Criminology and Criminal Justice, 5053–5063.* New York, NY: Springer Science—Business Media.

Bernhard, A., Martinelli, A., Ackermann, K., Saure, D., & Freitag, C. M. (2018). Association of trauma, posttraumatic stress disorder and conduct disorder: A systematic review and meta-analysis. *Neuroscience & Biobehavioral Reviews, 91*, 153–169.

Blair, C. (2010). Stress and the development of self-regulation in context. *Child Development Perspectives, 4*(3), 181–188.

Bridgett, D. J., Burt, N. M., Edwards, E. S., & Deater-Deckard, K. (2015). Intergenerational transmission of self-regulation: A multidisciplinary review and integrative conceptual framework. *Psychological Bulletin, 141*(3), 602.

Brouwers, A., & Tomic, W. (2000). A longitudinal study of teacher burnout and perceived self- efficacy in classroom management. *Teaching and Teacher Education, 16*(2), 239–253.

Burke, J., & Loeber, R. (2015). The effectiveness of the Stop Now and Plan (SNAP) program for boys at risk for violence and delinquency. *Prevention Science, 16*(2), 242–253.

Burke, J., & Loeber, R. (2016). Mechanisms of behavioral and affective treatment outcomes in a cognitive behavioral intervention for boys. *Journal of Abnormal Child Psychology, 44*(1), 179–189.

Carliner, H., Gary, D., McLaughlin, K. A., & Keyes, K. M. (2017). Trauma exposure and externalizing disorders in adolescents: Results from the National Comorbidity Survey Adolescent Supplement. *Journal of the American Academy of Child & Adolescent Psychiatry, 56*(9), 755–764.

Carr, C. P., Martins, C. M. S., Stingel, A. M., Lemgruber, V. B., & Juruena, M. F. (2013). The role of early life stress in adult psychiatric disorders: A systematic review according to childhood trauma subtypes. *The Journal of Nervous and Mental Disease, 201*(12), 1007–1020.

Cavanagh, M., Quinn, D., Duncan, D., Graham, T., & Balbuena, L. (2017). Oppositional defiant disorder is better conceptualized as a disorder of emotional regulation. *Journal of Attention Disorders, 21*(5), 381–389.

Charach, A., Bélanger, S. A., McLennan, J. D., & Nixon, M. K. (2017). Screening for disruptive behavior problems in preschool children in primary health care settings. *Paediatrics & Child Health, 22*(8), 478–484.

Child Development Institute. (2018a). *SNAP® boys group manual.* Toronto, ON: Child Development Institute.

Child Development Institute. (2018b). *SNAP® girls group manual.* Toronto, ON: Child Development Institute.

Child Development Institute. (2017). *SNAP® school based manual.* Toronto, ON: Child Development Institute.

Child Development Institute. (2016). *When you look at me, what do you see?* [Girls Video Script]. Toronto, ON: Child Development Institute.

Cohen, J. A., Berliner, L., & Mannarino, A. (2010). Trauma focused CBT for children with co- occurring trauma and behavior problems. *Child Abuse & Neglect, 34*(4), 215–224.

Cohen, M. A., & Piquero, A. R. (2009). New evidence on the monetary value of saving a high risk youth. *Journal of Quantitative Criminology, 25*(1), 25–49.

Cook, A., Spinazzola, J., Ford, J., Lanktree, C., Blaustein, M., Cloitre, M., . . . Mallah, K. (2005). Complex trauma in children and adolescents. *Psychiatric Annals, 35*(5), 390–398.

D'Andrea, W., Ford, J., Stolbach, B., Spinazzola, J., & van der Kolk, B. A. (2012). Understanding interpersonal trauma in children: Why we need a developmentally appropriate trauma diagnosis. *American Journal of Orthopsychiatry, 82*(2), 187–200.

Duckworth, A. L., Gendler, T. S., & Gross, J. J. (2014). Self-control in school-age children. *Educational Psychologist, 49*(3), 199–217.

Durlak, J. A., Weissberg, R. P., Dymnicki, A. B., Taylor, R. D., & Schellinger, K. B. (2011). The impact of enhancing students' social and emotional learning: A meta-analysis of school- based universal interventions. *Child Development, 82*(1), 405–432.

Earlscourt Child and Family Centre. (1986a). *Under 12 outreach project (SNAP) children's group manual.* Toronto, ON: Earlscourt Child and Family Centre.

Earlscourt Child and Family Centre. (1986b). *Under 12 outreach project (SNAP) parent group manual.* Toronto, ON: Earlscourt Child and Family Centre.

Earlscourt Child and Family Centre. (1996a). *Girls connection group (SNAP) manual: The girls club.* Toronto, ON: Earlscourt Child and Family Centre.

Earlscourt Child and Family Centre. (1996b). *Girls connection parent group (SNAP) manual.* Toronto, ON: Earlscourt Child and Family Centre.

Eisenberg, N., Spinrad, T. L., & Eggum, N. D. (2010). Emotion-related self-regulation and its relation to children's maladjustment. *Annual Review of Clinical Psychology, 6*, 495–525.

Erskine, H. E., Norman, R. E., Ferrari, A. J., Chan, G. C., Copeland, W. E., Whiteford, H. A., & Scott, J. G. (2016). Long-term outcomes of attention-deficit/hyperactivity disorder and conduct disorder: A systematic review and meta-analysis. *Journal of the American Academy of Child & Adolescent Psychiatry, 55*(10), 841–850.

Fallot, R., & Babout, R. (2012). Acknowledging and embracing 'the boy inside the man': Trauma informed work with men. In N. Poole & L. Greaves (Eds.), *Becoming trauma informed*. Toronto, ON: Centre for Addiction and Mental Health.

Farrington, D. P., & Koegl, C. J. (2015). Monetary benefits and costs of the Stop Now And Plan program for boys aged 6–11, based on the prevention of later offending. *Journal of Quantitative Criminology, 31*(2), 263–287.

Felitti, V. J., Anda, R. F., Nordenberg, D., Williamson, D. F., Spitz, A. M., Edwards, V., . . . Marks, J. S. (1998). Relationship of childhood abuse and household dysfunction to many of the leading causes of death in adults: The Adverse Childhood Experiences (ACE) Study. *American Journal of Preventive Medicine, 14*(4), 245–258.

Felitti, V. J., & Anda, R. F. (2010). The relationship of adverse childhood experiences to adult medical disease, psychiatric disorders, and sexual behavior: Implications for healthcare. In R. A. Lanius, E. Vermetten, & C. Pain (Eds.), *The impact of early life trauma on health and disease: The hidden epidemic* (pp. 77–87). Cambridge, UK: Cambridge University Press.

Fergusson, D. M., Boden, J. M., & Horwood, L. J. (2009). Situational and generalised conduct problems and later life outcomes: Evidence from a New Zealand birth cohort. *Journal of Child Psychology and Psychiatry, 50*(9), 1084–1092.

Fergusson, D. M., Horwood, L. J., & Ridder, E. M. (2005). Show me the child at seven: The consequences of conduct problems in childhood for psychosocial functioning in adulthood. *Journal of Child Psychology and Psychiatry, 46*(8), 837–849.

Ford, J. D., & Blaustein, M. E. (2013). Systemic self-regulation: A framework for trauma informed services in residential juvenile justice programs. *Journal of Family Violence, 28*(7), 665–677.

Ford, J. D., Chapman, J., Connor, D. F., & Cruise, K. R. (2012). Complex trauma and aggression in secure juvenile justice settings. *Criminal Justice and Behavior, 39*(6), 694–724.

Fox, B. H., Perez, N., Cass, E., Baglivio, M. T., & Epps, N. (2015). Trauma changes everything: Examining the relationship between adverse childhood experiences and serious, violent and chronic juvenile offenders. *Child Abuse & Neglect, 46*, 163–173.

Frick, P. J., & Nigg, J. T. (2012). Current issues in the diagnosis of attention deficit hyperactivity disorder, oppositional defiant disorder, and conduct disorder. *Annual Review of Clinical Psychology, 8*, 77–107.

Glick, B., & Goldstein, A. P. (1987). Aggression replacement training. *Journal of Counseling & Development, 65*(7), 356–362.

Gottfredson, M. R., & Hirschi, T. (1990). *A general theory of crime*. Redwood City, CA: Stanford University Press.

Gottfredson, G. D., Gottfredson, D. C., Payne, A. A., & Gottfredson, N. C. (2005). School climate predictors of school disorder: Results from a national study of delinquency prevention in schools. *Journal of Research in Crime and Delinquency, 42*(4), 412–444.

Hastings, R. P., & Bham, M. S. (2003). The relationship between student behavior patterns and teacher burnout. *School Psychology International, 24*(1), 115–127.

Hinshaw, S. P., & Lee, S. S. (2003). Conduct and oppositional defiant disorders. In E. J. Mash & R. A. Barkley (Eds.), *Child psychopathology* (2nd ed., pp. 144–198). New York, NY: Guilford Press.

Hoagwood, K., Burns, B. J., Kiser, L., Ringeisen, H., & Schoenwald, S. K. (2001). Evidence-based practice in child and adolescent mental health services. *Psychiatric Services, 52*(9), 1179–1189.

Huang, L. N., Flatow, R., Biggs, T., Afayee, S., Smith, K., & Clark, T. (2014). *SAMHSA's concept of trauma and guidance for a trauma-informed approach.* Rockville, MD: Substance Abuse and Mental Health Services Administration.

Hrynkiw-Augimeri, L. K. (1986). *Earlscourt child and family centre's outreach project report.* Toronto, ON: Earlscourt Child and Family Centre.

Hrynkiw-Augimeri, L., Pepler, D., & Goldberg, K. (1993). An outreach program for children having police contact. *Canada's Mental Health, 41*, 7–12.

Jaffee, S. R., Caspi, A., Moffitt, T. E., Dodge, K. A., Rutter, M., Taylor, A., & Tully, L. A. (2005). Nature×nurture: Genetic vulnerabilities interact with physical maltreatment to promote conduct problems. *Development and Psychopathology, 17*(1), 67–84.

Jiang, D., Walsh, M., & Augimeri, L. K. (2011). The linkage between bullying behavior and future offending. *Criminal Behavior and Mental Health, 21*(2), 128–135.

Kalb, L. M., & Loeber, R. (2003). Child disobedience and noncompliance: A review. *Pediatrics, 111*(3), 641–652.

Kim-Cohen, J., Caspi, A., Moffitt, T. E., Harrington, H., Milne, B. J., & Poulton, R. (2003). Prior juvenile diagnoses in adults with mental disorder: Developmental follow-back of a prospective longitudinal cohort. *Archives of General Psychiatry, 60*(7), 709–717.

Kim, J., & Cicchetti, D. (2010). Longitudinal pathways linking child maltreatment, emotion regulation, peer relations, and psychopathology. *Journal of Child Psychology and Psychiatry, 51*(6), 706–716.

Korpershoek, H., Harms, T., de Boer, H., van Kuijk, M., & Doolaard, S. (2016). A meta-analysis of the effects of classroom management strategies and classroom management programs on students' academic, behavioral, emotional, and motivational outcomes. *Review of Educational Research, 86*(3), 643–680.

Kretschmer, T., Hickman, M., Doerner, R., Emond, A., Lewis, G., Macleod, J., . . . Heron, J. (2014). Outcomes of childhood conduct problem trajectories in early adulthood: Findings from the ALSPAC study. *European Child & Adolescent Psychiatry, 23*(7), 539–549.

Lang, I. A., Marlow, R., Goodman, R., Meltzer, H., & Ford, T. (2013). Influence of problematic child-teacher relationships on future psychiatric disorder: Population survey with 3-year follow-up. *The British Journal of Psychiatry, 202*(5), 336–341.

Leflot, G., van Lier, P. A., Onghena, P., & Colpin, H. (2010). The role of teacher behavior management in the development of disruptive behaviors: An intervention study with the good behavior game. *Journal of Abnormal Child Psychology, 38*(6), 869–882.

Levene, K. S., Augimeri, L. K., Pepler, D. J., Walsh, M. M., Koegl, C. J., & Webster, C. D. (2001). *Early assessment risk list for girls: EARL-21G, Version 1, Consultation Edition.* Toronto, ON: Earlscourt Child and Family Centre.

Lewis, M. D., Granic, I., Lamm, C., Zelazo, P. D., Stieben, J., Todd, R. M., . . . Pepler, D. (2008). Changes in the neural bases of emotion regulation associate with clinical improvement in children with behavior problems. *Development and Psychopathology, 20*, 913–939.

Lipman, E. L., Kenny, M., Sniderman, C., O'Grady, S., Augimeri, L., Khayutin, S., & Boyle, M. H. (2008). Evaluation of a community-based program for young boys at risk of antisocial behavior: Results and issues. *Journal of the Canadian Academy of Child and Adolescent Psychiatry, 17*(1), 12–19.

Little, E., Hudson, A., & Wilks, R. (2000). Conduct problems across home and school. *Behavior Change, 17*, 69–77.

Loeber, R., Farrington, D. P., & Petechuk, D. (2003). *Child delinquency: Early intervention and prevention*. Washington, DC: US Department of Justice, Office of Justice Programs, Office of Juvenile Justice and Delinquency Prevention. Behavior Change, 17(2), 69–77.

Marlow, R., Hansford, L., Edwards, V., Ukoumunne, O. C., Norman, S., Ingarfield, S., . . . Ford, T. (2015). Teaching classroom management—A potential public health intervention? *Health Education, 115*(3/4), 230–248.

Matthys, W., & Lochman, J. E. (2016). *Oppositional defiant disorder and conduct disorder in childhood* (2nd ed.). West Sussex, UK: John Wiley & Sons, Ltd.

McClelland, M., Geldhof, J., Morrison, F., Gestsdóttir, S., Cameron, C., Bowers, E., . . . Grammer, J. (2018). Self-regulation. In N. Halfon, C. Forrest, R. Lerner, & E. Faustman (Eds.), *Handbook of life course health development* (pp. 275–298). Cham, Switzerland: Springer International Publishing.

McGinnis, E., Goldstein, A. P., Sprafkin, R. P., & Gershaw, N. J. (1984). *Skill-streaming the elementary school child: A guide for teaching prosocial skills*. Champaign, IL: Research Press.

Moffitt, T. E., Arseneault, L., Belsky, D., Dickson, N., Hancox, R. J., Harrington, H., . . . Sears, M. R. (2011). A gradient of childhood self-control predicts health, wealth, and public safety. *Proceedings of the National Academy of Sciences, 108*(7), 2693–2698.

Moffitt, T. E., Arseneault, L., Jaffee, S. R., Kim-Cohen, J., Koenen, K. C., Odgers, C. L., . . . Viding, E. (2008). Research review: DSM-V conduct disorder: Research needs for an evidence base. *Journal of Child Psychology and Psychiatry, 49*(1), 3–33.

Murray, J., & Farrington, D. P. (2010). Risk factors for conduct disorder and delinquency: Key findings from longitudinal studies. *The Canadian Journal of Psychiatry, 55*(10), 633–642.

Odgers, C. L., Moffitt, T. E., Broadbent, J. M., Dickson, N., Hancox, R. J., Harrington, H., . . . Caspi, A. (2008). Female and male antisocial trajectories: From childhood origins to adult outcomes. *Development and Psychopathology, 20*(2), 673–716.

Oliver, R. M., Wehby, J. H., & Reschly, D. J. (2011). *Teacher classroom management practices: Effects on disruptive or aggressive student behavior*. Evanston, IL: Society for Research on Educational Effectiveness.

Patterson, G. R. (1982). *Coercive family process*. Eugene, OR: Castalia.

Pepler, D., Walsh, M., Yuile, A., Levene, K., Vaughan, A., & Webber, J. (2010). Bridging the gender gap: Interventions with aggressive girls and their parents. *Prevention Science, 11*(3), 229–238.

Piquero, A. R., Jennings, W. G., Diamond, B., Farrington, D. P., Tremblay, R. E., Welsh, B. C., & Gonzalez, J. M. R. (2016). A meta-analysis update on the effects of early family/parent training programs on antisocial behavior and delinquency. *Journal of Experimental Criminology, 12*(2), 229–248.

Porche, M. V., Fortuna, L. R., Lin, J., & Alegria, M. (2011). Childhood trauma and psychiatric disorders as correlates of school dropout in a national sample of young adults. *Child Development, 82*(3), 982–998.

Rajca, E., Sewell, K., Levene, K., & Augimeri, L. K. (2018). Understanding SNAP: Transforming theoretical underpinnings into early intervention clinical practice. Manuscript in preparation.

Reaves, S., McMahon, S. D., Duffy, S., & Ruiz, L. (2018). The test of time: A meta-analytic review of the relation between school climate and problem behavior. *Aggression and Violent Behavior, 39,* 100–108.

Rocque, M., Posick, C., & Piquero, A. R. (2016). Self-control and crime. In K. D. Vohs & R. F. Baumeister (Eds.), *Handbook of self-regulation, third edition: Research, theory and applications* (pp. 514–532). New York, NY: The Guilford Press.

Rowe, R., Costello, E. J., Angold, A., Copeland, W. E., & Maughan, B. (2010). Developmental pathways in oppositional defiant disorder and conduct disorder. *Journal of Abnormal Psychology, 119*(4), 726–738.

Sabol, T. J., & Pianta, R. C. (2012). Recent trends in research on teacher—Child relationships. *Attachment & Human Development, 14*(3), 213–231.

Scott, S. (2015). Oppositional and conduct disorders. In A. Thapar, D. Pine, J. Leckman, S. Scott, M. Snowling, & E. Taylor (Eds.), *Rutter's child and adolescent's psychiatry* (pp. 913–930). West Sussex, UK: John Wiley & Sons, Ltd.

Scott, S., Augimeri, L., & Fifield, J. (2017). Early interventions in conduct disorders and oppositional defiant disorder. In S. Bailey, P. Tarbuck, & P. Chitsabesan (Eds.), *Forensic child and adolescent mental health* (pp. 239–253). Cambridge, UK: Cambridge University Press.

Shanker, S. (2010). Self-regulation: Calm, alert and learning. *Education Canada, 50*(3), 105–138.

Skaalvik, E. M., & Skaalvik, S. (2007). Dimensions of teacher self-efficacy and relations with strain factors, perceived collective teacher efficacy, and teacher burnout. *Journal of Educational Psychology, 99*(3), 611.

Sue, D. W., Capodilupo, C. M., & Holder, A. M. B. (2008). Racial microaggressions in the life experience of Black Americans. *Professional Psychology: Research and Practice, 39*(3), 329–336.

Teplin, L. A., Abram, K. M., McClelland, G. M., Dulcan, M. K., & Mericle, A. A. (2002). Psychiatric disorders in youth in juvenile detention. *Archives of General Psychiatry, 59*(12), 1133–1143.

Thomas, D. E., Bierman, K. L., Thompson, C., Powers, C. J., & Conduct Problems Prevention Research Group. (2008). Double jeopardy: Child and school characteristics that predict aggressive disruptive behavior in first grade. *School Psychology Review, 37*(4), 516–532.

Thomas, J. M., & Guskin, K. A. (2001). Disruptive behavior in young children: What does it mean? *Journal of the American Academy of Child & Adolescent Psychiatry, 40*(1), 44–51.

Thompson, R. A. (2014). Stress and child development. *The Future of Children, 24*(1), 41–59.

Underwood, L. A., & Washington, A. (2016). Mental illness and juvenile offenders. *International Journal of Environmental Research and Public Health, 13*(2), 228.

Vachon, D. D., Krueger, R. F., Rogosch, F. A., & Cicchetti, D. (2015). Assessment of the harmful psychiatric and behavioral effects of different forms of child maltreatment. *JAMA Psychiatry, 72*(11), 1135–1142.

van der Kolk, B. A. (2005). Developmental trauma disorder: Toward a rational diagnosis for children with complex trauma histories. *Psychiatric Annals, 35*(5), 401–408.

van der Laan, A. M., Veenstra, R., Bogaerts, S., Verhulst, F. C., & Ormel, J. (2010). Serious, minor, and non-delinquents in early adolescence: The impact of cumulative risk and promotive factors. The TRAILS study. *Journal of Abnormal Child Psychology, 38*(3), 339–351.

Webster-Stratton, C., Reid, M. J., & Hammond, M. (2001). Preventing conduct problems, promoting social competence: A parent and teacher training partnership in Head Start. *Journal of Clinical Child Psychology, 30*(3), 283–302.

Weinschenker, K. (2018, April 4). Why school shooters shoot: Depression to aggression. *Nexstar Broadcasting, Inc.* Retrieved from www.wtrf.com/news/health/why-school shooters-shoot-depression-to-aggression/1101748028

Wertz, J., Agnew-Blais, J., Caspi, A., Danese, A., Fisher, H. L., Goldman-Mellor, S., . . . Arseneault, L. (2018). From childhood conduct problems to poor functioning at age 18 years: Examining explanations in a longitudinal cohort study. *Journal of the American Academy of Child & Adolescent Psychiatry, 57*(1), 54–60.

Woltering, S., Granic, I., Lamm, C., & Lewis, M. D. (2011). Neural changes associated with treatment outcome in children with externalizing problems. *Biological Psychiatry, 70*(9), 873–879.

Woltering, S., & Lewis, M. D. (2013). Changing the neural mechanism of emotion regulation in children with behavior problems. In D. Hermans, B. Rime, & B. Mesquita (Eds.), *Changing emotions* (pp. 37–43). New York, NY: Psychology Press.

Woltering, S., & Shi, Q. (2016). On the neuroscience of self-regulation in children with disruptive behavior problems: Implications for education. *Review of Educational Research, 86*(4), 1085–1110.

School Shootings and School Lockdowns

8

Jeffrey A. Daniels and Whitney Hyatt

Although school shootings or hostage-taking events are statistically unlikely, schools are the chosen site for some individuals committing targeted mass violence (Stein, 2007). Since the Columbine High School massacre in 1999, there have been numerous school shootings and hostage-taking events in the United States (e.g., Sandy Hook Elementary, Marjory Stoneman Douglas High School, Santa Fe High School, Red Lake Senior High School, Cokeville Elementary School, and Marysville Pilchuck High School). Combined, the incidents at these schools resulted in 68 student casualties. Some researchers suggest, "With guns and their associated lethal violence increasingly finding their way into the lives of school-age children, the traditional view of schools as safe havens from violence can no longer be sustained" (Elliot, Hamburg, & Williams, 1998, p. 159). This chapter examines the research on school shootings and school lockdowns, as well as how schools are best able to deal with such events.

Prevalence of School Shootings

Over the past two decades, highly publicized and tragic school shootings have evoked widespread public fear that schools are dangerous places. On the contrary, schools are one of the safest places for children to be during the day. One study found that only 0.8% of mass-casualty homicides within the US occur in schools; multiple casualty homicides were much more likely to occur at residences (52%) or on the streets (24%) (Nekvasil, Cornell, & Huang, 2015). For child victims, school homicides account for only about 1% of US homicides for youth under 18 (Centers for Disease Control and Prevention, 2010). Students who carry out homicide attacks at school are a heterogeneous group and there is general agreement that no profile or set of risk factors are sufficiently specific that they can be used to profile a potential shooter (O'Toole, 2000; Rocque, 2012; Vossekuil, Fein, Reddy, Borum, & Modzeleski, 2002).

In an analysis of 37 acts of targeted school violence by 41 students, the US Department of Education and the US Secret Service found that many of these youths had been suicidal (78%), victims of bullying (71%), and intensely interested in violence (59%) (Vossekuil et al., 2002). On the other hand, many were active in peer groups, lived in two-parent homes, did well academically, and had not been in trouble at school (Vossekuil et al., 2002). Almost all of the school shooters (98%) experienced a major loss before the attack, including perceived failure or loss of status. Most notably, in 81% of the incidences, the youth had told at least one person that they were considering a school attack. In some instances, the shooter divulged the date, time, and location to others beforehand. This is a key finding, as it indicates an opportunity to prevent school shootings if threats are reported and subsequently investigated (Cornell & Malone, 2015).

Although the likelihood of a school shooting or hostage-taking event is slim-to-none, it is important for school personnel, including administrators, teachers, counselors, psychologists, police (or school resource officers), and nurses, to have a crisis response plan in place and regularly practiced. Children who witness firearm violence can suffer psychological trauma, and the impact of firearm injuries on children can adversely affect individual development and the educational climate in schools (Elliott, Hamburg, & Williams, 1998). Furthermore, adults in the school should be aware of acute stress disorder (ASD) and post-traumatic stress disorder (PTSD) symptoms that students may exhibit following a violent school experience.

Effects of School Violence, Shootings, Lockdowns, and Hostage-Taking Events

The impact of violence on children can be measured in terms of physical injury and death, psychological trauma to victims and witnesses, and disruption of the school learning environment. Evidence suggests the severity of a child's response to trauma is related to the physical distance between the child and the violent event, the child's relationship with the victim(s), and the presence of a parent or caretaker to help mediate the impact of the event on the child (Elliott et al., 1998). Next are examples of symptoms that may be experienced.

Acute Stress Disorder (ASD)

Acute stress reactions describe trauma-related symptomatology that occur between 3 days and 1 month following exposure to a traumatic event, and may be a precursor to a diagnosis of PTSD (American Psychiatric Association, 2013). According to the *Diagnostic and Statistical Manual of Mental Disorders, 5th edition* (DSM-5), a person may be diagnosed with ASD if: (1) they were exposed to trauma directly or through witnessing an event, learning that the event occurred to a close family member or friend, or repeated exposure to the details of an event; (2) nine or more symptoms from any of the five categories of intrusion, negative mood, dissociation, avoidance, and arousal are present; and (3) the duration of the disturbances is from 3 days to 1 month after exposure to the traumatic event. There are two other qualifiers, including experiencing significant distress or impairment, and the disturbance not being due to the effects of substances or a medical condition. The specific symptoms of ASD are listed in Table 8.1.

The Acute Stress Reaction Questionnaire (ASRQ) is a reliable instrument that can be used to distinguish between PTSD and ASD (Schupp, 2004). School personnel should be prepared to intervene through ensuring physical safety and providing mental health referrals if a student were to begin exhibiting ASD or PTSD symptoms in response to a school shooting or hostage-taking event.

Post-Traumatic Stress Disorder (PTSD)

Post-traumatic stress disorder, or PTSD, is a trauma or stressor-related disorder that may occur in individuals exposed to actual or threatened death. The exposure results from directly experiencing or witnessing the traumatic event, learning the traumatic event occurred to a close family member or friend, or experiencing first-hand repeated or extreme exposure to aversive details of the traumatic event including media and images (American Psychiatric Association, 2013). Students in a school that experience a lockdown for an active shooter or barricaded situation can develop PTSD despite not

Table 8.1 Symptoms of Acute Stress Disorder

Category	Symptoms
Intrusion	Recurrent, involuntary, and intrusive distressing memories of the traumatic event(s). **Note:** In children, repetitive play may occur in which themes or aspects of the traumatic event(s) are expressed.
	Recurrent distressing dreams in which the content and/or affect of the dream are related to the event(s). **Note:** In children, there may be frightening dreams without recognizable content.
	Dissociative reactions (e.g., flashbacks) in which the individual feels or acts as if the traumatic event(s) were recurring. (Such reactions may occur on a continuum, with the most extreme expression being a complete loss of awareness of present surroundings.) **Note:** In children, trauma-specific reenactment may occur in play.
	Intense or prolonged psychological distress or marked physiological reactions in response to internal or external cues that symbolize or resemble an aspect of the traumatic event(s).
Negative Mood	Persistent inability to experience positive emotions (e.g., inability to experience happiness, satisfaction, or loving feelings).
Dissociation	An altered sense of the reality of one's surroundings or oneself (e.g., seeing oneself from another's perspective, being in a daze, time slowing).
	Inability to remember an important aspect of the traumatic event(s) (typically due to dissociative amnesia and not to other factors such as head injury, alcohol, or drugs).
Avoidance	Efforts to avoid distressing memories, thoughts, or feelings about or closely associated with the traumatic event(s).
	Efforts to avoid external reminders (people, places, conversations, activities, objects, situations) that arouse distressing memories, thoughts, or feelings about or closely associated with the traumatic event(s).

(Continued)

Table 8.1   (Continued)

Category	Symptoms
Arousal	Sleep disturbance (e.g., difficulty falling or staying asleep, restless sleep).
	Irritable behavior and angry outbursts (with little or no provocation), typically expressed as verbal or physical aggression towards people or objects.
	Hypervigilance.
	Problems with concentration.
	Exaggerated startle response.

Note: Symptoms are quoted directly from https://psychiatryonline.org/doi/10.1176/appi.books.9781585625048.gg28

directly witnessing the violence. Hearing disturbing sounds (screaming, gunshots, people in distress), seeing pictures (news reports, videos), and interacting with students or other school personnel during and after the crisis can potentially trigger PTSD symptoms in children and adolescents, regardless of age and development.

A diagnosis of PTSD cannot be made until after 1-month post-exposure to the traumatic event. Like ASD, the symptoms must cause significant disturbance or impairment, and cannot be attributable to substances or medical conditions. Symptoms cluster into four main categories, which are provided in Table 8.2.

Students exhibiting PTSD could be feeling a sense of self-blame, intense fear, or helplessness. The memories of a traumatic event can suddenly or unexpectedly return weeks, months, or even years afterward. Mental Health First Aid (MHFA) should be used when the school professional becomes aware of the problem (Kitchner & Jorm, 2012). MHFA is elaborated in greater detail later in the chapter.

Definitions

The ideas presented in this chapter center around five issues that require definition: school violence, nonlethal school violence, lethal school violence, school shooting, and both direct and indirect victims.

Table 8.2 Symptoms of Post-Traumatic Stress Disorder

Category	Symptoms
One or more of the following:	Recurrent, involuntary, and intrusive distressing memories of the traumatic event(s). **Note:** In children older than 6 years, repetitive play may occur in which themes or aspects of the traumatic event(s) are expressed.
	Recurrent distressing dreams in which the content and/or affect of the dream are related to the traumatic event(s). **Note:** In children, there may be frightening dreams without recognizable content.
	Dissociative reactions (e.g., flashbacks) in which the individual feels or acts as if the traumatic event(s) were recurring. (Such reactions may occur on a continuum, with the most extreme expression being a complete loss of awareness of present surroundings.) **Note:** In children, trauma-specific reenactment may occur in play.
	Intense or prolonged psychological distress at exposure to internal or external cues that symbolize or resemble an aspect of the traumatic event(s).
	Marked physiological reactions to internal or external cues that symbolize or resemble an aspect of the traumatic event(s).
Persistent avoidance of stimuli associated with the traumatic event(s), beginning after the traumatic event(s) occurred, as evidenced by one or both of the following:	Avoidance of or efforts to avoid distressing memories, thoughts, or feelings about or closely associated with the traumatic event(s).
	Avoidance of or efforts to avoid external reminders (people, places, conversations, activities, objects, situations) that arouse distressing memories, thoughts, or feelings about or closely associated with the traumatic event(s).

(Continued)

Table 8.2 (Continued)

Category	Symptoms
Negative alterations in cognitions and mood associated with the traumatic event(s), beginning or worsening after the traumatic event(s) occurred, as evidenced by two (or more) of the following:	Inability to remember an important aspect of the traumatic event(s) (typically due to dissociative amnesia and not to other factors such as head injury, alcohol, or drugs).
	Persistent and exaggerated negative beliefs or expectations about oneself, others, or the world (e.g., "I am bad", "No one can be trusted", "The world is completely dangerous", "My whole nervous system is permanently ruined").
	Persistent, distorted cognitions about the cause or consequences of the traumatic event(s) that lead the individual to blame himself/herself or others.
	Persistent negative emotional state (e.g., fear, horror, anger, guilt, or shame).
	Markedly diminished interest or participation in significant activities.
	Feelings of detachment or estrangement from others.
	Persistent inability to experience positive emotions (e.g., inability to experience happiness, satisfaction, or loving feelings).
Marked alterations in arousal and reactivity associated with the traumatic event(s), beginning or worsening after the traumatic event(s) occurred, as evidenced by two (or more) of the following:	Irritable behavior and angry outbursts (with little or no provocation) typically expressed as verbal or physical aggression towards people or objects.
	Reckless or self-destructive behavior.

Category	Symptoms
	Hypervigilance.
	Exaggerated startle response.
	Problems with concentration.
	Sleep disturbance (e.g., difficulty falling or staying asleep or restless sleep).

Note: PTSD symptoms are quoted directly from https://dsm.psychiatryonline.org/doi/10.1176/appi.books.9780890425596.dsm07

School Violence

School violence involves any act of violence in a school building, on school grounds, on a school bus, or at a school-sponsored activity. Some authors also include violence that occurs to one or more students or faculty on their way to or from school (Vossekuil et al., 2002). School violence may be perpetrated by current or former students, faculty or staff, or external intruders (including domestic violence that spills into the school environment; Daniels & Bradley, 2011). School violence can be nonlethal or lethal.

Nonlethal School Violence

Nonlethal school violence is any school violence that does not result in loss of life. Specifically, nonlethal school violence "includes all bullying (physical, relational, cyber), threats, intimidation, harassment, assault, sexual assault, and property crimes" (Daniels & Haist, 2012, p. 335).

Lethal School Violence

In contrast to nonlethal school violence, lethal school violence consists of loss of life. Daniels and Bradley (2011) defined lethal school violence as school violence "that results in the death of one or more individuals" (p. 3). They included in their definition "suicide, domestic murder/suicide, gang-related deaths, fights that result in death, barricaded captive situations that end in one or more fatalities, and rampage school shootings" (p. 3).

School Shooting

A school shooting is one form of school violence. There are multiple terms for school shootings, including rampage school shootings (Newman, Fox, Harding, Mehta, & Roth, 2004) and school rampages (e.g., Rocque, 2012). In addition to different terms, there has been a lack of consensus in defining school shootings, with some authors adopting a broad definition of all homicides with a firearm including one or more victims (Kelly & May, 2011). Most commonly, school shooting and school rampage (or rampage school shooting) are defined as at least two victims injured or killed (e.g., Moore, Petrie, Braga, & McLaughlin, 2003). For their edited book on school shootings, Böckler, Seeger, Sitzer, and Heitmeyer (2013, pp. 7–8) offered a thorough definition of school shootings, which we use in this chapter:

- Location of violent incident was at a school (elementary or secondary) or an institution of further or higher education.
- Perpetrator was a current or former student at the educational facility.
- Use of a potentially lethal weapon (firearm, knife, explosives, etc.) to attempt to injure or kill *one or more persons*. The crucial criterion is not the outcome (actual number of victims) but the intent.
- The attack took place during school hours on school premises, usually in front of an audience composed of other students and/or members of the school staff.
- The shooter chose victims:

  1) Deliberately on the basis of conflictual relationships; and/or
  2) Randomly; and/or
  3) For their symbolic significance or status in the school's social system.

Direct and Indirect Victims

Following a school shooting or other traumatic occurrence (such as a barricaded captive-taking), survivors include both direct and indirect victims. Direct victims are those who were injured, in the "line of fire", or held captive. Indirect victims "are those not in the immediate vicinity of the shooting, friends and relatives of the victims, and others in the community who are negatively impacted" (Daniels & Page, 2013, p. 423).

Having defined key terms, we turn now to a description of the scope of the school shooting problem. We focus specifically on the prevalence of school shootings, including the discrepancy between the data and people's perceptions of school violence, which are often elevated by the intense media coverage of mass-casualty school shootings.

Nature of the Problem

As we detailed earlier in this chapter, school violence that requires school lockdowns is not common, despite public perceptions (e.g., Cornell, 2006). Borum, Cornell, Modzeleski, and Jimerson (2010) wrote: "the perception of school safety is easily influenced by frightening but isolated incidents like school shootings" (p. 27). Indeed, school shootings in general, and specifically school shootings that result in death, are statistically rare. Borum et al. (2010) presented the following:

> In the 10-year period from 1996–1997 to 2005–2006, 207 student homicides occurred in U.S. schools, an average of 21 deaths per year. Dividing the nation's approximately 125,000 elementary and secondary schools (U.S. Department of Education, 2008) by 21, any given school can expect to experience a student homicide about once every 6,000 years. And although 21 homicides per year is a distressingly large number, it represents less than 1% of the annual homicides of youth ages 5 to 18 in the United States.
>
> (Borum et al., 2010, p. 27)

Prevalence data for school shootings is difficult to attain. Although there are several websites that collect data on school shootings, many of these do not use reliable data collection methods, nor do they always use a standard definition of a school shooting. Many of these websites have the agenda of showing how out of control school shootings are, and advocate for gun control.

Perhaps a better statistic than the number of shootings is to examine the number of violent deaths at schools. This allows for consideration of weapons other than firearms and includes suicides at schools. The National Center for Education Statistics (NCES; Musu-Gillette et al., 2018) is the US government agency for education-related data, and they maintain yearly data on school violence. Data include violent deaths that were intentional rather than accidental. The most recent report from the NCES, *Indicators of School Crime and Safety: 2017*, presented the following:

- In the 2014–2015 school year, there were 1,168 youth homicides and 1,785 youth suicides in the US.

- Of these, 20 homicides and nine suicides occurred at school.
- This represents 1.7% youth homicides and 0.5% youth suicides.

These data support the conclusion by Borum et al. (2010) that schools remain one of the safest places for children and youth. Despite alarming statistics by activist organizations and media coverage, lethal school violence remains statistically rare in the US and throughout the world. Most of the school shootings occur within the US, but school shootings are not unique to US schools. Shootings have occurred in Canada, Germany, France, the UK, Finland, Brazil, and many other countries.

Understanding that the actual prevalence of school shootings is not as high as people often believe, we can try to ease the fears of students and their parents. One method of mitigating anxiety is to be prepared for an event. In the next section, we address lockdown procedures and drills as one such method of preparedness.

Lockdowns

Schools may call for lockdowns for a variety of crimes and threats, such as active shooters or threatened shootings. Schools also go on lockdown when a crime has occurred in a school's neighborhood during school hours, such as an armed robbery, and the perpetrator has not yet been apprehended (Dorn, Thomas, Wong, & Shepherd, 2004). We could not find any reports of the number of school lockdowns that occur each year. However, we offer some suggestions and considerations for practicing and for actual lockdowns. Specifically, we address lockdown preparedness (Dorn et al., 2004), how to teach lockdown procedures to young children (Dickson & Vargo, 2017), considerations for lockdown procedures for children with disabilities (Clarke, Embury, Jones, & Yssel, 2014), and the impact of rumors that spread via social media during a lockdown (Jones, Thompson, Schetter, & Silver, 2017).

In *Jane's Safe Schools Planning Guide for all Threats*, Dorn et al. (2004) identified two options for lockdowns—"a preventative or 'soft' lockdown and a full or 'hard' lockdown" (p. 123). The preventative lockdown involves locking access to the building while maintaining freedom to move throughout. This will occur when there is a violent suspect in the school's neighborhood or on school grounds. A full lockdown is called when there is an active shooter within the school, and includes locking classroom doors, turning the lights off, moving students away from windows and doors, and may include having students lie down on the floor.

In the only study of the effectiveness of lockdown training, Dickson and Vargo (2017) measured kindergarten children's adherence to lockdown procedures before and after behavioral skills training (BST). The BST occurred in three phases: (1) the teacher read the instructions to the class, using picture cards as supplements; (2) the teacher then modeled the correct lockdown steps, followed by the children's rehearsal of the steps; and (3) after the rehearsal, the teacher provided corrective feedback and "animated praise" (p. 409) for correct responding. Three to 4 days after the BST, children participated in a lockdown while observers recorded the extent to which they followed the established procedures. Children showed a noticeable enhancement in following the procedures and responding more quietly during the drill.

For the reader's information, the following seven steps were included in this study, and may be helpful for school administrators who are developing lockdown procedures (Dickson & Vargo, 2017, p. 408).

1. Students stop what they are doing and put all materials and supplies on the floor or table.
2. Students locate a concealed area and move quickly to that area without items.
3 While moving to the concealed area, students remain quiet or only whisper if speaking.
4. Students are located in the concealed area (bathroom with door closed) within 30 seconds of the announcement of a lockdown.
5. Students sit on the floor (crisscross style) in the concealed area.
6. Students remain seated in the same location until they are instructed that the lockdown is over (5 minutes).
7. Students remain quiet and do not talk or produce noises unless instructed by the experimenter.

When developing lockdown procedures, schools must include a special education teacher on the committee so she or he may add critical information about students with disabilities (Clarke et al., 2014). Some elements of a lockdown may be difficult for students with varying disabilities. For example, quickly getting to a safe place may be problematic for students with mobility problems; remaining quiet during a possible loud and chaotic time may be difficult for students with sensory processing disabilities; or remaining in lockdown for several hours may be especially challenging for students with special needs. In addition to including a special educator on crisis planning teams, Clarke et al. argued that a question be added to the students' individualized education program (IEP) meeting: "Is there a need for a specific plan for this student's individual needs if there were a crisis in the building?" (p. 170). There should be a specific plan for every special needs student for crises and lockdowns.

In a study of a rumors following a shooting at a US university, Jones et al. (2017) found that during the lockdown, false, incomplete, or contradictory information was spread across social media sites, thereby contributing to rumors. They also found that people who turned to social media for information about the shooting reported significantly greater distress than those who turned to more trusted sources of information. The authors suggested that during a crisis, such as a school shooting, officials should provide frequent updates to both the affected individuals (in this case, college students, faculty, staff, and administrators) and the public to mitigate rumors and distress.

Although there is no information that we could find linking lockdown drills and distress, we have offered some insights into special considerations for lockdowns in emergencies. However, research in other settings shows that preparedness is negatively related to fear during an actual event. Whealin, Ruzek, and Vega (2013) described preparatory education as an important factor in building resiliency in pre-deployment military personnel. That is, being prepared for a traumatic event will decrease "the intensity of emotional responses to subsequent fear-producing events" (p. 121). Having addressed lockdowns, we now turn to the short- and long-term consequences of traumatic events.

Short- and Long-Term Consequences

Following a traumatic school event, such as a barricaded captive-taking or school shooting, it is important to know that everyone affiliated with the school, including parents and spouses/partners of employees, may experience some level of trauma. It is also important to know that not everyone responds to traumatic events in the same way. We now outline some of the common effects of trauma, both immediately after an event and in the months or years since.

Short-Term Effects

In the hours and days following a traumatic event, some direct and indirect victims will experience a range of emotions. At the most extreme level, students and school personnel may develop symptoms of acute stress disorder (ASD, previously discussed). Symptoms may include "psychological numbing, feeling of being in a daze, derealization, depersonalization, and dissociative amnesia" (Daniels, Bradley, & Hays, 2007, p. 653). In addition, students may experience heightened, or even debilitating, fear and anxiety (Daniels & Bradley, 2011). School attendance among both students and teachers may also be impacted, with greater absenteeism (Newman et al., 2004).

Long-Term Effects

Left untreated, some traumatized people may develop post-traumatic stress disorder (PTSD, previously discussed). In a study of PTSD symptoms 7 months after a school shooting in Denmark, Elklit and Kurdahl (2013) found that 9.5% of the witnesses reported PTSD and 25% had subclinical symptoms of PTSD. Students who experienced "negative affectivity, persistent dissociation, and lack of social support ('feeling let down')" (p. 4) had the greatest level of symptomology. In a similar study following a shooting in a Finnish school, Murtonen, Suomalainen, Haravuori, and Marttunen (2012) reported that greater exposure to the shooting resulted in greater levels of symptomology, but that immediate crisis support was helpful in these students' recovery. In addition to students, following a school shooting in Kentucky, Newman and colleagues "found that teachers and administrators experienced multiple negative long-term consequences, including illness, divorce, burnout, and career change" (Daniels et al., 2007, p. 653).

After this brief review of the short- and long-term effects of exposure to school violence, we now turn to two related issues. First, the prevention of PTSD and other mental health disorders, and second, interventions to enhance students' coping.

Prevention and Intervention

Immediately Following an Event

Immediately following a school shooting, barricaded captive-taking, or other violent school event, there are actions school personnel should take to prioritize the affected students' needs. These responses may include getting the student to physical safety in a classroom, to a medical professional, or providing Mental Health First Aid (MHFA). Each member of the school crisis team should be trained in MHFA to effectively respond in cases of emergencies.

School Crisis Team

It is essential to have a school crisis team in place to provide a sound safety response following a violent school event. Crisis team members should consist of administrators, school psychologists, counselors, nurses, and other staff without class responsibilities. There are a variety of roles within a crisis team, including a team leader, counseling or intervention specialist, medical team representative, law enforcement or security representative, media representative, parent representative, and teacher representative (Adamson & Peacock, 2007). The team leader could be a principal or administrator and the counseling intervention specialist could be filled by the school psychologist or professional school counselor. A medical team representative should be the school nurse and the law enforcement representative can be the school resource officer (SRO). The media, parent, and teacher representatives should be decided prior to a crisis event to limit the amount of decisions needed to be made if a violent school event were to unfold.

Mental Health First Aid

General guidelines for providing MHFA to youth after a mass traumatic event, such as ensuring one's own safety before offering assistance to anyone else, is similar to the airlines', "Place your oxygen mask on before helping others". As a first aider providing services during and immediately following a school-wide crisis, it is important to keep yourself physically and psychologically safe and alert so you can be available to support those in need of assistance. If approaching a student you do not know, calmly introduce yourself and clearly state you are there to help keep them safe. Find out the student's name and use it regularly, as that may provide a sense of comfort and familiarity in a time of chaos. Direct the student away from being further traumatized by relocating them from traumatic sights and sounds like distressed students, injured or screaming people, and media images. If possible, reassure the student she or he will not be left alone. If you need to leave the student for any reason to provide MHFA services elsewhere, connect the student with another trusted adult. It is important to also stay aware of multicultural differences when comforting students, as some students may find hugging or swaddling more uncomfortable than placing a hand on their shoulder or refraining from physical touch altogether. In these cases, asking the student what they need to make them feel safe can help them regain a sense of control in a time of crisis. Providing first aid does not entail taking on a medical role; it is the school personnel's duty to identify those in need of physical assistance for injuries and connecting them with police, emergency medical technicians (EMTs), and other trained medical professionals. Even when students may seem physically or mentally stable, stay aware of potentially declining stability injuries that may reveal themselves more slowly due to the state of shock fading away over time. It is best practice to not make any promises you cannot keep to students, such as promising the youth they will go home soon or that their friends are okay. Comfort and communicate with the students in a direct and calm manner.

Talking with Students

When talking with students following a school shooting or mass traumatic event, it is important to be honest and use developmentally appropriate language. Allow the youth to ask questions while remaining patient and consistent if they repeat themselves, as their memory may be disrupted from the traumatic events they have just experienced. If the youth knows upsetting, accurate information, do not deny them. Respect cultural and religious beliefs by refraining from saying, "Went to heaven" or "God" when talking about people who may have died in the event, unless knowing the student's background. When referring to death, do not say, "Went to sleep", as children may become fearful of sleep. In all, if students want to talk, allow them the safe space to express themselves, but never coerce or force them to speak if they do not want to.

Indicators of the Need for a One-on-One Crisis Intervention Referral

In most cases, small-group crisis interventions will be the most effective in soothing and reaching multiple traumatized students at one time. Some students will exhibit more intense post-traumatic symptoms that would suggest a need for more individualized mental health support. Symptoms such as suicidal ideation or plans, inability to control emotional reactions, dissociation, excessive self-blame or intropunitive anger, and absence of emotional reactions in those who were close to or witnessed the traumatic event need immediate attention by a trained mental health professional (Larsson, Michel, & Lundin, 2000).

Small-Group Crisis Intervention

In times of crisis, it can be challenging to give extended attention to an individual student due to large groups of people being affected by one event. Small-group crisis interventions can be helpful in linking students together to encourage feelings of safety and community. These are best served in groups of 4–12 students (Brock, Lazarus, & Jimerson, 2002). Adults should facilitate directive discussions of healthy coping behaviors, such as deep breathing and positive thoughts. It is important to keep in mind people can differ in how they react to traumatic events: one person may perceive the event as deeply traumatic but another may not. A history of trauma can make some people more susceptible to being affected, whereas others become more resilient (Kitchner & Jorm, 2012). Depending on pre-trauma psychological stability, trauma reactions of students exposed to violence within their community may be triggered by a school shooting or may be less affected than their peers. Youth may respond differently than adults, depending on age and psychological maturity, so being aware of post-trauma symptoms is essential in providing crisis interventions in a small group.

Key Components in Crisis Response

Developing a crisis plan and training a crisis team prior to a violent school event occurring is key to a sound intervention strategy (Brock, Sandoval, & Lewis, 2001; Crepeau-Hobson, Sievering, Armstrong, & Stonis, 2012; Daniels & Page, 2012). Rehearsed lockdowns ensure that students and staff have the knowledge and ability to put appropriate safety protocols into place, thereby reducing panic and confusion should a crisis emerge (Gereluk, Donlevy, & Thompson, 2015). Mental health crisis intervention includes four main aspects: establishing safety and security, and providing ventilation and validation, prediction and preparation, and empathy and empowerment (Crepeau-Hobson et al., 2012). Establishment of safety and security includes connecting the student with parents or loved ones and helping him or her to establish a sense of control. Ventilation is providing the student an opportunity to tell her or his story, and validation is normalizing the student's reactions and feelings. Prediction and preparation are tasks for the crisis response team prior to an attack (Crepeau-Hobson et al., p. 214). Empathy is attempting to see a person's experience from her or his perspective. It may also include:

> attending to the needs of staff, students and the community, anticipating what they need to increase their sense of safety and security, and responding to their venting empathically. Empathy also involves being flexible and adjusting the mental health response as needed.
>
> (Crepeau-Hobson et al., 2012, p. 214)

Finally, empowerment involves helping the students develop self-worth and competence in psychologically surviving the trauma.

Another essential component following a school-wide crisis is the reunification process. The reunification process is an important aspect of the crisis response as the re-establishment of natural social support systems and is often the only crisis intervention needed for many individuals (Barenbaum, Ruchkin, & Schwab-Stone, 2004; Horowitz, McKay, & Marshall, 2005). The crisis team should have handouts ready and available to give to parents, families, and students to connect them to community resources. To be culturally responsive, handouts should be in all languages relative to the specific school.

A safe haven should be established shortly following the event. A safe haven is typically set up the day after the traumatic school-wide event (Crepeau-Hobson et al., 2012). A safe haven is "a designated gathering place for students, families, and staff aids in reaffirming physical health and safety and is strongly related to psychological safety and recovery" (Crepeau-Hobson et al., 2012, p. 213). Along with the safe haven being created, school counselors and other crisis team members should hold postvention roles. They can achieve this is by providing counseling services to students, informing parents of the incident, responding to their questions and concerns, and coordinating the efforts of school district and mental health professionals in the community (Daniels et al., 2007).

Shortly Following the Event

After the immediate needs of people are met, we enter the second phase of recovery. This time period spans roughly from the first 24–72 hours.

The First 72 Hours

The first 72 hours following the event are critical for large-group crisis intervention. Large-group crisis interventions are advantageous because they allow crisis team members to reach a larger number of students, and the group process promotes sharing and mutual support. The process of the group crisis intervention, also known as GCI, is the most effective in the classroom with sizes ranging from 15 to 30 students. It is important for teachers to identify the event and discuss it with their students. If, following a crisis, a teacher begins the school day by following the normal routine (without mentioning the trauma), it suggests to students that the trauma was not a significant event, which may lessen students' willingness to share (Armstrong et al., 1998). The student-teacher relationship can be critical for students expressing themselves shortly after the event; therefore, a ratio of one facilitator to every ten students is recommended (Armstrong et al., 1998). This recommendation is made because there should be at least one familiar adult in the GCI, whether that be a teacher, administrator, counselor, or psychologist.

There are six steps in the GCI process, which include an introduction, providing facts and dispelling the rumors, sharing stories, sharing reactions, empowerment, and the closing. In the introduction, the facilitator might start off by saying something like: "I'm sorry this happened to our school. When bad things like this happen, it is helpful to talk about it. So, we are going to spend some time today talking. From our discussion, we will have a better understanding of what happened, how it has affected us, and what we can do to help each other cope". Next, explain the GCI purpose, identify the facilitators, and finally review the rules of the group. Typical group rules are for students to have general respect for group members' thoughts and opinions, as everyone has differing experiences and backgrounds, and to avoid any blaming statements by using "I" statements, such as "I feel angry because . . ." instead of "You" statements. Following the introduction, provide the facts to the group, and dispel any rumors that the students might have heard. One way to dispel rumors is by stating, "We have experienced an event that was so unusual we might find it hard to understand. I would like to share with you what we know about this tragedy. Feel free to ask questions. It's important that you understand what happened". During this step, the goal is to assist students in approaching a reality-based understanding of the event.

The next step is sharing stories about the event. The purpose of this step is to help students feel less alone and more connected to classmates. A method of reaching that goal is by saying something such as: "Each person who gets through an event, such as the one we have just experienced, has a story. We are going to tell as many of these stories as we can today. Who wants to start?" Some facilitative questions may include: "Where were you when it happened? Who were you with? What did you see, hear, smell, taste, or touch at the time? What did you do? How did you react?" Sharing their stories is meant to get the conversation about the event started so the students can talk about their experiences. Once the students start to share their experiences, facilitators should validate all experiences and identify common themes and reactions. Sharing reactions is the step that then follows sharing stories. To initiate this step, the facilitator might say something like: "Following a trauma, such as the one we've experienced, it is not unusual for people to feel and behave differently for a while. Some common reactions are sadness, anger, grief, or loneliness. These are normal reactions to abnormal circumstances. Who has had some of these reactions?" Other facilitative questions may include: "What do you think will happen next? Will you, your friends, family continue to be affected? What concerns or worries you?" Everyone reacts differently to trauma, and the goal of this step is to normalize trauma reactions.

Empowerment is the next step, and it is used to help students regain a sense of control over their lives. Concrete action is taken or planned, and identifying what students have done in the past to cope with problems helps students gain awareness of their individual effective coping strategies. The facilitator may lead the discussion with: "Traumatic events can make us feel helpless. I would like to see us take action or make plans to repair trauma-related damage or prevent trauma from reoccurring". Emphasize positive coping strategies and offer alternatives to maladaptive techniques such as drinking, attacking the gunman, etc. The final step is the conclusion. This step is meant to help students think about placing the trauma behind them. The facilitator may engage this process by asking questions such as: "What can we do to begin to place this event behind us and move on with our lives?" Activities can be used to help students put the trauma behind them and enable students to begin the process of saying goodbye to that which was lost.

Facilitators should not only focus on the students, but they should focus on their own reactions and coping. Following the completion of the six steps of GCI, there must be a facilitators' debriefing session. The debriefing session allows discussion of student reactions and decisions regarding who will need one-on-one crisis intervention. After the GCI, follow-up activities should take place depending on the needs of each group. One or 2 weeks following the event, a meeting should be held with the entire school staff to review the events, allow for ventilation of feelings, and provide further information about grief, bereavement, or adjustment to trauma (Brock et al., 2002).

Long-Term Following the Event

After 72 hours, and remaining indefinitely, is the long-term recovery process. In the following pages, we describe considerations post-group crisis intervention (GCI), and long-term psychological and/or medical treatment.

Post-GCI
After GCI, it is very important that caregivers are informed about the actions they can take to continue the coping process. For instance, caregivers need to listen to and spend time with their child. Caregivers must offer to talk about the trauma and reassure their child that he or she is safe. It is beneficial for caregivers to offer assistance with everyday tasks and chores. Caregivers should respect their child's privacy and try not to take anger or other actions personally.

Long-Term Activities
There are three main long-term activities that should be implemented when helping the student(s) with the coping process. First, a pre-entry visit to the school can ease the fears about returning to school. The pre-entry visit should be done after school, on the weekend, or another time when people are not there. Second, family support is crucial to helping the child with the coping process. Parents who have lost a child should seek a support group, such as

Compassionate Friends (https://www.compassionatefriends.org/). A referral for more intensive intervention such as psychotherapy or family therapy may be needed. School counselors and personnel should be knowledgeable about the support resources available in the community to assist families. A third suggestion for long-term activities is group treatment. This refers to the cognitive-behavioral model used when counseling students with symptoms of PTSD.

In using the cognitive-behavioral model, evidence suggests following a ten-session format (Brock et al., 2002). The ten sessions include explaining PTSD, starting the assessment process, continued assessment, controlling thoughts, controlling physical reactions, replacing unwanted images, being safe, continuing to identify ways to be safe, and termination (Brock et al., 2002). The second session, in which the assessment process begins, includes identifying cognitions. The third session, which is continued assessment, includes identifying intrusive images. The fourth session, which is also referred to as continued assessment, includes identifying physical symptoms. The cognitive-behavioral model is then implemented in the remaining sessions, and can assist children and adolescents to have awareness and control over their thought processes to enable more positive, healthy coping behaviors.

Should the Youth Receive Professional Help?
Fortunately, not all youth will need professional help to recover from a traumatic event. However, if the child is exhibiting one or more of the following behaviors 4 or more weeks following the trauma, professional help is highly recommended. Although developmental differences occur in response to trauma, the diagnostic criteria provided in Tables 8.1 and 8.2 account for these. The behaviors to look for in the child include: being unable to enjoy life, displaying sudden or severe reactions to the trauma, being unable to escape intense, ongoing distressing feelings, withdrawing from caregivers or friends, feeling jumpy or having nightmares because of, or about, the trauma, and being unable to stop thinking about the event (Kitchner & Jorm, 2012). If any PTSD or ASD symptoms are displayed, as mentioned earlier in the chapter, the student needs to be referred to a mental health professional for psychological assessment.

Physiological Interventions
Mental health caregivers such as school counselors, psychologists, or nurses should provide physiological interventions for those students experiencing mild anxiety in school following a violent school event. Two main components

of physiological interventions include emphasizing the importance of sleep and implementing relaxation techniques. Children and adolescents especially need uninterrupted, routine sleep cycles to ensure optimal development (Schupp, 2004). Educating students on the benefits of positive, as well as the repercussions of poor, sleep habits can encourage healthier sleeping routines and ultimately assist in returning to pre-trauma functioning.

Most students and adults can benefit from learning relaxation techniques. Because of the increased arousal state that exists in many trauma survivors, the need for relaxation has heightened importance. Relaxation is person-specific, but it allows trauma survivors to engage themselves in an experience that causes them to temporarily lose track of time in a safe and comforting manner (Schupp, 2004). A few techniques school personnel can implement in the school setting include guided imagery, progressive relaxation, and breathwork.

Guided imagery is a directive activity wherein the adult leads the student(s) in envisioning a "happy place" where they feel safe and comfortable. The leader goes through the five senses (auditory, taste, touch, smell, and sight), helping the student develop a psychological safe haven they can re-visit in times of stress, anxiety, or fear. If the leader feels uncomfortable with leading a guided imagery activity,[1] there is access to free transcripts and recordings online they can use instead (e.g., https://www.innerhealthstudio.com/peaceful-place.html). It is important to note trust is a major concern with students who have been violated by another person, so they may not be comfortable allowing another individual to guide their thoughts. In this case, clients may record their own message, saying exactly what is wanted or needed. The familiarity of one's own voice is pleasing to the psyche and offers no resistance to the message (Schupp, 2004).

Progressive relaxation allows the student to have a sense of control and mastery over their physiological condition. The leader directs the student(s) to tighten different muscle groups in the body and then relax each group to accentuate the idea of "going with the tension" (Schupp, 2004). Typically, progressive relaxation begins with the feet and moves up the body, ending with clenching the face, scrunching the nose, and letting everything go at once.

Although breathwork, such as deep breathing, may seem universally relaxing, not everyone can use breathing techniques. Use caution when implementing breathing techniques with students exposed to violent, traumatic school events, as any activity that causes a person to gasp for breath can evoke traumatic memories and cause re-experiencing of the original event (Schupp, 2004). This difficulty in relaxation is called "relaxation-induced anxiety", which highlights the importance of the student's feeling safe due to a sense of vulnerability that comes with being relaxed (Schupp, 2004). If the student feels comfortable with practicing breathwork, diaphragmatic breathing can be implemented in any setting. When guiding diaphragmatic breathing, direct the student to sit comfortably in a chair placing feet flat on the floor with hands on their diaphragm directly below the ribcage. Using a calm voice, have the student inhale slowly through the nostrils, filling the lungs with oxygen. Instruct the student to then exhale slowly through the nostrils, using the diaphragm, repeating this technique for 5–10 minutes several times throughout the day as needed.

Suggestions for Elementary School Teachers Following a Traumatic School Event

Following a traumatic school event, there are five suggestions for elementary school teachers to help their students cope. First, seek help the moment you suspect a student in your classroom is suffering from symptoms of PTSD. Second, provide a classroom atmosphere that affords a feeling of acceptance and safety for all of your students. This includes consistency in establishing and maintaining respectful communication among all class members, as well as incorporating classroom routines and procedures that protect students from physical or emotional harm. Third, lend a compassionate, nonjudgmental listening ear to all children exposed to the traumatic event. Allowing children to speak, write, and draw about the event enables them to process their traumas. Fourth, traumas involve feeling a loss of control; therefore, offer students options to nurture a counteracting sense of control and safety. For example, provide students with opportunities to make simple, safe choices, such as completing the even or odd numbers for homework, selecting red or blue construction paper, etc. Finally, foster academic success for students with PTSD. Shortened assignments and the use of graphic organizers promote remembering, organizing, and focusing to foster academic success. Another suggestion for fostering academic success is offering additional time for assignments to reduce anxiety and stress (Ray, 2014).

Postvention Crisis Activities

There are many postvention crisis activities that may be advantageous to children and adolescents. Increased communication with parents is extremely important. Also, providing defusing and debriefing activities and offering counseling services can be beneficial for both individual and group recovery. Setting up a "crisis room" for students needing assistance is a great postvention crisis activity. Lastly, coordinating a partnership with community resources can enable a sense of empowerment through action for students affected by the violent school event (Studer & Salter, 2010).

CBITS: Cognitive Behavioral Intervention for Trauma in Schools
Cognitive Behavioral Intervention for Trauma in Schools, or CBITS, is a skills-based group intervention provided by a school counselor, psychologist, or other mental health professional (Crepeau-Hobson & Summers, 2011). CBITS is intended to relieve symptoms of PTSD by addressing maladaptive thought processes, and in turn altering unhealthy coping behaviors to more positive expressions of self (Jaycox, 2003).

SSET: Support for Students Exposed to Trauma
Support for Students Exposed to Trauma, better known as SSET, can be implemented by school personnel without a background in mental health training (https://ssetprogram.org). SSET is a series of ten lessons intended to reduce the distress resulting from exposure to trauma (Jaycox, Langley, & Dean, 2009). For example, one lesson addresses common reactions to trauma.

Critical Incident Stress Debriefing
A critical incident is defined as "a sudden and unexpected event that has the potential to overwhelm the coping mechanisms of a whole school or members of the school community" (Beeke, 2013, p. 3). Critical Incident Stress Debriefing (CISD) was developed to promote emotional processing through allowing individuals to express reactions and prepares individuals for possible experiences following a critical incident. CISD is a psycho-educational group approach with seven phases: introduction, facts, thoughts, reactions, symptoms, teaching, and re-entry. The group format also helps in identifying individuals who may require further intensive intervention (Mitchell & Everly, 1995).

Cognitive Behavioral Techniques (CBT)
Cognitive behavioral techniques, or CBT, work by uncoupling the pairing between the traumatic stimuli/cognitive events and the anxiety response and supplants the relaxation response and more logical thinking (Basco, Glickman, Weatherford, & Ryser, 2000). CBT combines stress management strategies, including breathing techniques, progressive muscle relaxation, thought stopping, and positive imagery (Herman, 1992). Although some of the principles

of CBT can be helpful for teachers who are aiding their students' recovery, CBT is best implemented by a trained psychologist or counselor.

School Reintegration

School reintegration is designed for those students with extended absences following the traumatic event. Reintegration includes establishing the relationship, PTSD recovery education, individualized plan development, facilitated integration, and independent integration (Cook-Cottone, 2004).

Self-Care

The Importance of Processing and Reflecting Personal Experiences

It is especially important to process and reflect personal experiences for self-care following a traumatic event. It is also critical that any first aider prioritizes their own emotional well-being, similar to the MHFA guideline of ensuring your individual safety before helping others. When absorbing another person's sadness and trauma, there can be vicarious trauma or compassion fatigue that occurs in the aider's well-being. The aiders must pay attention to their own physical needs, such as maintaining a proper diet and sleep. They should ask for help from social support networks and, most importantly, allow time for healing and reflection in the self-care process (Brock et al., 2002).

Compassion Fatigue

As a psychological trauma advisor, self-care needs to be consistently monitored. Secondary traumatic stress (STS), or compassion fatigue, results from an intense and caring involvement with a traumatized person (Schupp, 2004). It is essential for those providing support services after a traumatic event to keep their self-care routines a high priority. Breaks and lunches should be taken and restful places provided; mental health days should be provided. Schools need to be worker-friendly and sensitive to the needs of trauma-care providers and aware of compassion fatigue symptoms that may occur in crisis team members or other school personnel following a school shooting or captive-taking situation (Schupp, 2004).

Compassion fatigue is a possible response for psychological first aiders and there are many symptoms referred to as "burnout symptoms" (Schupp, 2004).

The effects can be cognitive, emotional, behavioral, spiritual, personally relational, somatic, and of work performance. Cognitive symptoms are displayed as a lowered concentration at work, apathy, and preoccupation with the trauma. Emotional effects consist of feelings of powerlessness, survivor guilt, and fear. The behavioral changes exhibit impatience, nightmares, elevated startle responses, and withdrawal. Loss of purpose, questioning of prior religious beliefs, and greater skepticism are a few spiritual symptoms that may be experienced. Personal relations are changes wherein the individual feels a decreased interest in intimacy or sex, mistrust, and isolation from others. Somatic symptoms include breathing difficulties, sweating, rapid heartbeat, and other feelings of panic or anxiety. Lastly, work performance includes low morale or motivation, negativity, staff conflicts, absenteeism, and exhaustion. Debriefing sessions and an emphasis on self-care can alleviate some of the burnout symptoms in trauma-care providers and should be prioritized throughout the post-trauma recovery.

Conclusion

Although school shootings and captive-taking events are statistically rare, their impact is far-reaching. Partially due to the intense media coverage most of these events garner, many people do not feel that their children are safe at school. However, as we have shown in this chapter, data demonstrate that schools remain the safest place for children and adolescents during the day. This chapter has detailed the effects of traumatic events on school-aged children, and provides an overview of important considerations for school professionals to help students recover.

There is much that the school can do to help children in the immediate aftermath of a school shooting or other school-based trauma. However, it is important that school personnel practice self-care so they can be effective in aiding children's recovery. It is also important that traumatized school personnel have access to brief or ongoing psychological help. Finally, we remind school personnel that many students, staff, or administrators may need more long-term treatment as well. It is imperative that these individuals be referred to professionals outside of the school community for treatment.

Although we cannot yet prevent schools from being the targets of persons desiring to do harm, we can take measures proven to mitigate the immediate and long-term effects of these events. Through training, preparation, and resources, we can help all members of the school community recover after a school-based attack.

Key Messages

1. Lethal school violence is statistically uncommon, and schools remain the safest places for children and youth.
2. Some students may develop symptoms of acute stress disorder (ASD) in the days following a traumatic school attack.
3. Some students may develop symptoms of post-traumatic stress disorder (PTSD) in the months, or even years, after a school attack.
4. School personnel, family members, and individuals in the community are not immune from developing ASD or PTSD.
5. Individualized plans need to be in place for implementation of lockdowns and other crisis procedures, including plans for special needs students in the school.
6. There are research-validated psychological interventions that can aid individuals and groups in recovering from traumatic events.
7. School personnel who are helping children to recover need to practice good self-care, which may include attending to their own psychological treatments.

Appendix 8.1

Resource Materials for Teachers, Parents, and School Administrators

- American Counseling Association: https://www.counseling.org/knowledge-center/coping-in-the-aftermath-of-a-shooting
- American Psychological Association: https://www.apa.org/helpcenter/aftermath.aspx and https://www.apa.org/helpcenter/mass-shooting.aspx
- Cognitive Behavioral Intervention for Trauma in Schools: https://cbitsprogram.org/
- The Compassionate Friends—support for families after a child dies: https://www.compassionatefriends.org/
- Critical Incident Stress Debriefing (CISD): https://www.info-trauma.org/en/e-library
- Guided Imagery Exercises: https://www.innerhealthstudio.com/peaceful-place.html
- International Critical Incident Stress Foundation, Inc.: https://icisf.org/
- National School Safety Center: https://www.schoolsafety.us/home
- National Center for Education Statistics, *Indicators of School Crime and Safety: 2017*: https://nces.ed.gov/pubsearch/pubsinfo.asp?pubid=2018036
- Safe Havens International, campus security resources: http://safehavensinternational.org/
- Support for Students Exposed to Trauma (SSET): https://ssetprogram.org

Appendix 8.2

Guided Imagery Script: "Peaceful Place"

www.innerhealthstudio.com/peaceful-place.html

The purpose of this peaceful place relaxation script is to relax your mind and guide you to imagine your own peaceful, safe place. This place will be an imaginary area that you can visualize to help calm and relax your mind when you are feeling stressed.

Begin by setting aside a few minutes so that you can relax without having anything else you need to focus on. Find a comfortable position.

For the next few moments, focus on calming your mind by focusing on your breathing. Allow your breathing to center and relax you. Breathe in . . . and out.

In . . . out. . .

In . . . out. . .

Continue to breathe slowly and peacefully as you allow the tension to start to leave your body.

Release the areas of tension, feeling your muscles relax and become more comfortable with each breath.

Continue to let your breathing relax you. . .

Breathe in . . . 2. . . 3. . . 4. . . hold . . . 2. . . 3. . . out . . . 2. . . 3. . . 4. . . 5

again . . . 2. . . 3. . . 4. . . hold . . . 2. . . 3. . . out . . . 2. . . 3. . . 4. . . 5

Continue to breathe slowly, gently, comfortably. . .

Let the rate of your breathing become gradually slower as your body relaxes.

Now begin to create a picture in your mind of a place where you can completely relax. Imagine what this place needs to be like for you to feel calm and relaxed.

Start with the physical layout of the place you are imagining . . . where is this peaceful place? You might envision somewhere outdoors . . . or indoors . . . it may be a small place or large one . . . create an image of this place.

(pause)

Now picture some more details about your peaceful place. Who is in this place? Are you alone? Or perhaps you are with someone else? Are there other people present? Animals? Birds? Imagine who is at your place, whether it is you only, or if you have company.

(pause)

Imagine even more detail about your surroundings. Focus now on the relaxing sounds around you in your peaceful place.

Now imagine any tastes and smells your place has to offer.

Imagine the sensations of touch . . . including the temperature, any breeze that may be present, the surface you are on . . . imagine the details of this calming place in your mind.

Focus now on the sights of your place—colors, shapes, objects . . . plants . . . water . . . all of the beautiful things that make your place enjoyable.

To add further detail to this relaxing scene, imagine yourself there. What would you be doing in this calming place? Perhaps you are just sitting, enjoying this place, relaxing. Maybe you imagine walking around . . . or doing any other variety of activities.

Picture yourself in this peaceful place. Imagine a feeling of calm . . . of peace . . . a place where you have no worries, cares, or concerns . . . a place where you can simply rejuvenate, relax, and enjoy just being.

(pause)

Enjoy your peaceful place for a few moments more. Memorize the sights, sounds, and sensations around you. Know that you can return to this place in your mind whenever you need a break. You can take a mental vacation to allow yourself to relax and regroup before returning to your regular roles.

In these last few moments of relaxation, create a picture in your mind that you will return to the next time you need a quick relaxation break. Picture yourself in your peaceful place. This moment you are imagining now, you can picture again the next time you need to relax.

When you are ready to return to your day, file away the imaginary place in your mind, waiting for you the next time you need it.

Turn your attention back to the present. Notice your surroundings as your body and mind return to their usual level of alertness and wakefulness.

Keep with you the feeling of calm from your peaceful place as you return to your everyday life.

Note

1. A sample guided imagery exercise is included in Appendix 8.2.

References

Adamson, A. D., & Peacock, G. G. (2007). Crisis response in the public schools: A survey of school psychologists' experiences and perceptions. *Psychology in the Schools, 44*(8), 749–764.

American Psychiatric Association. (2013). *Diagnostic and statistical manual of mental disorders* (5th ed.). Washington, DC: Author.

Armstrong, K. R., Zatzick, D., Metzler, T., Weiss, D. S., Marmar, C. R., Garma, S., . . . Roepke, L. (1998). Debriefing of American Red Cross personnel: Pilot study on participants' evaluations and case examples from the 1994 Los Angeles earthquake relief operation. *Social Work in Health Care, 27*, 33–50.

Barenbaum, J., Ruchkin, V., & Schwab-Stone, M. (2004). The psychological aspects of children exposed to war: Practice and policy initiatives. *Journal of Child Psychology and Psychiatry, 45*, 41–62.

Basco, M. R., Glickman, M., Weatherford, P., & Ryser, N. (2000). Cognitive-behavioral therapy for anxiety disorders: Why and how it works. *Bulletin of the Menninger Clinic, 64*, A52–A71.

Beeke, M. (2013). Critical incidents: Exploring, theory, policy and practice. *Institute of Education Research Bulletin, 1,* 3.

Böckler, N., Seeger, T., Sitzer, P., & Heitmeyer, W. (2013). School shootings: Conceptual framework and international empirical trends. In N. Böckler, T. Seeger, P. Sitzer, & W. Heitmeyer (Eds.), *School shootings: International research, case studies, and concepts for prevention* (pp. 1–24). New York, NY: Springer.

Borum, R., Cornell, D. G., Modzeleski, W., & Jimerson, S. R. (2010). What can be done about school shootings? A review of the evidence. *Educational Researcher, 39,* 27–37. doi:10.3102/0013189X09357620

Brock, S. E., Sandoval, J., & Lewis, S. (2001). *Preparing for crises in the schools: A manual for building school crisis response teams* (2nd ed.). New York, NY: Wiley.

Brock, S., Lazarus, P., & Jimerson, S. (2002). *Best practices in school crisis prevention and intervention.* Bethesda, MD: National Association of School Psychologists.

Centers for Disease Control and Prevention. (2010). *National violent death reporting system.* Retrieved from www.cdc.gov/violencePrevention/NVDRS/index.html

Clarke, L. S., Embury, D. C., Jones, R. E., & Yssel, N. (2014). Supporting students with disabilities during school crises: A teacher's guide. *Teaching Exceptional Children, 46*(6), 169–178. doi:10.1177/0014402914534616

Cook-Cottone, C. (2004). Childhood posttraumatic stress disorder: Diagnosis, treatment, and school reintegration. *School Psychology Review, 33*(1), 127–139.

Cornell, D. G. (2006). *School violence: Facts versus fears.* Mahwah, NJ: Lawrence Erlbaum Associates.

Cornell, D. G., & Malone, M. (2015). Child and adolescent homicide. In V. Van Hasselt-and & M. Bourke (Eds.), *Handbook of behavioral criminology.* New York, NY: Springer.

Crepeau-Hobson, F., Sievering, K., Armstrong, C., & Stonis, J. (2012). A coordinated mental health crisis response: Lessons learned from three Colorado school shootings. *Journal of School Violence, 11,* 207–225.

Crepeau-Hobson, F., & Summers, L. (2011). The crisis response to a school-based hostage event: A case study. *Journal of School Violence, 10,* 281–298.

Daniels, J. A., & Bradley, M. C. (2011). *Preventing lethal school violence.* New York, NY: Springer.

Daniels, J. A., Bradley, M., Cramer, D., Winkler, A., Kinebrew, K., & Crockett, D. (2007). In the aftermath of a school hostage event: A case study of one school counselor's response. *Professional School Counseling, 10*(5), 482–489.

Daniels, J. A., Bradley, M. C., & Hays, M. (2007). The impact of school violence on school personnel: Implications for psychologists. *Professional Psychology: Research and Practice, 38,* 652–659. doi:10.1037/0735-7028.38.6.652

Daniels, J. A., & Haist, J. (2012). School violence and trauma. In L. Lopez Levers (Ed.), *Trauma counseling: Theories and interventions* (pp. 335–348). New York, NY: Springer Publishing Company.

Daniels, J. A., & Page, J. (2012). School-barricaded captive-taking: A literature review and critique. *Aggression and Violent Behavior, 17,* 140–146.

Daniels, J. A., & Page, J. (2013). Averted school shootings. In N. Böckler, T. Seeger, P. Sitzer, & W. Heitmeyer (Eds.), *School shootings: International research, case studies, and concepts for prevention* (pp. 421–439). New York, NY: Springer.

Dickson, M. J., & Vargo, K. K. (2017). Training kindergarten students lockdown drill procedures using behavioral skills training. *Journal of Applied Behavior Analysis, 50,* 407–412.

Dorn, M., Thomas, G., Wong, M., & Shepherd, S. (2004). *Jane's safe schools planning guide for all hazards*. Surrey, UK: Jane's Information Group.

Elklit, A., & Kurdahl, S. (2013). The psychological reactions after witnessing a killing in public in a Danish high school. *European Journal of Psychotraumatology, 4*, 1–7. http://dx.doi.org/10.3402/ejpt.v4i0.19826

Elliott, D., Hamburg, B., & Williams, K. (1998). *Violence in American schools*. Cambridge, UK: Cambridge University Press.

Gereluk, D. T., Donlevy, J. K., & Thompson, M. B. (2015). Normative considerations in the aftermath of gun violence in schools. *Educational Theory, 65*(4), 459–474.

Herman, J. L. (1992). *Trauma and recovery: The aftermath of violence—From domestic abuse to political terror*. New York, NY: Basic Books.

Horowitz, K., McKay, M., & Marshall, R. (2005). Community violence and urban families: Experiences, effects, and directions for intervention. *American Journal of Orthopsychiatry, 75*, 356–368.

Jaycox, L. H. (2003). *CBITS: Cognitive behavioral intervention for trauma in schools*. Longmont, CO: Sopris West Educational Services

Jaycox, L. H., Langley, A. K., & Dean, K. L. (2009). *Support for students exposed to trauma: The SSET Program*. Retrieved from www.rand.org/pubs/technical_reports/2009/RAND_TR675.pdf

Jones, N. M., Thompson, R. R., Schetter, C. D., & Silver, R. C. (2017). Distress and rumor exposure on social media during a campus lockdown. *PNAS—Proceedings of the National Academy of Sciences of the United States of America, 114*, 11,663–11,668. Retrieved from www.pnas.org/cgi/doi/10.1073/pnas.1708518114

Kelly, E., & May, D. (2011). Increases in school shootings: Reality or myth? *International Journal of Sociological Research, 4*, 45–57.

Kitchner, B. A., & Jorm, A. F. (2012). *Youth mental health first aid USA: For adults assisting young people*. Baltimore, MD: Mental Health Association of Maryland.

Larsson, G., Michel, P., & Lundin, T. (2000). Systematic assessment of mental health following various types of posttrauma support. *Military Psychology, 12*, 121–135.

Mitchell, J. T., & Everly, G. S. (1995). *Critical Incident Stress Debriefing (CISD): An operations manual for the prevention of traumatic stress among emergency service and disaster workers* (2nd ed.). Ellicott City, MD: Chevron Publishing Corporation.

Moore, M. H., Petrie, C. V., Braga, A. A., & McLaughlin, B. L. (Eds.). (2003). *Deadly lessons: Understanding lethal school violence*. Washington, DC: National Academies Press.

Murtonen, K., Suomalainen, L., Haravuori, H., & Marttunen, M. (2012). Adolescents' experiences of psychosocial support after traumatisation in a school shooting. *Child and Adolescent Mental Health, 17*, 23–30. doi:10.1111/j.1475-3588.2011.00612.x

Musu-Gillette, L., Zhang, A., Wang, K., Zhang, J., Kemp, J., Diliberti, M., & Oudekerk, B. A. (2018). *Indicators of School Crime and Safety: 2017* (NCES 2018-036/NCJ 251413). Washington, DC: National Center for Education Statistics, US Department of Education, and Bureau of Justice Statistics, Office of Justice Programs, US Department of Justice.

Nekvasil, E. K., Cornell, D. G., & Huang, F. L. (2015). Prevalence and offense characteristics of multiple casualty homicides: Are schools at higher risk than other locations? *Psychology of Violence, 5*, 236–245. doi:http://dx.doi.org/10.1037/a0038967

Newman, K. S., Fox, C., Harding, D. J., Mehta, J., & Roth, W. (2004). *Rampage: The social roots of school shootings*. New York, NY: Basic Books.

O'Toole. (2000). *The school shooter: A threat assessment perspective*. Quantize, VA: National Center for the Analysis of Violent Crime, Federal Bureau of Investigation.

Psychiatry Online. (2018). *DSM Library, Trauma- and stressor-related disorders*. Retrieved from the world wide web May 29, 2018 from https://dsm.psychiatryonline.org/doi/10.1176/appi.books.9780890425596.dsm07 https://doi.org/10.1176/appi.books.9780890425596.dsm07

Ray, J. (2014). Posttraumatic stress disorder in children: What elementary teachers should know. *Kappa Delta Pi Record, 50*(3), 109–113.

Rocque, M. (2012). Exploring school rampage shootings: Research, theory, and policy. *The Social Science Journal, 49*, 304–313. doi:10.1016/j.soscij.2011.11.001

Schupp, L. J. (2004). *Assessing and treating trauma and PTSD*. Eau Claire, WI: PESI HealthCare.

Stein, T. M. (2007). Mass shootings. In D. E. Hogan & J. L. Burnstein (Eds.), *Disaster medicine* (2nd ed.). Philadelphia, PA: Lippincott Williams & Wilkins.

Studer, J. R., & Salter, S. E. (2010). *The role of the school counselor in crisis planning and intervention*. Retrieved from http://counselingoutfitters.com/vistas/vistas10/Article_92.pdf

Vossekuil, B., Fein, R., Reddy, M., Borum, R., & Modzeleski, W. (2002). *The final report and findings of the safe school initiative: Implications for prevention of school attacks in the United States*. Washington, DC: US Department of Education, Office of Elementary and Secondary Education, Safe and Drug-Free Schools Program and US Secret Service, National Threat Assessment Center.

Whealin, J. M., Ruzek, J. I., & Vega, E. M. (2013). Cognitive behavioral methods for building resilience. In R. R. Sinclair & T. W. Britt (Eds.), *Building psychological resilience in military personnel: Theory and practice*. Washington, DC: American Psychological Association.

Exposure to Terrorism and Political Violence   **9**

Judith A. Myers-Walls

This chapter addresses working with children who have been exposed to the potential trauma of terrorism and political violence. It defines the relevant terms and then describes the levels at which children's lives might be influenced by these events and some possible consequences of exposure. It goes on to explore resilience in children and outline ways that schools could play preventive and restorative roles with children and their families when they face terrorism and political violence. The chapter ends with a list of related resources.

Definition of Terms

Danger is generally defined as the possibility or likelihood of harm or injury or of the occurrence of something unwelcome or unpleasant. A logical assumption is that the threats that are more likely are also of more concern. However, Witte (1994) has said that the key issue for impact on people's well-being is not objective threat, but what is *perceived* to be a threat. The perception of threat seems to bypass cognitive processes and lead to emotion-based responses and instinctive self-preservation (Chemtob, Roitblat, Hamada, Carlson, & Twentyman, 1988).

Terrorism is all about fear and threat. Merriam-Webster defines *terrorism* as "the systematic use of terror especially as a means of coercion" (https://www.merriam-webster.com/dictionary/terrorism). Pereda (2013) has further pointed out that terrorist acts are "unpredictable and episodic, and imply an undefined threat" (p. 182) and that terrorism combines two characteristics particularly unsettling for adults and children: (1) acts are intentional and (2) they seem random. When examining the effect of terrorism on the average adult or child in countries without active armed violence, the distinction between objective and perceived threat is especially relevant. Although a person in the United States between 2002 and 2017 was almost six times more likely to be killed in a shark attack than by a refugee terrorist (and the likelihood of dying in a shark attack is only 1 in 8 million), the Federal Government has taken significant steps to limit the acceptance of refugee immigrants (People.com, 2017). It follows that objective threat is not the primary danger of terrorism in the United States and similar locations; we cannot assume that only true objective threat will compromise children's well-being. There are many ways that children may be touched by terrorism/political violence.

The term *political violence* was added to the title of this chapter because the differentiation between terrorism and political violence or war is sometimes related to a person's perceptions more than an objective difference. Whether the armed conflict is seen as primarily aimed at instilling fear and terror or is seen as legitimate force to achieve a political objective (or "war") is of little importance to those who need to deal with its consequences. Terrorism, state-sponsored armed aggression, and wars all increasingly use similar tactics. The seeming randomness and unpredictability are important aspects of terrorism that keep people around the world on edge. Therefore, although terrorism/political violence may be less likely to physically harm children than other kinds of violence, the likelihood is not the most relevant characteristic to consider. Not all threats of violence have the same outcomes, however. A contrast between war/terrorism and other violence such as child abuse is that child abuse/domestic violence and targeted school shootings, for instance, have a personal or relational focus whereas political violence and terrorism reflect intergroup conflicts. As Cairns (1996) defined it, political violence is "violence perpetrated by one set or group of people on another set or group of people who were often strangers to each other before the violence occurred" (p. 10). Individuals become dangerous and threatening to each other not because of some previous interaction or personal vendetta but simply because of group membership.

How Children's Lives and Well-Being Might Be Touched by Terrorism and Political Violence

UNICEF has estimated that more than one billion children worldwide (more than half of the world's children) live in countries affected by armed conflict (VOANews, 2014). There are many risks to consider when examining the dangers of terrorism/political violence for children; I have outlined six levels of exposure (Myers-Walls, 2004, 2010). It could take place at home, in the child's neighborhood or community, or in schools. The levels are: (1) direct exposure to armed violence and physical harm, (2) displacement or refugee status due to armed conflict, (3) experiencing the deployment of family and/ or friends, (4) suffering from economic sanctions or military expenditures, (5) observing armed conflict through mass media, and (6) being subjected to propaganda and enemy images. I will discuss each level individually, although children and families could be exposed to several levels either consecutively or simultaneously.

Direct Exposure to Armed Violence and Physical Harm

War zones are messy places, and direct experience in them is the most visible and potentially devastating of the levels of exposure. There are several ways that children can become direct victims of war (Garreau, 2012; Santa Barbara, 2006):

- *Civilian victims.* Some injuries from armed conflict may be due to accidental collateral damage inflicted by weapons such as land mines and unexploded ammunition, but at other times, children are purposely targeted as a means to terrorize and demoralize a group of people (Shaheen & Graham-Harrison, 2016).
- *Child soldiers.* Young people under the age of 18 who are recruited or conscripted into service in armies and militias are classified as child soldiers (UNICEF, 2009). Younger children are often placed in support roles, whereas older children are taught to fight and kill or participate in terrorist acts like suicide bombings. Child soldiers may be liberated and returned to their homes, but they are often shunned or rejected.
- *Displaced children and orphans.* The chaos of war and armed conflict often separates children from the adults who have cared for them, due either to parental death or untraceable relocations. Separations can happen within a war zone and outside of it.

- *Wounded, ill, or handicapped children.* Because armed conflict is not restricted to limited locations and instead is aimed at civilian populations, serious civilian injuries and maiming are common (UNICEF, 2009). At the same time, infrastructure and support systems are generally disrupted in war zones, making both medical and mental-health care inadequate and difficult to locate.
- *Imprisoned children.* The terrorist tactic of abducting children can be as effective as, or more effective than, killing children in manipulating a population. Abduction leads to *ambiguous loss* (Boss, 1999), which can keep parents and communities in a frozen state, not knowing whether to grieve or search for the children. The abducted children themselves also experience ambiguous loss, not knowing whether they will be returned or whether their parents continue to care about them or are even still alive.
- *Exploited children (sexual exploitation or forced labor).* Sexual contact with children is another way to take something valuable—children and their childhood—from those on the other side of the conflict, and pregnancies can be a way to conquer another ethnic group and contribute to genocide and the obliteration of the enemy (Machel, 1996). Mistreatment and pregnancies continue to be traumatizing even if the victims are returned to their home communities where they and their offspring may be rejected (Leithead, 2016).

Displacement or Refugee Status

Families and children often flee armed conflict, leaving all that is familiar, which might feel more dangerous to the children than staying in the war zone. The United Nations High Commission on Refugees (UNHCR) reported that 65.6 million people worldwide were displaced by conflict or persecution at the end of 2016 (Edwards, 2017). More than 28 million children were among those numbers (McKirdy, 2016). UNHCR says that half of all refugees are children (Edwards, 2017).

Some of these children and families find themselves in new and generally secure situations, but finding true safety and security can be very difficult. Many refugees undergo significant stress and trauma in conflict zones before and during their escapes, and that legacy can travel with them to their new homes and schools. Many young people and their families are left with symptoms of post-traumatic stress disorder (PTSD) and/or depression (Berthold, 2000). Refugee camps can be as bad or worse than war zones with danger and deprivation still present. Refugees often dream of returning home to the motherland, which can leave children feeling rootless and unsettled.

Experiencing the Deployment of Family and/or Friends

In 2011, more than 1.2 million dependent children lived in active-duty military families in the United States (Clever & Segal, 2013). There is unfortunately limited research on how living in a home with a deployed parent has affected children. Published studies, mostly from the United States, have found that, although some children show negative outcomes related to their family situation, others do well and show considerable resilience. Approximately one-third of children with combat-deployed parents have shown clinically significant levels of depression, anxiety, or externalizing symptoms (Flake, Davis, Johnson, & Middleton, 2009; Lester et al., 2010). It is important to note that some of these effects remained even after the parents returned from combat (Lester et al., 2010). Important factors predicting child adjustment difficulties were parents' poor mental health levels and a high number of times a parent had been combat-deployed. At least one study found that deployment can be associated with poor parent-child attachment (Posada, Walker, Cardin, Nyaronga, & Schwarz, 2015). In one interview study (Chandra, Martin, Hawkins, & Richardson, 2009), school personnel reported that they saw many children in the United States who had fears and worries about their deployed parents, increased home responsibilities, concerns about the mental health of the non-deployed parent, and difficulties with getting mental health assistance. All of these conditions can lower the ability of children to thrive in school.

Suffering from Economic Sanctions or Military Expenditure

Military economic costs are objective dangers of which most children would not be aware, but are important risks that could threaten children's futures and often their school careers. Because of their physical and social vulnerability, children often bear the brunt of the impact from fiscal shortfalls resulting from a country's military expenditures and/or sanctions (Arnove, 2000). The redirection of funds away from healthcare, education, infrastructure, and recreation may be experienced by some children and families as dangers and threats, and they have consequences for the upcoming generations (Watson Institute, 2017).

Observing Armed Conflict Through Media

It would seem logical that children exposed to terrorism/political violence only through mass media would be in less danger of negative outcomes than those who are closer to the armed violence, but that is not the case. In fact, Holman, Garfin, and Silver (2014) found that individuals with a heavy diet of media exposure to the terror attacks at the Boston Marathon had *higher* psychological stress symptoms than those who experienced the attacks directly. Comer and Kendall (2007) call that *second-hand terrorism*. Young people are some of the heaviest users of some mass media—especially social media, a format that facilitates the goal of instilling terror in the largest possible population and in continually innovative ways (Comer, Furr, Beidas, Weiner, & Kendall, 2008). In addition, at least one study found that print media were actually associated with more trauma than television (Pfefferbaum et al., 2005), suggesting that all media sources should be monitored.

Young children are especially challenged with knowing the difference between media and reality (Carrick, Quas, & García Coll, 2006); that confusion becomes even more blurred when entertainment media are based on actual news events, and news ("fake" or real) is spread on Facebook, Twitter, and Instagram, along with the perspectives and interpretations of many lay individuals. These media settings can be ideal for terrorist efforts by providing low-cost, uncensored, and immediately global outlets for disrupting the security and well-being of adults and children.

Being Subjected to Propaganda and Enemy Images
Closely related to the previous topic is exposure to propaganda related to creating an image of the "enemy". Defining a country or group of people as "other" and dangerous in some way can occur as a precursor to or as a result of a conflict and can be constructed in family, peer group, and societal settings (Oppenheimer, 2006). Children are not born knowing enemies. As Hesse put it, "We go through a long and subtle process of political and ideological education in childhood and adolescence during which we learn to identify the heroes and villains in our own country and in international politics" (1989, p. 1). The image-building is usually insidious and includes methods as varied as school lessons, children's toys and entertainment, media campaigns, and parental comments (Hesse, 1989; Oppenheimer, 2006, Vriens, 1999).

Building an image of an enemy is sometimes a method of managing the stress and trauma of war or armed conflict. Some researchers found that the definition of the enemy becomes integral to children's definitions of themselves: "[T]hose raised in the greatest conflict . . . have organized their self-definitions (identity) around participation in the conflict" (Elbedour, Bastien, & Center, 1997, p. 227). That suggests that some children grow up knowing themselves best in juxtaposition with those they hate. Although this process can help children deal with trauma at some level by finding meaning in difficult situations, it can plant the seeds for greater problems in the future. As Garbarino (1991) put it, the enemy image-building can "set in motion the dark forces of the human spirit . . . The same ideology that gives meaning to life in a war zone may also lead to a process of dehumanization" (p. 22). That can lead to greater likelihood of future conflicts throughout the children's and community's lives.

In addition, a belief that the world is dangerous can be a self-sustaining mindset. Muris, Ollendick, Roelofs, and Austin (2014) discovered that adolescents who showed high levels of fear tended to actively seek confirmation of that fear. The more anxious they were, the more likely they were to notice events that supported their belief that their fears were justified. Those fears can then become even more resistant to change if family members, friends, and societal messages support the anxiety. This exposure can also lead to adolescents taking greater risks than others (Pat-Horenczyk et al., 2007).

Consequences of Child Exposure to Terrorism and Political Conflict

The consequences from exposure to terrorism/political violence vary quite widely. Next, four primary categories of potential consequences are described: (1) threats to physical health, safety, and well-being; (2) disruptions in psychological/emotional health and well-being; (3) restrictions in life experiences and developmental opportunities; and (4) problematic world views and beliefs.

Physical Health, Safety, and Well-Being

Physical well-being and health are at risk in several levels of exposure. In 1996, Machel reported that more than 2 million children had been killed in armed conflict in the previous decade and approximately three times that number had been seriously injured or physically maimed. Some analyses suggest that the rate of child deaths and injuries as a result of armed conflict could continually rise as the nature of conflicts becomes increasingly civilian-based (UNICEF, 2009).

Physical injuries and deaths have been connected with exposure to weapons aimed directly at children and other civilians (Shaheen & Graham-Harrison, 2016) or with accidental or incidental death or injury due to dangers such as land mines or unexploded munitions (UNICEF, 2009). Some physical health consequences can also arise from disruptions in healthcare services as a result of direct or indirect attacks on institutions (Rosenau, Chalk, McPherson, Parker, & Long, 2009, UNICEF, 2009), living in refugee camps or other locations with multiple health risks and poor or non-existent healthcare facilities

(Luxemburger, Rigal, & Nosten, 1998), or dislocation to sites in which refugees are not eligible for services (see, e.g., Philbrick, Wicks, Harris, Shaft, & Van Vooren, 2017). Finally, health service availability could be reduced when military expenditures redirect funds away from healthcare (Watson Institute, 2017).

Psychological or Emotional Health and Well-Being

Psychological well-being could be at risk at any of the exposure levels listed in the previous section. Stress, depression, fear or anxiety, and post-traumatic stress disorder (PTSD) are referenced in many reviews of the impact of terrorism/political violence on children. As stated earlier, children with high levels of fear are also likely to take excessive risks (Pat-Horenczyk et al., 2007). Direct exposure to armed violence that leads to personal injury or loss of a parent has been most closely related to extreme stress reactions in children, especially young ones (Cohen, Chazan, Lerner, & Maimon, 2010). Over time, the effects of witnessing violence appear to fade, but not the effects of personal injury and loss of a parent.

Some studies found levels of PTSD in children that ranged from 13% to 40% (Anonymous, 2003; Peltonen, Qouta, Diab, & Punamaki, 2014; Pfefferbaum et al., 2005; Veronese, Pepe, Jaradah, Murannak, & Hamdouna, 2017). However, a review of 17 studies of children's psychological well-being after exposure to war and political violence (Attanayake et al., 2009) found the range for PTSD—the most frequent reaction measured and reported—to be from 4.5% to 89.3%, with an overall pooled estimate of 47%. The authors explained the significant variability among reports as being due to methods of measurement, study locations, or length of time since exposure. The ages of children being assessed, types and amounts of exposure to violence, moderating factors, and training and perspectives of those assessing the symptoms are other possible explanations of variability. Similar variability has been found in measures of psychological reactions such as depression, anxiety, and behavior problems. Clearly, there is a potential for PTSD and other psychological distress when children are exposed to war or political violence, but it is not inevitable or universal.

Restrictions in Life Experiences and Developmental Opportunities

Restrictions could occur in war zones and locations of active armed aggression and among refugees when schools and other community programs are closed, parents' workplaces cannot function, or transportation and utilities are disrupted (Jordans et al., 2010; Klingman, 1992; UNICEF, 2009). It is conceivable that restrictions in children's lives could occur at other levels of exposure as well if parents and other adults respond to the threats and potential dangers of terrorism/political violence by reducing children's freedom of movement and range of exploration in an effort to keep them safe (Foster, Villanueva, Wood, Christian, & Giles-Corti, 2014). In addition, whenever disruptive events occur, even if they are short term, routines and rituals are interrupted, making life difficult for children who thrive on predictability. Another common outcome in communities facing political violence is the expectation that children are required to take on additional responsibilities that interfere with school and other developmentally appropriate activities (Hick, 2001).

Influence on Children's World Views and Beliefs

Impacting children's world views and beliefs can take place at any level of exposure. Children may learn from their exposure that the world is a dangerous place, some people or groups of people cannot be trusted, and one must be ready to fight for survival (Belsky, 2008; Hesse, 1989; Oppenheimer, 2006; Vriens, 1999). These attitudes can be connected with children's psychological well-being, leading to high anxiety and hypervigilance, and can be passed from one person or generation to the next. Belsky (2008) suggests that this inheritance can be realistic and adaptive, but Garbarino, Kostelny, and Dubrow (1991) propose that these world views can contribute to deeply ensconced conflict that is highly resistant to peacemaking efforts. Of course, it needs to be recognized that some children respond to exposure to terrorism/political violence with resilience and a commitment to growth.

Resilience in Children and Families Exposed to Terrorism and Political Violence

Accomplishing the goal of reducing or eliminating terrorism/political violence would be ideal, but it is very difficult and not likely to be fully achieved in the near future. Therefore, professionals need to know what to do when children and families experience the negative consequences previously discussed. To explore possible prevention or restorative actions, it can help to examine resilience among children who are exposed to terrorism/political violence.

Although the negative outcomes experienced by many children are serious and demand treatment and mitigation, it is critical that individuals and societies do not despair and assume that the worst outcomes are inevitable (Peltonen et al., 2014). There is significant variability in how children respond to both exposure and restorative efforts, and children themselves provide the motivation for action and hope for the future. As Graça Machel (1996) stated:

> I have learned . . . that despite being targets in contemporary armed conflict, despite the brutality shown towards them and the failure of adults to nurture and protect them, children are both our reason to eliminate the worst aspects of armed conflict and our best hope of succeeding in that charge. In a disparate world, children are a unifying force capable of bringing us all together in support of a common ethic.
>
> (UNICEF, 2009, p. 5)

Moderating Factors and Characteristics of Resilience

Several characteristics of settings or events have been identified as mediating or moderating factors in children's outcomes, including the kind, frequency, and duration of exposure; how widespread it is; what protective factors were in place before, during, and after the event; the meaning that the child is able to make of the event; and whether it is associated with significant vs. limited amounts of deprivation of basic needs and services (Magid & Boothby, 2013; Shaw, 2003). In addition, there are characteristics of individuals, families, and communities that predict resilience and positive outcomes (e.g., Peltonen et al., 2014; Tol, Jordans, Kohrt, Betancourt, & Komproe, 2013; Walsh, 2016) and can provide guidance in ways to improve the outcomes for greater numbers of children and youth.

The theoretical perspectives of three resilience frameworks (Peltonen et al., 2014; Tol et al., 2013; Walsh, 2016), along with other theoretical and empirical studies, suggest keys to lowering the incidence of negative consequences among exposed children and maximizing positive outcomes: individual child factors; relationships with families, peers, and other components of children's immediate environments; community conditions; and the broad cultural and societal context.

Individual Factors

Although resilience is conceptualized as built into the relationship and context, and not technically an individual characteristic (Boss, 1999; Walsh, 2016), some individual factors have been identified (Peltonen et al., 2014; Tol et al., 2013) as contributing to children's resilience, such as creativity, problem-solving skills, and intelligence—characteristics that help children and youth establish perspective, understand the situation, and use cognitive coping strategies. Age and maturity of the child have also been associated with resilience, which highlights the particular needs of young children for targeted support and assistance with building resilience.

Family, Peers, and Children's Immediate Environment

Connectedness and attachments with families, peers, schools, and neighborhoods were important factors identified for facilitating resilience in multiple studies (Klingman, 1992; Magid & Boothby, 2013; Pfefferbaum et al., 2005). As central figures in that network, parents or caregivers are especially important sources of social support for all ages of children dealing with terrorism/political violence and are a critical presence for young children. Peers become increasingly important as children grow older (Peltonen et al., 2014). Flexibility and adaptiveness within families and schools are also important qualities that serve to counterbalance violent events that disrupt normal life (Walsh, 2016). Supportive peers and family members can also help with establishing and maintaining belief systems and finding meaning in difficult situations (Veronese, Pepe, Jaradah, Murannak, & Hamdouna, 2017). As mentioned earlier, however, although meaning-making is helpful in managing stress, there are complications if those beliefs are ideologically inflexible and based on promoting negative images of the "other" and pitting different social groups against each other.

Community Institutions and Cultural Institutions

Religion, government, and culture can provide comforting support for children and families in violent situations (Jordans et al., 2010; Magid & Boothby, 2013; Peltonen et al., 2014). Activities and rituals that are familiar and promote a sense of belonging can contribute to restoring normalcy and boosting resilience (Klingman, 1992). Schools and community centers may be seen as safe havens that are politically neutral and open to all. Government programs that provide food, healthcare, shelter, and other emergency-assistance resources can contribute to resilience—as long as the government is functioning and its help is available to all who need it.

Cultural Values, Beliefs, and Practices

Values and beliefs help children and families make meaning of difficult situations, provide a backdrop for how people will respond to terrorism/political violence, and play a part in how and when these violent events occur (Jordans et al., 2010; Tol et al., 2013; Webster & Harris, 2009). One important issue is whether the environmental situation and expectations in which the children find themselves are familiar and comfortable. Basic lifestyle conditions such as food, sleeping arrangements, and hygiene are likely to serve as comfort if they are recognizable as similar to home, whereas significant changes in those amenities could contribute to additional stress and difficulty with coping. Cultural practices like music, dance, art, and holiday rituals can be reassuring and restorative. Some cultural practices could help prepare children for the conditions in which they might find themselves in relation to terrorism/political violence and thereby contribute to resilience (Magid & Boothby, 2013). Familiarity breeds comfort.

All cultural groups have practices and rituals related to self-identity and the identification of and relationships with insiders and outsiders. Resilience in the context of cultural diversity is related to whether the primary focus is on differences or shared values and beliefs inherent in the cultures (Garbarino et al., 1991). Even children under 1 year of age have been found to recognize whether a person is gentle and supportive or rejecting and mean to other people (de Waal, 2008; Hamlin, Wynn, & Bloom, 2007). Positive emotional contagion and empathy can be reassuring and build resilience even when directed at other people, whereas witnessing exclusion and rejection can contribute to uneasiness and fear.

Recommendations for Educational Institutions

The information provided so far provides a foundation for recommendations in the following eight categories that can be applied by schools and other educational or community institutions: (1) self-examination and caring for educators and other school personnel; (2) reuniting families and reintegrating social support systems; (3) preventing armed conflict and advocating for children; (4) providing safe spaces; (5) talking with children about terrorism and political violence; (6) screening children for specialized services; (7) monitoring the educational environment; and (8) teaching children peacemaking skills. It should be noted, however, that there is significant overlap across the categories and each deserves attention using a comprehensive approach.

1. Self-Examination and Caring for Educators and Other School Personnel

Times of political violence and terrorist events are unsettling for everyone, including educators (Institute of Medicine, 2014). As research has shown, improving the well-being of caregiving adults is one of the most powerful ways to enhance children's adjustment (Toros, 2013), as it helps teachers, administrators, and other caregivers put on their metaphorical oxygen masks first so they can help the children (McInerney & McKlindon, n.d.; TSA, n.d.).

As frequent first or second responders to children when terrorism/political violence occurs, educators are tasked with figuring out how to satisfy their own needs and at the same time provide reassurance to children. They need to resist the temptation to turn on a live newsfeed in the classroom, where children will be exposed to unfiltered and potentially traumatic information. When I was a child, a live radio announcement was broadcast over the school loudspeaker that President Kennedy had been shot. For thousands of children as young as kindergarten-age across the country on September 11, 2001, there was live TV coverage of the terrorist attacks in New York City and Washington, DC. (Kingade, 2011).

Recommendations:

- Make sure that children are as safe as possible. Follow emergency protocols.
- Practice emergency procedures in a routine and comfortable way for both children and adults. Avoid introducing trauma during drills.
- Monitor your own reactions. Use stress management strategies (e.g., deep breathing) to be able to provide a secure base for the children. Avoid emotion contagion of stress, fear, or anger reactions from adults to children.
- Recognize your own needs. If you find that you are unable to manage your own reactions, plan how to pass the care of the children to someone else.
- Consider establishing pairs or small groups of personnel to share the care of the children as necessary. This will allow the adults to alternate between managing the children and meeting their own needs.
- Keep track of critical events as necessary, but keep the primary focus on the children.
- Avoid taking sides on sensitive issues. Accept a wide variety of children's attitudes and reactions.

2. Reuniting Families and Reintegrating Social Support Systems

In times of terrorism and political violence, families can often be separated (Centers for Disease Control and Prevention, 2017; REMS, n.d.). Both children and parents are likely to think immediately about family. They want to know where other family members are and whether they are safe. Facilitating the reunification of families is critical because "the risk of trauma or danger experienced by children increases with the time that they remain separated from their family" (REMS, n.d., p. 1).

Schools should be sure that their emergency operations plans (EOPs) include procedures for family reunification. Readiness and Emergency Management for Schools (REMS; n.d.) notes that schools are involved in reunification between parents and children every day and can build on those plans in emergencies. Collaboration with other community resources can maximize positive outcomes for children and families and avoid communication gaps. Schools are also ideal institutions to bring together community networks and support systems. Supporting whole family healing and well-being is a powerful way to support the children (Jordans et al., 2010; Webster & Harris, 2009). Schools are local and familiar, but their reach is across households, helping to reduce family isolation when normal routines are interrupted.

Recommendations:

- Establish plans for dealing with emergencies, including terrorism and political violence. Include reunification of families in those plans.
- Avoid drills that are graphic and frightening. Try to normalize the emergency procedures and make them comfortable and even special in some way to prepare children to react calmly.
- Identify other relevant local community resources available to your school and its families and build collaborative relationships.
- Consider how the school can serve as a central, neutral meeting site for the surrounding community. This can help with immediate reunification and later rebuilding.
- Consider providing educational programs and workshops for families on preparation and recovery.
- Partner with families and communities when making plans. Gather input from families about needs and preferences and inform families about plans and resources.

- Be sensitive to a variety of family forms. In addition to pre-existing diversity, family forms may be changed as a result of violence that causes death or dislocation of family members. Be respectful of how individuals define their own families and support their efforts to renegotiate boundaries and roles after disruption.

3. Becoming Advocates to Prevent Armed Conflict and Support Children

Preventing terrorism/political violence is a more powerful way to achieve positive outcomes for children and families than trying to pick up the pieces after they have been negatively affected. Wexler, Branski, and Kerem (2006) focused on the roles of medical professionals in preventing terrorism/political violence, and their recommendations could be adapted to educational professionals. Like medical caregivers, educators are likely to be some of the first to recognize if children are suffering ill effects of exposure to terrorism/political violence. They also are likely to notice signs of atrocities or actions that violate international law, and could report the abuses to appropriate authorities. Educators are also likely to have contact with parents and professionals on multiple sides of political conflicts and may be able to facilitate dialogue that could lead to positive outcomes. Finally, educators can help give a voice to the children and tell their stories of the impact of the violence on the younger generation. They also can highlight when children's needs are being met in times of terrorism/political violence, and can advocate for public spending priorities that serve children.

Recommendations:

- Report any indications that children have suffered from atrocities or actions that violate international law. Know where and how to report those actions.
- Bring together parents and community members on different sides of political struggles when possible. Build on the community base of public schools and focus on shared interests and goals.
- Tell the stories of children who are coping with any level of terrorism and political violence. When possible, include the voices of children by sharing children's drawings, dramas, or quotes or allowing children to speak for themselves.

4. Providing Child-Friendly Spaces

One of the most challenging results of children's exposure to terrorism/political violence is the loss of predictability and routine (Jordans et al., 2010). An important way to support children is for schools to remain open and in session whenever possible and offer some kind of program. Klingman (1992) confirms, "Individuals and institutions . . . should continue to function as much as possible in as many aspects of life as before the crisis" (p. 378).

The goal is to create "child-friendly spaces" (CFSs) for children and families (Ager & Metzler, 2012). These are used by agencies to protect children from risk, promote their psychosocial well-being, and support a community's efforts to strengthen its child-protection efforts. They are "protected environments in which [children] participate in organized activities to play, socialize, learn, and express themselves as they rebuild their lives" (Save the Children, 2008, p. 1). The key characteristics of CFSs, based on the United Nations Convention of the Rights of the Child and on literature about resilient children, could be followed in creating restorative environments. Even when schools are closed, school personnel and/or other community professionals could take advantage of the centrality and familiarity of the school building to offer children a child-friendly haven with caring people who support the qualities of tolerance, respect, and peacemaking in the midst of the threat or actual presence of terrorism/political violence.

Recommendations:

- Restore structure and routine for children and families as soon as possible.
- Create places that connect children with caring, supportive adults and community support networks.
- Minimize exposure to live media, especially news coverage.
- Facilitate children's active play and participation in creative, culturally appropriate activities.
- Guide children in making decisions and adapting to changes.
- Provide opportunities for children to take actions to help themselves and others.

5. Talking with Children About Terrorism and Political Violence

Talking to children about terrorism/political violence is not easy, but important (Myers-Walls, n.d.). My colleagues and I have found that children as young as 3 know something about war and peace, but often their bits of information are partial or confused (Myers-Walls, 2004). If adults do not make themselves available to talk about these issues, there is a possibility for what I call the "cycle of silence" (Myers-Walls, 2004). When adults and children have both experienced a stressful event, children's first reaction is often to try to get back to normal. The adults' interpretation may be that the children did not notice the stressful event. Therefore, the adults might decide it is not necessary to talk to the children. However, although it is common for children to try to get back to normal at first, they are likely to have questions later. The children's interpretation of the adult's silence, however, might be that it is not OK to talk about terrorism/political violence. Thus begins the cycle of silence. To avoid that cycle, adults should make themselves available to children and answer their questions when the children are ready to explore the issue.

Another principle of talking to children is to be honest. Although some professionals and lay people recommend that adults tell children that "nothing bad will happen" or "everything will be all right", those are promises that adults cannot keep. Relationships between adults and children can lose trust when some uncontrollable thing does occur in spite of those promises. Instead, adults can say they will do everything they can to keep children safe. Very close adults and parents can reassure children that they will always love them and be with them no matter what happens. People of faith can also share their belief in the care of a higher power. That kind of reassurance can provide the support children need.

It also is important to acknowledge children's fears and worries, but not stop there (Myers-Walls, 2004). Fear and worry are not the only responses in children. Children have been shown to be likely to talk about being sad, worried for the well-being of others, and angry about the violence as well. Adults should recognize and affirm these reactions that reflect care for many people beyond themselves and find actions that can be taken by the children, adults, or both together (Veronese et al., 2017). Taking such actions increases feelings of optimism, hope, and control.

Finally, research regarding children and the processing of trauma has found that "talking it out" is a different process for children compared to adults (Cohen et al., 2010). Although adults can benefit from support groups and directly facing traumatic events, young children do not have the cognitive defense mechanisms to manage those discussions. Children need to know that communication lines are open, but be given opportunities for creative expression using play, art, music, or drama to express their feelings. They also need to feel free to ignore the events. They may be prepared to talk about them later, or might never want to do so. In the case of children, that can be healthy.

Recommendations:

- Do not assume that children do not know anything about terrorism/political violence. Clarify misunderstandings.
- Do not promise anything you cannot deliver. Tell children you will do whatever you can to keep them safe.
- Reassure children, but recognize that they also may feel sadness, anger, and worry about people they do not know.
- Identify actions that children and adults can take to improve the situation and make peace.
- Let children take the lead. Do not count on one single talk. Keep talking, but do not worry about having all the answers. Find answers together as necessary.
- Do not require young children to talk about traumatic experiences.
- Share stories of caring, rescue, and rebuilding amidst the violence.

6. Screening Children for Specialized Services

Children who have been exposed to terrorism/political violence have a wide range of needs. Although the majority of children and families are likely to rebound with basic community care, some will need para-professional group, focused, or specialized care. Screening procedures should be in place to determine which children and families require more intensive levels of care (Jordans et al., 2010). Toros (2013) argued, "Early identification of traumatized children in school and timely referral to appropriate treatment will likely . . . improve outcomes for many of these children" (p. 229).

The mental health professionals already in place in schools may be ideal for heading up efforts to screen children and families (Klingman, 1992). More training might be necessary for others and has been successful in at least one project (Toros, 2013).

Recommendations:

- Identify trained personnel to screen children and families in need of specialized services. Consider offering training to a larger group of educational professionals to assist in the screening.
- Train all personnel to recognize basic signs of manageable stress. Train them to respond to the stress-related needs of children and families who are coping adequately.

- Create a list of community resources and professionals who can assist with children and families requiring group-based, targeted, or specialized services. Train staff to make appropriate referrals.

7. Monitoring the Educational Environment

In times of significant exposure to terrorism/political violence, the school day may not be normal. Children who have experienced potentially traumatic events are likely to demonstrate learning problems (Streeck-Fischer & van der Kolk, 2000). They may not be able to determine how to direct their attention, may interpret many stimuli as traumatic or shut them out, be overwhelmed and overstimulated by new problems or experiences, and insist on boring sameness as a way to manage stress. They could also have difficulty processing auditory or visual stimuli, leading to poor reading and writing skills.

Educators should be aware that both individuals and groups are exposed to terrorism and political violence, so they may need to use both individual and group strategies to help students learn. Strategies for reaching traumatized children have been shared by several groups (McInerney & McKlindon, n.d.; TSA, n.d.). The common thread among the recommendations is to provide predictability, avoid punitive responses in disciplinary settings, build relationships among students and between students and staff, be aware of the type of trauma experienced by the children and the type of events that may now be difficult for them, and maintain open communication across the system.

Recommendations:

- Assess your own current and past experiences with trauma and adversity and how they might impact your relationship with the children.
- Communicate openly and consciously with the children and their families. Listen carefully and be aware of both your verbal and non-verbal messages and how they may be received.
- Break learning into small steps and provide encouraging feedback at each step.
- Provide students with choices and a sense of control in the learning setting.
- Remember anniversaries, meaningful locations, words and music, or people who may carry special meaning for the children. Those meanings may be positive or negative, and some children may understand those events or experiences in different ways from others. Help the children process them while respecting each other.

- Avoid disciplinary practices that exclude or "criminalize" students. Use positive discipline.

8. Teaching Children Peacemaking Skills

Children who have been exposed to terrorism/political violence might not be able to imagine alternatives to that violence, leaving them feeling hopeless or fearful. Studies have shown that children of parents who are active in peacemaking in some way are more likely to identify alternatives to war and feel more optimistic about the future than other children (Myers-Walls, 2001). Providing children with alternatives to violence is also consistent with stress management techniques and with recommendations made by many of the authors who have discussed resilience. Schools are an ideal place to provide some of this training either in response to concerns about children's exposure to terrorism/political violence or as a preventive technique to build resilience or prevent future violent conflicts. Topics related to peacemaking can be infused into virtually every subject matter in the curriculum.

Many specific topics are included in various peace-focused curricula. Fountain (1999) reviewed the peace education initiatives that had taken place under the direction of UNICEF and grouped them into the following categories: children's rights/human rights education; education for development; gender training; global education; landmine awareness; life skills education; and psycho-social rehabilitation. Although these topics are not all necessary in all areas, this provides a helpful outline. Another agency in the United Nations, UNESCO, prepared a report outlining recommended directions in curriculum reform in education for peace (Choi, Marope, & Lewis, 2013). The Peace Education Foundation (n.d.) provides educational materials and research related to crisis intervention, conflict management, and peer mediation. School systems should review a variety of resources and materials already in place to increase the availability of education for peace in a way that will fit the needs of the community.

Recommendations:

- Review the existing curricula to identify how existing school programs currently address peace education/learning.
- Conduct trainings for educational personnel regarding basic principles of communication, conflict management, appreciation of diversity, empathy, community-building, and cooperation.

- Adapt curricula to respond to the abilities and interests of children at different developmental levels.
- Begin peace education at an early age and continue throughout the students' school journeys.
- Examine the consistency between the peace education/learning concepts and the policies and practices of the school environment, including discipline policies and staff employment practices.

Children's exposure to terrorism/political violence occurs at many levels and in a wide variety of cultural and political contexts. The effects of that exposure are interwoven with their school lives and experiences, through which they can receive support and guidance from caring and prepared staff. Educational professionals can feel overwhelmed with supporting children who are or could be exposed, but the information presented in this chapter helps by identifying some starting points.

Key Messages

1. Children can be exposed to terrorism/political violence at several different levels.
2. The consequences of exposure for children can include: (1) threats to physical health, safety, and well-being; (2) disruptions in psychological/emotional health and well-being; (3) restrictions in life experiences and developmental opportunities; and (4) problematic world views and beliefs.
3. Many children are resilient in spite of exposure to terrorism/political violence, and educators can support the factors that lead to resilience.
4. Educators and educational institutions are in a position to take several actions to prevent and minimize negative impacts of exposure and restore healthy functioning after exposure occurs.

Appendix 9

Resources for School Personnel and Parents

Disaster and Terrorism Preparedness

- Homeland Security Advisory System Recommendations for Schools
  These recommendations explain the five levels of security advisories used
  by the Department of Homeland Security.
- Ridge Launches Terror Preparedness Campaign
  CNN.com offers this information from the federal Department of Homeland Security about how citizens should prepare for a possible terrorist attack.
- American Red Cross Disaster Services: Educator's Information
  Included here is a link to *Masters of Disaster*, a Red Cross K–8 curriculum
  for teaching students about natural and human-caused disasters.

Trauma and PTSD

- Grosse, S. G. (2001). *Children and Post Traumatic Stress Disorder: What Classroom Teachers Should Know*. ERIC Digest. https://eric.ed.gov/?id=ED460122 This fact sheet is specifically for classroom teachers.
- National Child Traumatic Stress Network: https://www.nctsn.org/trauma-types/terrorism. This publication lists an extensive collection of resources regarding terrorism.

Peace Education/Learning

- UNESCO: Education for Peace: Planning for Curriculum Reform: http://unesdoc.unesco.org/images/0023/002336/233601e.pdf. This publication from the United Nations is billed as *Guidelines for integrating Education for Peace curriculum into education sector plans and policies*.
- Teachers Without Borders: *Peace Education Initiative: Waging Peace One Teacher at a Time*: https://teacherswithoutborders.org/child-friendly-spaces/. This is downloadable curriculum from Teachers Without Borders.
- Peace Education Foundation: https://www.peace-ed.org/. This site provides links to educational materials, training, research, and other links.
- *Peace Education in UNICEF*: https://www.unicef.org/education/files/PeaceEducation.pdf. This paper is from the Peace Education Working Group of the United Nations in 1999 but still stimulates discussion.

Child-Friendly Spaces

- *Child-Friendly Spaces: A Structured Review of the Current Evidence Base*: https://reliefweb.int/sites/reliefweb.int/files/resources/CFS_Literature_Review_final_Aug_2012.pdf
- Handbooks and facilitator training manuals for child-friendly spaces by Save the Children: http://toolkit.ineesite.org/toolkit/INEEcms/uploads/1152/How2_Save_the_%20Children_2008.pdf
- Save the Children: https://resourcecentre.savethechildren.net/library/child-friendly-spaces-emergencies-handbook-save-children-staff. This link also is connected to a number of related resources.

Trauma-Informed Education

- The National Child Traumatic Stress Network (https://www.nctsn.org/) provides resources for a variety of audiences, including school personnel.
- *Child Trauma Toolkit for Educators* (https://www.nctsn.org/sites/default/files/assets/pdfs/Child_Trauma_Toolkit_Final.pdf) provides information about responding to a school crisis, school safety, the effects of trauma, disaster response, and service interventions. A list of web resources is also available.
- The National Center for Trauma-Informed Care (https://www.samhsa.gov/nctic/about.asp) is operated by the Substance Abuse and Mental Health Services Administration (SAMHSA). The website provides information on trauma-informed care, links to models that could be adapted for implementation by schools, and information on training and technical assistance support.
- The Safe Start Initiative (http://www.safestartcenter.org/) is operated by the Office of Juvenile Justice and Delinquency Prevention and works to prevent and reduce children's exposure to violence and expand understanding of evidence-based practices.
- The Toolkit for Schools (http://www.safestartcenter.org/infographics/infographic_cev-in-school.php) is a collection of resources for teachers and school administrators that provide information on the prevalence and consequences of children's exposure to violence and ways they can help.

State Resources

- Massachusetts's *Helping Traumatized Children Learn*: http://www.massadvocates.org/documents/HTCL_9-09.pdf

- Washington's *The Heart of Learning and Teaching: Compassion, Resiliency, and Academic Success*: http://www.k12.wa.us/CompassionateSchools/pubdocs/TheHeartofLearningandTeaching.pdf
- Wisconsin's Creating Trauma-Sensitive Schools to Improve Learning Toolkit: https://dpi.wi.gov/sspw/mental-health/trauma/modules•
  Sanctuary Model®: http://www.sanctuaryweb.com/schools.php. This model focuses on changing organizational culture to be more sensitive to the impacts of trauma on individuals and families served as well as staff members.
- RiskingConnections®:http://www.riskingconnection.com/.Thistrauma-informed model emphasizes the importance of "RICH" relationships (i.e., relationships marked by respect, information sharing, connection, and hope) and self-care for service providers working with individuals who have experienced trauma.
- Trauma-Informed Organizational Self-Assessment: http://www.family homelessness.org/media/90.pdf. This self-assessment tool was designed for use by homeless services providers but could be adapted and used in the school setting to evaluate and improve practices to better support students who have experienced trauma.
- National Child Traumatic Stress Network Learning Center: http://learn.nctsn.org/. Registering for this free online learning center provides access to several archived sessions of interest to education professionals. One of these resources is the Schools and Trauma Speaker Series (https://learn.nctsn.org/file.php/1/pdf/Schools_and_Trauma_Speaker_Series.pdf), which has five archived sessions: (1) trauma-informed IEPs, (2) evidence-based practices, (3) sudden death on a school campus, (4) trauma-informed understanding of bullying, and (5) school/mental health partnerships classroom tools.
- Southwest Michigan Children's Trauma Assessment Center's School Intervention Project Curriculum: The resource includes background information on trauma and trauma-informed principles and provides several trauma-informed lesson plans that can be adapted for use with different age groups.
- Trauma-specific information and interventions. Several online resources profile evidence-based and promising education and practices for trauma intervention that can be adapted and used by schools, including National Child Traumatic Stress Network's link for parents and caregivers https://www.nctsn.org/audiences/families-and-caregivers. Or for school personnel https://www.nctsn.org/audiences/school-personnel. These links provide factsheets related to specific and general trauma situations from the National Child Traumatic Stress Network centers.

- RAND Corporation's *How Schools Can Help Students Recover from Traumatic Experiences Toolkit*: http://www.rand.org/content/dam/rand/pubs/technical_reports/2006/RAND_TR413.pdf. This toolkit provides a menu of programs that schools can implemented to help children recover from trauma, categorized by type of trauma. Recommendations for securing program funding are also provided.
- *Support for Students Exposed to Trauma*: http://www.rand.org/pubs/technical_reports/TR675.html. This trauma-specific intervention was designed for implementation by teachers and school counselors, and the program manual—including lesson plans—is available for download.

Talking with Children

- Purple Wagon: https://extension.purdue.edu/purplewagon. This is a collection of fact sheets, activities, interviews, and materials for researchers connected with children, war, and peace.

References

Ager, A., & Metzler, J. (2012). *Child friendly spaces: A structured review of the current data-base.* Columbia University Mailman School of Public Health. Retrieved from https://reliefweb.int/sites/reliefweb.int/files/resources/CFS_Literature_Review_final_Aug_2012.pdf

Anonymous. (2003). Effects of terrorism on very young children. *Psychosocial Nursing and Mental Health Services, 41*(7), 10.

Arnove, A. (Ed.). (2000). *Iraq under siege: The deadly impact of sanctions and war.* Cambridge, UK: South End Press.

Attanayake, V., McKay, R., Joffres, M., Singh, S., Burkle Jr, F., & Mills, F. (2009). Prevalence of mental disorders among children exposed to war: A systematic review of 7,920 children. *Medicine, Conflict and Survival, 25*(1), 4–19. doi:10.1080/13623690802568913

Belsky, J. (2008). War, trauma and children's development: Observations from a modern evolutionary perspective. *International Journal of Behavioral Development, 32*(4), 260–271.

Berthold, S. M. (2000). War traumas and community violence. *Journal of Multicultural Social Work, 8*(1–2), 15–46. doi:10.1300/J285v08n01_02

Boss, P. (1999). *Ambiguous loss: Learning to live with unresolved grief.* Boston, MA: Harvard University Press.

Centers for Disease Control and Prevention (CDC). (2017). *Reunification.* Retrieved from www.cdc.gov/childrenindisasters/reunification.html

Cairns, E. (1996). *Children and political violence.* Cambridge, MA: Blackwell.

Carrick, N., Quas, J. A., & García Coll, C. (2006). Effects of discrete emotions on young children's ability to discern fantasy and reality. *Developmental Psychology, 42*(6), 1278–1288.

Chandra, A., Martin, L. T., Hawkins, S. A., & Richardson, A. (2009). The impact of parental deployment on child social and emotional functioning: Perspectives of school staff. *Journal of Adolescent Health, 46*, 218–223. doi:10.1016/j.jadohealth.2009.10.009

Chemtob, C. M., Roitblat, H. L., Hamada, R. S., Carlson, J. G., &Twentyman, C. T. (1988). A cognitive action theory of post- traumatic stress disorder. *Journal of Anxiety Disorders, 2*, 253–275.

Choi, S. H., Marope, M., & Lewis, S. G. (2013). *Education for peace: Planning for curriculum reform.* New York, NY: UNESCO. Retrieved from http://unesdoc.unesco.org/images/0023/002336/233601e.pdf

Clever, M., & Segal, D. R. (2013). The demographics of military children and families. *Future of Children.* Retrieved from https://pdfs.semanticscholar.org/c567/b17bc58e83e93e68e28f1cfe270473593a48.pdf

Cohen, E., Chazan, S., Lerner, M., & Maimon, E. (2010). Posttraumatic play in young children exposed to terrorism: An empirical study. *Infant Mental Health Journal, 31*(2), 159–181.

Comer, J. S., Furr, J. M., Beidas, R. S., Weiner, C. L., & Kendall, P. C. (2008). Children and terrorism-related news: Training parents in coping and media literacy. *Journal of Consulting and Clinical Psychology, 76*(4), 568–578.

Comer, J. S., & Kendall, P. C. (2007). Terrorism: The psychological impact on youth. *Clinical Psychology: Science and Practice, 14*, 179–212.

deWaal, F. B. M. (2008). Putting the altruism back in altruism: The evolution of empathy. *Annual Review of Psychology, 59*, 279–300.

Edwards, A. (2017). Forced displacement worldwide is at its highest in decades. *UNHCR.* Retrieved from www.unhcr.org/afr/news/stories/2017/6/5941561f4/forced-displacement-worldwide-its-highest-decades.html

Elbedour, S., Bastien, D. E., & Center, B. A. (1997). Identity formation in the shadow of conflict: Projective drawings by Palestinian and Israeli Arab children from the West Bank and Gaza. *Journal of Peace Research, 34*(2), 217–231.

Flake, E. M., Davis, B. E., Johnson, P. I., & Middleton, L. S. (2009). The psychosocial effects of deployment on military children. *Journal of Developmental & Behavioral Pediatrics, 30*, 271–278.

Foster, S., Villanueva, K., Wood, L., Christian, H., & Giles-Corti, B. (2014). The impact of parents' fear of strangers and perceptions of informal social control on children's independent mobility. *Health & Place, 26*, 60–68.

Fountain, J. (1999). *Peace education in UNICEF.* New York, NY: UNICEF. Retrieved from www.unicef.org/education/files/PeaceEducation.pdf

Garbarino, J., Kostelny, K., & Dubrow, H. (1991). *No place to be a child: Growing up in a war zone.* Lexington, MA: D. C. Heath and Company.

Garreau, O. (2012). Children in war: Child victims of armed conflicts. *Humanium.* Retrieved from www.humanium.org/en/children-in-war/

Hamlin, J. K., Wynn, K., & Bloom, P. (2007). Social evaluation by preverbal infants. *Nature, 450.* doi:10.1038/nature06288

Hesse, P. (1989). *The world is a dangerous place: Images of the enemy on children's television.* Cambridge, MA: Harvard University Center for Psychological Studies in the Nuclear Age.

Hick, S. (2001, May). The political economy of war-affected children. *The Annals of the American Academy of Political and Social Science; Children's Rights, 575*, 106–121.

Holman, E. A., Garfin, D. R., & Silver, R. C. (2014). *Media's role in broadcasting acute stress following the Boston Marathon bombings.* Retrieved from www.pnas.org/content/111/1/93

Institute of Medicine. (2014). *Preparedness, response, and recovery considerations for children and families: Workshop summary.* Washington, DC: National Academies Press. Retrieved from www.ncbi.nlm.nih.gov/books/NBK174835/

Jordans, M. J. D., Tol, W. A., Komproe, I. H., Susanty, D., Vallipuram, A., Ntamatumba, P., ... & Joop T. V. M. (2010). Development of a multi-layered psychosocial care system for children in areas of political violence. (Research Report). *International Journal of Mental Health Systems, 4*, 15.

Kingade, T. (2011). The other first responders: How teachers dealt with 9/11 unfolding in their classrooms. *Huffpost*. Retrieved from www.huffingtonpost.com/2011/09/09/teachers-dealt-with-september-11_n_950916.html

Klingman, A. (1992). School psychology services: Community-based, first-order crisis intervention during the Gulf War. *Psychology in the Schools, 29I*, 376–384.

Leithead, A. (2016). Boko Haram abductions: Freed "bride" tells of stigma ordeal. *BBC*. Retrieved from www.bbc.com/news/world-africa-36041860

Lester, P., Peterson, K., Reeves, J., et al. (2010). The long war and parental combat deployment: Effects on military children and at-home spouses. *Journal of the American Academy of Child & Adolescent Psychiatry, 49*(4), 310–320. doi.org/10.1016/j.jaac.2010.01.003

Luxemburger, C., Rigal, J., & Nosten, F. (1998, 1 April). Health care in refugee camps. *Transactions of The Royal Society of Tropical Medicine and Hygiene, 92*(2), 129–130.

Machel, G. (1996). *Impact of armed conflict on children*. Retrieved from www.unicef.org/graca/a51-306_en.pdf

Magid, B., & Boothby, N. (2013). Promoting resilience in children of war. In C. Fernando & M. Ferrari (Eds.), *Handbook of children in war* (pp. 39–49). New York, NY: Springer.

McInerney, M., & McKlindon, A. (n.d.). *Unlocking the door to learning: Trauma-informed classrooms & transformational schools*. Education Law Center. Retrieved from www.elc-pa.org/wp-content/uploads/2015/06/Trauma-Informed-in-Schools-Classrooms-FINAL-December2014-2.pdf

McKirdy, E. (2016). Nearly 50 million children are refugees or migrants, says UNICEF. Retrieved from www.cnn.com/2016/09/07/world/unicef-report-on-child-refugees-and-migrants/

Muris, P., Ollendick, T. H., Roelofs, J., & Austin, K. (2014). The short form of the fear survey schedule for children-revised (FSSC-R-SF): An efficient, reliable, and valid scale for measuring fear in children and adolescents. *Journal of Anxiety Disorders, 28*(8), 957–965.

Myers-Walls, J. S. (n.d.). *Talking with children about terrorism*. West Lafayette, IN: Purdue University Cooperative Extension. Retrieved from https://extension.purdue.edu/purplewagon/PARENTS/Resources/TalkwChildrenAboutTerrorism.pdf

Myers-Walls, J. A. (2001). The parents' role in educating about war and peace. In J. A. Myers-Walls & P. Somlai with R. N. Rapoport (Eds.), *Families as educators for global citizenship* (pp. 191–202). Aldershot: Ashgate.

Myers-Walls, J. A. (2004). Children as victims of war and terrorism. *Journal of Aggression, Maltreatment & Trauma, 8*(1/2), 41–62.

Myers-Walls, J. A. (2010). *Children and the stress of disasters and political violence*. Presented at Development and equity for a global society: Emerging concerns for social work, Madras School of Social Work, Chennai, Tamil Nadu, India.

Oppenheimer, L. (2006). The development of enemy images: A theoretical contribution. *Peace and Conflict: Journal of Peace Psychology, 12*(3), 269–292.

Pat-Horenczyk, R., Peled, O., Miron, T., Brom, D., Villa, Y., & Chemtob, C. M. (2007). Risk-taking behaviors among Israeli adolescents exposed to recurrent terrorism: Provoking danger under continuous threat? *The American Journal of Psychiatry, 164*(1), 66–72.

Peace Education Foundation. (n.d.). Retrieved from www.peace-ed.org/

Peltonen, K., Qouta, S., Diab, M., & Punamaki, R.-L. (2014). Resilience among children in war: The role of multilevel social factors. *Traumatology, 20*(4), 232–240.

People.com. (2017). *How many terrorist attacks in the U.S. have been carried out by immigrants from the 7 banned Muslim countries?* Retrieved from http://people.com/politics/donald-trump-refugee-muslim-ban-terrorist-attack-us-statistics/

Pereda, N. (2013). Systematic review of the psychological consequences of terrorism on child victims. *International Review of Victimology, 19*(2), 181–199. doi:10.1177/0269758012472771

Pfefferbaum, B. J., Devoe, D. R., Stuber, J., Schiff, M., Klein, T. P., & Fairbrother, G. (2005). Psychological impact of terrorism on children and families in the United States. *Journal of Aggression, Maltreatment & Trauma, 9*(3–4), 305–317.

Philbrick, A. M., Wicks, C. M., Harris, I. M., Shaft, G. M., & Van Vooren, J. S. (2017). Make refugee healthcare great [again]. *American Journal of Public Health, 107*(5), 656–658. doi:10.2105/AJPH.2017.303740

Posada, G., Walker, D., Cardin, J.-F., Nyaronga, D., & Schwarz, R. (2015). Maternal perspectives on deployment and child-mother relationships in military families. *Family Relations, 64*, 651–664.

Readiness and Emergency Management for Schools (REMS). (n.d.). *Creating, practicing, and implementing plans for family reunification before, during, and after an emergency.* Retrieved from https://rems.ed.gov/Resources_EM%20Functions_Reunification.aspx.

Rosenau, W., Chalk, P., McPherson, R., Parker, M., & Long, A. (2009). Doing Business in Zones of Conflict. In *Corporations and Counterinsurgency* (pp. 3–8). RAND Corporation. Retrieved from www.jstor.org.ezproxy.lib.purdue.edu/stable/10.7249/op259.8

Santa Barbara, J. (2006). Impact of war on children and imperative to end war. *Croat Medical Journal, 47*, 891–894. Retrieved from www.ncbi.nlm.nih.gov/pmc/articles/PMC2080482/

Save the Children. (2008). *Child friendly spaces for children in emergencies: A handbook for save the children staff.* Retrieved from www.unicef.org/french/videoaudio/PDFs/Guidelines_on_Child_Friendly_Spaces_-_SAVE.pdf

Shaheen, K., & Graham-Harrison, E. (2016, November 16). Children's hospital in Aleppo hit by airstrikes. *The Guardian.* Retrieved from www.theguardian.com/world/2016/nov/16/horror-has-come-back-to-aleppo-airstrikes-continue-in-rebel-held-east

Shaw, J. A. (2003). Children exposed to war/terrorism. *Clinical Child and Family Psychology Review, 6*(4), 237–246.

Streeck-Fischer, A., & van der Kolk, B. A. (2000). Down will come baby, cradle and all: Diagnostic and therapeutic implications of chronic trauma on child development. *Australian and New Zealand Journal of Psychiatry, 34*, 903–918.

Tol, W. A., Jordans, M. J. D., Kohrt, B. A., Betancourt, T. S., & Komproe, I. H. (2013). Promoting mental health and psychosocial well-being in children affected by political violence: Part I—current evidence for an ecological resilience approach. In C. Fernando & M. Ferrari (Eds.), *Handbook of children in war* (pp. 12–37). New York, NY: Springer.

Toros, M. (2013). School-based intervention in the context of armed conflict: Strengthening teacher capacity to facilitate psychosocial support and well-being of children. *International Journal of Humanities and Social Science, 3*(7), 228–237.

Treatment and Services Adaptation Center (TSA). (n.d.) *What is a trauma-informed school?* Retrieved from https://traumaawareschools.org/traumainschools

UNICEF. (2009). *Machel study 10-year strategic review: Children and conflict in a changing world.* New York, NY: UNICEF.

Veronese, G., Pepe, A., Jaradah, A., Murannak, F., & Hamdouna, H. (2017). "We must cooperate with one another against the Enemy": Agency and activism in school-aged children as protective factors against ongoing war trauma and political violence in the Gaza Strip. *Child Abuse & Neglect, 70,* 364–376.

VOA (Voice of America) News. (2014). *UNICEF says children main victims of war.* Retrieved from www.voanews.com/a/unicef-says-children-main-victims-of-war/2459908.html

Vriens, L. (1999). Children, war, and peace. In A. Raviv, L. Oppenheimer, & D. Bar-Tal (Eds.), *How children understand war and peace* (pp. 27–58). San Francisco, CA: Jossey-Bass.

Walsh, F. (2016). *Strengthening family resilience* (3rd ed.). New York, NY: Guilford Press.

Watson Institute. (2017). *Costs of war: About.* Retrieved from http://watson.brown.edu/costsofwar/about

Webster, P. S., & Harris, Y. R. (2009) Working with children who have experienced war, terrorism, and disaster. *Childhood Education, 85*(6), 364–369. doi:10.1080/00094056.2009.10521402

Wexler, I. D., Branski, D., & Kerem, E. (2006). War and children. *Journal of the American Medical Association, 295*(5), 579–581.

Witte, K. (1994). Fear control and danger control: A test of the extended parallel process model (EPPM). *Communication Monographs, 61*(2), 113–134. doi:10.1080/03637759409376328

Implementing School-Based Programs   **10**

Jonathan Pettigrew and Diana E. Gal

The trick to having tested, effective prescriptions is to follow them well. Consider an illustration from medicine. Imagine two different people become sick and go to a doctor. Both of them are prescribed a 10-day antibiotic regimen. Both patients feel improvement after 4 days of treatment. Feeling better, Patient 1 decides to stop taking antibiotics on the fifth day, whereas Patient 2 continues the entire 10-day treatment. In the short term, there may be no major differences between the two patients; however, taking only part of the treatment regimen can lead to substantial differences in the long term. Patient 1 is more likely than Patient 2 to relapse with the same or similar sickness. Another result is that Patient 1's disease may mutate and become resistant to antibiotic treatment (e.g., MRSA virus). Although only an analogy, the point remains: following effective prescriptions well can lead to the best outcomes.

This book presents a number of evidence-based prescriptions for dealing with dangers and trauma facing children and youth at school. For each, both immediate and long-term coping strategies have been suggested. The question that remains is how can these strategies, suggestions, and prescriptions be best implemented? This is the question our chapter addresses.

We emphasize three points about implementation that transcend the specific contexts that have been addressed in this book. First, *effective implementation is practically as important as effective content.* A good recipe in the hands of a bad chef can make for an unsavory meal. So, too, evidence-based content can be delivered ineffectively, leading to negative instead of positive outcomes. Second, *changes need to be made to ensure fit with each new context.* An evidence-based strategy developed in urban southern California may not work in rural northern Maine. Programs, strategies, and practices need to be customized or aligned to specific features and contingencies of each context. Third, *planning, training, and ongoing support are key to being able to respond in the face of and aftermath of danger.* As the adage goes, failing to plan is planning to fail. For school-based interventions, planning how to deliver programs, by whom, and in coordination with which salient entities (e.g., families, neighborhoods, community groups, legal authorities, etc.) is key to enacting effective interventions. In sum, attending to implementation issues can not only prevent good intervention material from inadvertently being squandered but also prepare school personnel to serve children and youth in effective, thoughtful, and compassionate ways.

Effective Implementation Is Practically as Important as Effective Content

Implementation quality is a broad term that generally refers to how programs are delivered in real-world settings and how the delivery is related to program outcomes. As Miller-Day and colleagues (2013) insightfully observe, real-world implementation of school-based programs "is a negotiation" that synthesizes "the curriculum, teachers' classroom management and interests, students' behaviors and needs, and administrative influence" (p. 325). Frameworks for understanding implementation (e.g., Wandersman et al., 2008) consider how broader contextual factors influence program delivery. For example, political and budgetary decisions have ramifications for how, when, and which programs are implemented. Other contexts, such as media, also have a profound influence on children and youth, which has inspired some (e.g., Biglan, 2016) to call for academics, schools, practitioners, and others interested in improving youth outcomes to join together to influence these social forces. Broadband community support is necessary to effectively and efficiently implement sustainable programs that will keep children and youth safe in schools. In many situations, however, broad, multisector support is difficult to muster and social forces like media are resistant to influence. Hence, we focus on aspects of implementation quality more in the purview of schools.

Classroom Implementation

Classroom implementation is critical for achieving desirable outcomes for youth, families, schools, and communities. Dusenbury, Brannigan, Falco, and Hansen (2003) stress that poor classroom implementation may explain the null findings in some studies that examine intervention effects. Good programs implemented poorly should not expect positive results. Classroom implementation encompasses aspects of a program, its delivery, and its recipients. All three domains intersect to drive outcomes. Great program content is necessary, but not sufficient. Wonderful teaching makes program content accessible, but cannot force positive change. Finally, without students enacting a program's prescriptions and practices, it cannot result in positive outcomes. Existing reviews of implementation quality (e.g., Berkel, Mauricio, Schoenfelder, & Sandler, 2011) help elucidate each of these dimensions. We briefly describe components of the program, delivery, and participants. We then present a model for maximizing effective implementation of manualized behavior-change programs.

Program Elements: Designing Effective Curricula
Aspects of a program that can affect outcomes for children and youth are its scope and dosage. These elements can determine a program's reach (e.g., for whom a program is developed) and uniqueness (i.e., how a program differentiates from others). A program's scope and dosage determine how much content is delivered, how often, and through which mechanisms. For example, a program might have ten lessons, 45 minutes each, delivered once per week, or may include quarterly fire drills. If only one of the ten lessons is delivered, students receive only 10% of the program. If four annual fire drills are done during the first month of classes, students may not recall their classroom's designated safe-zone towards the end of the year. The implementation structures of evidence-based programs are intentional and theoretically driven while attempting to balance practical considerations facing schools, teachers, and classrooms (Pettigrew & Hecht, 2015). That is, the number of sessions and recommended delivery have been thoughtfully considered and researched by the program developers, and modifications to these designs may result in unwanted consequences. Schools should consult with program developers to ensure that any particular program's scope is adequate to address the needs or targeted outcomes with an appropriate dose delivered over a suitable schedule and time frame.

Delivery Elements: Teaching for Behavior Change
To achieve their goals, programs also must be communicated or delivered in some way. Curricula must be taught. Sirens or flashing lights must alert building occupants of a fire drill. This "communication link" (Fixsen, Naoom,

Blase, Friedman, & Wallace, 2005) is the second key dimension of implementation quality that relates to outcomes.

Existing research and reviews show that delivery can be done with high or low quality (e.g., Dusenbury et al., 2003; Pettigrew et al., 2013), and a substantial body of work attests to the fact that *how* programs are delivered affects desired outcomes (for review, see Durlak & Dupre, 2008). Tobler and Stratton (1997) performed a meta-analysis of 120 interventions and clearly demonstrated that knowledge-only programs were ineffective for health promotion compared to approaches that utilized interactive teaching. Other implementation research has shown that desirable outcomes are more likely for after-school programs when their delivery is SAFE: *sequenced* ("connected and coordinated set of activities"), *active* ("employs engaged learning techniques"), *focused* ("devoted to developing personal or social skills"), and *explicit* ("targets specific skills"; Durlak, Weissberg, & Pachan, 2010, p. 298). These reviews clearly demonstrate that incorporating skill-practice and interactive teaching tactics into program implementation is part of what makes evidence-based programs work.

Despite the fact that many evidence-based programs are structured using evidence-based delivery principles, only about half of schools utilize these programs (Ringwalt et al., 2011) and evidence from studies of implementation (e.g., Ennett et al., 2003) and adaptation (e.g., Miller-Day et al., 2013) suggests that many schools that use evidence-based programs do not follow prescribed interactive teaching methods. The goals of health-promotion interventions are different from the goals of other forms of instruction. They aim for changed behavior, not acquired knowledge. Hence, behavior-change interventions require pedagogical tactics that allow students to internalize and apply knowledge while developing skills. To facilitate teaching towards behavior change, we present a practical model for how to implement classroom programs. Framed by ideas of communication competence (Spitzberg & Cupach, 1984), extensive observations of teachers delivering health-promotion curricula (Pettigrew et al., 2013), and experience adapting and developing prevention programming (Colby et al., 2013), we suggest teachers use the engaged delivery framework (Figure 10.1).

The framework incorporates three dimensions of communication competence—concept knowledge, behavioral skills, and motivation—and represents three domains of instruction required to teach towards behavior change. Implementing programs to promote healthy and safe environments relies on learning new concepts as well as acquiring new skills. Teachers are invited to take both the role of instructor by sharing new information as well as the coach by helping students develop new abilities. Also included in the model are prototypical learning activities: presenting and reviewing

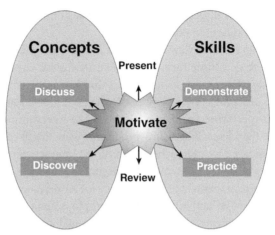

Figure 10.1 Engaged Delivery Framework

are integral to learning both knowledge and skills; discussion and discovery align with mastering concepts; and demonstration and practice align with skill acquisition. Thus, concepts can be presented, discussed, discovered, and reviewed, whereas skills can be presented, demonstrated, practiced, or reviewed through a mixture of class and individual assignments.

Central to the model is motivation. Without it, little can be accomplished. Inspiring, encouraging, and convincing students to learn, although difficult and not necessarily linear, is key to health promotion. Motivation may take place through engaging youth with stories, evolve from demonstrating immediate personal or social relevance of the material, or grow from adept teaching strategies that engage students. To be most effective, these strategies will be tailored to the age of the students. For example, although sharing personal stories is an effective motivational strategy for all ages, instructors must be sensitive to include developmentally appropriate stories and share them in ways that capture the interests of their particular age group. Demonstrating the social relevance of materials might include more peer examples for adolescents and more family and sibling examples for younger students. Sticker charts and rewards for participation may be more effective with younger rather than older students. Implementers should use the best available strategies for good teaching, but it is important to keep in mind that, however it develops, motivation is key to quality delivery of school-based programs for all ages.

The engaged delivery framework can be a useful guide for lesson plan creation for curriculum developers as well as teachers. Program logic models are diagrams that show how behavior-change theories are integrated into specific components of an intervention (see Julian, Jones, & Deyo, 1995). Logic models determine *what* kinds of concepts and skills should be taught. The framework presented here proposes *how* that material can be effectively delivered to students in classrooms. Lesson plans should integrate framework elements in meaningful ways so that there are reinforcing assignments and activities that take place in individual and collective settings in age-appropriate ways. In so doing, school-based implementers can best position themselves to witness practical change in target outcomes.

Participant Elements: Adopting, Adapting, and Enacting

A third aspect of implementation that affects program outcomes recognizes that participants are not passive recipients of programs, practices, or curricula (Pettigrew, Segrott, Ray, & Littlecott, in press). Participants engage or disengage based on a wide variety of factors and how they respond can act like a gatekeeper between good program delivery and desired outcomes (Berkel et al., 2011). The best content delivered in the most effective way may lead to nothing if participants do not attend lessons, grasp the material, or practice the program content. One strategy for increasing the likelihood that interventions can achieve their desired outcomes is to implement "priming" interventions that alter the climate of a school or community. For example, before introducing a drug use prevention intervention that relies on small-group sharing, it might be necessary to first focus on increasing the warmth and social connectedness of classrooms (i.e., increase factors that lead to better small-group sharing). Such community-wide or school-wide interventions may "prime the pump" for participants to accept intervention prescriptions (Pettigrew et al., in press). Although systematic research has yet to shine light on how participant adaptation affects program outcomes, it is safe to say that unless participants respond to program content (i.e., enact the behaviors summoned by an intervention), little progress can be expected.

Implementation Summary

The purpose of the health-promotion curriculum is not academic but practical; the goal is to shape behaviors and influence outcomes that make for safe environments and individuals. How a program is delivered is practically as important as what content is included. We describe a broad view of implementation, cover aspects of program design, present an engaged delivery framework for classroom interventions, and recognize the central importance of participants' decisions in changing behaviors. This section, taken as a whole, underscores that effective implementation is practically as important as effective content.

Changes Need to Be Made to Ensure Fit with Each New Context

Although the importance of high-quality implementation cannot be overstated, how a program is implemented at different times and from place to place requires sensitivity to the temporal and local needs. Students everywhere need to be motivated to engage with intervention content, but specific strategies or tactics a teacher might employ to motivate students in one location will look very different from those used in another. In this regard, there is no one-size-fits-all approach to implementation. Said another way, effectively and efficiently implementing practices and programs described throughout this book will require thoughtful, principled local adaptations. These adaptations might be changes in the actual content through adaptation to the lessons themselves, or to the delivery of the content such as changing a small-group assignment to an individual one.

Research into school-based adaptations has identified common types and reasons for making changes (Miller-Day et al., 2013). In this study, the biggest barrier to delivering the program as intended was time. Teachers felt constrained because of multiple, often competing, demands placed on them as educators of the next generation. In addition to time constraints, teachers experienced personal, institutional, and technical constraints. Each of these thwarted teachers' abilities to deliver the program and necessitated adaptations, whether to the content or the format of the program. Content adaptations included omitting parts of lessons, partially omitting lesson components, adding new content to lessons, or substituting content in the lessons with other material. Format adaptations included changes to the way lesson components were delivered: completing a homework assignment as a class activity, changing group activities into individual activities, spending more time on one part of a lesson, or changing the order/time for when lesson components were delivered.

Changes to the way a program is delivered are less consequential than changes to the program content. Changes to content may be the most important to carefully consider. On the one hand, programs are intentionally designed with specific components that address particular skills or attitudes, which research has verified lead to desired outcomes. Omitting or changing the content, even in small ways, may result in programs with no effect. It is especially problematic if changes are made by picking and choosing only easy-to-apply parts of one or several programs because doing so may miss the theoretically important core components of the intervention (Van der Kreeft, Jongbloet, & Van Havere, 2014). On the other hand, changes to the content may be especially important to make the program relevant and engaging for new or different age groups.

It is an error to blindly transport a program from one context to a new one without adapting to the "school, local habits, or regional cultural traits" (Van der Kreeft et al., 2014). For example, elementary school children in rural farm areas may have limited exposure to row homes or shopping malls. If a program is full of examples from urban settings, these examples likely will not connect easily with rural students. Another problem can occur when taking a middle-school program and implementing it with elementary school students or using a high-school program with other age groups. Because rapid development occurs throughout childhood, early adolescence, and late adolescence, the risks experienced by these distinct age groups differ widely. The primacy of different relationship types also changes as children age through adolescence, moving from family and same-sex, platonic peer relationships to peer and romantic attachments. Evidence-based programs account for these differing risk and relational realities. Transporting a program to a new population necessitates appropriate adaptations for these and other age-based differences. Outdated material also may be a barrier to kids fully engaging with a program. In these cases, it might be useful to make changes to program content. Although it is important to change content to make it culturally appropriate, age appropriate, timely, and relevant to a particular classroom or school, it is equally important to maintain the active ingredients of a program. These active ingredients can be identified through collaboration with the program developers and by developing an understanding of the program's theory of change.

Researchers and thinkers are just beginning to develop a "science of adaptation". For example, Castro and Yasui (2017) suggest that if teachers or other implementers have a "thorough understanding" of an intervention's goals and the theory that underlies how these goals are achieved, thoughtful and well-planned adaptations can be made that still stay true to the program's core components (p. 624). These authors argue for a "both/and" approach that embraces thoughtful adaptation while adhering to the theoretical principles of the program. In other words, teachers, schools, and other implementers should make changes that help programs fit local contexts as long as they carefully maintain the spirit of the intervention.

Balancing innovation and fidelity requires in-depth knowledge about how a program works as well as the target population. Whoever is tasked with making local adaptations needs to understand the core components of a program that lead to desired effects as well as how the program introduces, sequences, reinforces, and practices these components. Adapters also need insider knowledge about the target population. They should readily be able to identify who will receive the program and how the participants will best become vested in the concepts and skills advocated by the program. This may involve changing scenarios used in lessons. It may mean translating some content into local vernacular. It likely also means ensuring that new concepts are not added, but, instead, that the behavior-change components of the original intervention are maintained in the adapted program. Local adaptation can and should be done, but needs to be completed cautiously and wisely.

Planning for Success

As with following all good recipes, planning and preparation are key to the success of an intervention. The first step in planning for implementation of an intervention is choosing the right program for a particular community. After identifying the most suitable program for the community, the most critical steps for preparation are identifying personnel, coordinating quality training, and devising a plan for ongoing monitoring, support, and evaluation.

Selecting a Program

With the abundance of programs and approaches available, it can quickly become overwhelming to know which to choose. To narrow down the options, it is important to first define the program's objective and scope. What will it ultimately achieve? Some programs seek to help specific students in response to a need, others aim to impact the entire school. Clarifying the specific needs an intervention might address and its scope can help narrow the options available. Next, consider the resources available for implementation and the related costs. Program cost, duration, needed personnel, and training requirements should factor into this decision. Most programs require a licensing fee, teacher materials, student materials, and training certification. Some charge based on a per capita fee whereas others can be purchased for a certain duration.

There are also opportunity costs to using various programs over others. For example, choosing to implement a particular program will mean that teachers need to learn new material or activities, which can limit their capacity to train on other topics. Creating some stability is also important. School staff are often faced with a "program du jour", in which boards, superintendents, principals, or other outside forces impose new methods or programs each year. These impositions frustrate school staff and almost certainly require new training, workshops, and meetings. This instability and constant influx of new programs leaves staff feeling lambasted with the latest.

To effectively introduce a new intervention, it is important to provide staff with a rationale of the need for a new program, demonstrate the value added over existing practices, examine how the program fits into school structures and staffing, and clearly explain how the program will lead to the desired outcomes. The best choice of program will most efficiently maximize available resources and be sustainable for at least 3–5 years, if not longer. Finally, consider the populations for whom the program was developed and in which the program has been tested. The most effective programs will be those developed and tested in populations that most closely resemble the school, community, and culture of local students. For example, rural communities should locate a program that was developed for and targets rural, not urban, schools and vice versa (Castro, Barrera Jr, & Martinez, 2004; Hecht et al., 2003). Choosing the right program is an essential planning step that should not be overlooked.

In addition to the programs and practices overviewed in this book, various lists and tools (e.g., Blueprints, http://www.blueprintsprograms.com/programs, and NREPP, http://www.samhsa.gov/nrepp) have been developed to aid in selecting different programs for particular populations. It is important to note that inclusion on these "lists" is both a political process as well as a scientific one. Decision makers should be aware that there are debates about what counts as "evidence-based". Different scientific traditions (e.g., sociology, developmental psychology) may have differing definitions of what counts as evidence for effectiveness. These differences can lead to confusing criteria for what programs can and cannot be included on these curated lists. Even so, such lists can be helpful starting points for identifying appropriate programs. Although the field of prevention science has articulated rigorous standards for evidence (e.g., Flay et al., 2005; Gottfredson et al., 2015), few programs can (or should) meet all of these criteria.Therefore, others advocate for pragmatic and flexible approaches to developing an evidence base (e.g., Wandersman, Alia, Cook, Hsu, & Ramaswarny, 2016). We believe that local community and school personnel are in a good position to consider the threats or risks students face and to use good judgment and information from trusted sources (such as those identified in this book) to determine if a program fits student and administrative needs.

Identifying Personnel

Personnel planning involves deciding who will be involved in delivering the intervention and how by identifying all the potential stakeholders. When identifying personnel who will be involved, it is especially useful to think of all existing structures that could help reach intended audiences. Consider who is involved in the lives of these students on a daily basis. Here, it is important to keep in mind the scope of a program. If implementing a program for only students in danger of selling drugs on campus, potentially fewer individuals will need to be involved than if the program will be implemented school-wide. When identifying personnel, it is important to cast the net beyond teachers, and consider everyone who might be involved, as well as what strengths each of these individuals might contribute. This could include school counselors, school safety officers, administrators, playground monitors, coaches, after-school program staff, and cafeteria staff. Some successful programs go as far as including bus drivers and janitorial staff in their implementation (Shetgiri, Espelage, & Carroll, 2015). It is also useful to consider what community resources can be included in this effort. Organizations like local police and county sheriff's offices, social workers, neighborhood churches, community libraries, local businesses, charities, and after-school program coordinators may all be willing and able to contribute towards programs that benefit children and youth. Involving the community and creating community coalitions often leads to stronger implementation and better program outcomes (Barrera, Berkel, & Castro, 2017; Brown, Feinberg, & Greenberg, 2010).

Once the potential personnel have been identified, it is important to map the experience and capacity of these individuals and systems. At this stage, it is helpful to identify how key personnel's existing knowledge, abilities, and influence could be leveraged to implement a program. This experience and capacity mapping can then be used to narrow down who will be involved in the process and clearly define each individual's or organization's role. Having a clearly defined and established role in the implementation process reduces stress and enables personnel to most effectively deliver programs (Booth, 2017).

Coordinating Training

Once the program is chosen and personnel are identified, the next step is to plan for training. Often, schools have to juggle many different types of training needs for staff. Prioritizing training and making time to support the implementation of a new program can be challenging, but is absolutely critical to the successful implementation of an intervention. It is imperative to identify the core elements of the intervention that will be implemented and allow sufficient time for training. Consider how many training sessions should be ideally conducted and how many can be conducted feasibly. Identify if it is preferable to have several short training sessions or one longer one and if it is better to spread training out over time or do it only once. Making these decisions will likely require balancing the ideal amount of training against the practical considerations of time.

Successful training involves all staff who will be part of the implementation, provides models of skills and gives participants hands-on opportunities to practice the skills being taught, builds staff buy-in, and clearly communicates program goals and expectations. Training led by enthusiastic instructors that give staff time to practice skills leads to more successful program implementation (Fagan & Mihalic, 2003). Moreover, the importance of generating staff buy-in during training is demonstrated by a study that found that middle school teachers who believed their school needed a bullying intervention were more likely to implement the program with high quality than those who did not believe in the importance of the intervention (Kallestad & Olweus, 2003; Wanless, Groark, & Hatfield, 2015). To foster general enthusiasm for the program, it is also helpful to have a program "champion" among the implementation staff (Fagan & Mihalic, 2003). This is an individual who believes in the need for the program, and will foster communication among staff as well as between staff and administration. Finally, administrator and leadership enthusiasm and involvement is also key to providing quality training. When staff perceive that their leaders value the new program and will support them in implementing it, the program is implemented with higher quality (Collaborative for Academic Social and Emotional Learning, 2006). Similarly, Cooper, Bumbarger, and Moore (2015) found that administrative buy-in, financial support, and advanced planning all relate to more effective program outcomes.

A cost-benefit analysis of quality training should balance initial investment against ongoing returns. Initial training investments may be needed to cover costs of a qualified trainer, funds for a substitute teacher while primary implementers attend the training, and administrative time to purchase or produce program materials. This initial cost must be weighed against the benefits that pass down to students year after year. We also recommend planning to utilize a new program for at least 3 years. This allows for a real return on investment (in terms of training costs), whereas participating in a one-off training and implementation likely will not benefit as much or as many. Finally, for some programs, it may be prudent to trial them on a limited scale and evaluate the trial before rolling it out school-wide. This may prevent costly investments in programs that do not fit the needs of students or staff. Trialing a program on a small scale also helps establish a system for monitoring, support, and evaluation.

Monitoring, Supporting, and Evaluating

Implementation is best coupled with ongoing support and monitoring. At this stage, it is important to consider what ongoing support needs to be provided to staff who will be implementing the program once training is complete. Mentorship, personalized coaching, and ongoing technical support models may be particularly useful for maintaining high-quality implementation, but can be costly and time consuming (Odom, 2009; Reinke, Stormont, Herman, & Newcomer, 2014; Stormont, Reinke, Newcomer, Marchese, & Lewis, 2015). Other ongoing support models include facilitating learning communities among the implementation staff using small-group discussions to support one another, share challenges and success, and maintain enthusiasm for the program. Other opportunities to gather and ask questions and share ideas may be booster trainings conducted throughout the year or other informal gatherings. Remember that, as with training, involvement and support from leadership is essential to the success of a new program. Leadership can be key in helping staff have the time to implement and the resources necessary to do so.

Finally, before beginning any implementation, it is essential to identify what processes will be put in place to monitor the implementation and effects of the program. Monitoring the effects of the program on outcomes helps indicate if the efforts are having the desired results and may help inform modification of implementation strategies. Practically, monitoring the effects of the program for the target population may include surveys administered to the students who are being reached, observations in the school setting, or monitoring metrics such as attendance, academic performance, or disciplinary referrals. Monitoring the program implementation might include self-assessment checklists distributed to the personnel implementing the program or live and/or recorded observations. To establish a low-cost monitoring system, it might be preferable to use metrics already collected (e.g., test scores, attendance, suspensions, disciplinary referrals) as student or school-level outcomes and to use administrative staff as supervisors who attend trainings and then visit classrooms to monitor the program implementation. As with all steps in the planning process, the monitoring process will be specific to the program chosen, and will vary in magnitude based on the scope of the program. Biglan (2016) recommends ongoing monitoring be built into every intervention. We note that all interventions become dated and need to be refreshed from time to time. Creating a system for continuous quality improvement (e.g., Wandersman et al., 2016) is a useful way to ensure that outcomes persist in moving in the right direction.

Planning Summary

Planning for success requires attention to the details with a clear vision of how any particular program fits into ongoing efforts to teach and support students. Identifying goals, selecting an appropriate program, training implementers, developing ongoing support systems, preparing monitoring and evaluation plans, and ensuring continuous quality improvement are difficult but necessary steps. Taking time to plan what will be done, by whom, and when is crucial for success.

Conclusion

In this chapter, we outlined an approach to understanding quality implementation of school-based programs, including aspects of teaching for behavior change, the process of making program adaptations, and planning for program choice, personnel, training, and ongoing support and evaluation. Practically, implementing a new program always requires a balance between the ideal needs and realistic constraints of available resources. It is often more effective to start with smaller programs and implement them intentionally and carefully than ineffectively implement a large-scale program. Trialing a program in each new context is a great practice. We present the following as key points.

Key Messages

1. High-quality implementation is essential for optimal program outcomes.
2. Quality implementation that promotes behavior change requires teachers to motivate, instruct, and coach.
3. Changes to the program content are sometimes necessary but must always be made thoughtfully and with caution. Specifically, adapters need to consider the program logic model and the needs of their new target audience.
4. Planning for implementation of a program is key for success and involves: (1) selecting the best fitting program for the local population, needs, and available resources; (2) thoughtful consideration of the personnel who can most efficiently and effectively deliver program content; (3) quality training that builds staff buy-in and motivation; and (4) ongoing monitoring for quality implementation and program outcomes.

References

Barrera, M., Berkel, C., & Castro, F. G. (2017). Directions for the advancement of culturally adapted preventive interventions: Local adaptations, engagement, and sustainability. *Prevention Science, 18*, 640–648. doi:10.1007/s11121-016-0705-9

Berkel, C., Mauricio, A. M., Schoenfelder, E., & Sandler, I. N. (2011). Putting the pieces together: An integrated model of program implementation. *Prevention Science, 12*, 23–33. doi:10.1007/s11121-010-0186-1

Biglan, A. (2016). The ultimate goal of prevention and the larger context for translation. *Prevention Science, 19*, 328–336. doi:10.1007/s11121-016-0635-6

Booth, S. L. (2017). *Professional development as a means to increase teacher fidelity and improve teacher and student outcomes.* Master's Thesis, California State University, San Bernardino, CA.

Brown, L. D., Feinberg, M. E., & Greenberg, M. T. (2010). Determinants of community coalition ability to support evidence-based programs. *Prevention Science, 11*, 287–297.

Castro, F. G., Barrera Jr, M., & Martinez Jr, C. R. (2004). The cultural adaptation of prevention interventions: Resolving tensions between fidelity and fit. *Prevention Science, 5*, 41–45. doi:10.1023/B:PREV.0000013980.12412.cd

Castro, F. G., & Yasui, M. (2017). Advances in EBI development for diverse populations: Towards a science of intervention adaptation. *Prevention Science, 18*, 623–629. doi:10.1007/s11121–017–0809-x

Colby, M., Hecht, M. L., Miller-Day, M., Krieger, J. L., Syvertsen, A. K., Graham, J. W., & Pettigrew, J. (2013). Adapting school-based substance use prevention curriculum through cultural grounding: A review and exemplar of adaptation processes for rural schools. *American Journal of Community Psychology, 51*, 190–205. doi:10.1007/s10464-012-9524-8

Collaborative for Academic Social and Emotional Learning. (2006). *CASEL practice rubric for schoolwide SEL implementation.* Collaborative for Academic Social and Emotional Learning. Retrieved from http://casel.org/wp-content/uploads/2011/04/Rubric.pdf

Cooper, B. R., Bumbarger, B. K., & Moore, J. E. (2015). Sustaining evidence-based prevention programs: Correlates in a large-scale dissemination initiative. *Prevention Science, 16*, 145–157. doi:10.1007/s11121-013-0427-1

Durlak, J. A., & DuPre, E. P. (2008). Implementation matters: A review of research on the influence of implementation on program outcomes and the factors affecting implementation. *American Journal of Community Psychology, 41*, 327–350. doi:10.1007/s10464-008-9165-0

Durlak, J. A., Weissberg, R. P., & Pachan, M. (2010). A meta-analysis of after-school programs that seek to promote personal and social skills in children and adolescents. *American Journal of Community Psychology, 45*, 294–309.

Dusenbury, L., Brannigan, R., Falco, M., & Hansen, W. B. (2003). A review of research on fidelity of implementation: Implications for drug abuse prevention in school settings. *Health Education Research, 18*, 237–256.

Ennett, S. T., Ringwalt, C. L., Thorne, J., Rohrbach, L. A., Vincus, A., Simons-Rudolph, A., & Jones, S. (2003). A comparison of current practice in school-based substance use prevention programs with meta-analysis findings. *Prevention Science, 4*, 1–14. doi:10.1023/A:1021777109369

Fagan, A. A., & Mihalic, S. (2003). Strategies for enhancing the adoption of school-based prevention programs: Lessons learned from the Blueprints for Violence Prevention replications of the Life Skills Training program. *Journal of Community Psychology, 31,* 235–253. doi:10.1002/jcop.10045

Flay, B. R., Biglan, A., Boruch, R. F., Castro, F. G., Gottfredson, D., Kellam, S., . . . Ji, P. (2005). Standards of evidence: Criteria for efficacy, effectiveness and dissemination. *Prevention Science, 6,* 151–175.

Fixsen, D. L., Naoom, S. F., Blase, K. A., Friedman, R. M., & Wallace, F. (2005). *Implementation research: A synthesis of the literature.* Tampa, FL: University of South Florida, Louis de la Parte Florida Mental Health Institute, The National Implementation Research Network (FMHI Publication #231). Retrieved from http://nirn.fmhi.usf.edu/resources/publications/Monograph/pdf/monograph_full.pdf

Gottfredson, D. C., Cook, T. D., Gardner, F. E. M., Gorman-Smith, D., Howe, G. W., Sandler, I. N., & Zafft, K. M. (2015). Standards of evidence for efficacy, effectiveness, and scale-up research in prevention science: Next generation. *Prevention Science, 16,* 893–926. doi:10.1007/s11121-015-0555-x

Hecht, M. L., Marsiglia, F. F., Elek, E., Wagstaff, D. A., Kulis, S., Dustman, P., & Miller-Day, M. (2003). Culturally grounded substance use prevention: An evaluation of the keepin'it REAL curriculum. *Prevention Science, 4,* 233–248. doi:10.1023/A:1026016131401

Julian, D. A., Jones, A., & Deyo, D. (1995). Open systems evaluation and the logic model: Program planning and evaluation tools. *Evaluation and Program Planning, 18,* 333–341. doi:10.1016/0149-7189(95)00034-8

Kallestad, J. H., & Olweus, D. (2003). Predicting teachers' and schools' implementation of the Olweus Bullying Prevention Program: A multilevel study. *Prevention & Treatment, 6.* doi:10.1037/1522-3736.6.1.621a

Miller-Day, M., & Hecht, M. L. (2013). Narrative means to preventative ends: A narrative engagement framework for designing prevention interventions. *Health Communication, 28,* 657–670. doi:10.1080/10410236.2012.762861.

Miller-Day, M., Pettigrew, J., Hecht, M. L., Shin, Y., Graham, J., & Krieger, J. (2013). How prevention curricula are taught under real-world conditions: Types of and reasons for teacher curriculum adaptations. *Health Education, 113,* 324–344. doi:10.1108/09654281311329259

Odom, S. L. (2009). The tie that binds: Evidence-based practice, implementation science, and outcomes for children. *Topics in Early Childhood Special Education, 29,* 53–61. doi:10.1177/0271121408329171

Pettigrew, J., & Hecht, M. L. (2015). Developing school-based prevention curricula. In K. Bosworth (Ed.), *Prevention science in school settings: Complex relationships and processes* (pp. 151–174). New York, NY: Springer.

Pettigrew, J., Miller-Day, M., Shin, Y., Hecht, M. L., Krieger, J. L., & Graham, J. W. (2013). Describing teacher-student interactions: A qualitative assessment of teacher implementation of the 7th grade *keepin' it REAL* substance use intervention. *American Journal of Community Psychology, 51,* 43–56. doi:10.1007/s10464-012-9539-1

Pettigrew, J., Segrott, J., Ray, C. D., & Littlecott, H. (in press). Social interface model: Theorizing ecological post-delivery processes for intervention effects. *Prevention Science.* doi:10.1007/s11121-017-0857-2

Reinke, W. M., Stormont, M., Herman, K. C., & Newcomer, L. (2014). Using coaching to support teacher implementation of classroom-based interventions. *Journal of Behavioral Education, 23*, 150–167. doi:10.1007/s10864-013-9186-0

Ringwalt, C. L., Vincus, A., Hanley, S., Ennett, S., Bowling, J., & Haws, S. (2011). The prevalence of evidence-based drug use prevention curricula in U.S. middle schools in 2008. *Prevention Science, 12*, 63–69. doi:10.1007/s11121-010-0184-3

Shetgiri, R., Espelage, D. L., & Carroll, L. (2015). *Practical strategies for clinical management of bullying*. New York, NY: Springer.

Spitzberg, B. H., & Cupach, W. R. (1984). *Interpersonal communication competence*. Beverly Hills, CA: Sage.

Stormont, M., Reinke, W. M., Newcomer, L., Marchese, D., & Lewis, C. (2015). Coaching teachers' use of social behavior interventions to improve children's outcomes: A review of the literature. *Journal of Positive Behavior Interventions, 17*, 69–82.

Tobler, N. S., & Stratton, H. H. (1997). Effectiveness of school-based drug prevention programs: A meta-analysis of the research. *Journal of Primary Prevention, 18*, 71–128. doi:10.1023/A:1024630205999

Van der Kreeft, P. van der, Jongbloet, J., & Havere, T. V. (2014). Factors affecting implementation: Cultural adaptation and training. In Z. Slaboda & H. Petras (Eds.), *Defining prevention science* (pp. 315–334). Boston, MA: Springer.

Wandersman, A., Duffy, J., Flaspohler, P., Noonan, R., Lubell, K., Stillman, L., . . . Saul, J. (2008). Bridging the gap between prevention research and practice: The interactive systems framework for dissemination and implementation. *American Journal of Community Psychology, 41*, 171–181. doi.org/10.1007/s10464-008-9174-z

Wandersman, A., Alia, K., Cook, B. S., Hsu, L. L., & Ramaswamy, R. (2016). Evidence-based interventions are necessary but not sufficient for achieving outcomes in each setting in a complex world: Empowerment evaluation, getting to outcomes, and demonstrating accountability. *American Journal of Evaluation, 37*, 544–561. doi.org/10.1177/1098214016660613

Wanless, S. B., Groark, C., & Hatfield, B. (2015). Assessing organizational readiness. In J. Durlak, R. Weissburg, & T. Gullotta (Eds.), *Handbook of social emotional learning* (pp. 360–376). New York, NY: Guilford Publications.

Schools   11

An Ideal Setting for Talking About Trauma

Philip J. Ritchie

In 1996, at the Democratic National Convention, Hillary Clinton famously stated, "It takes a village to raise a child". Although the provenance of such a statement may be unclear (Goldberg, 2016), its sentiment rings true for many people. Those who grew up in small towns and villages even a generation ago can attest to the lack of anonymity they experienced in such settings, particularly if they were engaged in activity their family (including parents, grandparents, aunts, uncles, cousins, siblings, etc.), clergy, shopkeepers, fishmongers, etc. might not condone. In contrast to the relative comfort this connectivity afforded, in the 21st century, many people are now discovering the downside of public scrutiny, as videos captured by phone, past social media posts, and intimate pictures and the like are shared for all to see. The benevolence implied in the village quote is easily lost, in that the absence of extended family and neighbors who have a vested interest in your success as an integral member of that family or community may instead be replaced by online trolls who willingly wreak havoc on unsuspecting targets, often in the absence of obvious transgressions, not to mention context or accuracy.

News organizations increasingly appear to struggle when it comes to credibility and perceived accuracy. A recent survey published as the 2018 Edelman Trust Barometer (Edelman, 2018) suggests that less than half the surveyed sample in 20 of 28 countries (total sample size of 33,000) believe they can trust news organizations to provide an accurate depiction of events occurring at the local, national, and international levels. However, the lack of reliable sources of information does not negate a family's hunger for information when dealing with a child confronted by illness, bullying, mental health issues, or a range of other difficulties.

Schools are responsible for the education of a society's children and youth. In many ways, the very future of a community depends on the success of schools in meeting their mission. Albert Einstein is credited with saying, "Education is what remains after one has forgotten what one has learned in school". The United Nations Educational, Scientific, and Cultural Organization (UNESCO) defines the role of education as "a means to empower children and adults alike to become active participants in the transformation of their societies. Learning should also focus on the values, attitudes and behaviors which enable individuals to learn to live together in a world characterized by diversity and pluralism" (United Nations Educational, Scientific, and Cultural Organization, n.d.).

Why School Is the Place to Talk to Children and Youth About Danger

Schools are experienced and credible when it comes to talking with children about danger, with such conversations often happening right from the beginning of kindergarten. Children may even be offered "courses" on how to be safe getting on and off a school bus—in some cases, before the first day of kindergarten. With the first days of classes, there are fire alarms and lockdown drills to be practiced, and depending on where you live, earthquake and tornado drills may also take place. In short, schools have been teaching children how to deal with danger from their earliest days as a student.

It should come as no surprise, then, that schools are ideally placed to teach children and youth about all manner of danger or trauma. Teachers and other educational professionals are trained in the principles of pedagogy, and delivering such an evidence-based curriculum falls well within their scope of practice. Said another way, that is what teachers do—they teach. This means that teachers have experience in talking to children about potentially frightening subjects, and experience in reassuring them, recognizing and easing their anxiety as it emerges.

Teachers also are ideally placed to deal with such matters because they are a consistent, known presence in the lives of their students, at least for the better part of a school year, and often much longer. The importance of someone who is familiar to children and youth, particularly in a nurturing role such as teaching, is integral to recognizing and supporting the anxious student (Perry,

2007). Why this is relevant when it comes to speaking about trauma is discussed in greater detail later in this chapter.

Another related principle considered involves the range of reactions one might see in students when trauma is discussed. Some students may be triggered and respond with a great deal of anxiety, whereas others may "shut down". A key indicator that a student of any age might be struggling is when there are otherwise unexplained noticeable changes in behavior, academics, peer relations, and attitudes. Teachers, as part of their responsibility for students, and grounded in their relationships with them, will generally monitor each of these areas of functioning, with formal and informal evaluations occurring on an ongoing basis. If significant changes in functioning do occur that are suggestive of difficulties, teachers are in a very good position to make contact with families and, if necessary, mental health professionals working within the educational system.

Educating children about potential dangers should be inclusive—the more students that can be reached, the greater the impact. The education system offers the potential to reach the vast majority of school-aged children and youth. In Canada, depending on the province, the percentage of school-aged children attending public schools ranges from 87% to 98% (Van Pelt, Clemens, Brown, and Palacios, 2015). Similarly, the US Department of Education (2016) reports that approximately 90% of American school-age children attend public schools.

UNESCO's stated goal of preparing people to live in a diverse and pluralistic society should not be considered a mere platitude. Today's public schools provide a microcosm of our society and, as such, are increasingly multicultural. Teachers and other educational professionals ideally are also a reflection of this diversity, and well accustomed to working with children and youth of all cultural and socio-economic backgrounds. It would be counterintuitive, not to mention unethical, to suggest that anyone should be omitted when it comes to preparing children and youth to deal with an assortment of potential dangers. Publicly funded schools in North America are a reflection of today's society, and have ready access to 90% or more of the school-aged population. It is difficult to imagine any other publicly funded system able to reach such a large and representative percentage of a targeted population.

Schools and Early Intervention

With so many children attending public schools, it is inevitable that some will have been directly affected by the topics of concern discussed throughout this book. Recognizing these affected children and getting them the help they need early on can be of paramount importance to a healthy outcome. For example, a student that has witnessed or experienced violence in the home may be triggered by a related discussion; if an atypical reaction to the topic is noted by a teacher or other professional, this could lead to a follow-up discussion with that student and, in turn, earlier intervention. Kessler and colleagues (2007) reviewed the World Health Organization's (WHO) survey conducted by World Mental Health and concluded there is clear evidence that mental disorders most frequently emerge in childhood or adolescence. They argued that individuals often suffer for 10 years or more with symptoms of mental illness before getting help, adding that early identification and intervention might attenuate the severity and duration of primary disorders and, ideally, disrupt the development of secondary disorders.

Anxiety is typically the first of the mental illnesses to present; it is also the most frequent. The *Diagnostic and Statistical Manual of Mental Disorders, 5th edition* (DSM-5; American Psychiatric Association, 2013) defines separation anxiety disorder as "developmentally inappropriate and excessive fear or anxiety concerning separation from those to whom the individual is attached" (p. 190). It may become apparent with a child's initial presentation at school. Although it is easy to normalize children having a difficult time separating from parents when they first begin school, teachers have ready access to comparative data (i.e., the behavior of all their other students) they can use to determine if a child's behavior is possibly "developmentally inappropriate". As part of their training, they have also frequently received instruction in normal and exceptional child development as well as mental health.

Although anxiety can present from an early age, psychosis typically emerges from adolescence through to early adulthood, and high school teachers may be among the first to observe such disorders in their students. Marshall & Rathbone (2011), in a Cochrane Review of early intervention programs and psychosis, recognized the goals of early intervention as twofold: first, to identify those who show prodromal symptoms or early signs of a psychotic illness and attempt to prevent the actual onset of schizophrenia; second, to offer evidence-based interventions to those in the early stages of schizophrenia, with a goal of limiting the severity and duration of any psychotic episode. These authors reported that studies support the use of early intervention in psychosis, noting that it is now used throughout the developed world, although the studies cited have not been ruled conclusive and further investigation is required.

The value of early intervention is not restricted to the identification and treatment of mental illness. The earlier we recognize and intervene in cases of child abuse, child neglect, child exploitation, and even bullying behavior, the better the odds of preventing further damage being inflicted upon a child, as well as limiting or even preventing the victimization of additional children by the same perpetrator.

Early identification can also mitigate the impact of the abuse of alcohol and other substances by youth. Ali et al. (2011) examined the merits of early identification of illicit drug and alcohol use by teens, noting that the risks of such behaviors going unchecked include "motor vehicle accidents, risky sexual behaviors, increased suicidality, homicides, mental health problems, and high rate of school dropout" (p. 24). They note that punitive measures after the fact have typically been ineffective and recommended adopting preventive strategies. Ali et al. (2011) conclude, in part, that "there is an urgent need for parents, school teachers, and healthcare providers to be familiar with the early signs and symptoms of drug and substance abuse to be able to implement preventive measures" (p. 26).

Schools and Family Engagement

Clearly, education in contemporary society encompasses so much more than merely imparting knowledge, or teachers would readily be replaced by smartphones and education would stop once a child's wi-fi access started. Furthermore, the US Department of Education, among others, has recognized the importance of education in enabling all people to flourish in a diverse and pluralistic society. The Department of Education also recognized family engagement as an essential component in promoting equity in that society (www.ed.gov).

There is an expectation that education, as part of fulfilling its various roles and responsibilities, will be delivered in a safe and caring environment—one that affords dignity and respect to each student. Schools have been given the responsibility of acting *in loco parentis*, having responsibility for all manner of care for a student once that student arrives on their doorstep. There would seem to be an implicit understanding that this care does not cease with the end of the school day (although, arguably, perhaps any legal responsibility for that care might), as students at the very least are generally expected to continue with their school-assigned work at home. An incontrovertible corollary, of course, is that a parent's care does not stop upon dropping their child off at school. Family engagement becomes easier when teachers and parents recognize and identify their common goals, including the care of children both in school and out.

Care cannot be completely parsed out. We expect families to be vested in the total care of their children at home and beyond, including their physical, emotional, vocational, moral, and cognitive well-being. Similarly, school needs to be inclusive when it comes to defining its role in caring for that child. Accordingly, schools have stepped into the breach in attempting to provide support and answer questions of students as well as their families in response to a wide range of challenges, from individual education plans for students deemed to have exceptional needs to large-scale disasters affecting entire communities and, occasionally, the world as we know it (e.g., 9/11). But to do this effectively, we have to understand who these families are.

The educational system now understands that much like the society we live in, families look different than they used to, to the point where the description of a "typical family" becomes oxymoronic. Today, the family a student returns to at day's end looks very different than it did even one generation ago. Belkin (2011), writing in the *New York Times*, notes: "statistically, (family) is no longer a mother, a father and their biological children living together under one roof (and certainly not with Dad going off to work and Mom staying home)".

The Vanier Institute of the Family has been studying Canadian families for more than 50 years. It recognizes the dynamic nature of today's society and defines family as "any combination of two or more persons who are bound together over time by ties of mutual consent, birth and/or adoption or placement" (Mirabelli, 2015, p. 14). Members of the family join to assume some or all of a number of responsibilities, including "physical maintenance and care of each other . . . addition of new members (including through adoption), socialization of children, social control of members, production, consumption, distribution of goods and services, (and) love" (p. 14). For the purposes of the current discussion, the term "family engagement" includes research and other articles that make reference to "parent engagement", unless these works specifically state otherwise, and the expectation is that society's definition of "family" will continue to change; accordingly, this chapter interprets family using an inclusive perspective.

This engagement between families and schools sometimes occurs quite naturally and early in the student's educational journey. Many parents report having' capitulated to the urge to jump into their car and follow the school bus or peek in the classroom windows to make sure that a son or daughter was really in safe and capable hands on that first day of school. An understanding smile from that kindergarten teacher (if not the school bus driver, whose eyes parents would presumably prefer to remain on the road) who sees those parents peeking in may set a welcoming tone for the new parent-school relationship. The challenge for schools is to reach those parents and families who may not already feel engaged, including those whose lack of resources may limit their involvement (not everyone has a car or time to follow a school bus), as well as sustain engagement in those who already are.

Why Is Family Engagement Important?

The importance of parent or family engagement in supporting children and youths' mental health was reviewed by the Ontario Centre of Excellence for Child and Youth Mental Health (2016). Family engagement was defined as "an active partnership between families and service providers, which involves listening to what families have to say, engaging in two-way communication and seeing the families as partners and allies in children and youths' mental health" (Ministry of Child and Youth Services, 2013). Family engagement was associated with improved psychological adjustment in children and youth and decreased parenting stress (Bellin, Osteen, Heffernan, Levy, & Snyder-Vogel, 2011), improved child management skills and more effective use of resources (MacKean et al., 2012), increased community awareness of children's mental health concerns (Ferreira, 2011), and reduced stigma (Ferreira, Hodges, & Slaton, 2013), issues that will be re-visited later in this chapter.

Aside from its beneficial impact on mental illness, engagement between families and the school system has also been the subject of formal investigation; and, again, it has been demonstrated to result in robust benefits. These benefits include better student behavior (e.g., El Nokali, Bachman, & Votruba-Drzal, 2010; Epstein & Sheldon, 2002), improved academic achievement (e.g., Fan & Chen, 2001; Jeynes, 2007), and reduced incidence of cigarette, alcohol, and illicit drug use (e.g., Guilamo-Ramos et al., 2010; Perry et al., 1996).

Gonzalez-DeHass, Willems, and Holbein (2005) conducted a review of studies that examined the impact of parental involvement on student motivation and concluded that students of involved parents report greater effort, concentration, and attention when it comes to school and "are more likely to take personal responsibility for their learning" (p. 117). These authors were cautious not to imply there is a causal relationship between involvement and motivation. They speculated that parental involvement boosts students' perceived sense of control and competence, contributes to an important sense of security and connectedness to students, and helps students internalize the importance of education. Alternatively, they suggested that parents may be more responsive to the needs of children they perceive to be motivated.

The National Association of School Psychologists (NASP) recognized the importance of family engagement, developing a position statement on school-family partnering (NASP, 2012). They stated, "the goal of enhancing student competence cannot be accomplished by schools or educators alone . . . Families are essential in this endeavor" (p. 1). The author noted there is evidence that the benefits of family engagement for students include: improved attitudes, achievement, attendance, and test scores; increased homework completion; improved participation in school activities; and, interestingly, reduced demand for intensive (and expensive) services, such as special education. In addition, engaged families report improved self-efficacy as parents, better understanding and relationships with school personnel, and better communication with their children. Educators working in a system that fosters family engagement report higher job satisfaction, improved evaluations by parents and administrators, and, not surprisingly, better relationships with families (NASP, 2012).

Family engagement also appears to be linked to improved physical health. The Centers for Disease Control and Prevention (2012) reviewed the impact of family-school engagement on students' health, stating that "it is essential for school staff, parents, and community partners to recognize the advantages of working together to guide children's health and learning" (p. 10). They noted that in addition to benefits specifically linked to school achievement and behavior, there are a number of health-related advantages that students from engaged families accrue. These include less likelihood of emotional distress, unhealthy eating behavior, and suicidal thinking or behavior. Furthermore, students with parents who volunteer at their school are less likely to smoke and more likely to engage in healthy levels of physical activity.

We know from the work of Bandura (1977) and many others that the behavior of one individual can influence that of another. Any effort to explain a behavior is almost inevitably followed by a "nature-nurture" debate. The impact of available family resources and educational level may also affect an individual's health. So it comes as no surprise that unhealthy behaviors can run in families.

Vander Ploeg, Maximova, McGavock, Davis, and Veugelers (2014) recognized the impact of family on a number of health-related factors, including obesity, eating habits, and smoking behavior. They were particularly interested in the role of socio-economic status on children's health and expressed concern that school-mediated health programs may inadvertently serve to exaggerate pre-existing differences in health-related behaviors; in other words, families in which the risk is greatest, including those identified as lower socio-economic status, are least likely to benefit from programs meant to target certain unhealthy behaviors. Vander Ploeg et al. (2014) specifically examined the behavior of children attending schools in a socio-economically disadvantaged neighborhood. Results of their study indicated that it was "with the involvement of key stakeholders including parents, students, staff, and community" (p. 81) that they were able to effect positive and enduring changes in at-risk students' behavior.

Unhealthy behavior is not always limited to the children in a family, so it makes sense that effective interventions need to be inclusive of all family members, as well. Bailey, Hill, Oesterle, and Hawkins (2006) demonstrated that adolescents with smoking parents were twice as likely to adopt that habit as those with non-smoking parents. Hardy, Wadsworth, and Kuh (2000) discussed the link between parents' body mass index (BMI) and that of their children, recognizing the impact of parents as models for their children in food selection, feeding practices, and the development of eating patterns and behaviors.

Schuck, Otten, Engels, Barker, and Kleinjan (2013) demonstrated that the relationship between parents and youth smoking is bi-directional. Specifically, they determined that not only does the smoking behavior of parents influence that of their youth, the converse is true, as well. If this bi-directional relationship exists between other health-related behaviors of students and their parents, then by implication, an effective educational program that improves the health of students potentially could have a positive impact on the same health-related behavior in their parents. Encouragingly, this has recently been shown to be the case with respect to interventions targeting health-related behaviors (e.g., Gunawardena et al., 2016; Kato et al. 2015).

Unfortunately, studies looking to encourage healthy behavior in students, and possibly their parents, have not always had the desired impact, particularly with those most at-risk. As Vander Ploeg et al. (2014) acknowledge, some programs may only serve to exacerbate pre-existing inequities. Holdsworth and Robinson (2013) questioned the efficacy of smoking programs that assume parental smoking behavior is the result of ignorance, particularly in the face of evidence to the contrary (e.g., Thompson, Pearce, and Ross Barnett, 2007). Holdsworth and Robinson concluded from their own interviews (including talking with parents who smoke) that educational programs that fail to properly understand the diverse nature of families, and fail to engage those families, are likely to have minimal impact on those most in need of intervention. It is unclear if better family engagement would improve the effectiveness for programs directed towards at-risk children and their parents.

Working Towards Family Engagement

The Centers for Disease Control and Prevention (2012), or CDC, embraced a definition of parent engagement as "parents and staff working together to support and improve the learning, development, and health of children and adolescents" (p. 6). The CDC endorsed the importance of general principles of teachers and other school personnel working to establish a relationship with families and making them feel welcome in their children's schools. In addition, they identified six specific solutions to common problems that interfere with family engagement:

1. Parent involvement in activities and meetings can improve with parent-centered scheduling and incentives, such as child care and food or refreshments; alternative ways for parents to access information and communicate with school staff (e.g., email, listserv, and social media) can also improve participation.
2. Providing transportation to events or holding them online improves access to meetings and activities for those families lacking transportation.
3. Having students as well as staff welcoming parents to informal events, such as presentations on topics of interest at the school, can improve the comfort level of those with previously negative school experiences (as student or parent).
4. Providing translators and written information in the languages spoken by a school community and communicating in simple language can improve access to information for non-English-speaking families and those who may have literacy barriers.
5. Offering professional development activities for teaching staff around parent engagement affirms family engagement as a priority and can improve the competence and comfort of teaching staff in collaborating effectively with parents.
6. Finally, the CDC suggested mobilizing parents and school staff through an evidence-informed approach to demonstrating the significant positive impact on children's health and education to improve school administrative and financial support for family engagement.

NASP (2012) itemized three basic components to family engagement: "joint problem-solving, two-way communication and shared decision-making" (p. 1). In addition, NASP emphasized the role of trust in developing and maintaining family engagement, with evidence suggesting that trust is built over time, and improved through positive communication. Adams and Christenson (2000) demonstrated that the nature of parent-school communication (i.e., positive versus neutral or negative) was seen as more important than the frequency with respect to building and maintaining trust between families and schools. The Ontario Centre for Excellence in Child and Youth Mental Health's (2016) review concluded that "applying a strength-based lens to treatment can influence the extent to which parents actively engage in services while also increasing their hope and optimism" (p. 8). In other words, families appear more willing to engage when those who are working with them look to emphasize and harness an individual's or family's strengths rather than merely focus on a given problem.

Conversely, research suggests that family engagement is not effective when it is problem-focused. Fan and Williams (2010) found that, in addition to parents' educational aspirations for their children, school-initiated "benign" communication (such as newsletters, classroom updates, etc.) with parents had a positive impact on students' engagement, self-efficacy, and motivation in different subject areas. However, when parent-school contact was initiated in response to negative situations, such as academic or behavioral concerns, student motivation was negatively affected in all domains that were examined. In short, waiting until there is a problem may have a negative impact on outcome, and parent or family engagement may be more effective when communication between home and school is strength-based.

NASP (2012) identified several responsibilities that schools can assume in working towards improved family engagement. These include providing a positive environment in which schools view families as equal partners in a child's education, including those families who may be more difficult to engage for a wide range of factors. Educators are expected to promote engagement through valuing different kinds of parent participation, including input into decisions about how a given school is run. Family engagement was considered particularly important in working with those from diverse backgrounds, in part because students from these families interpret the alignment of home and school as a reflection of both working to enable that student's success. Finally, NASP suggested that family engagement should encourage a view whereby education is a shared responsibility: "[W]hen problems arise, they are addressed jointly by families, students, and educators in a respectful, collaborative, solution-focused manner" (p. 4).

Sex Ed and What We Can Learn from It (Other Than the Obvious)

From the previous examples, we see that well-intended programs may not always have the desired impact on the most at-risk students. Effective family engagement includes accurately assessing what those families' needs might be. The teaching of sexual health education (SHE) in the classroom allows for two valuable object lessons with respect to these needs: the first involves the importance of evaluating the impact of a given program (i.e., does it work?); the second involves ensuring that programs accurately reflect the needs of students and their families (i.e., is this really what students and their families want and need?).

Although talking with children and youth about sexual health may not constitute a topic of direct "trauma", that would not preclude it from being a topic of controversy. Earlier chapters of this book examine sexuality-related topics, including the safety of LGBTQ+ kids and dangers surrounding sexual abuse and exploitation. Additional discussion of the teaching of SHE also illustrates the merits of family engagement when it comes to any school-based discussion related to a topic of danger.

In the United States, the history of SHE began largely as an endorsement of Victorian values that "sexual activity in the marital bedroom for purposes of procreation was the only truly acceptable form of sexual activity" (Elia, 2009, p. 34). The social hygiene movement of the early 1900s was promoted by a wide range of professionals, including physicians, social reformers, philanthropists, and, importantly, educators (Imber, 1984). In the classroom, efforts were directed towards the prevention of sexually transmitted infections (STIs) and the eradication of masturbation and prostitution, while continuing to confine sexual expression to marriage (Elia, 2009).

More recently, efforts at promoting this rather narrow—and some would argue puritanical—view of sexuality education continue. In 1981, the US Adolescent Family Life Act was established to promote "chastity (and) self-discipline", incorporating morally charged language such as "virgin" and "chaste" (Santelli et al., 2017). Funding of these programs was contingent on there being no discussion of contraception except for the emphasis on their failure rates (Haskins & Bevan, 1997). Santelli et al. (2017) note that between the fiscal years of 1982–2017, approximately $2 billion US was spent by the American government on such abstinence-only-until-marriage (AOUM) initiatives. AOUM is promoted as the only sure-fire method of avoiding pregnancy outside of marriage, as well as STIs. The US government similarly imposed AOUM requirements on the funding of sexuality-related initiatives in developing countries (Santelli et al., 2017).

Several reviews and meta-analyses have evaluated the effectiveness of AOUM-based education initiatives (e.g., Denforth, Abraham, Campbell, & Busse, 2017; Kirby, 2007; Underhill, Operario, & Montgomery, 2007). The conclusions of these reviews are consistent and unequivocal: AOUM-based programs are not effective in delaying age of initiating intercourse, encouraging abstinence even among youth who express this as a goal, or reducing unwanted pregnancies or STIs.

Perhaps it could be argued that, although ineffective, AOUM programs reflect the values of the community at-large and, as such, can be justified. Again, a review of literature seems to contradict this. Studies have demonstrated that the vast majority of parents want SHE taught in schools, "including abstinence as a behavioral goal—but also including information about condoms, contraception, and access to condoms and contraception for sexually active adolescents" (Santelli et al., 2017). Even in Mississippi, a state readily identified as politically conservative, results indicate that more than 90% of parents support sex-related education that includes discussion of the transmission and prevention of HIV and STIs, and how to get tested for these; more than 80% want information provided on where to obtain birth control; and more than 70% wanted a demonstration on the correct use of condoms (McKee, Ragsdale, & Southward, 2014).

Similar findings were also obtained when Canadian parents' attitudes were surveyed. McKay, Byers, Voyer, Humphreys, and Markham (2014) found that almost 90% of parents of Ontario students supported SHE being taught in school, and 84% of those surveyed indicated that the teaching of SHE should begin no later than middle school. Parents also demonstrated significant support for the teaching of all 13 of the suggested sexual health topics in the survey, including methods of contraception, STIs, reproduction, correct anatomical terms, sexual orientation, and media literacy. Interestingly, among parents surveyed, only 2% believed SHE should not be taught in the school system at all.

Family engagement, by definition, involves communication between school and home—a two-way process. It cannot be restricted to schools merely telling parents what it is they are teaching their children; it requires the accurate assessment and evidence-based response to the needs of students and their families. McKay et al. (2014) comment on the Ontario government in 2010 suspending a decision to update the SHE curriculum "in the wake of media news reports and commentaries implying or claiming that a large percentage of Ontario parents were opposed to broadly-based SHE in the schools"—clearly the data would not support such a decision. Sex-ed in the schools offers a poignant reminder that there is no substitute for family engagement, and that a paternalistic approach in which assumptions are made about what is in the best interests of students, and by extension their families, risks jeopardizing student health and safety, while misjudging the needs of the community those schools serve. Similarly, effective engagement must work to engage all families, and not just those who are most vocal, as evidence suggests that at least in the case of SHE, the most vocal parents may not necessarily reflect the values of the community.

Talking About Danger and Trauma-Informed Care

Children's brains, like those of adults, can be significantly affected by exposure to stress (Felitti et al., 1998). Certain responses can be adaptive, like quicker reaction time when pursued by a predator, whereas other reactions may interfere with a child's or youth's ability to process and follow through with information provided. The Adverse Childhood Experiences (ACE) study demonstrated how exposure to extreme, acute traumatic stress (e.g., the loss of a primary caregiver) in some cases can have a profound and lasting impact on the brain's development even in infants (Felitti et al., 1998); on the other hand, exposure to moderate, predictable levels of stress has long been recognized as a pillar of resilience (e.g., Perry, 2007).

Any in-class discussion about how to avoid potential dangers may understandably result in heightened anxiety for students and, in turn, perhaps their families. Although covering such topics is unlikely to be perceived as extreme stress by most children, there may be those who are "triggered" by such discussions, based on a number of factors. Without going into a detailed discussion of all factors, the most obvious involves a history of previous exposure to trauma, particularly if that trauma is related to the topic at hand (e.g., Perry & Pollard, 1998). These authors elaborate that "following an acute stress response, the brain creates a set of memories from the event. These memories are reactivated when the child is exposed to a specific reminder of the traumatic event . . . Furthermore, these memories can be reactivated when the child simply thinks about or dreams about the event" (p. 42).

Practically speaking, presenting the perils of drug use to a classroom may be triggering for a child who lives with a parent or sibling with a substance abuse disorder. Similarly, a discussion of the prevention of sexual abuse will likely be heard very differently by the child who already is a victim of abuse. This is not to imply that potential at-risk children should be excluded from such discussions. Indeed, one may wish to ensure that these children are included, as such discussions will include support for those who are at-risk or have already experienced trauma, and provide guidelines on how to tell a trusted adult and, ideally, prevent further trauma. However, understanding which children are at risk and recognizing reactions that may indicate that a child has a history of trauma should be part of training for any teachers leading these discussions, as recognizing the at-risk child can be essential to getting that child help.

Family engagement is a logical first step in identifying an at-risk child, whether dealing with physical illness (e.g., anaphylactic nut allergy), mental illness (e.g., post-traumatic stress disorder, or PTSD), or vulnerability (e.g., a recent break up of a marriage). A parent that understands that their child's school is as committed to that child's overall well-being as they are will be more likely to share important information relevant to that child's care (Ontario Centre for Excellence in Child and Youth Mental Health, 2016). That information may include letting a teacher know if there has been a history of trauma, and if there are specific triggers to be aware of or avoid.

Alternatively, it is important that parents and teachers understand that not all stress is aversive: "Children, given the opportunity for moderate, controlled exposures to stress during childhood—with a consistent, available and safe caregiver to serve as 'home-base' can become inoculated against future more severe stressors". Furthermore, the levels of arousal and "'stress' associated with novelty and safe exploratory behavior help build a healthy child" (Perry, 2007, p. 2). The value of family engagement becomes even more important in that family and teachers may each fulfill the role of "consistent, available and safe caregiver".

In addition to the complex role that stress can play in a child's development, teachers and other educational professionals may be required to distinguish between normal responses to a stressful situation that may still require support, versus responses requiring immediate action. Normal responses requiring support include children or youth who are anxious about a violent event in a school, or who are grieving the sudden death of a family or staff member, or peer. An individual who dissociates or experiences psychotic symptoms to the point that they can no longer tell what is real and what is not (including whether they themselves are real) is an example of reactions that are not considered "normal" and require emergent intervention. Similarly, a student who expresses homicidal or suicidal ideation, or intent in the wake of a significant stressor, is also in need of immediate evaluation by a mental health professional.

Therefore, because the same event is toxic for one child but inoculating for another, and some "normal" responses still require additional support, it is important that teachers understand and recognize concerning signs and symptoms of distress in children. In response to violence or deaths in schools and communities, organizations like the American Red Cross and the National Child Traumatic Stress Network (Brymer et al., 2006), among many others, offer suggestions on how to support children and youth in the aftermath of traumatic events. The American Psychological Association (2001) consolidated their recommendations in the wake of 9/11, the result of which included guidelines to understanding children's reactions from a developmental perspective. NASP similarly provides up-to-date and evidence-informed suggestions on how to talk with children and youth about difficult subjects. These resources are family-friendly, providing tips for parents and school staff alike; they also reflect the multicultural environment of the school community, as they are available in English and at least nine other languages.

Developmental level or age can also influence whether an event is interpreted as stressful or traumatizing; understanding this can inform educators and parents in how to recognize that a child or youth is affected, as well as how best to support them. But such support must be offered bearing in mind the principles of beneficence (help those in need) and nonmaleficence (do no harm). Although such principles at first glance may seem redundant, one need only look at the listed possible side-effects on a medication bottle to recognize that, at times, attempts to remediate one problem may inadvertently create others.

There does appear to be the potential for harm when providing support to traumatized individuals in the immediate aftermath of an event. A review of literature examining the use of debriefings with adults following traumatic events suggests that, under some circumstances, such interventions can make things worse (Rose, Bisson, Churchill, & Wessely, 2002). However, doing nothing in the wake of these incidents could be perceived as a lack of social support, something that has been associated with the subsequent development of PTSD in adults (Ozer, Best, Lipsey, & Weiss, 2003), and may contribute to some degree of confusion for teachers.

Bandura's (1977) social learning theory suggests that we learn from each other through observing, imitating, and modeling of behavior. Ironically, asking someone to "calm down" is quite possibly the surest, fastest way of having the opposite impact on an individual's behavior, regardless of age (if you are not sure, try it out some time on a significant other), quite likely because it stems from that individual's own distress in attempting to cope with a situation—in essence, becoming co-dysregulation. In contrast, co-regulation refers to the positive, bi-directional process of emotional regulation that occurs between two or more people. Van der Kolk (2005) described how children who enjoy secure attachment with a calm, predictable caregiver have the "experience of feeling understood (which) provides them with the confidence that they are capable of making good things happen and that, if they do not know how to deal with difficult situations, they can find people who can help them (p. 403). Morris, Silk, Steinberg, Myers, and Robinson (2007) demonstrated that a sensitive and responsive parenting approach that included discussing and modeling appropriate emotional responses could contribute to healthy emotion regulation in children.

Teachers, mental health professionals, and other educational staff must be aware of the impact of their own emotions, particularly when discussing distressing or traumatic events. Tears would generally seem to be an appropriate and understandable reaction to a sad event and it can be validating for those students who are sad to see a teacher or other adult cry. Other understandable reactions to trauma can include anxiety, anger, doubt, and a myriad of others. Again, there is nothing wrong with teachers and others demonstrating such emotions. However, such expression should not be at the expense of that adult's emotional regulation. Ideally, the emotion is presented in the context of remaining calm and in control, in spite of any emotional reactions (and quite possibly in contrast to some of the inner turmoil they may be experiencing), particularly if a goal is to facilitate students' own emotional regulation.

Psychological first aid (PFA) is an evidence-informed approach to offering immediate aid to those who may be experiencing trauma. Similar in principle to medical first aid, in which one intervenes in a medical crisis prior to the arrival of first responders or other healthcare providers, PFA looks to mitigate the impact of potentially traumatizing events through care by those who are not necessarily mental health professionals. PFA is described as "basic, nonintrusive pragmatic care with a focus on: listening but not forcing talk; assessing needs and ensuring that basic needs are met; encouraging but not forcing company from significant others; and protecting from further harm" (Bisson & Lewis, 2009, p. 3). These authors reviewed studies of PFA as a response to acute, post-trauma distress and concluded that although there is an absence of direct evidence of efficacy, indirect evidence does support such a program "consistent with research evidence on risk and resilience . . . appropriate for developmental levels across the lifespan; and culturally informed and delivered in a flexible manner" (p. 15).

Although PFA represents a comprehensive psycho-social response to people of all ages who have experienced trauma, and to some extent may seem to be over-kill with respect to supporting children talking about danger, erring on the side of caution appears to be warranted and consistent with the principles of trauma-informed care. With this in mind, PFA for schools (PFA-S) has been developed, including access to a free, online manual (National Child Traumatic Stress Network, n.d.).

Recapitulating, although not all classroom discussions of danger will result in traumatized children, that potential remains. Having a clear understanding of this potential can inform the appropriate response of teachers, mental health professionals, and other educational staff offering support in the class-room. Based on the work of the NCTSN, APA, and NASP, the following developmental considerations are proffered.

Some responses to traumatic events can be seen in students of all ages. These include:

- *Regression.* It can be particularly important to educate families about this, as they can become quite distressed when young children start wetting the bed or adolescents climb into their parents' bed in the middle of the night; understanding such behavior as a normal response to a traumatic event can be reassuring to parents and children/youth alike.
- *Increased somatic complaints,* such as headaches and stomach aches. There can be a secondary gain for children with these symptoms, as they may take comfort from being able to stay home with parents and other family members, rather than attend school.
- *Emotional lability,* including increased anxiety, preoccupation with safety, teariness, irritability, and hostility.
- *Behavioral changes in addition to regression,* including difficulties sustaining attention, jumpiness or hypervigilance, and impulsivity.
- *Loss of interest in normal activities.*
- *Decline in academic functioning.*
- *Children and youth may be acutely sensitive to any changes in routine,* including the physical environment (e.g., lighting, seating plans, classrooms, etc.), resulting in additional anxiety.
- *Resilience.* Most children, adolescents, and adults who have experienced a traumatic event demonstrate resilience, or an ability to bounce back. Among those who have difficulty bouncing back, some will struggle with distress and confusion, and as a consequence, begin to re-examine their values and beliefs, a process that can lead to post-traumatic growth (Collier, 2016). For most, recovery is normal, and resilience and growth can be seen across the lifespan.

Some reactions to trauma can occur more frequently in children and youth of a particular age. A developmental understanding of how children and youth experience distress and trauma can be helpful for those in the school.

- *Young children (up to 5 years of age).* The potential for profound and lasting impact of early childhood trauma on both the mental and physical well-being of that individual has been demonstrated in the ACE study (Felitti et al., 1998). Young children are prone to re-experiencing traumatic events in nightmares, new fears, or actions (including play-related) that re-create the event. They are particularly dependent on parents and caregivers to protect them, and the effects of trauma may be compounded if parents or caregivers are similarly traumatized by an event. Young children may have greater difficulty expressing themselves verbally, and often a change in their behavior is the first sign of struggling. They also may have somewhat magical thinking, believing somehow that their own thoughts or actions led to the event, or that parents or caregivers are to blame for not keeping them safe, something that may compound the guilt that those same care-givers (including teachers) may be experiencing in its wake. For traumatic events that involve death, other magical thinking may revolve around a belief that death is reversible. Ongoing reassurance that children are not responsible for the event and are safe should be provided by a known, con-sistent caregiver as an important component of supporting young children in the wake of a traumatic experience. Activity-based strategies (e.g., play, drawing) may be particularly helpful for this population in light of this age group having less-developed verbal skills.

- *Elementary students.* Once into the elementary school years, children are better able to understand that death is not reversible. These children can often fixate on concrete details associated with a traumatic event. Their hunger for understanding can lead to them asking questions that adult caregivers may find distressing (e.g., requesting specifics about the exact manner in which someone may have died). It can be important for these children to be able to demonstrate their own experience in dealing with distressing events (sometimes leading to "war stories" that involve every relative and pet that they are aware of that has died or even been injured). Adults may need to validate the emotional experiences of these children, but after everyone has had an opportunity to ask questions, they can move the conversation along. Answering questions honestly and with appropri-ate details is recommended. For example, it is not necessary to go into "gory details" when asked how someone died; rather, indicating that because of their injuries, "their heart stopped beating and they stopped breathing" generally will satisfy the one posing the question. Children of this age also want to know what they can control. They can do well to write cards or draw pictures for anyone who has been traumatized.

- *Middle and high school students.* Pre-adolescents and adolescents share much in common in their experience of trauma. They generally have a good understanding of trauma, and may experience similar emotional reactions that adults might, although they lack the context that can help adults get through difficult times. These youths often need to appear knowledgeable, and are particularly sensitive to how they may be perceived by their peers; unfortunately, their seeking of answers and understanding is sometimes undermined by a reluctance to ask questions, lest they be judged by peers as naïve and inexperienced. In many cases, those working with youth should offer group-based interventions to avoid anyone feeling singled out; normalizing possible reactions and appropriate self-disclosure (e.g., "I'm really having a hard time understanding this, too") can be helpful. Anticipating and answering probable questions is also of benefit, as it provides information without requiring the youth to ask questions. Ensuing discussions frequently provide clues as to the worries and additional questions that may require attention from adults working with these youths. Teachers, mental health professionals, and others should be aware that exposure to traumatic events can give rise to existential and spiritual concerns, particularly among older adolescents. This group is at greater risk of developing and using unhealthy coping strategies to help regulate difficult emotions, and schools need to know where their students are during the school day, even in the wake of trauma. Drug and alcohol use, self-harm, suicidal thinking, and unprotected sex are all behaviors that should be addressed.

Trauma shows no respect for age, religion, gender, sexual orientation, race, culture, or language. Any of these factors can have a significant impact on how a child or family experiences a traumatic event. They can also influence how individuals cope in the aftermath, mourning rituals, and even willingness to accept the advice and services of mental health professionals. The impact of trauma may be compounded by a group's history of any number of variables, including war, abuse, suicide, racism, and other forms of discrimination. For these reasons, it is essential that interventions be offered in a culturally sensitive, inclusive manner, and that as much as possible, those adults offering support be a reflection of the greater community. Enlisting the help of community leaders, including clergy and other spiritual leaders, can improve the representative nature and, in turn, understanding of those adults who are supporting children and youth at such difficult times.

Talking About Trauma and Stigma

Stigma in and of itself may not always be objectionable. Few would argue that there should not be some reproach for those convicted of murder or pedophilia. However, in many instances, stigma may be unwarranted, and is best thought of as a reflection of the difficulty some people have in accepting others who are different, even when those differences do not constitute a threat to well-being. Stigma may also be the proverbial elephant in the room—particularly if it has a negative impact—when it comes to discussing a wide range of topics in the classroom, including several touched on in this book.

Kurzban and Leary (2001) suggest that some stigmatization may at least in part be attributed to an evolutionary process whereby people are endowed with disease-avoidance strategies predisposed to be over-inclusive due to the potential consequences (i.e., illness or death) of underestimating risk. Park, Van Leeuwen, and Chochorelou (2013) demonstrated how this process unfairly targets those who pose no risk of harm, providing an example of individuals presenting with facial birthmarks, yet no perceived threat of contagion, who experienced similar avoidance as those thought to have more infectious conditions.

Link and Phelan (2006), in reviewing the impact of stigma, suggest there is a social selection process that determines which human differences are considered to be significant, and which are inconsequential. They contrast the social significance of these differences and, in turn, stigma associated with a variety of medical conditions, such as hypertension, bone fractures, and melanoma versus those of incontinence, AIDS, and schizophrenia.

Link and Phelan (2006) further suggest that the discrimination associated with stigma is comprised of three major forms. By way of example, *direct discrimination* occurs when an individual refuses to hire or rent a property to someone whose differences (e.g., race, gender, religion, sexual orientation, ability) they see as objectionable. A subtler form, *structural discrimination*, occurs when the pool of candidates considered for a position or property rental is influenced by employers or landlords giving preferential treatment to those referred by friends and associates from similar backgrounds—in essence, there is no direct denial to visible minorities, but their chances of being considered for a job or apartment are significantly undermined. Finally, there is the *impact on the stigmatized* (self-stigma), whereby they feel more stress and less willingness to socialize, knowing that others discriminate against them, potentially leading them to greater social isolation, an unwillingness to apply for some positions or dwellings, un- or under-employment, and poorer self-esteem.

Stigma has been demonstrated to interfere with individuals seeking help for a wide range of conditions, such as mental illness (Corrigan & Watson, 2002), living in poverty (Allen, Wright, Harding, & Broffman, 2014), obesity (Puhl & Heuer, 2010), substance abuse disorders (Smith, Earnshaw, Copenhaver, & Cunningham, 2016), and HIV (Venable, Carey, Blair, & Littlewood, 2017). The Centers for Disease Control and Prevention (2016), or CDC, recognized the negative impact of homophobia, stigma, and discrimination with respect to the health of students who may be targeted. Among the CDC's recommendations, they incorporated suggestions specifically for schools, including the creation of a positive environment where students feel safe. A safer school environment was associated with the prevention of bullying and harassment, and promotion of school connectedness and parent engagement.

The Role of Schools in Stigma Reduction

Thornicroft, Rose, Kassam, and Sartorius (2007) describe the three pillars of stigma as "knowledge (ignorance), attitudes (prejudice) and behavior (discrimination)". The educational system is well placed to address all three: its ability to impart knowledge is self-evident, and recall the UNESCO statement that "learning should also focus on the values, attitudes and behaviors which enable individuals to learn to live together" (op cit.). Therefore, schools appear to already possess the mandate and skills to address the ignorance, prejudice, and discrimination that defines stigma.

Corrigan, Morris, Michaels, Rafacz, and Rüsch (2012) completed a meta-analysis of interventions directed at reducing stigmatizing attitudes held by community members towards those with mental illness. They concluded that face-to-face contact tended to be a more effective strategy for reducing stigma among adults, whereas education efforts worked better with adolescents.

Griffiths, Carron-Arthur, Parsons, and Reid (2014) conducted a similar overview involving randomized controlled trials (RCTs) and concluded that "educational interventions alone or when combined with other interventions were consistently associated with a reduction in personal stigma for different types of mental disorders", although not schizophrenia/psychosis.

The MHCC also examined stigma and mental illness (Koller, Chen, Lamantia, & Stuart, 2013). Their findings suggest that a program involving face-to-face contact between high school students and volunteers with lived experience of mental illness had a positive impact on the reduction of stigma towards this population; however, the magnitude of change may have been greater if earlier education sessions had not already targeted stigma among this sample of high school students.

Finally, Thornicroft et al. (2016) reviewed a number of programs geared towards reducing stigma. They identified school-based programs that incorporate education with or without contact (i.e., with those who have lived experience with mental illness) as effective at changing knowledge, although long-term effects were not as clear, and may not be as strong over time.

As previously noted, Thornicroft et al. (2007) describe the pillars of stigma as ignorance, prejudice, and discrimination. Schools would seem to be the natural choice of venues in which to address the issue and its consequences. From the first days of kindergarten, they provide knowledge to counter ignorance, offer guidance to encourage positive attitudes and challenge prejudice, and, finally, model and practice this in an inclusive, multicultural environment where, in theory, all are welcome and, indeed, all are expected. Family engagement by definition requires two-way communication between school and home. A school system that is well engaged with families offers a unique opportunity to educate parents and other family members as well as children. Such intervention may be crucial when it comes to addressing stigma, as it seems likely that the ignorance, prejudice, and discrimination of the children may reflect, at least in part, the knowledge, attitudes, and behavior of those around them (Kang & Inzlicht, 2012).

Conclusion

Schools appear to provide an ideal setting in which to educate children and their families about life's dangers and how to deal with them. Schools bring with them a long history of talking to kids about how to stay safe. They have the potential to reach almost all children and youth. In addition, educational and mental health professionals are trained in providing education and support, while recognizing when a child or youth requires additional intervention.

Schools also have a mandate to work with families—through homework, parent-teacher meetings, school advisory committees, and the like. Family engagement requires more than this, however. Parents and other family members must be recognized for their expertise when it comes to understanding their children, and engagement with family members begins from a strengths-based perspective.

Talking with children about danger may provoke anxiety in students and teachers, and perhaps even in staff. A trauma-informed approach provides for anxious and even traumatized children to be given the same information as their peers, something that is particularly helpful when it comes to talking about danger—especially because those conversations may include information for students about how to ask for help. Tackling stigma head-on ensures that the challenges posed by various dangers are not compounded by the ignorance, prejudice, and discrimination of others.

Finally, lessons learned from the teaching of SHE demonstrate that we cannot take program efficacy or parent and family preferences for granted. Although schools might be a "natural choice" when it comes to talking about danger, proper family engagement and outcome evaluation continues to be in order. Finally, although schools cannot provide a world free from danger, they can offer the skills needed to deal with such danger, so students and their families can move forward in an informed and hopeful manner.

Key Messages

1. Schools are experienced and credible when it comes to teaching students and families about issues pertaining to their safety; using an approach consistent with trauma-informed care is recommended.
2. Teachers and other educational professionals recognize deviations from normal development; this can allow for early identification and intervention with a wide range of concerns.
3. Schools have become a hub for many communities, and with family engagement, can reach out beyond their students to the community at large.
4. Schools are well versed at evaluating and influencing the knowledge, behavior, and attitudes of their students, all three of which are considered integral components in mitigating the negative impact of stigma.

Appendix 11

Resource Materials For Parents, Teachers, School Administrators, Pediatricians and Others Who Work with Youths

The following list of resources provides a sampling of material available online. This list is not in any way comprehensive. Rather, it offers a few suggestions on how and where to get started, as well as additional resources (e.g., books) that may be of help.

- anxietybc.com
  Information for parents, youth, and professionals on coping with anxiety.
- ementalhealth.ca
  Information for parents, children, youth, and professionals about mental illness and how to get support. Links to specific support sources available in Canada are also provided.
- mghclaycenter.org/parenting-concerns
  Information for parents of children from infants and toddlers through to young adults. Topics include children with mental illness, learning disorders, and ADHD, as well as additional concerns.
- nasponline.org
  The website of the National Association of School Psychologists provides information for psychologists and other educational professionals, and families, on a wide range of topics including but not limited to school safety, bullying, substance abuse, trauma-informed care, school response to traumatic events, mental illness, and learning disorders.
- nctsn.org
  The website of the National Child Traumatic Stress Network provides information for parents and professionals on a wide range of topics including individual and group trauma, school response to traumatic incidents, and trauma-informed care. A detailed description of psychological first aid (PFA) is also available through NCTSN.
- parentbooks.ca
  Information for parents and professionals on suggested books. Topics include children with special needs, parenting and family life, education, and mental health.
- prevnet.ca
  Information for parents, children, youth, and professionals about bullying prevention and cyberbullying.

- redcross.org
  Information for families, schools, and communities on emergency preparedness and response.
- worrywisekids.org
  Information for parents and professionals on how to support children struggling with anxiety disorders.

References

Adams, K., & Christenson, S. L. (2000). Trust and the family-school relationship: Examination of parent-teacher differences in elementary and secondary grades. *Journal of School Psychology, 38*(5), 477–497.

Ali, S., Mouton, C. P., Jabeen, S., Ofoemezie, E. K., Bailey, R. K., Shahid, M., & Zeng, Q. (2011). Early detection of illicit drug use in teenagers. *Innovations in Clinical Neuroscience, 8*(12), 24–28.

Allen, H., Wright, B. J., Harding, K., & Broffman, L. (2014). The role of stigma in access to health care for the poor. *The Milbank Quarterly, 92*(2), 289–318.

American Psychiatric Association. (2013). *Diagnostic and statistical manual of mental disorders* (5th ed.). Arlington, VA: American Psychiatric Publishing.

American Psychological Association. (2001, September 14). *Coping with terrorism.* Retrieved from helping.apa.org/daily/terrorism.html

Bailey, J. A., Hill, K. G., Oesterle, S., & Hawkins, J. D. (2006). Linking substance use and problem behavior across three generations. *Journal of Abnormal Child Psychology, 34*(3), 263–282.

Bandura, A. (1977). *Social learning theory.* Englewood Cliffs, NJ: Prentice Hall.

Belkin, L. (2011, February 23). A "normal" family. *The New York Times.* Retrieved from www.nytimes.com

Bellin, M. H., Osteen, P., Heffernan, C., Levy, J. M., & Snyder-Vogel, M. E. (2011). Parent and health care professional perspectives on family-centered care for children with special health care needs: Are we on the same page? *Health and Social Work, 36,* 281–290.

Bisson, J. I., & Lewis, C. (2009). *Systematic review of psychological first aid.* Geneva, Switzerland: World Health Organisation.

Brymer, M., Layne, C, Jacobs, A., Pynoos, R., Ruzek, J., Steinberg, A., Vernberg, E., & Watson, P., National Child Traumatic Stress Network and National Center for PTSD. (2006). *Psychological First Aid: Field operations guide* (2nd ed.) California: National Center for PTSD.

Centers for Disease Control and Prevention (CDC). (2012). *Parent engagement: Strategies for involving parents in school health.* Atlanta, GA: US Department of Health and Human Services.

Centers for Disease Control and Prevention (CDC). (2016, February 29). *Stigma and discrimination.* Retrieved from www.cdc.gov/msmhealth/stigma-and-discrimination.htm

Collier, L. (2016). Growth after trauma: Why are some people more resilient than others— and can it be taught? *Monitor on Psychology, 47*(10). Retrieved from www.apa.org/monitor/2016/11/index.aspx

Corrigan, P. W., Morris, S. B., Michaels, P. J., Rafacz, J. D., & Rüsch, N. (2012). Challenging the public stigma of mental illness: A meta-analysis of outcome studies. *Psychiatric Services, 63*(10), 963–973.

Corrigan, P. W., & Watson, A. C. (2002). Understanding the impact of stigma on people with mental illness. *World Psychiatry, 1*(1), 16–20.

Denforth, S., Abraham, C., Campbell, R., & Busse, H. (2017). A comprehensive review of reviews of school-based interventions to improve sexual-health. *Health Psychology Review, 11, 33–52.*

Edelman, R. (2018). *2018 Edelman trust barometer.* Retrieved from www.edelman.com/trust-barometer

El Nokali, N. E., Bachman, H. J., & Votruba-Drzal, E. (2010). Parent involvement and children's academic and social development in elementary school. *Child Development, 81*(3), 988–1005.

Elia, J. (2009). School-based sexuality education: A century of sexual and social control. In E. Schroder & J. Kuriansky (Eds.), *Sexuality education—Past, present, and future, volume one—History and information* (pp. 33–57). Westport, CT: Praeger.

Epstein, J., & Sheldon, S. (2002). Present and accounted for: Improving student attendance through family and community involvement. *The Journal of Educational Research, 95*(5), 308–318.

Fan, X., & Chen, M. (2001). Parental involvement and students' academic achievement: A meta-analysis. *Educational Psychology Review, 13*(1), 1–22.

Fan, W., & Williams, C. M. (2010). The effects of parental involvement on students' academic self-efficacy, engagement, and intrinsic motivation. *Educational Psychology, 30*(1), 53–74.

Felitti, V. J., Anda, R. F., Nordenberg, D., Williamson, D. F., Spitz, A. M., Edwards, V., Koss, M. P., & Marks, J. S. (1998). Relationship of childhood abuse and household dysfunction to many of the leading causes of death in adults: The Averse Childhood Experiences (ACE) study. *American Journal of Preventive Medicine, 14*(4), 245–258.

Ferreira, K. (2011). *Actualizing empowerment: Developing a framework for partnering with families in system level service planning and delivery.* Graduate Theses and Dissertations. Retrieved from http://scholarcommons.usf.edu/etd/3103

Ferreira, K., Hodges, S., & Slaton, E. (2013). The promise of family engagement: An action plan for system-level policy and advocacy. In A. McDonald Culp (Eds.), *Child and family advocacy* (pp. 253–268). New York, NY: Springer.

Goldberg, J. (2016, July 30). *National public radio—It takes a village to determine the origins of an African proverb.* Retrieved from www.npr.org/sections/goatsandsoda/2016/07/30/487925796/it-takes-a-village-to-determine-the-origins-of-an-African-proverb

Gonzalez-DeHass, A. R., Willems, P. P., & Holbein, M. F. D. (2005). Examining the relationship between parental involvement and student motivation. *Educational Psychology Review, 17*(2), 99–123.

Griffiths, K. M., Carron-Arthur, B., Parsons, A., & Reid, R. (2014). Effectiveness of programs for reducing the stigma associated with mental disorders. A meta-analysis of randomized controlled trials. *World Psychiatry, 13*(2), 161–175.

Guilamo-Ramos, V., Jaccard, J., Dittus, P., Gonzalez, B., Bouris, A., & Banspach, S. (2010). The linking lives health education program: A randomized clinical trial of a parent-based tobacco use prevention program for African American and Latin Youths. *American Journal of Public Health, 100*(9), 1641–1647.

Gunawardena, N., Kurotani, K., Indrawansa, S., Nonaka, D., Mizoue, T., & Samarasinghe, D. (2016). School-based intervention to enable school children to act as change agents on weight, physical activity and diet of their mothers: A cluster randomized controlled trial. *Journal of Behavioral Nutrition and Physical Activity, 13*, 45.

Hardy, R., Wadsworth, M., & Kuh, D. (2000). The influence of childhood weight and socio-economic status on change in adult Body Mass Index in a British national birth cohort. *International Journal of Obesity, 24*, 725–734.

Haskins, R., & Bevan, C. S. (1997). Abstinence education under welfare reform. *Child Youth Services Review, 19*, 465–484.

Holdsworth, C., & Robinson, J. (2013). Parental smoking and children's anxieties: An appropriate strategy for health education? *Children's Geographies, 11*(1), 102–116.

Imber, M. (1984). The first world war, sex education, and the American Social Hygiene Association's campaign against venereal disease. *Journal of Educational Administration and History, 16, 1*, 47–56.

Jeynes, W. H. (2007). The relationship between parental involvement and urban secondary school student academic achievement: A meta-analysis. *Urban Education, 42*, 82–110.

Kang, S. K., & Inzlicht, M. (2012). Stigma building blocks: How instruction and experience teach children about rejection by outgroups. *Personality and Social Psychology Bulletin, 38*(3), 357–369.

Kato, S., Okamura, T., Kuwabara, K., Matsuzono, K., Yokota, C., Takekawa, H., . . . Minematsu, K. (2015). Effects of a school-based stroke education program on stroke-related knowledge and behaviour modification—School class-based intervention study for elementary school students and parental guardians in a Japanese rural area *BMJ Open, 7*(12), 1–7.

Kessler, R. C., Amminger, G. P., Aguilar-Gaxiola, S., Alonso, J., Lee, S., & Ustun, T. B. (2007). Age of onset of mental disorders: A review of recent literature. *Current Opinion in Psychiatry, 20*(4), 359–364.

Kirby, D. (2007). *Emerging answers 2007: Research findings on programs to reduce teen pregnancy and sexually transmitted diseases.* Washington, DC: The National Campaign to Prevent Teen and Unplanned Pregnancy: 2007: Report No.: 1586710370

Koller, M., Chen, S.-P., Lamantia, A., & Stuart, H. (2013). *Opening minds in high school: Results of a contact-based anti-stigma intervention.* Ottawa, ON: MHCC.

Kurzban, R., & Leary, M. R. (2001). Evolutionary origins of stigmatization: The functions of social exclusion. *Psychological Bulletin, 127*, 187–208.

Link, B. G., & Phelan, J. C. (2006). Stigma and its public health implications. *Lancet, 367*, 528–529

MacKean, G., Spragins, W., L'Heureux, L., Popp, J., Wilkes, C., & Lipton, H. (2012). Advancing family-centered care in child and adolescent mental health: A critical review of the literature. *Healthcare Quarterly, 15*, 64–75.

Marshall M., & Rathbone J. (2011). Early intervention for psychosis. *Cochrane Database of Systematic Reviews, 6.* Art. No.: CD004718. doi: 10.1002/14651858.CD004718.pub3.

McKay, A., Byers, E. S., Voyer, S. D., Humphreys, T. P., & Markham, C. (2014). Ontario parents' opinions and attitudes towards sexual health education in the schools. *The Canadian Journal of Human Sexuality, 23*(3), 159–166.

McKee, C., Ragsdale, K., & Southward, L. H. (2014). What do parents in Mississippi really think about sex education in schools? Results of a state-level survey. *Journal of Health Disparities Research and Practice, 7*(1), 97–119.

Ministry of Child and Youth Services. (2013). *Draft: Child and youth mental health service framework.* Retrieved from www.children.gov.on.ca/htdocs/English/documents/topics/specialneeds/mentalhealt h/ServiceFramework.pdf

Mirabelli, A. (2015). What's in a name? Defining family in a diverse society. *Transition, 44*(4), 14–15.

Morris, A. S., Silk, J. S., Steinberg, L., Myers, S. S., & Robinson, L. R. (2007). The role of the family context in the development of emotion regulation. *Social Development, 16*(2), 361–388.

National Association of School Psychologists. (2012). *School—Family partnering to enhance learning: Essential elements and responsibilities* [Position Statement]. Bethesda, MD: Author.

National Child Traumatic Stress Network. (n.d.). *Psychological First Aid for Schools (PFA-S).* Retrieved from www.nctsn.org/content/psychological-first-aid-schoolspfa

Ontario Centre for Excellence in Child and Youth Mental Health. (2016). *Evidence in-sight: Best practices in engaging families in child and youth mental health.* Retrieved from www. excellenceforchildandyouth.ca/sites/default/files/resource/EIS_Family_Engagement_EN.pdf

Ozer, E. J., Best, S. R., Lipsey, T. L., & Weiss, D. S. (2003). Predictors of posttraumatic stress disorder and symptoms in adults: A meta-analysis. *Psychological Bulletin, 129*(52–73).

Park, J. H., Van Leeuwen, F., & Chochorelou, Y. (2013). Disease-avoidance processes and stigmatization: Cues of substandard health arouse heightened discomfort with physical contact. *Journal of Social Psychology, 153*, 212–228.

Perry, B. (2007). *Stress, trauma and post-traumatic stress disorders in children: An introduction.* Retrieved from https://childtrauma.org/wp-content/uploads/2013/11/PTSD_Caregivers.pdf

Perry, B. D., & Pollard, R. (1998). Homeostasis, stress, trauma, and adaptation: A neurodevelopmental view of childhood trauma. *Child and Adolescent Psychiatric Clinics of North America, 7*(1), 33–51.

Perry, C. L., Williams, C. L., Veblen-Mortenson, S., Toomey, T. L., Komro, K. A., Anstine, P. S., & Wolfson, M. (1996). Project Northland: Outcomes of a communitywide alcohol use prevention program during early adolescence. *American Journal of Public Health, 86*(7), 956–965.

Puhl, R. M., & Heuer, C. A. (2010). Obesity stigma: Important considerations for public health. *American Journal of Public Health, 100*(6), 1019–1028.

Rose, S., Bisson, J., Churchill, R., & Wessely, S. (2002). Psychological debriefing for preventing post traumatic stress disorder (PTSD). *The Cochrane Database of Systematic Reviews,* 2. Art. No.: CD000560. doi: 10.1002/14651858.CD000560 *(3)*.

Santelli, J. S., Kantor, L. M., Grilo, S. A., Speizer, I. S., Lindberg, L. D., Heitel, J., . . . Ott, M. A. (2017). Abstinence-only until marriage: An updated review of U.S. policies and programs and their impact. *Journal of Adolescent Medicine, 61*, 273–280.

Schuck, K., Otten, R., Engels, R. C., Barker, E. D., & Kleinjan, M. (2013). Bidirectional influences between parents and children in smoking behavior: A longitudinal full-family model. *Nicotine & Tobacco Research, 15*, 44–51.

Smith, L. R., Earnshaw, V. A., Copenhaver, M. M., & Cunningham, C. O. (2016). Substance use stigma: Reliability and validity of a theory-based scale for substance-using populations. *Drug and Alcohol Dependence, 162*, 34–43.

Thompson, L., Pearce, J., & Ross Barnett, J. (2007). Moralising geographies: Stigma, smoking islands, and responsible subjects. *Area, 39*(4), 508–517.

Thornicroft, G., Mehta, N., Clement, S., Evans-Lacko, S., Doherty, M., Rose, D., . . . Henderson, C. (2016). Evidence for effective interventions to reduce mental-health-related stigma and discrimination. *The Lancet, 387*(10023), 1123–1132.

Thornicroft, G., Rose, D., Kassam, A., & Sartorius, N. (2007). Stigma: Ignorance, prejudice or discrimination? *The British Journal of Psychiatry, 190*(3), 192–193.

Underhill, K., Operario, D., & Montgomery, P. (2007). Abstinence-only programs for HIV infection prevention in high-income countries. *Cochrane Database Systems Review,* 2007:Cd005421.

United Nations Educational, Scientific, and Cultural Organization. (n.d.). Retrieved from www.unesco.org/new/en/social-and-human-sciences/themes/fight-against-discrimination/role-of-education/

US Department of Education, National Center for Education Statistics. (2016). *Digest of Education Statistics, 2015 (NCES 2016–014), Chapter 1.* Retrieved from https://nces.ed.gov/fastfacts/display.asp?id=65

van der Kolk, B. (2005). Developmental Trauma Disorder: Towards a rational diagnosis for children with complex trauma histories. *Psychiatric Annals, 33*(5), 401–408.

Van Pelt, D., Clemens, J., Brown, B., & Palacios, M. (2015, October 6). *Where our students are educated: Measuring student enrolment in Canada.* Retrieved from www.fraserinstitute.org/studies/where-our-students-are-educated-measuring-student-enrolment-in-canada

Vander Ploeg, K. A., Maximova, K., McGavock, J., Davis, W., & Veugelers, P. (2014). Do school-based physical activity interventions increase or reduce inequalities in health? *Social Science and Medicine, 112*, 80–87.

Venable, P. A., Carey, M. P., Blair, D. C., & Littlewood, R. A. (2017). Impact of HIV-related stigma on health behaviors and psychological adjustment among HIV-positive men and women. *AIDS and Behavior, 10*, 473–482.

Conclusion

Joanna Pozzulo and Craig Bennell

At this point, you have likely read the chapters you were interested in, or perhaps you read the entire book. First, we would like to thank you for being a dedicated and caring teacher or school administrator, or concerned caregiver or community member. Second, we hope you found the chapters useful in helping your students navigate the challenges facing them to ultimately achieve their best possible outcomes. Third, you may be dealing with an "active" trauma; if so, we recommend that you use some of the wonderful resources that have been included in the appendices by our contributors. Finally, we congratulate you for having the courage to affect change within your students, our children, and youth. This volume was designed to assist you in helping our children and youth who have either experienced trauma directly or indirectly (e.g., by having friends that have been traumatized or through the media).

The Traumas

We brought together experts, including academics and professionals working in the field, to provide the most current evidence-based practices on how to help students who may have experienced or witnessed trauma (or may currently be experiencing or witnessing trauma). We have presented research and advice for nine traumas: (1) bullying; (2) drugs and alcohol; (3) sexual abuse; (4) mental health; (5) lesbian, gay, bisexual, transgender, and queer (LGBTQ) safety; (6) stranger danger; (7) childhood disruptive behaviors; (8) school shootings and lockdowns; and (9) exposure to terrorism. Some traumas are more prevalent than others in terms of personal experiences, but our children and youth are likely to be indirectly exposed to all of them through television or the Internet. Because we expect that successful strategies ultimately require effective implementation, we included a chapter focused on how to implement a school safety program. Moreover, a theme we believe has been echoed throughout the book is that schools cannot deal with these issues alone; effective strategies engage family members and the broader community. Hence, we also included a chapter on how schools can partner with families and the communities they reside in to bring about positive change. All this work pays close attention to cultural and religious sensitivity, socio-economic variabilities, diversity issues, and developmental stages.

Take-Home Messages

Every chapter presents a set of key messages useful for quickly identifying elements that should be considered when addressing each trauma. As a reminder, dealing with trauma can be an ongoing endeavor—you may need to address it more than once in a school year or for several consecutive days, or over several successive years. Strategies you find in this book may be different than the ones you are currently using or similar to your current practices. The authors of these chapters were asked to provide strategies grounded in empirical research and based on current thinking and studies. We hope you will give these strategies a try. Both the short- and long-term impacts of the trauma are also included in the chapters to encourage our readers to keep in mind that, even though an event may have appeared to pass, it can still have an impact on the student. More information on a particular trauma, approach, or implementation can be found in the appendices available at the end of each chapter. Finally, the contributions highlight the importance of paying close attention to the students' developmental stage and the context in which the trauma is occurring or being experienced.

Remaining Challenges

Despite the wonderful contributions to this book, and all the pearls of wisdom included in each chapter, a number of remaining challenges exist. For one, as much as we know, there remains much to be discovered and learned. Some traumas feel like they have been around since the beginning of time, such as bullying. However, this particular trauma may be expressed in a different manner now than it has been in the past—rather than the school yard bullying that many readers may have experienced, children and youth today also have to deal with cyberbullying. Thus, although this long-standing form of trauma is not new, the expression of it is morphing and may require different strategies. We also need to better understand what strategies work best. For example, we may need to develop legislation that provides intervention approaches that cross borders to effectively deal with cyberbullying. In addition, we need to conduct more research on the impact of trauma over the long term. We must also dedicate more effort (including research) towards prevention programs of bullying and other traumas so that our children and youth do not have to experience these traumas in the first place. Moreover, some traumas are relatively "new" to the Western world, such as terrorism, but no less pervasive and distressing. Here, too, we need to advance what we know about how to effectively deal with the trauma, but also how to do so in a culturally and religiously sensitive manner. Finally, we need to keep studying how we can address all of the traumas mentioned in this book in an age-appropriate manner.

A core element of dealing with all trauma is bringing schools and communities together to provide inclusive prevention and intervention approaches. You may have read across the chapters that the richest dialogues and optimal solutions are likely to emerge when we bring students together with various "stakeholders", whether these consist of school personnel, parents, or community members. Solutions that cut across the school-home divide are likely to have the greatest likelihood of success; as such, we need to understand how to effectively engage all those affected by trauma to produce optimal outcomes.

A reality of our time is the decreased budgets that many schools have to work with. We believe that the content offered in this book, and in the appendices, is for the most part inexpensive, and often free. There are a number of resources we provide that can be accessed and used without any expense incurred by schools or individuals. We think all would agree, however, that there is a time commitment that comes at a cost. By using some of the strategies our contributors have outlined when working with your students, we hope this book ensures that your investment of time is offset by the long-term benefits our children and youth will experience. We hope you will access the resources available in the public domain and take the time needed to become familiar with this material and implement it.

Closing Remarks

When we started down the path of producing this volume, we wanted to provide something that was not readily available elsewhere. We also wanted to develop something that could be read and reread, and could be used in practice to increase the likelihood that all children and youth who have experienced trauma have the greatest likelihood of positive, long-term happiness. We rallied and pushed our contributors to give us empirically grounded approaches, with age parameters, for a variety of traumas, presented in such a manner that they could be readily applied by school professionals. We did not want a book so far removed from the perspective of a teacher standing in front of his/her class that it would gather dust on a shelf. In the forefront of our mind, we imagined a fourth-grade teacher, walking into her class after a school shooting took place in a neighboring city, who was going to be confronted with difficult questions by her young students. Or the tenth-grade teacher who has a student in his class dealing with gender identity issues, who feels that he cannot talk to his parents about it. We need to recognize that these issues—these traumas—are real and that students from all over are affected by these experiences in obvious and non-obvious ways. We are proud of the volume that has been produced and for all the contributions made by our colleagues. Although we would rather there be no need for such a book, we hope we have delivered an accessible resource for our school professionals that care so much about our children and youth.

Index

Page numbers in *italic* indicate a figure and page numbers in **bold** indicate a table on the corresponding page.